EDITH WHARTON IN CONTEXT

Edith Wharton was one of America's most popular and prolific writers, becoming the first woman to win the Pulitzer Prize for Fiction in 1921. In a publishing career spanning seven decades, she lived and wrote through a period of tremendous social, cultural, and historical change. Bringing together a team of international scholars, this volume provides the first substantial text dedicated to the various contexts that frame Wharton's remarkable career. Each essay offers a clearly argued and lucid assessment of Wharton's work as it relates to seven key areas: life and works, critical receptions, book and publishing history, arts and aesthetics, social designs, time and place, and literary milieux. These sections provide a broad and accessible resource for students coming to Wharton for the first time while offering scholars new critical insights. Of interest to English and American studies departments, the volume will also appeal to researchers in gender studies, film studies, book history, art history, and transatlantic studies.

LAURA RATTRAY is Senior Lecturer in American Literature at the University of Hull. She is editor of the two-volume *The Unpublished Writings of Edith Wharton* (2009) and *Edith Wharton's* The Custom of the Country: *A Reassessment* (2010). She is on the editorial board of the *Edith Wharton Review* and has recently been awarded a Leverhulme Fellowship for a new study of Wharton and Genre.

EDITH WHARTON IN CONTEXT

Edited by

LAURA RATTRAY

University of Hull

CAMBRIDGE
UNIVERSITY PRESS

CAMBRIDGE UNIVERSITY PRESS
Cambridge, New York, Melbourne, Madrid, Cape Town,
Singapore, São Paulo, Delhi, Mexico City

Cambridge University Press
32 Avenue of the Americas, New York, NY 10013-2473, USA

www.cambridge.org
Information on this title: www.cambridge.org/9781107010192

First published 2012

Printed in the United States of America

A catalog record for this publication is available from the British Library.

Library of Congress Cataloging in Publication data
Edith Wharton in context / [edited by] Laura Rattray, University of Hull.
p.   cm.
Includes bibliographical references and index.
ISBN 978-1-107-01019-2
1. Wharton, Edith, 1862–1937–Criticism and interpretation.   I. Rattray, Laura.
PS3545.H16Z6453   2012
813'.52–dc23   2012012617

ISBN 978-1-107-01019-2 Hardback

Contents

Illustrations

Notes on Contributors

JOHN DENNIS ANDERSON, a Performance Studies scholar, focuses his research in the area of narrative theory and performance. He is the author of *The Student Companion to William Faulkner* (2007). In addition to publishing articles in *Text and Performance Quarterly*, he has served as Book Review Co-Editor for the journal. He performs nationally in his one-person shows as authors Henry James, William Faulkner, Washington Irving, Lynn Riggs, and Robert Frost. Dr. Anderson is a former Chair of the Performance Studies Division of the National Communication Association and served as Director of the Honors Program at Emerson College, Boston, for ten years.

WILLIAM BLAZEK is Senior Lecturer in English and American Literature at Liverpool Hope University. He co-edited (with Michael K. Glenday) the essay collection *American Mythologies: Essays on Contemporary Literature* (2005) and (with Laura Rattray) the volume *Twenty-First-Century Readings of* Tender Is the Night (2007). His recent publications include three essays on Wharton's World War I writings and a study of masculine aesthetics in *The Custom of the Country*. He is also a founding co-editor of *The F. Scott Fitzgerald Review*.

LINDA COSTANZO CAHIR is Associate Professor and co-editor of the *Edith Wharton Review* at Kean University, and a contributing editor to *Literature/Film Quarterly*. Her publications include numerous articles and the books *Society and Solitude in the Works of Herman Melville and Edith Wharton* (1999) and *Literature into Film: Theory and Practical Approaches* (2006).

SHARON KEHL CALIFANO is Assistant Professor of English and Co-Chair of the Liberal Studies Department at Hesser College, in Manchester, New Hampshire. She has written on James, Wharton, and Morton Fullerton for the *Critical Companion to Henry James: A*

Literary Reference to His Life and Work (2009), contributed entries for the *Facts on File Companion to the American Novel* (2006), and wrote the Introduction to the Barnes and Noble Digital World Edition of Edith Wharton's *The House of Mirth* (2002).

DONNA CAMPBELL is Associate Professor of English at Washington State University. She is the author of *Resisting Regionalism: Gender and Naturalism in American Fiction, 1885–1915* (1997), which includes sections on Wharton's early fiction, *Ethan Frome*, and *The House of Mirth*. Focusing primarily on Wharton's naturalism and her relationship to other writers, her recent essays on Wharton have appeared in the *Edith Wharton Review, Studies in American Naturalism, A Companion to the American Short Story*, and *Twisted from the Ordinary: Essays on American Literary Naturalism*. Her current book project is titled *Bitter Tastes: Naturalism, Early Film, and American Women's Writing*.

HELENA CHANCE began her career as an Art Editor and Picture Researcher in book publishing. Following the completion of her doctorate at Oxford University in 2010, she was appointed Senior Lecturer in Visual and Material Culture at Buckinghamshire New University in High Wycombe. Her research focuses on the relationship between architecture and landscape and the design and representation of the industrial landscape in Britain and the United States from 1880 to 1939.

MELANIE DAWSON is Assistant Professor of English at the College of William and Mary, where she teaches courses in late nineteenth-century and early twentieth-century literature, women's environmental literature, and masculinity studies. She is the author of *Laboring to Play: Home Entertainment and the Spectacle of Middle-Class Cultural Life* (2005), co-editor of *The American 1890s* (2000), and editor of Gertrude Atherton's *Black Oxen* (2012). She is currently at work on a project focused on women and ageism in early twentieth-century literature.

LINDA DE ROCHE is Professor of English and American Studies at Wesley College in Dover, Delaware. She is a former Fulbright scholar and holds a doctorate from the University of Notre Dame. A specialist in American literature, she has published on Willa Cather, Gail Godwin, F. Scott Fitzgerald, and Erich Segal. Her books include *A Student Companion to F. Scott Fitzgerald* (2002), *A Student Companion to Willa Cather* (2006), and *Mary Higgins Clark: Life and Letters* (2010).

ANNE-MARIE EVANS is Lecturer in Literature at York St. John University. Her main area of interest is early twentieth-century American literature. She completed her PhD at the University of Sheffield where her thesis examined the work of women writers such as Wharton, Ellen Glasgow, Gertrude Stein, Fannie Hurst, and Zora Neale Hurston in terms of literature, consumerism, and the articulation of female identity. Current projects involve working on a monograph based on her thesis and on a new research project exploring contemporary literary and cultural responses to the American Civil War.

SUSAN GOODMAN is the H. Fletcher Brown Chair of Humanities at the University of Delaware. Her books include *Edith Wharton's Women: Friends and Rivals* (1990), *Edith Wharton's Inner Circle* (1994), *Ellen Glasgow: A Biography* (1998, 2003), and *Civil Wars: American Novelists and Manners, 1880–1940* (2003). With Carl Dawson, she has co-authored two biographies: *William Dean Howells: A Writer's Life* (2005) and *Mary Austin and the American West* (2009). Her most recent book is a cultural history of *The Atlantic Monthly* and its writers titled *Republic of Words* (2011). She has received a number of fellowships, including awards from the Andrew W. Mellon Foundation, the National Endowment for the Humanities, and a Guggenheim Fellowship for Biography.

JENNIFER HAYTOCK is Associate Professor of English at SUNY The College at Brockport. She has published the monographs *At Home, At War: Domesticity and World War I in American Literature* (2003) and *Edith Wharton and the Conversations of Literary Modernism* (2008) as well as essays on Wharton, Ernest Hemingway, John O'Hara, and Willa Cather.

ADAM JABBUR is Assistant Professor of English at Towson University, where he teaches courses in all periods of American literature. His publications include "Narrating the Sublime in *Absalom, Absalom!* and *The Unvanquished*" (2011), "Tradition and Individual Talent in Willa Cather's *Death Comes for the Archbishop*" (2010), and "'Land of Contrasts,' Land of Art: Morocco and the Imagination of Edith Wharton" (2010). His current project focuses on twentieth-century American historical fiction.

KATHERINE JOSLIN is the author of *Edith Wharton and the Making of Fashion* (2009), a winner of an American Library Association Choice Award. Her other books include *Jane Addams, A Writer's Life* (2004);

and *Edith Wharton* (1991). A founding member of the Edith Wharton Society, she directed a conference on Wharton in Paris in 1991 and then edited with Alan Price *Wretched Exotic: Essays on Edith Wharton in Europe* (1993). She is a Distinguished Faculty Scholar and Professor of English at Western Michigan University.

PAMELA KNIGHTS is Honorary Senior Lecturer at Durham University. She is the author of *The Cambridge Introduction to Edith Wharton* (2009) and co-author of *Edith Wharton's* The House of Mirth (2006). Other publications on Wharton include chapters in *The Cambridge Companion to Edith Wharton* (1995), *Edith Wharton's* The Custom of the Country: *A Reassessment* (2010), and *"This Strange Dream upon the Water": Venice and the Cultural Imagination* (2012). She has also written introductions to editions of *The House of Mirth* and *Ethan Frome*. She is currently working on a book, *Reading Dance and Performance Narratives for Children: Critical Moves*, for Palgrave Macmillan.

HEIDI M. KUNZ is Professor and Chair of the Department of English at Randolph College in Lynchburg, Virginia. She has written numerous articles on American literature, most recently in *F. Scott Fitzgerald in Context* (2011) and *Scientific Discourses and Cultural Difference* (forthcoming). She is currently working on a book, *The Mitchell Phenomenon: Celebrity Science and Cultural Memory*.

JESSICA SCHUBERT MCCARTHY teaches English at Washington State University. Her essay, "'It's Better to Watch': Compulsive Voyeurism in *The Custom of the Country*," appeared in *Edith Wharton's* The Custom of the Country: *A Reassessment* (2010). She has also published essays in *Studies in American Naturalism* and the *Journal of Scholarly Publishing*.

BONNIE SHANNON MCMULLEN has taught English literature at universities in the United States, Canada, and the United Kingdom, including more than twenty years' tutorial teaching at the University of Oxford. She has a particular research interest in the short story. She is the author of scholarly articles on F. Scott Fitzgerald, Wharton, Edgar Allan Poe, John Howison, and George Eliot. She recently contributed "'Don't Cry – it ain't that Kind of a Story': Wharton's Business of Fiction, 1908–13" to *Edith Wharton's* The Custom of the Country: *A Reassessment* (2010).

CECILIA MACHESKI is Professor Emerita at LaGuardia Community College of The City University of New York. She is co-editor of *Fetter'd or Free? British Women Novelists 1670–1820* (1985) and *Curtain Calls: British and American Women and the Theater 1660–1820* (1991). She has presented conference papers on a wide range of subjects, most recently on Wharton and Candace Wheeler. As a Fulbright Senior Scholar, she has taught American literature and Women's Studies in New Zealand and Norway.

MAUREEN E. MONTGOMERY is Associate Professor in American Studies at the University of Canterbury, New Zealand. She is the author of *"Gilded Prostitution": Status, Money, and Transatlantic Marriages, 1870–1914* (1989) and *Displaying Women: Spectacles of Leisure in Edith Wharton's New York* (1998), and she has published several articles dealing with Wharton's New York fiction. Her current work addresses the cultural work of novels of manners, etiquette, and travel writings in constructing U.S. national identity as white and civilized at a time of heightened debate around issues of "race," immigration, and empire.

ELSA NETTELS is Emeritus Professor of English at the College of William and Mary in Virginia. She is the author of *James and Conrad* (1977); *Language, Race, and Social Class in Howells's America* (1988); and *Language and Gender in American Fiction: Howells, James, Wharton, and Cather* (1997).

JULIE OLIN-AMMENTORP is Professor of English at Le Moyne College in Syracuse, New York, where she teaches a range of authors from Jane Austen to Jhumpa Lahiri. She is the author of *Edith Wharton's Writings from the Great War* (2004) and of essays on Henry James, Wharton, and Willa Cather. She is a past president of the Edith Wharton Society and is currently working on a comparative study of Wharton and Cather.

EMILY J. ORLANDO is Assistant Professor of English at Fairfield University. She is the author of *Edith Wharton and the Visual Arts* (2007), which earned a *Choice* Outstanding Academic Title Award in 2008. She also has published essays on literature and visual culture that have appeared in *American Literary Realism, Women's Studies: An Interdisciplinary Journal, New Voices on the Harlem Renaissance,* and other essay collections on American literature and culture. She was co-director of "Edith Wharton in Florence," the June 2012 international conference of the Edith Wharton Society.

ROBIN PEEL is Associate Professor of English at the University of
Plymouth in the UK. The focus of his recent research has been the
relationship between the work of Massachusetts women writers and
contemporary discourses. He is the author of *Writing Back: Sylvia
Plath and Cold War Politics* (2002); *Apart from Modernism: Edith
Wharton, Politics and Fiction* (2005); and *Emily Dickinson and the Hill
of Science* (2011). He is currently researching the impact of science on
nineteenth-century transatlantic travel writing and he coordinates the
Transatlantic Exchanges Forum at Plymouth.

MELISSA M. PENNELL is Professor of English at the University of
Massachusetts, Lowell. She is the author of the *Student Companion to
Nathaniel Hawthorne* (1999), the *Student Companion to Edith Wharton*
(2003), and *Masterpieces of American Romantic Literature* (2006) and
co-editor of *American Literary Mentors* (1999). She serves as a consulting scholar to museums in Lowell and Concord, Massachusetts, and
regularly delivers lectures on a variety of literary subjects, including the
life and works of Wharton, at public libraries and local schools.

LAURA RATTRAY is Senior Lecturer in American Literature at the
University of Hull. In addition to *Edith Wharton in Context*, she is the
editor of the two-volume *The Unpublished Writings of Edith Wharton*
(2009) and *Edith Wharton's* The Custom of the Country: *A Reassessment*
(2010). She is on the editorial board of the *Edith Wharton Review* and
has recently been awarded a Leverhulme Fellowship for a new study
of Wharton and genre, to be published by Palgrave Macmillan. Other
publications include work on F. Scott Fitzgerald, Josephine Johnson,
the Hollywood novel, Horace McCoy, and a forthcoming monograph
on 1930s American fiction.

JUDITH P. SAUNDERS is Professor of English at Marist College in
New York State. Her scholarship addresses a wide range of literary figures and topics, from Benjamin Franklin to Elizabeth Bishop, and it
includes numerous articles on the work of Wharton. She is the author
of *Reading Edith Wharton through a Darwinian Lens: Evolutionary
Biological Issues in Her Fiction* (2009).

SHARON SHALOO is the Executive Director of the Massachusetts
Center for the Book. A former board member of the Edith Wharton
Society, she was the co-director of the Society's conference in Newport
(2000) and London (2003). She has taught at Indiana University,
Bloomington; University of Massachusetts, Lowell; Wheaton College

(Norton, MA); and the University of Kent at Canterbury. She has published on Wharton and on topics in the history of the book and publishing studies, an interest sparked by several years' experience in a New York literary agency.

GAIL D. SINCLAIR is Executive Director and Scholar-in-Residence of the Winter Park Institute at Rollins College. Her chief academic focus is the representation of female characters in modern literature, and her latest publications include co-editing *Key West Hemingway: A Reassessment* (2009) along with essays in *Approaches to Teaching Fitzgerald's* The Great Gatsby (2009) and *Teaching Hemingway's* A Farewell to Arms (2008). She is currently on the board of directors for the Ernest Hemingway Foundation and Society and the F. Scott Fitzgerald Society.

CAROL J. SINGLEY is Professor of English and Director of Graduate Studies at Rutgers University-Camden, where she teaches American literature and culture, childhood studies, and children's literature. She is the author of *Edith Wharton: Matters of Mind and Spirit* (1995) and *Adopting America: Childhood, Kinship, and National Identity in Literature* (2011). She is the editor or co-editor of six volumes, including three on Wharton. She is a past president of the Edith Wharton Society and author of the bibliographic essay on Wharton for the annual *American Literary Scholarship*.

MARGARET TOTH is Assistant Professor at Manhattan College, where she teaches American literature and film. Her research interests focus on imperialism and race in early twentieth-century American fiction and visual culture. She has published in *Legacy: A Journal of American Women Writers* and *Studies in American Indian Literatures* and is currently working on a project on Wharton and Orientalism.

GARY TOTTEN is Associate Professor of English at North Dakota State University and President of the Edith Wharton Society. He has published essays on Wharton and her contemporaries and is the editor of *Memorial Boxes and Guarded Interiors: Edith Wharton and Material Culture* (2007). He currently is working on two book-length projects, one exploring issues of mobility in transatlantic African-American travel narratives and another on Theodore Dreiser's travel narratives.

LINDA WAGNER-MARTIN has been Hanes Professor of English and Comparative Literature at The University of North Carolina at Chapel

Hill since 1988; she recently retired. The recipient of Guggenheim, Rockefeller, National Endowment for the Humanities, and other fellowships, she received the Hubbell Medal for lifetime work in American Literature in 2011. She wrote several books on Wharton for the Twayne series and edited *The Portable Edith Wharton* for Penguin (2003). Her biographies include books on Zelda Fitzgerald, Sylvia Plath, Gertrude Stein, Barbara Kingsolver, and Ernest Hemingway.

Abbreviations

VD   *The Valley of Decision* (New York: Charles Scribner's Sons, 1902).

WF   *The Writing of Fiction* (New York: Charles Scribner's Sons, 1925).

SECONDARY SOURCE ABBREVIATIONS

Benstock   Shari Benstock, *No Gifts from Chance: A Biography of Edith Wharton* (New York: Charles Scribner's Sons, 1994).

CR   *Edith Wharton: The Contemporary Reviews*, eds. James W. Tuttleton, Kristin O. Lauer, and Margaret P. Murray (Cambridge: Cambridge University Press, 1992).

Lee   Hermione Lee, *Edith Wharton* (New York: Alfred A. Knopf, 2007).

Lewis   R. W. B. Lewis, *Edith Wharton: A Biography* (New York: Harper & Row, 1975).

Wolff   Cynthia Griffin Wolff, *A Feast of Words: The Triumph of Edith Wharton* (New York: Oxford University Press, 1977).

Preface

January 2012 marked the 150th anniversary of the birth of Edith Wharton. While many economies continued to flounder, this author's stock proved notably resilient. Anniversary events included radio dramatizations, day-schools, interviews with enthusiasts and scholars, newspaper and magazine articles on both sides of the Atlantic, a major academic conference in Florence for the Wharton Society, and an online birthday tribute. (Edith Wharton is, of all things, an established Facebook and Twitter presence.) In an article for the *Sunday Telegraph* to mark the occasion ("A 'lonely-hearted' heiress with a fearless eye"), Anita Brookner even targeted the British literary grail to propose Wharton as "a corrective to the national obsession with Jane Austen."[1]

In the pithy phrasing on the website of the author's home, The Mount, "After all of these years, Wharton still packs a cultural wallop." In the twenty-first century, the writer, born during the U.S. Civil War, infiltrates contemporary popular culture to a remarkable degree – and one imagines Wharton, insistently attuned to the marketplace and the "regular click of coin in [her] savings-box" (*Letters* 592), would have appreciated the financial, if not always the artistic, rewards. Her name, image, and writings inflect a wide array of popular cultures, spanning television, film, radio, music, and magazines. These range from *Gossip Girl*, *Entourage*, and the *Gilmore Girls*, to *The Nanny Diaries*, *Vogue*, the entertainment guides of Martha Stewart, the writings of Candace Bushnell, and the music of Suzanne Vega. Julian Fellowes' transatlantic television success, *Downton Abbey*, invited fruitful parallels to his predecessor, providing a cultural shorthand for its socially elite world, and Fellowes has cited Wharton among his favorite writers.

Long after her death in August 1937, Wharton remains a marketable asset. A collection of her letters sold at a Christie's auction in June 2009 for $182,500, while the surviving half of her library raised an eye-watering $2.6 million in 2006. Mass-marketed gift items, such as key rings, bookmarks, and photograph frames on sale in bookstores in the United States, carry two beautifully conceived lines from her dramatic monologue, "Vesalius in Zante": "There are two ways of spreading light; to be / The candle or the mirror that reflects it" (*Poems* 43). "In context," however, the lines swiftly lose their consumer-friendly allure. The assertion, after all, is not "Wharton's," but that of the physician-scientist speaker whose death-bed "confession" to the dissection of a girl still living ("pinioned hand and foot") admits no regrets: "Think what she purchased with that one heart-flutter / That whispered its deep secret to my blade!" (*Poems* 36).[2] While on the one hand chillingly inappropriate, on the other the market-ing line provides an apt reminder that Wharton's work, especially when it comes in period camouflage, is not always as it first seems.

In terms of Wharton scholarship, Helen Killoran labeled the years 1938 to 1975 "The Lull," while Cynthia Griffin Wolff, in the revised 1995 edition of her biography, hailed the "dazzling resurrection" of the writer's reputa-tion.[3] Hermione Lee offered a more nuanced appraisal in 2007, conclud-ing in her acclaimed biography that "[f]or all this massive interest among general readers and academics, much still remains to be done with the posthumous life of Edith Wharton" (Lee 758). *Edith Wharton in Context* addresses one such omission, by bringing together Wharton scholars to provide the first substantive volume focused exclusively on the social, lit-erary, cultural, and historical contexts that produced the writer and her long and prolific career. The collection considers the question of con-text through seven sections: Life and Works; Critical Receptions; Book and Publishing History; Arts and Aesthetics; Social Designs; Time and Place; and Literary Milieux. Contributors include the authors of: *Edith Wharton's Women: Friends and Rivals*; *Edith Wharton: Matters of Mind and Spirit*; *Edith Wharton's Writings from the Great War*; *Edith Wharton and the Visual Arts*; *The Cambridge Introduction to Edith Wharton*; *Displaying Women: Spectacles of Leisure in Edith Wharton's New York*; *Edith Wharton and the Making of Fashion*; *Apart from Modernism: Edith Wharton, Politics and Fiction*; and *Edith Wharton and the Conversations of Literary Modernism*. Also writing for the volume are the co-editor of the *Edith Wharton Review*, members of the Wharton Society board, the co-director of the sesquicentennial Wharton international conference, and the editors of *The Portable Edith Wharton*, *Memorial Boxes and Guarded Interiors: Edith Wharton and Material Culture*, and *The Unpublished Writings*. All leading Wharton scholars, their focus spans archival research, biography, publishing history, material culture, performance and the visual arts, gender studies, sociology and politics, and cultural studies. Each writer brings his or her expertise to build collectively the most sustained attempt to deepen our understanding of the ways in which Wharton lived and worked with, through, and sometimes against the contexts that impressed themselves upon her.

I would like to thank Ray Ryan for commissioning this volume for Cambridge University Press, Louis Gulino and Marielle Poss for seeing the book through production, and Jennie Kassanoff for her support from the outset of this project. I am grateful to the Beinecke Rare Book and Manuscript Library and its expert staff, especially Adrienne Sharpe and Anne Marie Menta; the British Association for American Studies; and the Edith Wharton Society. I would like to thank Elizabeth Ammons, Irene Goldman-Price, Laurah Heafield, Pam Knights, and Margaret Murray. My thanks go to all of the contributors to this volume for their expertise and enthusiasm for the project, from Wharton's Gobi Desert to the Cresta Run. I would also like to thank Julia Masnik at the Watkins/Loomis agency for facilitating permissions. Excerpts from unpublished Wharton writings are reprinted by permission of the estate of Edith Wharton and the Watkins/Loomis Agency. Special thanks to Julie Ellam, Susan Goodman, Linda Wagner-Martin, and the Rattray Club.

NOTES

1. A. Brookner, "A 'lonely-hearted' heiress with a fearless eye," *Sunday Telegraph*, January 15, 2012, 28.
2. My thanks to Clare Colquitt for alerting me to this marketing campaign.
3. H. Killoran, *The Critical Reception of Edith Wharton* (Rochester, NY: Camden House, 2001), 6; C. G. Wolff, *Edith Wharton: A Feast of Words* rev. ed. (Reading, MA: Addison Wesley, 1995), xxiii.

PART I

Life and Works

CHAPTER I

Edith Wharton: Contextual Revisions

Laura Rattray

> I don't believe there is any greater blessing than that of being pierced
> through & through by the splendour or sweetness of words, & no
> one who is not transfixed ... has known half the joy of living.[1]

In a recently recovered letter to her German teacher, Anna Bahlmann,
the fourteen-year-old who would become Edith Wharton pens a memorable self-portrait as she sits weeping tears of alcohol from a dripping
bandage, a wet cloth tied over an inflamed eye, leaving the correspondent
only her "very short-sighted" eye to guide her as she writes. Yet write she
does, and not a polite note – but, in "very bad writing," an eight-page
letter, detailing her poetry-in-progress, stanza choice, line and language
variants, translation, current reading, and literary criticism. "For two
or three days my eyes have been ailing, & reading & writing forbidden
pleasures, but now they are well again & I have got a new pen & I am
quite comfortable," assures the young correspondent. "Please, if it be
not troubling you too much, tell me which lines you *do not like*, in your
next letter" (my emphasis).[2] The evocative image conveyed through poor,
sight-strained penmanship reminds us in force that, whatever the obstacles, the youth who wrote as Eadgyth, David Olivieri, and Edith Jones
was resolutely determined to write. Indeed, from earliest childhood, stories, reading, and "making up" inspired "rhythmic raptures" (*BG* 38) and
"ecstasy" (*BG* 42) – "almost a form of illicit sexual indulgence" suggests
Elaine Showalter[3] – while at twenty-seven the author proclaims the blessing of "being pierced through & through by the splendour or sweetness
of words." Whatever course her life would take – a life she later described
as a series of "adventures with books"[4] – Edith Wharton's primary love
affair appears always to have been with language.

Filtered through the contexts of both her own age and those of subsequent generations, images of Wharton and her work continue to realign.
Louis Auchincloss memorably titled his 1971 study *Edith Wharton: A*

Woman in Her Time, yet the subject was also a woman *of* her time. And what a time. "The world is a welter and has always been one," she writes in the concluding "And After" section of her 1934 memoir, *A Backward Glance* (379). Born during the United States' Civil War, and dying as Europe broached World War II, Wharton witnessed dramatic social, economic, literary, cultural, and historic transformations. She lived through the Gilded Age, the Progressive Era, the surging expansion of the railroads, and a second industrial revolution. Her generation saw the building of immense industry monopolies, the seemingly unassailable power of financiers and bankers, the invention of the telephone and the incandescent bulb, divorce reform, the birth of film, the United States' expansionist endeavors, waves of immigration and immigration selection, Einstein's theory of relativity, and the arrival of the car. Wharton had a front seat at many of the cataclysmic events of World War I, while she viewed (from a distance) the onset of Prohibition in 1919, Amendment 19 (Woman's Suffrage in the United States) in 1920, a resurgent Ku Klux Klan, the Jazz Age, a series of Wall Street panics followed by the Crash, heralding the onset of the Great Depression. She witnessed the birth of modern celebrity culture, the coming of age of the modern consumer era, the rise of magazines, and revolutions in publishing, architecture, and interior design. In the arts, she outlived many of a phenomenal cast of leading talents. In an appreciation published in the week of the writer's death on August 11, 1937, the *New York Times* attempted to convey a sense of her extraordinary longevity in its opening lines: "Edith Wharton survived several literary generations. It is easier to realize how much of change she spanned in her creative life when one recalls that four of her poems, written at the age of 15, won the approval of Longfellow and, through his recommendation, appeared in *The Atlantic* of 1880."[5] Although she would be accused of failing to apply the theory to practice in her late writings, Wharton's "First Word" of *A Backward Glance* proclaims, "one *can* remain alive long past the usual date of disintegration if one is unafraid of change" (vii).

Wharton was a writer whose fiction often captured the very moment of social transition. She charted, for example, the course of new money, which threatened to dwarf the old inherited income of the genteel classes, heralding a dynamic shift in the makeup of elite social circles. She depicted the newly minted seeking to trade their wares on the marriage market for the lustre of social acceptance, alongside the erosion of traditional values and an increasing tolerance of divorce. With ambition and unsophisticated talent storming the bastions of the old, established order, social context is very quickly established as a primary character of a number of Wharton's most renowned society novels. *The Custom of the Country*, first published in 1913, the prophecy and warning text of rampant materialism, assumes a breathtakingly contemporary relevance in the burning embers of the economic meltdown post 2008. In the society novels, Wharton's narrator gives voice to the context, often translating for the reader the complex signings of an unfamiliar, closed world. May Archer's knowing instruction to her husband in *The Age of Innocence* that he "must be sure to go and see Ellen," her rival, memorably unleashes a page of narrative translation explicating this complex "mute message," "the code in which they had both been trained" (*AI* 269–70). Motoring to Le Bréau at the outset of World War I, Wharton commented on mysterious road "advertisements," which were in fact concealed plans of the principal French towns and the environs. The advertisements, noted the curious author, required viewers to look "at the picture at a certain angle" before "seeing the map come out" – and it is context itself that often proves the secret to unravelling her own narrative world.[6]

While elevated society proves its most insistent focus, Wharton's narrative realm does not deal exclusively with the preserve of the wealthy. The author was aware of the assumption that she wrote "only about the rich," despite "a list of ... tales, which deal with divers classes of people."[7] She certainly witnessed poverty and exploitation firsthand, in both urban and rural settings, in Europe and the United States, and notably criticized her predecessors, Mary Wilkins and Sarah Orne Jewett, for their "rose-coloured" distortions of country life (*BG* 293). She was well informed about the insalubrious working conditions facing factory workers and the damage those conditions inflicted on their health. Her (often less familiar) work considers those "divers classes" on a sliding scale of privilege from shabby gentility to the working poor and beyond – into the bowels of America's underclass and the destitute: her first published poem, "Only a Child" (focused on a child, locked up in a reformatory, who commits suicide); her first published story, "Mrs. Manstey's View"; the early rejected novella, *Bunner Sisters*. Her protagonists of privilege may also look into that social abyss: Lily Bart, always vulnerable and playing for high stakes, gambles, loses, and leaves the game to face New York's "rubbish heap" (*HM* 498). Wharton's plays also descend the social scale: an untitled play – one of the most intriguing, raw additions to her oeuvre – concerns an unmarried, pregnant maid and the social horrors and hypocrisies raining down on her from her elevated employers and their circle, one of whom is also pregnant by a lover. She, however, is a married woman protected by position, money, and class.[8] Hypocrisy thrives in Wharton's narrative milieu, even as it is mercilessly exposed. In a November 1905 letter to the *New York Times Saturday Review of Books*, reader Joseph D. Holmes forcefully objected to *The House of Mirth* "as a representation of New York society," and lamented the paper's praise for the novel:

Certainly Mrs. Wharton should apologize for introducing us to a set of people we would never meet twice voluntarily and making roués, divorcées, and gamblers her samples of the inhabitants of the "purlieus" of Fifth Avenue and Rhinebeck. Doesn't Mrs. Wharton know some of our big-hearted, athletic, clean-living men, prominent in church and social work, as in society and business? Doesn't she know some of our bright, broad-minded women, the true leaders of New York's "best" circles – generous, witty, "smart" in the best sense? ... And the pity of it is that it should go out to the Nation and abroad with the praise of the Outlook and THE NEW YORK TIMES SATURDAY REVIEW OF BOOKS.[9]

However, Wharton scholarship was slow to acknowledge that its writer was also tainted to varying degrees by the prejudices of her age. Early-twentieth-century anxieties about "race suicide" and hybridity deeply informed Wharton's aesthetic practices. Yet it is only in recent years that scholars have considered thoroughly the sometimes conflicting and profoundly uncomfortable discourses of race and imperialism that inflected both her world and her work, with important studies by Elizabeth Ammons and Jennie Kassanoff, among others.[10] This writer's palette fashioned an array of female protagonists unrivaled in the history of American letters, yet their creator proved at times remarkably dismissive of women and women's rights. These views often came in the guise of casual remarks and witticisms in her correspondence. When encouraged by Mary Berenson to read her daughter Ray Strachey's volume, *The Cause* (1928), charting the history of the British women's movement, Wharton countered: "To read a book called 'The Cause' (& *that* cause!) will require all my affection for you." After glancing at the volume, she retorted: "I, who think that women were made for pleasure & procreation, note with satisfaction that the leaders of the movement, judging from their photos, all look unfitted for the first, & many for both functions!" (quoted in Lee 611–12). The writer's career spanned a period that witnessed extraordinary changes and progressions in the social, sexual, economic, and political arenas for women, while at the same time, in practice, women's lives continued in many aspects to be conflicted and curtailed. (Few authors have employed images of imprisonment and entrapment to such devastating effect.) Here too was a woman whose vividly evocative travel descriptions, breathing nuance and sensitivity, could transport her reader to the very sites: the silver lamps flickering in the side chapels of the Santa Maria Novella in Florence, the "powdered" pine woods of St. Moritz with their suspended white waterfalls, magical Moroccan bazaars, and "enchanting" Greek Islands. At the same time, she could dismiss its people, the inhabitants of such wondrous places, in a facile, arrogant stroke: "filthy," "noisy," "brutal," and "detestable." ("'Only man is vile' ought to have been written of Southern Italy instead of Ceylon's Isle.")[11] Such prejudices were largely left out of the Lewis edition of the letters (Lee is too charitable in deeming their absence "a polite misrepresentation" [613]); only recently have these prejudices been reclaimed as part of the record.

The stuffy grande dame, rigid realist, tentative modernist – a variety of reductive labels have attached themselves to Wharton over the years. "When a critic thinks up a good label for me it lasts about ten years," she observed to an interviewer a year before her death.[12] Some of the epithets, however, were self-attached – for instance, writing of herself to younger contemporaries as representing "the literary equivalent of tufted furniture and gas chandeliers" (*Letters* 481) or "the Mrs. Humphry Ward of the Western Hemisphere" (*Letters* 445) – and these tags then proved stubborn to remove. And "Mrs. Wharton" was undoubtedly concerned about image: while she arranged papers "for my biographer," in private or intimate matters she proved determined to cover her tracks. She was notably anxious that her letters to her former lover Morton Fullerton should be returned (they were not), whilst in the midst of grief for her "so devoted" Anna Bahlmann, who gave more than forty years' service before her death in 1916, the "heart-broken" author had the presence of mind to request of Bahlmann's niece that all her letters be destroyed.[13] Sally Norton left a note that in the event of her death her correspondence was to be returned to the writer for her to destroy it, as she could not bring herself to do so.[14] Wharton was a prolific correspondent throughout her life: following a short trip in 1924, she found sixty-five letters awaiting her return, "the incoming mail over three days" (*Letters* 3), while in August 1905 she described herself as "overwhelmed" by correspondence and missing the "faithful hand" of Anna Bahlmann who was in Paris. The Lewis edition of her correspondence, while immensely valuable, reproduces only four hundred of many thousands of extant letters (these many thousands despite significant casualties, not least the author's destruction of most of her letters to Walter Berry and the burning of many of her letters by James), and it is inconceivable that there are not further discoveries still to be made in the United States and Europe, notably in France, where she made her home for more than twenty-five years.

Wharton scholarship has witnessed both important new discoveries and misdirections. Landmarks in the scholarship include R. W. B. Lewis' 1975 biography, which capitalized on the opening of the Yale archives, and Hermione Lee's internationally lauded 2007 study, which regenerated widespread interest both within and beyond the confines of academia. Biography has long been the showcase genre of Wharton scholarship, which in certain regards proves both a blessing and a curse: it opens up the critical vista on a life, while indirectly perpetuating determinedly biographical readings of her work. (The BBC Radio 4 adaptation of *Ethan Frome*, broadcast in January 2012, even recasts its narrator as "*Miss* Wharton.") The ongoing appreciation of Wharton's later writing, and of her less familiar works generally, has been greatly welcome, placing an extended range of texts under the critical spotlight. An emerging interest in the author's contribution to genre underscores her extraordinary dexterity, spanning both fiction and non-fiction: poetry, plays, novels, novellas, short stories, translation, architecture and design manuals, critical writings, memoirs, travel writing, and cultural history. Other ties have been loosened or unfastened entirely – most mercifully, perhaps, the link to Henry James that at one time threatened, like *Ethan Frome*, to bind "hand and foot." In a prescient 1967 article, Louis Auchincloss bemoaned the comparison ("ad nauseam") of the writers' backgrounds, when Wharton's, he claimed, "couldn't have been more different if she'd been born in the dust bowl": the female writer from a "cultivated ... [yet] totally uncreative family ... had to fight for her own expression, whereas Henry James would have been practically slapped over the fingers with a ruler had he not started writing at an early age."[15] Unexpected archival discoveries have also captured the imagination – the purchase of the Fullerton letters by the University of Texas at Austin, the recovery in France of Wharton's account of her cruise on the *Vanadis*, and the evergreen, seemingly prurient interest in the graphic Yale "Beatrice Palmato" fragment – even, in the last case, as boxes of substantial writings in the Beinecke archive continued to be overlooked.

Gaps have remained, however, and more than 150 years after the writer's birth, ongoing discoveries are still required to supply missing pieces of the puzzle. Despite the vast extant correspondence, R. W. B. and Nancy Lewis conclude that "Edith Wharton was thirty-eight years old, [and] had been publishing fiction for nine years ... before someone other than her Scribners editors thought her letters worth retaining" (*Letters* 4). As a result, they explain, there is only a single letter in their volume from Wharton's youth and childhood, then "[a]lmost twenty years must pass before another letter [dated 1893] ... comes into view" (*Letters* 27), throwing a veil over the writer's childhood, young adulthood, and the early years of the Wharton marriage. Similarly, Lee speculates on years when the biographical trail runs cold: "[F]ive poems [appeared] in *The Atlantic Monthly* when she was eighteen. And then something happened. It would be nine years before a few more poems appeared.... It was another seven years before her first book publication, and eight years before her first volume of stories.... The huge creativity of this exceptional young girl was somehow halted" (Lee 46).

There are surprises, however. Two years after the publication of Lee's biography, Wharton scholarship witnessed the extraordinary recovery of the writer's correspondence to Anna Bahlmann, her German teacher, secretary, early literary advisor, and sometime confidante. Auctioned at Christie's in 2009, purchased for the archive at the Beinecke, and only recently available to scholars, the collection includes 132 letters from Wharton to Bahlmann and spans a period of 41 years. The earliest missive was written at Pencraig, Newport, on May 31, 1874, when Edith Jones was just twelve; the last, dated December 29, 1915, was mailed from Paris, where the fifty-three-year-old writer was subsumed by her relief work during World War I, and with a lifetime's experiences in between. While covering more than four decades, many of the letters are focused on the mystery years of her youth and early married life, before and during the emergence of the professional author. Like the advertisements that concealed secret maps over which Wharton puzzled in the French countryside, this fascinating new resource opens up a series of altered images, realigning our understanding of the family dynamics, her youthful voice and ambitions, and calls into question her retrospective depiction of both people and events. Even where the clinical facts remain the same, the contexts from which those facts are mined can be transformed.

As Melanie Dawson identifies in her essay on biography for this volume, in later life Wharton depicted herself as having been a shy, solitary, intense child. In her memoir draft, "Life and I," the author self-consciously accentuated the portrayal, even amending her manuscript from "very shy" to "painfully shy self-conscious child" (*LI* 198). Wharton depicts a girl beset by anxieties and phobias, living "in a state of chronic fear" and "terror," "some dark undefinable [sic] menace, forever dogging [her] steps" in a "species of hallucination" that lasted "seven or eight years" (*LI* 191–92). The witty exuberance of *Fast and Loose* always appeared to run counter to such a claim, and the earliest letters to Bahlmann are charmingly animated, humorous, and high-spirited. Written from Newport, Rhode Island, the early correspondence presents a delightful picture of the pastimes of the young Edith Jones, as well as opening up the contextual vista on her social world. The familiar image of the author as the stately older woman entirely gives way not just to the girl, but to the girl unfettered by the potentially skewed perspective of her mature self, and she is a welcome new presence in Wharton research.

In the first letter of the Bahlmann correspondence, the twelve-year-old has been "commissioned" to write by "Mamma." Newport is "delightful" and they are ready and will be "very very glad indeed" to see "dear Miss Anna," with the "[e]ver your very affectionate" E. N. Jones requesting that she be a long time putting the house in order. In correspondence written between the ages of twelve and fifteen, she also makes her best "dancing school curtsey," she is pestered by her young niece Trix to whom she is "Aunt Eduff," and she feels really "beatific," having "practiced violently one of Beethoven's waltzes, (a species of funereal hymn) made two rosettes for a new pair of slippers & generally behaved ... – a sensation having still the charm of novelty." At fourteen, Edith Jones is about to join an archery club, and she also provides "dearest Tonni" with a charming description of lawn tennis, the sport young people gather most afternoons to play: "It is a most fascinating game; difficult, tiresome, & destructive to pretty dresses, & to the complexion, but nevertheless delightful."[16] She was evidently an energetic, athletic child and young woman, with skating, bicycling, and sleigh-rides also referenced among her leisure pursuits.

During this period, the breathtaking range of reference and learning that pervades the correspondence of the mature Wharton is already well fermented. She is an avid reader, facing the "horrid" task of having to decide which books will accompany her to New York, unwilling to leave a single volume behind, but unable to take them all to the city. Longfellow, Browning, Marlowe, Shakespeare, Dante, George Eliot, Goethe, and Schiller's correspondence are among those referenced, with Edith Jones urging Bahlmann to return so they can read German together. She will often critique a work for its lack of "passion," suggesting, for example, that Longfellow's poetry reminds her of a lifeless, "chilly" sculpture. Although Wharton would later claim that her mother largely forbade the reading of novels (*BG* 65), George Eliot's fiction is evidently on her younger self's reading list: *Daniel Deronda*, her "beloved" *Romola*, and in a charming summation of *Middlemarch* she once again bemoans a lack of passion, this time between Will Ladislaw and Dorothea, concluding, "When it was so dangerous to love at all, they might have loved a little more!"[17]

Edith Jones' avid reading is surpassed only by her avid writing. The author may not have published her first collection of stories until the age of thirty-seven, or her first novel until she was forty – Louise Collier Wilcox, writing in *The Outlook* in 1905, was thankful that "a writer had come who . . . had reversed the order of the day, and learned to write before she wrote"[18] – but she was, without doubt, a child prodigy. Alongside the youthful exuberance, mixed with a sharpening dash of self-deprecation, runs a serious side, intensely focused on her writing. The same letters of 1876 convey a remarkable creative precocity, and Bahlmann is an interested, engaged reader, enabling the young writer to discuss her work in great detail: "I do not like the 'do' you suggest"; "I can only use a word of one syllable"; the "rhymes are very difficult . . . especially in the third stanza"; "I would not spoil the last line." At fourteen, discussing her work "Mignon," she concludes she has been more than "rewarded" by Bahlmann's "frank criticism," which she finds a greater compliment than a polite, unmeaning "Oh, it's lovely," which she notes she is accustomed to hearing when she begs for an honest opinion. The focus of those literary efforts is all-important: this is an early apprenticeship in poetry and, to a lesser degree, translation – another genre in which Wharton would prove adept throughout her career.

Wharton's first and last books were volumes of poetry. *Verses* (1878) would be published privately, when the writer was just sixteen, while a collection of love poems, selected by Wharton and Robert Norton with the collaboration of Gaillard Lapsley, was published posthumously in 1938. In between came two other volumes of her own poetry – *Artemis to Actaeon* (1909) and *Twelve Poems* (1926) – while single poems were published throughout her lifetime in publications including *The Atlantic Monthly*, the *New York World*, and *Scribner's Magazine*.

At some of the most dramatic moments of her life, Wharton rejected all other genres to channel her emotion through poetry: an erotic tryst with a lover ("Terminus," "The Room"); an outpouring of grief at the death of her beloved Walter Berry (drafted in her diary on the day of Berry's death, and later published as "Garden Valedictory" in *Scribner's Magazine* in January 1928), while anguish at the senseless barbarity and casualties of World War I resulted in a mix of propagandist verse and deeply personal tributes to lost, young friends. When she was at the height of her commercial success in the 1920s, renowned for her ruthless playing off of one publisher against another and for serializing her work in the most lucrative magazines, she also negotiated with the Medici Society in London for the publication of her volume, *Twelve Poems*, in 1926, with a miniscule print run of 130 copies. Wharton agreed to buy thirty copies and receive a royalty of 25 percent on the sale of the remaining 100. The royalty statements are revealing: recorded sales of nine copies in 1927; a single copy in 1928; seven copies in 1929, earning the author a three-year total of eight pounds, eighteen shillings and sixpence. In the midst of Wharton's fierce commercialism, however, this was both a labor of love, and a marker of esteem. In her recent study of *The Atlantic Monthly* and its writers, Susan Goodman charts the writer's enthusiasm for publishing in the magazine, long after it first featured her work in 1880. Fresh from the success of her first novel, *The Valley of Decision* (1902), she was the one who made the approach ("I am tired of waiting"), willing to sacrifice her usual fee of $500 per story for the magazine's going rate in the cause of prestige and reaching out to a new audience.[19] Wharton was evidently prepared to make exceptions to her commercial rule. In 2005, the Library of America published a selection of the author's poetry, edited by Louis Auchincloss, yet the volume did not bring about a widespread reevaluation of the writer's work in this genre. The focus of the discussions with Bahlmann underlines the gravity of the omission. In recent years, Wharton scholarship has suggested the importance of playwriting to her early professional career, and the Bahlmann letters now in turn illuminate the primacy of poetry throughout her youth, underlining the fact that Wharton research has still to engage fully with the writer's extraordinary dexterity and range of genre.

In *A Backward Glance*, Bahlmann's early role as the writer's "Supreme critic"[20] was largely subsumed by Wharton's determined, loving recognition of Walter Berry: "Others praised, some flattered – he alone took the trouble to analyze and criticize" (*BG* 116). Certainly her influence waned. When the seventeen-year-old Jones has work accepted in *The Atlantic Monthly*, she is for the most part simply informing her governess of her success, not seeking her advice, as evidenced by the casual "By the way did I or did I not tell you that I have four things coming out in the 'Atlantic'?"[21] Bahmann's role changed to secretary, rather than advisor, but in a study of the early apprenticeship this newly discovered correspondence offers ample evidence that she invaluably provided her charge with a secure, yet critically rigorous environment in which she could be taken seriously and hone her craft.

Another revelation of the correspondence lies in its indication of a closer, more supportive family environment than Wharton would later concede. She appears close to "Mama," while Papa is an "angel" transcribing her work (a task she later delegates to Bahlmann). She conveys a "special message from Papa & Mama"; "Mama sends much love"; the parents join with their daughter to "beg" Bahlmann to agree to their joint plan for her to visit.[22] In a letter dated October 16, 1879, written from Pencraig, the seventeen-year-old opens by explaining that she has been spending time reading and translating Bahlmann's long letter to her mother, suggesting some of her governess's letters were written in German for language practice for her pupil. The Lucretia Jones of the acidic "Drawing-rooms are always tidy" response to her daughter's first novel, written at the age of eleven (*BG* 73), is nowhere in evidence here. On the contrary, as indicated by her earlier letter, Edith Jones is accustomed to being told her work is "lovely" – although this clearly brought its own set of frustrations. Later, during the Whartons' early married life, her mother is often with them or close by, in both the United States, with the living arrangements at Pencraig, but also in France; at times Wharton is "very much worried" about her mother's health, while letters from Paris in 1891 recount their custom of spending every afternoon together.

Undoubtedly, the relationship changed, and its souring appears to have its origins in the fall out from her brother Frederic's divorce. Wharton writes to Bahlmann of her sister-in-law "having been obliged" to divorce her brother, and the "deluded & perverted view" of the situation which her mother had been influenced to take. Like the narrator of *Ethan Frome*, each protagonist appears persuaded by an individual, uncorroborated "vision."[23] Whatever the precise cause of the rift, the mother-daughter relationship never recovered. Wharton's manuscript word selection and amendments of "Life and I," targeting Lucretia many years after her death (see *Unpublished Writings* xxi–ii; 228–30), were still those of a daughter with issues unresolved, and her late recollections increasingly appear as reinventions, perhaps perversely reminiscent of Percy Lubbock's twisted posthumous "portrait" of her. When Lucretia died in Paris after a long illness, during which, her daughter recounted, she had been "paralyzed & unconscious" for nearly a year, there was understandable relief all round at the release. In a letter to Sally Norton of June 3, 1901, Wharton opens with an explanation of the black-bordered paper and expresses "thankfulness" at the sudden conclusion, before continuing: "But my object in writing is to say that I was glad to hear the drive to Pittsfield was not <u>too</u> uncomfortable." Nine days later, Wharton wondered who was responsible for the "barbarous" notion of conveying grief in gloves and passementeries.[24] There were no reminiscences, no fond memories shared, no regrets. The death of Wharton's dogs drew forth anguished descriptions and exchanged condolences; the death of her mother was presented as a release, but also a digressive aside.

Teddy Wharton, meanwhile, has traditionally been portrayed as the most unsatisfactory of Edith Wharton's unsatisfactory men: "[h]is collapses were in part, one surmises, ways of drawing attention to himself in the midst of his wife's widespread recognition and her achieved independence and well-being" (Lewis 273); "explosive"; "he 'foamed at the mouth'"; "[s]he was 'pinching' herself at the prospect that the nightmare would soon be over" (Benstock 239, 126, 277); "[i]t is not difficult to identify the good-natured but callous husband as Teddy" (Wolff 73); "[t]he awful comedy of Teddy's performance is like a grotesque parody of her own restlessness" (Lee 396). Readings of the late, collapsing marriage have at times been read as the whole. Familiar with such portraits, a reader of the Bahlmann correspondence might be forgiven for a double take when realizing the following descriptions are also of Teddy. There is effusive recognition from the woman who married him: "it seems almost incredible that a man can be so devoted, so generous, so sweet-tempered & unselfish"; "he is one of the people whose charm makes itself felt at once"; Teddy is as "sweet-tempered" as ever; he is as "patient as an angel."[25] Through the Bahlmann letters, the bold black and white strokes of biographical fact take on the more complex shadings of real life. The epithet of "charm" is attached to Teddy. He is athletic, energetic, and personable; his wife notably enjoys the attention he receives, for example with his skating prowess in St. Moritz. He is sweet, attentive, and concerned not to leave his wife when she is ill (albeit a potentially mixed blessing), and offers more sympathy than she musters for him when positions are reversed.

The picture of the Wharton marriage, conveyed through the writer's own words, is of a comfortable, compatible partnership before the ravages of his illness take their toll. Notably, Teddy is prepared to indulge his wife's passion for travel, and marriage offered Mrs. Wharton a passport to more exotic, dangerous destinations, places she could not easily have visited as a single woman. (To the woman known as "Mrs. Wharton" for a generation, "Mrs. Wharton" to her was, for a long time, Teddy's mother.) The author writes of the risks of a number of their expeditions during the *Vanadis* cruise, accounts of visitors murdered and the U.S. consul unable to venture out without an armed escort.[26] Writing appeared to have been sidelined during the upheaval over her father's illness and the broken engagement to Harry Stevens. During the early years of marriage, writing generally continued to be sidelined in favor of social amusements, adjustments to married life, travel, and the couple's love of exercise, but it also surfaced in a different form in this period, through breathtakingly vivid accounts of her travels in the correspondence.[27] On the one hand, these descriptions would prove a valuable dress rehearsal for the later travel books, but on the other, Wharton would never quite recapture the youthful immediacy and spontaneity of these early accounts in the studied brilliance and determined authority of the published books. It was Teddy Wharton who made this life possible. He was capable, amenable, and more than a little intimidated by his wife's talent, writing to Sally Norton that he was not on her "high plain of thought."[28] While his wife had a dazzling array of learning, culture, and languages at her fingertips, Teddy's correspondence is of simple sentence structure, misplaced and missing apostrophes and grammar, although the content speaks kindly: in his sole extant letter to Bahlmann, he encourages her to enjoy her travels and invites her to cable him if she requires money,[29] while the letter to Sally Norton, referenced above, also conveys messages from "Puss," expresses concern for her health and satisfaction that the "servants" are all receiving French lessons. As the marriage disintegrated, his wife's letters adopted an unforgiving tone: accusatory, self-justifying, condescending. Teddy is patronized as "Dear Old Man"; she summarizes her actions and his response, making copies of her letters for her version of the record.[30] Yet, however the final years unraveled, there was clearly for many years another side to the marriage, and another Teddy, on view through the Bahlmann letters.

The letters of the marriage also record a litany of ill-health, and are a reminder that Wharton's could so easily have been a different story, like that of so many women who could not find a way through the domestic, social, and gender conflictions of their age. The heavily-laced wit of self-deprecation ("my vile body") is at times reminiscent of Alice James, the sister in the shadows who in many respects chose invalidism as a vocation, and literally invalidated herself in the process. Illness was part of the fabric of Wharton's early married life. One letter from Paris on October 23, 1884, for example, runs the gamut, describing the writer's health, the health of her mother, that of Toots the dog, as well as informing Bahlmann that she was being sent a "wonderful" new medicine designed for the suppression of uric acid. The advertising contexts of this period and of the writer's early career provide a graphic reminder that illness was fashionable and its treatment big business, and Wharton took treatments in Switzerland, Italy, and the United States during her early married life. A newspaper clipping in the Beinecke, penciled the *Saturday*

Evening Sun of March 1, 1902, carries a favorable review of *The Valley of Decision*, while its reverse boasts an extensive advertisement for "Lydia E. Pinkham's Vegetable Compound," promising a cure for "Nervous Prostration," aimed at its target audience of women: "The relation of woman's nerves and generative organs is very close; consequently nine tenths of the nervous prostration, nervous despondency and nervous irritability of women arise from some derangement of the organism which makes her a woman."

Genuine ill health blighted Wharton's life at this time, even as she maintained an active social life. In 1908, she looked back in a letter to Sally Norton to recall: "for *twelve* years I seldom knew what it was to be, for more than an hour or two of the twenty four, without an intense feeling of nausea, & such unutterable fatigue ..." (*Letters* 139–40). The Bahlmann correspondence records a list of illnesses, ailments and treatments. Wharton is advised to be "absolutely quiet"; she takes courses of electric baths and massage therapy; she is to follow a "regime"; she is placed on a special diet that leaves her "starved"; there are repeated references to "cure," "rest," and "after-cure" – but certainly no rest cure with Silas Weir Mitchell and not a forbidding of writing – the correspondence itself is testimony to that. (During a "cure" in Paris, she writes of plans to take French lessons and to study in the Cabinet d'Estampes.) In one letter from Land's End, she reports that if her improvement continues her doctor has determined there is to be no "rest-cure," but he also forbids traveling to Europe on account of the effects of the sea voyage on her heart. While the letters name Teddy's early ailments as "malaria," "neurasthenia," and "bad nervous attacks," Wharton's own illnesses are variously diagnosed as: "nervous dyspepsia," "indigestion," "colds," "a state of extreme depression caused by anaemia & goutiness," "insomnia," "a relapse," "un peu de faiblesse," "bad hay-fever," "migraine," and "rheumatism."[31] Ill health was a regular houseguest. Even reports of wellness carried qualifications, for example, when writing to Bahlmann from Land's End on August 27, 1893: "But – there is always a but with us ..." Wharton was not subjected to Mitchell, but she was certainly subjected to unsuitable, debilitating treatments. Although the writer mined the account for comedy, her new doctor, after being shown a table of his patient's diet, informed her husband she had been "starved" and promptly instructed her to eat "everything."[32] Wharton in turn notified Bahlmann that she was now "eating wildly right & left." Being underweight was evidently a concern throughout the writer's health record. From the age of seventeen there are delighted notes of her weight gain: a weight of 123 pounds, aged seventeen; joy at having gained three pounds; weight of 128 pounds, her highest in years. After excessive traveling, the author suggested she was fit to exhibit at Barnum's as the Thin Lady. Meanwhile, a jacket she had sent to Bahlmann was too small, prompting the loaded comment: "I am glad, however, that you are getting fat."[33]

Throughout the letters of the years before and as Wharton emerges as a professional writer, there runs a strong sense of someone determined to find a way through – an individual who describes life as "charming," "nomadic," but "purposeless." In 1896 she writes of wanting to overcome the "restlessness" that has overcome her since she has been ill – a trait that would mark many of her protagonists.[34] For a woman who in many ways would become synonymous with Europe – and one recalls the often-quoted letter to Sally Norton in 1903, describing herself as feeling "out of sympathy with everything" in America (*Letters* 84) – there are notably strong, earlier expressions of homesickness for the United States. The home desired is Newport: she is "crazy" to return she confesses from Paris in April 1891.[35] At this stage of her life, Wharton was, like *The Custom of the Country*'s Undine Spragg of Apex, still U.S.-branded, having "taken its creases" more than she realized. In the same letter in which she discusses the aftermath of Minnie's divorce in 1896 and the polarized family responses, Wharton writes that she means to make the "best" of her life. Scattered references to writing slowly build: in August 1889, the *Century* editor accepts "The Sonnet on the Sonnet"; "Mrs. Manstey's View" is accepted in 1890; "The Fulness of Life" is initially rejected in 1891; verses on Chartres are published in *Scribner's* in August 1893, while in a letter of November 15, 1893 the author encloses the fee for "That Good May Come," explaining her ability to send a Christmas present of her own earning is one of the few high spots in a series of "melancholy" months. By 1898, the output has become a cascade of productivity, and Wharton lists her achievements in a letter simply marked "Sunday": imminent publication of "The Pelican"; acceptance of "The Muse's Tragedy," and the completion of "Souls Belated," as she does indeed find, as advertised in the title of her first collection of short stories, "The Greater Inclination."

With the emergence of the efficient, business professional, a familiar picture of Wharton re-emerges. Conditions for writing were rarely ideal: she suffered from insomnia, but drugs rendered her unfit to work the following morning. She writes of "Niagara days" in 1905 when everything comes at a rush from morning to night.[36] In the one letter in the Bahlmann collection from Teddy, dated August 27, 1908, he writes from The Mount that no one can stop "Puss" working. Tellingly, conditions were seldom entirely conducive to Wharton's protagonists with artistic leanings, among them Ralph Marvell, Vance Weston, and Claud Hartwood. In her early play, *The Man of Genius*, the author even appears to mock the very concept of "ideal": the writer Hartwood is frustrated by constant interruptions and conflicting demands, yet when conditions are perfected, his every whim catered for, he is simply frustrated and bored. Wharton embraces the discipline, and although illness returns at intervals, her phenomenal creativity is never stemmed.

The Wharton-Bahlmann correspondence comes to an abrupt end with the latter's unexpected death in April 1916 while she was visiting family in the United States. The author's personal bereavements around this time were heavy, but at the same time they represented only one woman's casualties in a world descending into barbarism. The final batch of letters provide a detailed insight into Wharton's work and the output from her workroom at the outset of World War I. "Mrs." Wharton was a grafter, recording long days "steeped" in her relief work, when she could "eat, sleep, talk, think" only ouvroir.[37] The writer was thoroughly committed and involved, and her newspaper appeals for funds are notable for their use of possessives: "my 735 destitute children of Flanders," "my 160 helpless old people and nuns."[38] One newspaper headlined her special dispatch "In the Land of Death" with the assertion that "No woman, probably no man not engaged in military service, has seen so much of the war."[39] This is the same woman who, postwar, would be increasingly regarded as a throwback to the past, while a number of young male modernists wore their shrapnel wounds as a badge of legitimacy, or forever regretted a lack of battle experience. Her correspondence can be graphic: in a September 9, 1914 letter to Bahlmann, Wharton relayed "authenticated" accounts of Belgian children arriving in Paris with their hands cut off, a man with his eyes put out, a Belgian woman with her ears cut off, a girl gang raped. The detail of the first eighteen months of the relief efforts recorded in the correspondence before Bahlmann's death underscores the importance of the discussion of Wharton's war work and writings conducted by Julie Olin-Ammentorp, Alan Price, and others. As with millions of veterans, the securities and certainties of life exploded on the battlefield, forever lost, and one of the most poignant items of the writer's vast archive at the Beinecke library is a fragment of glass from the bombed Rheims cathedral – a fragment rescued in the chaos, from all that had been lost.

We will never know whether our views of the final twenty-one years of Wharton's life would have similarly realigned had Bahlmann survived for the correspondence to extend beyond its extant forty-one years.

The author is reported to have enjoyed her friends' perception of her as "self-made," an epithet that Auchincloss endorsed in his article "Edith Wharton and Her Letters": "Not that she did not inherit things, but she did not inherit the things she *wanted* to inherit. She did not like New York architecture; she did not like New York culture; she did not like New York society. She had to find her own books, her own friends, her own country (which was, eventually, France [Auchincloss 2])." Yet, as the ongoing archival discoveries and scholarly reevaluations remind us, this was no immaculate conception; Wharton was also a product of her age. In much of the writer's oeuvre, to deny context is shown to deny meaning: in removing the Marvell family jewels from their age-old setting and orchestrating the eventual sale of the de Chelles' tapestries, *The Custom of the Country*'s relentless Undine Spragg violates context and "destroy[s] the identity" (CC 214). Context is the Goliath glue that binds together the writer's social, economic, literary, aesthetic, historical whole. She repeatedly attempted to thwart and mislead: destroying letters, requesting others to do the same, reinventing events and circumstances of her life for the record. Even as she covers her tracks, however, Edith Wharton rarely fails to leave an impression.

NOTES

1. Unpublished letter from Edith Wharton to Anna Bahlmann (Tonni), August 24, 1889, written in Newport. Anna Catherine Bahlmann Papers Relating to Edith Wharton. Yale Collection of American Literature, Beneicke Rare Book and Manuscript Library, Yale University. All of the Wharton-Bahlmann letters cited are from the Beinecke archive.
2. Letter from E. Jones to Bahlmann, Newport, August 1876 (no day).
3. E. Showalter, "The Death of the Lady (Novelist)," reprinted in E. Ammons (ed.), *The House of Mirth* (New York: Norton, 1990), 357–72; 371.
4. Among the Wharton papers at the Beinecke are two fragments of memoirs, both titled "Adventures with Books." See L. Rattray (ed.), *The Unpublished Writings of Edith Wharton* (London: Pickering and Chatto, 2009), vol. II, vii, xxiv, n. 2. Subsequent references to this volume are included in the text.
5. *New York Times*, August 13, 1937. Clipping, Beinecke.
6. Letter from Wharton to Bahlmann, written from the "Ouvroir de Mme Wharton," October 17, 1914.
7. E. Wharton, "A Cycle of Reviewing," *Spectator*, November 3, 1928, reprinted in F. Wegener (ed.), *Edith Wharton: The Uncollected Critical Writings* (Princeton University Press, 1996), 159–63; 161–62.
8. "Untitled" in L. Rattray (ed.), *The Unpublished Writings of Edith Wharton* (London: Pickering and Chatto, 2009), vol. I, 67–89.

9. Letter to the *New York Times Saturday Review of Books*, Joseph D. Holmes "On board SS. Cretic, Gibraltar," November 13, 1905. Clipping, Beinecke.

10. See E. Ammons, "Edith Wharton and the Issue of Race" in M. Bell (ed.), *The Cambridge Companion to Edith Wharton* (Cambridge University Press, 1995), 68–86; E. Ammons, "The Myth of Imperiled Whiteness and *Ethan Frome*," *The New England Quarterly*, LXXXI: I (March 2008), 5–33; and J. Kassanoff, *Edith Wharton and the Politics of Race* (Cambridge University Press, 2004), 1–7.

11. Letter from Wharton to Bahlmann, dated March 27 [1887].

12. Paris edition of the *New York Herald Tribune*, November 1936. Clipping, Beinecke.

13. See telegram from Wharton to Minnie Jones, April 20, 1916, and letters to Mrs. Charles Parker, dated April 17, 1916, and September 15, 1917. Bahlmann Papers, Beinecke.

14. See Sally Norton's handwritten note with the request, dated November 1906. Folder 896, Edith Wharton Collection. Yale Collection of American Literature, Beneicke Rare Book and Manuscript Library, Yale University.

15. L. Auchincloss, "EW and Her Letters," *The Hofstra Review* (Winter 1967), 1–7; 3. Subsequent references to this work are included in the text.

16. See letters to Bahlmann, dated May 31, 1874; November 13, 1875; August 1876 (no day); September 17, 1876; September 23, 1876. Wharton scholarship will be indebted to Irene Goldman-Price, whose edition of the Bahlmann correspondence is forthcoming from Yale University Press.

17. See letters to Bahlmann dated November 13, 1875; August 1876 (no day); September 17, 1876; September 23, 1876; September 2 [1878].

18. L. C. Wilcox, "Literary Personalities," *The Outlook*, November 25, 1905, 719–24; 719. Beinecke.

19. S. Goodman, *Republic of Words: The Atlantic Monthly and Its Writers 1857–1925* (Hanover and London: University Press of New England, 2011), 216–18.

20. Letter from Wharton to Bahlmann, Pencraig, October 17, n.y.

21. Letter from Wharton to Bahlmann, Pencraig, October 16, 1879. Wharton lists the four pieces as "A Failure," "Patience," "Wants," and "A Parting Day." In a burst of creativity, the young author records in the same letter that she has also completed two sonnets and a 196-line work, but is "too lazy" to copy them.

22. See letters from Wharton to Bahlmann, dated September 17, 1876 and September 23, 1876.

23. Letter from Wharton to Bahlmann, from Milan, written over two days, June 3 and 4 [1896].

24. Letters from Wharton to Sally Norton, from Lenox, dated June 3, 1901 and June 12, 1901. Wharton Papers, Beinecke.

25. Letters from Wharton to Bahlmann: "Sunday" [1885, announcing engagement]; "Tuesday eve" [1885]; September 7, 1894; September 27 [1894].

26. Letter from Wharton to Bahlmann, April 12 [1888], written from the yacht *Vanadis*.

27. See especially the following letters to Bahlmann: March 27 [1887]; April 12 [1888]; March 13, 1890; January 11, n.y.
28. Letter from Edward (Teddy) Wharton to Sally Norton, February 26, 1907, written from Rue de Varenne, Paris. Wharton Papers, Beinecke.
29. Letter from Teddy Wharton to Anna Bahlmann, August 27, 1908, written from the Mount. Bahlmann Papers, Beinecke.
30. See Wharton's correspondence of folder 941, Beinecke, with copies of letters from the writer to her husband during 1911–12, addressing Teddy's health, his "nervous breakdown," and difficult/impossible behavior, including his reluctance to concede control of her trust fund and management of her financial affairs.
31. See especially the following letters from Wharton to Bahlmann: September 7 [1894] from Paris; January 11, n.y. from St. Moritz; June 1 [1899] from London; September 20 [1898] from Land's End; November 1 [1898] from Philadephia; January 24 [1899] from Washington.
32. See letters from Wharton to Bahlmann, written from London on June 1 and June 5, 1899.
33. See the following letters to Bahlmann: October 16, 1879; August 26, 1880; April 13 [1907]; April 14, n.y.
34. Letter from Wharton to Bahlmann, June 4 [1896], written from Turin.
35. Letter from Wharton to Bahlmann, April 18, 1891, written from Paris.
36. Letter from Wharton to Bahlmann, September 1905, written from The Mount.
37. Letter from Wharton to Bahlmann, October 9, 1914, written from Rue de Varenne, Paris.
38. "Mrs. Wharton's Appeal. To the Editor of *The New York Times*," written December 1, 1916. Clipping, Beinecke.
39. E. Wharton, "In the Land of Death," *The Sun*. Undated clipping, Beinecke.

CHAPTER 2

Chronology: Wharton in Cultural and Historical Context

Pamela Knights and Laura Rattray

The majority of Wharton's writings first appeared in magazines, as did those of many of her contemporaries. This list includes all the books she published in her lifetime, with selected other writings, omitting translations of her works.

Date	Edith Wharton (EW)	Cultural contexts	Historical contexts
1861			**1861–65**: U.S. Civil War; defeat of the Southern Confederacy; Emancipation Proclamation; assassination of President Abraham Lincoln (1865).
1862	Edith Newbold Jones (ENJ) born January 24, New York City, youngest child of Lucretia Rhinelander Jones (1825–1901) and George Frederic Jones (1821–82); two brothers: Frederic (Freddy) (1846–1918) and Henry (Harry) (1850–1922). ENJ nicknamed "Pussy," "Lily," and "John." Baptized at Grace Church, New York.	Anthony Trollope, *North America*.	Development of the Holmes Stereopticon.
1863		George Eliot, *Romola*.	

Date	Edith Wharton (EW)	Cultural contexts	Historical contexts
1865	Given white spitz puppy (Foxy), first of many adored small dogs.	First exhibition of Edouard Manet's *Olympia* at the Paris Salon. Charles Dodgson (Lewis Carroll), *Alice's Adventures in Wonderland*.	
1866	Joneses move to Europe, conserving income in post-war economic depression; Hannah Doyle ("Doyley"), ENJ's Irish nurse, accompanies them. The family spends six years in Italy, Spain, France, and Germany.	Fydor Dostoyevesky, *Crime and Punishment*.	Founding of the American Society for the Prevention of Cruelty to Animals, New York.
1867			The United States buys Alaska from Russia for $7.2 million.
1868		Louisa May Alcott, *Little Women*; Wilkie Collins, *The Moonstone*.	Founding of National Woman Suffrage Association. First transcontinental railroad; railroads extend throughout the century, with clearances of Native American tribes from the Great Plains. Retail merchant A. T. Stewart commissions $3 million mansion on Fifth Avenue and 34th Street.
1869		Leo Tolstoy, *War and Peace*.	Prohibition Party founded in Chicago. Suez Canal opened.
1870	Gains sister-in-law Mary (Minnie) Cadwalader Rawle (1850–1935); friendship endures Minnie and Freddy's divorce (1896).		First Married Women's Property Act, UK. John D. Rockefeller establishes Standard Oil Company. Franco-Prussian war (1870–71).

(continued)

Date	Edith Wharton (EW)	Cultural contexts	Historical contexts
1871		Charles Darwin, *The Descent of Man*; Edward B. Tylor, *Primitive Culture*.	Paris Commune.
1872	Family returns to the United States. Birth of Beatrix, only child of Minnie and Freddy Jones.	George Eliot, *Middlemarch*.	Society leader, Mrs Astor, with Ward McAllister, launches exclusive dances for the "400," the pinnacle of old New York families.
1873	The Joneses employ Anna Bahlmann, a young woman of German ancestry, to tutor their daughter. Bahlmann encourages her young charge in her prolific reading and writing of literature (notably the writing of poetry) and translations. It marks the start of a relationship that would endure for more than forty years. Bahlmann would later return to the Wharton household as secretary and assistant.	Samuel Clemens (Mark Twain) and Charles Dudley Warner, *The Gilded Age: A Tale of To-Day*; Walter Pater, *Studies in the History of the Renaissance*; Arthur Rimbaud, *A Season in Hell*; Jules Verne, *Around the World in Eighty Days*.	Panic on Wall Street; widespread business failure and unemployment. Comstock Law prohibits trade in "obscene literature" and "immoral articles"; targets include birth control, abortion, and sexual information.
1874		First exhibition of *Impression, Sunrise* by Claude Monet with Anonymous Society of Painters, Sculptors, Printmakers, etc in Paris.	New York financier's daughter, "beauty" Jennie Jerome, 20, marries Lord Randolph Churchill; mother to future British Prime Minister, Winston Churchill.
1875		Première of Georges Bizet's *Carmen*, Paris. Publication of Heinrich Schliemann's *Troy and Its Remains* [*Trojanische Alterthümer*, 1874], about his purported discovery of the site of Troy and of "Priam's Treasure" at	

Date	Edith Wharton (EW)	Cultural contexts	Historical contexts
		Hissarlik, Turkey, in 1873. Christina Rossetti, *Poems*.	
1876		First Bayreuth Festival, with first complete cycle of *The Ring of the Nibelung* by Wagner. Tchaikovsky composes *Swan Lake*. Herbert Spencer, *The Principles of Sociology* appears in three volumes between 1876 and 1897.	Invention of telephone (Alexander Graham Bell). Battle of Little Big Horn.
1877	Completes *Fast and Loose*, "novelette," using the pseudonym David Olivieri (30,000 words; first publication, 1977).	Henry James, *The American*.	Cornelius Vanderbilt dies, leaving $105 million.
1878	*Verses* (Newport: C. E. Hammett, Jr.): [anonymous] twenty-nine poems, privately printed. First publication.		
1879	Poem, "Only a Child," published under the pseudonym "Eadgyth" in *New York World*. Makes social debut in private ballroom on Fifth Avenue. Longfellow shows ENJ's poems to William Dean Howells at *The Atlantic Monthly*.	Fydor Dostoyevsky, *The Brothers Karamazov*; Henry George, *Progress and Poverty* advocates redistribution of wealth; Henrik Ibsen, *A Doll's House*; Henry James, *Daisy Miller*.	Thomas Edison invents incandescent bulb.
1880	Five poems published in *The Atlantic Monthly*: "Areopagus," "Patience," "Wants," "The Parting Day," and "A Failure." Concerns over father's health; the family seeks better climate in France.	Rise of magazines – *Cosmopolitan*, the *Ladies' Home Journal*, *McClure's*. Rodin creates *The Thinker*. Henry James, *Washington Square*; Vernon Lee, *Studies of the Eighteenth Century in Italy*; Emile Zola, *Nana*.	Growth of women's clubs throughout the 1880s; labor unrest – almost 10,000 strikes and lockouts; electricity for private homes; rise of department stores. Taylor's "time-study" experiments.
1881		George M. Beard, *American Nervousness*; Helen Hunt	

(continued)

Date	Edith Wharton (EW)	Cultural contexts	Historical contexts
1881		Jackson, *A Century of Dishonor*; Henry James, *The Portrait of a Lady*; Dante Gabriel Rossetti, *Ballads and Sonnets*; Walt Whitman prepares 6th edition of *Leaves of Grass*. *Century* begins serialization of William Dean Howells' "divorce" novel, *A Modern Instance* (to October 1882). Book published October 1882.	New York population, swelled by immigration, tops one million. New England Divorce Reform Society founded.
1882	Father dies in Cannes. ENJ inherits over $20,000. Engaged briefly to Harry Stevens. (His mother opposes marriage.) Engagement announced in August and broken off in October.		First New York central power plant (Edison, backed by J. P. Morgan); steam-heating in private homes. Second Married Women's Property Act, UK.
1883	Returns to the United States with mother. Briefly becomes close to law student, Walter Van Rensselaer Berry (1859–1927), later her dearest and life-long friend. Meets Edward Wharton (Teddy), popular Bostonian socialite (supported by family on annual allowance of $2,000).	New Metropolitan Opera House opens with performance of *Faust*, sung by Christine Nilsson. *Life* magazine established. *The Atlantic Monthly* reviews Margaret Lee's novel, *Divorce: Or, Faithful and Unfaithful*. Friedrich Nietzsche, *Thus Spoke Zarathustra* (1883–85).	Working Girls' Vacation Society founded in New York. Introduction of "Standard Time" in the United States. Krakatoa volcano explosion. Maiden trip of Orient Express.
1884	Catherine Gross employed as ENJ's maid; remains as housekeeper until her death (1933).	John Singer Sargent, portrait of *Madame X* (Mme. Gatreau). Mark Twain, *Adventures of Huckleberry Finn*.	Fabian Society established.
1885	Marries Teddy Wharton in private ceremony, 29 April.	William Dean Howells, *The Rise of Silas Lapham*.	Death of William Henry Vanderbilt, richest man in the world.

Date	Edith Wharton (EW)	Cultural contexts	Historical contexts
1886		Frances Hodgson Burnett, *Little Lord Fauntleroy*; Robert Louis Stevenson, *Kidnapped*, *The Strange Case of Dr Jekyll and Mr Hyde*.	The Statue of Liberty dedicated in New York harbor.
1887		Arthur Conan Doyle, *A Study in Scarlet*; Mary E. Wilkins [Freeman], *A Humble Romance and Other Stories*.	Queen Victoria's Golden Jubilee.
1888	Whartons lavish $10,000 on four-month Aegean cruise on steam yacht, *Vanadis*. (Journal of voyage published, 1992.) EW inherits $120,000 from distant cousin, Joshua Jones.		
1889	Whartons rent house on Madison Avenue, New York. *Scribner's Magazine* accepts more poems, including "The Last Giustiniani."	Vincent Van Gogh, *Starry Night*. Andrew Carnegie's essay, "Wealth" (published in book form as *The Gospel of Wealth* in 1900).	Jane Addams founds Hull Settlement House, Chicago. Opening of the Eiffel Tower, commemorating the centennial of the French Revolution.
1890	Throughout the decade, EW suffers from recurring bouts of low health, including respiratory troubles and depression, while maintaining an active social life. In 1908, EW looks back to describe a form of "neurasthenia" as having "consumed" the "best years" of her youth (*Letters* 140).	Henrik Ibsen, *Hedda Gabler*; William James, *Principles of Psychology*; Jacob Riis, *How the Other Half Lives: Studies among the Tenements of New York*.	Louis Sherry opens restaurant at Fifth Avenue and 37th Street, rival to famous Delmonico's. Massacre at Wounded Knee, South Dakota.
1891	First published story, "Mrs. Manstey's View" (*Scribner's Magazine*, July). Whartons live at Pencraig Cottage on her mother's	Emily Dickinson's poems published posthumously (1891 and 1892); Thomas Hardy, *Tess of the d'Urbervilles*; Oscar Wilde, *The Picture of*	

(continued)

Date	Edith Wharton (EW)	Cultural contexts	Historical contexts
	grounds at Newport. Purchase townhouse in Park Avenue, New York. Suicide of William Craig Wharton (Teddy's father).	*Dorian Gray*; Mary E. Wilkins [Freeman], *A New England Nun and Other Stories*.	
1892	*Bunner Sisters* [30,000 word novella] rejected by *Scribner's Magazine* (published, *Xingu and Other Stories*, 1916).	First issue of *Vogue* magazine, a society weekly. Charlotte Perkins Stetson [Gilman], "The Yellow Wall-paper."	*New York Times* prints Ward McAllister's list of the "400." Suppression of Homestead Strike results in widespread anti-union campaign. Jay Gould, financier, dies; worth $77 million.
1893	*Scribner's Magazine* publishes "The Fulness of Life" [story] (December) and accepts two further stories (published in 1894 and 1895). Buys Land's End, on Atlantic front at Newport for $80,000. Becomes friends with French novelist, Paul Bourget.	Stephen Crane, *Maggie: A Girl of the Streets*.	Panic of 1893: Wall Street collapse. Economic depression for next four years. World Columbian Exposition, Chicago, where Edison demonstrates his Kinetoscope. Anti-Pinkerton Act curtails Federal Government's power to hire private security and strike-breaking agencies.
1894	"That Good May Come" [story] (*Scribner's Magazine*, May). Travels in Italy. Meets British expatriate writer Vernon Lee (Violet Paget).	Claude Debussy, *Prélude à l'après-midi d'un faune*. George Du Maurier, *Trilby*.	Alfred Dreyfus arrested for spying; given life sentence on Devil's Island in January 1895, exonerated 1906. Pullman Strike.
1895	"The Lamp of Psyche" [story] (*Scribner's Magazine*, October). Invited to Alva Smith Vanderbilt's famous ball at Marble House, Newport.	Oscar Wilde imprisoned, sentenced to two years' hard labor. Première of *Guy Domville* by Henry James. Joseph Breuer and Sigmund Freud, *Studies on*	Booker T. Washington: Atlanta Exposition Speech. Auguste and Louis Lumière give first public showing of a film, *Lunch Break at*

Date	Edith Wharton (EW)	Cultural contexts	Historical contexts
		Hysteria; Stephen Crane, *The Red Badge of Courage*; H. G. Wells, *The Time Machine*.	the *Lumière Factory*. Wilhelm Conrad Röntgen discovers X-rays.
1896	"The Valley of Childish Things" [set of fables] (*Century*, July).	Nobel Prizes established. Sousa composes "The Stars and Stripes Forever." Henri Bergson, *Matter and Memory*; Anton Chekhov, *The Seagull*; Paul Laurence Dunbar, *Lyrics of Lowly Life*; Sarah Orne Jewett, *The Country of the Pointed Firs*.	Utah joins the Union, with full suffrage rights granted to women. Democratic convention: William Jennings Bryan's "Cross of Gold" speech. Separate-but-equal doctrine upheld by the Supreme Court in Plessy v. Ferguson case.
1897	First book, *The Decoration of Houses* [a treatise on interior design] (Scribner's), with architect Ogden Codman, Jr.	The Bradley Martins host Louis XV costume ball at New York Waldorf Hotel, boasted to cost $370,000. Opening of Tate Gallery, London. Henry James, *What Maisie Knew*; Bram Stoker, *Dracula*.	Rockefeller retires, worth c. $200 million.
1898		Based in Fifth Avenue studio, Childe Hassam founds the Ten American Painters Group. Publication of "J'accuse!" by Emile Zola, in defence of Dreyfus. Henry James, *The Turn of the Screw*; Oscar Wilde, "The Ballad of Reading Gaol."	Outbreak of Spanish-American war.
1899	First story collection, *The Greater Inclination* (Scribner's); continues throughout career to publish individual stories in magazines. Travels in Europe. From 1899 to 1902, EW works	New York society weekly, *Town Topics*, claims a subscription list of 140,000. Kate Chopin, *The Awakening*; Frank Norris, *McTeague*; Olive Schreiner, *The Woman*	Philippine-American war (1899–1902).

(continued)

Date	Edith Wharton (EW)	Cultural contexts	Historical contexts
	on at least four plays: a social comedy, *The Tight-Rope*; a stage adaptation of *Manon Lescaut*; a second original play, *The Man of Genius*; and a translation of Herman Sudermann's drama, *Es Lebe das Leben*.	*Question*; Thorstein Veblen, *The Theory of the Leisure Class*.	
1900	*The Touchstone* [novella] (Scribner's). Travels in Europe.	Publication of *European Travel for Women* by sister-in-law, Mary Cadwalader Jones. Universal Exhibition in Paris. L. Frank Baum, *The Wonderful Wizard of Oz*; Joseph Conrad, *Lord Jim*; Theodore Dreiser, *Sister Carrie*; Sigmund Freud, *The Interpretation of Dreams* [1899] (3rd edition translated into English by A. A. Brill, 1913).	Eugene Debs, former trade-union leader, runs for president on a Socialist platform.
1901	*Crucial Instances* [stories] (Scribner's). Buys 113-acre estate in Lenox, Massachusetts. Plans large house and gardens, comes to be known as The Mount; architect Francis V. L. Hoppin. Mother dies in Paris. Inherits trust of $90,000; Teddy and brother Harry are co-trustees.	Clyde Fitch's *The Climbers* at the Bijou Theater.	President McKinley dies, shot by anarchist. Presidency of Theodore Roosevelt (to 1909); Roosevelt promises anti-trust legislation. First billion-dollar trust, U.S. Steel (Big Steel).
1902	First novel, *The Valley of Decision* (2 volumes, Scribner's). Becomes friends with Theodore Roosevelt. Begins correspondence with Henry James (1843–1916).	Joseph Conrad, *Heart of Darkness*; André Gide, *L'Immoraliste*; Henry James, *The Wings of the Dove*; Owen Wister, *The Virginians*.	

Date	Edith Wharton (EW)	Cultural contexts	Historical contexts
	Moves into The Mount, Lenox in September. Teddy shows signs of nervous illness.		
1903	*Sanctuary* [novella] (Scribner's). Travels in Europe with Teddy. First of many visits to Salsomaggiore (Italian spa) for "inhalations" and rest.	Marie Curie awarded first Nobel Prize, for Physics. Bernard Berenson, *The Drawings of the Florentine Painters*; W. E. B. Du Bois, *The Souls of Black Folk*; Jack London, *The Call of the Wild*, *The People of the Abyss*; Frank Norris, *The Pit*.	The United States strengthens immigration selection. Wright brothers' first flight.
1904	*Italian Villas and Their Gardens* [collection of articles on landscaping and architectural design] (Century); *The Descent of Man and Other Stories* (Scribner's). Buys first automobile. Travels through England and France. Works on *The House of Mirth* throughout busy summer at The Mount. Guests include Henry James.	Ellen Glasgow, *The Deliverance*.	Railroad engineer, John F. Wallace, accepts appointment to supervise building of Panama Canal. Two-thirds of adult male workers in the United States receive average wage of less than $600 per year. Banking houses of Morgan, Rockefeller, Vanderbilt, and Baker control business and commercial life of the United States.
1905	*The House of Mirth* [novel] (Scribner's); serialized, January–November; EW finishes writing in March; book published October 14. Becomes best-seller (140,000 copies by the end of the year). *Italian Backgrounds* [collection of travel essays] (Scribner's). Lunches at the White House with President Roosevelt.	Exhibition of Matisse's *Woman with the Hat* at Salon D'Automne; critic referred to him and others as "les fauves." Thomas Dixon, Jr.'s *The Clansman: An Historical Romance of the Ku Klux Klan* is *The House of Mirth*'s best-selling rival.	Eugene Debs involved in formation of the International Workers of the World. Albert Einstein's theory of relativity.

(continued)

Date	Edith Wharton (EW)	Cultural contexts	Historical contexts
1906	Travels through England and France. Charles Du Bos translates *The House of Mirth* into French. Stage adaptation of *The House of Mirth* (with Clyde Fitch). Whartons attend successful opening in Detroit; play fails in New York.	Upton Sinclair, *The Jungle*.	President Roosevelt requests new census on marriage and divorce; tells Congress that marriage is "at the very foundation of our social organization."
1907	*Madame de Treymes* [novella] (Scribner's); *The Fruit of the Tree* [novel] (Scribner's). Whartons and Henry James tour France in a motorcar. Developing relationship with Morton Fullerton (1865–1952); begins a "Love Diary." Divides her time between Paris and Lenox.	Pablo Picasso, *Les Demoiselles d'Avignon*. Henry Adams, *The Education of Henry Adams*; Frances Hodgson Burnett, *The Shuttle*; Henry James, *The American Scene*.	
1908	*The Hermit and the Wild Woman and Other Stories* (Scribner's); *A Motor-Flight through France* [travelogue] (Scribner's); affair with Fullerton (1908–10); continues love diary, letters, and love poems.	Zona Gale, *Friendship Village*.	First Model T Ford car assembled.
1909	*Artemis to Actaeon and Other Verse* (Scribner's). Friendship formed with Bernard Berenson. Worsening rifts with Teddy, whose mental and emotional condition deteriorates. In November, discovery of Teddy's embezzlement of $50,000 of EW's money.	First season of Sergei Diaghilev's *Ballet Russes*, Paris. Sigmund Freud and Carl Jung give invited lectures at Clark University, Massachusetts. Charlotte Perkins Gilman founds feminist periodical, the *Forerunner* (to 1916).	Founding of National Association for the Advancement of Colored People.

Date	Edith Wharton (EW)	Cultural contexts	Historical contexts
1910	*Tales of Men and Ghosts* [stories] (Scribner's). Rents apartment in Paris; Teddy dispatched on world tour.	*Manet and the Post-Impressionists* exhibition in London, curated by Roger Fry. *The American Magazine* begins serialization of Frances Hodgson Burnett's *The Secret Garden* (November 1910 to August 1911; book published 1911). Jane Addams, *Twenty Years at Hull House*; E. M. Forster, *Howards End*.	Strikes in garment industry in New York; Women's Trade Union League helps strikers.
1911	*Ethan Frome* [novella] (Scribner's). Final stay at The Mount, which is then sold. EW and Walter Berry visit the Berensons in Florence. Tries and fails to secure Nobel Prize for Henry James.	Theodore Dreiser, *The Financier*, first volume of the *Trilogy of Desire*; Charlotte Perkins Gilman, *Herland*, *The Man-Made World, Our Androcentric Culture*; Frederick Taylor, *The Principles of Scientific Management*.	Roald Amundsen reaches South Pole.
1912	*The Reef* [novel] (Scribner's).		French protectorate imposed in Morocco. *Titanic* sinks on maiden voyage, April 15. Election of President Woodrow Wilson.
1913	*The Custom of the Country* [novel] (Scribner's) serialized January–November (serialization begins months before EW has completed the story); book published October 18. On April 16, divorce is finalized in Parisian court and EW retains her married name. Travels with Walter Berry in Sicily and Bernard Berenson in Germany.	The International Exhibition of Modern Art, also known as the Armory Show, in New York. Première of *The Rite of Spring*, Paris. Alain-Fournier, *Le Grand Meaulnes*; Marcel Proust, *Du Côté de Chez Swann* (*À la Recherche du Temps Perdu* 1913–27). Beatrix [Jones] Farrand designs new gardens at the White House for the	Suffragette Emily Davison killed after running out in front of the King's horse at Epsom Derby, UK.

(continued)

Date	Edith Wharton (EW)	Cultural contexts	Historical contexts
	Last visit to the United States for ten years to attend wedding celebrations of niece, Beatrix Jones, in New York.	wife of Woodrow Wilson. Later projects include the campus gardens at Yale and Princeton and in the UK at Glyndebourne.	
1914	Travels in Spain (July). **1914–19:** Based in Paris, tireless fundraising and other work for unemployed women, refugees, homeless children, and tuberculosis convalescents. Visits the front, and writes articles for *Scribner's Magazine*.	Geoffrey Scott, *The Architecture of Humanism*.	**1914–18:** World War I. Woodrow Wilson declares policy of U.S. neutrality (August). First Battle of the Marne (September); first Battle of Ypres (October–November). Rising publicity in the United States for new method of pain relief in childbirth, and founding of the National Twilight Sleep Association (NTSA).
1915	*Fighting France, from Dunkerque to Belfort* [essays] (Scribner's); compiles *The Book of the Homeless* [collection of poetry, drawings, articles by renowned contemporaries] (Scribner's, 1916). Organizes Children of Flanders Rescue Committee.	Henry James renounces American citizenship. Film of *The Birth of a Nation*.	Allied landings at Gallipoli (April); second Battle of Ypres. German submarine sinks the *Lusitania* (May).
1916	*Xingu and Other Stories* (Scribner's). Death of Henry James, February 28. EW made Chevalier of French Legion of Honour. Death of Anna Bahlmann in Kansas City.	The term "Dada" is invented.	Easter Rising, Dublin. Battle of the Somme (July–November). Woodrow Wilson re-elected.
1917	*Summer* [novella] (Appleton). Tours Morocco with Walter Berry	Leonard and Virginia Woolf establish The Hogarth Press (Bloomsbury, London). David Graham	Germany announces unrestricted submarine warfare (January). The

Date	Edith Wharton (EW)	Cultural contexts	Historical contexts
	(September–October). American Red Cross takes over many of her war charities.	Phillips, *Susan Lenox: Her Fall and Rise*.	United States declares war on Germany (April). First American troops arrive in France (June). Third Battle of Ypres (Passchendaele) begins (July). Revolution in Russia.
1918	*The Marne* [novella] (Appleton). Buys house (Pavillon Colombe) outside Paris. Death of brother Freddy. Silent film of *The House of Mirth*.	Willa Cather, *My Ántonia*; Booth Tarkington, *The Magnificent Ambersons* (Pulitzer Prize 1919).	Germany launches major offensives on the Western Front (Spring). Former Tsar, Nicholas II, and wife and family executed by the Bolsheviks (July). Hundred Day Offensive by Allies; German army in retreat (August to November). Armistice signed (November 11). Spanish influenza pandemic.
1919	*French Ways and Their Meaning* [essays] (Appleton); rents château at Hyères on Riviera.	Expatriate American Sylvia Beach opens bookshop in Paris, Shakespeare and Company, which will become a center for modernist experimental writing. The United Artists Corporation is formed by Charles Chaplin, Douglas Fairbanks, D. W. Griffith and Mary Pickford. Sigmund Freud, "The Uncanny"; Amy Lowell, *Pictures of the Floating World*.	Signing of the Treaty of Versailles (June). 18th Amendment (Prohibition).

(continued)

Date	Edith Wharton (EW)	Cultural contexts	Historical contexts
1920	*The Age of Innocence* [novel] (serialized in *Pictorial Review*); book published by Appleton. *In Morocco* [travelogue] (Scribner's).	Harlem Renaissance (into the 1930s). Robert Wiene directs *The Cabinet of Dr Caligari*. F. Scott Fitzgerald, *This Side of Paradise*; Sinclair Lewis, *Main Street*; Katherine Mansfield, *Bliss, and Other Stories*; Anzia Yezierska, *Hungry Hearts*.	League of Nations formed. 19th Amendment (Woman's Suffrage). Soaring membership of a resurgent Ku Klux Klan in the 1920s (an estimated five million members by 1924).
1921	Wins Pulitzer Prize for the novel, *The Age of Innocence* – the first awarded to a woman.	*Ladies' Home Journal* asks: "Does Jazz Put the Sin in Syncopation?" Percy Lubbock, *The Craft of Fiction*.	Moroccans struggle for independence in Rif War (1921–26).
1922	**1922–31**: Continues to travel; buys her Hyères home. Publication of *The Old Maid* [novella] (serialized in *Red Book Magazine*); *The Glimpses of the Moon* [novel] (Appleton) written for *Pictorial Review*. (F. Scott Fitzgerald will work on film version.) Death of brother Harry.	Willa Cather, *One of Ours*; T. S. Eliot, *The Waste Land*; F. Scott Fitzgerald, *The Beautiful and Damned*; James Joyce, *Ulysses*; Sinclair Lewis, *Babbitt* (dedicated to EW); May Sinclair, *The Life and Death of Harriett Frean*.	Signing of the Anglo-Irish Treaty and the establishment of the Irish Free State. Benito Mussolini comes to power in Italy.
1923	*A Son at the Front* [novel] (Scribner's). Visits the United States to receive honorary Doctorate of Letters from Yale University; first woman to receive the award. Last visit to the United States. Film adaptation of *The Glimpses of the Moon*.	Bessie Smith makes first recording, including "Down Hearted Blues." Willa Cather, *A Lost Lady*; Jean Toomer, *Cane*.	The Munich Putsch and the arrest of Adolf Hitler.
1924	*Old New York* [novella sequence]: *False Dawn (The 'Forties), The Old Maid (The 'Fifties), The Spark (The 'Sixties)*, and *New Year's Day (The 'Seventies)* (Appleton).	Debut of George Gershwin's "Rhapsody in Blue," New York.	Ramsay MacDonald elected first Labour Prime Minister of UK.

Date	Edith Wharton (EW)	Cultural contexts	Historical contexts
	Awarded Gold Medal by [U.S.] National Institute of Arts and Letters; the first female recipient. Silent film of *The Age of Innocence*.		
1925	*The Mother's Recompense* [novel] (Appleton); *The Writing of Fiction* [essays] (Scribner's). Hosts F. Scott Fitzgerald to unsuccessful tea at Pavillon Colombe.	The *New Yorker* is established. Charles Chaplin stars in *The Gold Rush*. Josephine Baker performs in *La Revue Nègre*, Paris. Alain Locke edits anthology, *The New Negro: An Interpretation*. Willa Cather, *The Professor's House*; Theodore Dreiser, *An American Tragedy*; F. Scott Fitzgerald, *The Great Gatsby*; Franz Kafka, *The Trial*; Anita Loos, *Gentlemen Prefer Blondes*; Gertrude Stein, *The Making of Americans*; Virginia Woolf, *Mrs Dalloway*.	The Scopes "monkey" trial. Growing concerns throughout the 1920s about the ethics of consumerism lead to rise of "The Truth-in-Advertising Movement" and similar efforts of self-regulation.
1926	*Here and Beyond* [stories] (Appleton); *Twelve Poems* (London: Medici Society). Ten-week Mediterranean cruise with friends on the *Osprey*.	Book-of-the-Month Club enrolls members. Ernest Hemingway, *The Sun Also Rises* (*Fiesta*).	The General Strike in the United Kingdom.
1927	*Twilight Sleep* [novel] (Appleton). Death of Walter Berry.	The Academy of Motion Picture Arts and Sciences founded. Warner Brothers releases *The Jazz Singer*, the first feature film with synchronized speech as well as music, using the Vitaphone sound-on-disc system. Clara Bow stars in Paramount's adaptation of Elinor Glyn's *It*;	Sacco and Vanzetti sentenced to death and executed in the United States. Charles Lindbergh makes first solo, nonstop flight across the Atlantic.

(continued)

Date	Edith Wharton (EW)	Cultural contexts	Historical contexts
		becomes known as the "It girl," icon of the "Roaring Twenties." In Paris, Harry and Caresse Crosby consolidate the Black Sun Press. Natalie Barney promotes the writing of women with *L'Académie des Femmes*, Paris. (Her salon has been a feature of Parisian culture since 1909.)	
1928	*The Children* [novel] (Appleton), a Book-of the-Month choice. The book earns EW $95,000; filmed as *The Marriage Playground* (1929). Publisher congratulates her on high earnings this year. Death of Teddy in February. Stage adaptation of *The Age of Innocence*.	UK obscenity trial over the publication of *The Well of Loneliness* by Radclyffe Hall. Nancy Cunard founds Hours Press in Paris. Bertolt Brecht and Kurt Weill, *Threepenny Opera*. Nella Larsen, *Quicksand*; D. H. Lawrence, *Lady Chatterley's Lover* (private publication); Margaret Mead, *Coming of Age in Samoa*.	Amelia Earhart is the first woman to fly across the Atlantic (first woman to fly it solo in 1932).
1929	*Hudson River Bracketed* [novel] (Appleton); awarded Gold Medal by American Academy of Arts and Letters. Seriously ill and difficulties working first months of the year.	Jean Cocteau, *Les Enfants Terribles*; William Faulkner, *The Sound and the Fury*; Robert Graves, *Goodbye to All That*; Ernest Hemingway, *A Farewell to Arms*; Nella Larsen, *Passing*; Erich Maria Remarque, *All Quiet on the Western Front*.	Valentine's Day Massacre, Chicago. Textile strikes in Tennessee and the Carolinas. New York Stock Market crash, October.
1930	*Certain People* [stories] (Appleton). Meets Kenneth Clark and Aldous Huxley. During 1930s, visits England, Austria, Netherlands, and Scotland.	Motion Pictures Producers and Distributors of America form a Production Code (commonly referred to as the Hays Code; more widely used from 1934). Release of *The Blue Angel*; exhibition of Grant Wood's *American Gothic*.	The United States lurches into its Great Depression, leading to a decade of widespread destitution. Continuing unemployment, further collapse of banks, industries and farms, and rising popular protests.

Date	Edith Wharton (EW)	Cultural contexts	Historical contexts
1931		"Star-Spangled Banner" made official U.S. national anthem. Warner Brothers release gangster films *The Public Enemy* and *Little Caesar*. Pearl Buck, *The Good Earth* (wins Pulitzer Prize).	Completion of Chrysler Building and Empire State Building.
1932	*The Gods Arrive* [novel] (Appleton), sequel to *Hudson River Bracketed*. Godmother to son of Kenneth and Jane Clark.	Ellen Glasgow, *The Sheltered Life*; Aldous Huxley, *Brave New World*.	Beginnings of catastrophic drought in the U.S. plains (1932–35), and of "Dust Bowl" migrations. U.S. unemployment higher than 20%. Franklin Delano Roosevelt elected president.
1933	*Human Nature* [stories] (Appleton). Deaths of EW's long-time maid, Elise Duvlenck and housekeeper, Catherine Gross.	Warner Brothers release *Gold Diggers of 1933*. Songs include "We're in the Money."	Repeal of Prohibition. Roosevelt initiates radical measures for economic recovery, including founding of Federal Emergency Relief Administration (FERA). Adolf Hitler becomes Chancellor of Germany.
1934	*A Backward Glance* [memoir] (Appleton-Century); serialized (1933), *Ladies' Home Journal*. Writes "postscript": "A Little Girl's New York," published posthumously (*Harper's Magazine,* March 1938). Film of *The Age of Innocence*, with sound.	*Four Saints in Three Acts* opens in Broadway; composed by Virgil Thomson and libretto by Gertrude Stein. F. Scott Fitzgerald, *Tender is the Night*; Josephine Johnson, *Now in November* (wins Pulitzer Prize 1935).	General Textile Strike, United States; over 400,000 workers involved.
1935	*The Old Maid*, adapted by Zoë Akins, wins Pulitzer Prize for drama.	Works Progress Administration and Federal Arts Project, United States.	Italy invades Ethiopia.

(continued)

Date	Edith Wharton (EW)	Cultural contexts	Historical contexts
	EW suffers stroke. Death of sister-in-law, Minnie Jones.	1930s Hollywood dominated by the "Big Five" or "the Majors" of the studio system: Paramount, Metro-Goldwyn-Mayer, 20th Century Fox (so named following a studio amalgamation in 1935), Warner Brothers, and RKO. 1935–38 Shirley Temple is the number-one box-office star in the United States. Release of Leni Riefenstahl's *Triumph of the Will*.	
1936	*The World Over* [stories] (Appleton-Century). *Ethan Frome* dramatized. Attends performance of *Don Giovanni* at Glyndebourne.	Sergei Prokofiev composes *Peter and the Wolf*. William Faulkner, *Absalom, Absalom!*; Margaret Mitchell, *Gone With the Wind*.	Abdication of Edward VIII. Spanish Civil War (1936–39).
1937	Writes final short story, "All Souls'." Suffers another stroke in June. Dies August 11. Buried at Versailles near grave of Walter Berry. *Ghosts* [stories] (Appleton-Century), published posthumously, October; includes "All Souls'."	Nazis open the "Degenerate Art" exhibition in Munich (July to November). Pablo Picasso's *Guernica* displayed in the Spanish Pavillion at the International Exhibition in Paris. Zora Neale Hurston, *Their Eyes Were Watching God*.	Golden Gate Bridge completed, San Francisco.
1938	Final novel (unfinished), *The Buccaneers* (Appleton-Century).		
1939	*Eternal Passion in English Poetry* [anthology of love poems] (Appleton-Century). Selected by EW and Robert Norton with the collaboration of Gaillard Lapsley.	Metro-Goldwyn-Mayer releases *The Wizard of Oz* and *Gone With the Wind*.	1939–45: World War II.

CHAPTER 3

Biography

Melanie Dawson

While Edith Wharton protected her privacy throughout her life, she was particularly determined to do so in 1927, immediately after the death of her close friend, Walter Berry – the "most important person in her life," according to her recent biographer (Lee 11). After the funeral, Wharton approached Berry's sister, gained entrance to his apartment, and burned more than forty years' worth of her correspondence to him, preserving only a few of the least personal letters. Whereas Wharton was willing to share information about her travels, houses, and well-known associates and to discuss her participation in social, professional, and international contexts, she was determined to shield her relationships (of all kinds) from prying eyes. Even her autobiography, *A Backward Glance* (1934), is far from revelatory about her private concerns.

During her lifetime, Wharton, who preferred to be addressed as "Mrs. Wharton," not "Mrs. Edward Wharton" (particularly after her divorce), and certainly not the more familiar "Mrs. Edith Wharton," privileged formal address, which allowed her to maintain a degree of privacy as she circulated socially.[1] Wharton's reserve, an element of her formality, was described as formidable by friends and associates, while her manners, always aristocratic, were fashioned as a means of creating distance between herself and others.

Dimensions of Wharton's carefully guarded privacy are traceable to her social training in an elite American society. Born to the branch of the New York Jones family with which the phrase "keeping up with the Joneses" was said to have originated, Wharton grew up in a protected and privileged class, and in a socially ambitious family.[2] From an early age, she was deeply attuned to the intricacies of high society's forms, from introductions and social debuts to ritualized engagements and painfully public initiations characterized by social rites of acceptance and inclusion. As Nancy Bentley notes of the manners of the moneyed classes of Wharton's era, "Patterns of social habit and convention emerged as a 'second nature,' a reality unable to be stripped away and awaiting its own yet to be discovered casual laws."[3] Provided with this "second nature" by her upbringing, Wharton had chilling encounters with strangers, even those with whom she would seem to have much in common. She could appear stiff, as in her introduction to F. Scott Fitzgerald, (reportedly drunken and at his most performative at the time), who disastrously visited Wharton in Paris in 1925, and with individuals who would become close friends later, including Henry Adams, Henry James, and Bernard Berenson (Lee 622).

Born in her parents' older age, Wharton was their third child and only daughter, as well as the youngest by twelve years. Neither her mother nor brothers were deeply intellectual, nor were they especially motivated by art, travel, or literature. In "Life and I," Lucretia Rhinelander Jones is described by her daughter as "wholly indifferent to literature" (*LI* 191). Lucretia Jones was a conventional woman who is seen as influencing her daughter's marriage to Teddy Wharton and a figure about whom Wharton wrote little; the glimpses sighted in "Life and I" promise a less-than-flattering portrayal. Wharton's self-portrait as a solitary artist reads as an implicit critique of her childhood milieu, for as she wrote in her older age, "I have often sighed, in looking back at my childhood, to think how pitiful a provision was made for the life of the imagination behind those uniform brownstone facades, and then have concluded that since, for reasons which escape us, the creative mind thrives best on a reduced diet, I probably had the fare best suited to me."[4] Wharton, who later described herself as painfully shy, writes that she sequestered herself in rooms to read and compose as a young child. Both aesthetics and the nature of her literary work would lead to a finely developed sense of personal space, or space that was both worthy of admiration and suitable for the laborious work of writing. As an adult, Wharton would design various homes where she worked and entertained guests; although no recluse, she typically reserved mornings for work, secluding herself from even her closest associates until she was ready to transition from writer to host.

Characters in Wharton's fiction, like their creator, are typically concerned about the consequences of circulating publicly. They keep secrets, allowing themselves to be known only in partial and controlled ways; many depart from their homes or their associates with secrets unshared and unjudged. In an early and prescient novella, *The Touchstone* (1900), the love letters sent by the famous author Margaret Aubyn to Stephen Glennard, her correspondent of many years, are made public by Glennard, who sells them to an eager publisher. These letters are then read as scandalous not because of any impropriety in their content, but because they expose Aubyn's unrequited affection for their recipient. As one reader asserts after reading them, "'I believe it *is* a vice, almost, to read such a book as the *Letters* ... It's the woman's soul, absolutely torn up by the roots – her whole self laid bare; and to a man who evidently didn't care; who couldn't have cared. I don't mean to read another line: it's too much like listening at a keyhole.'"[5] Yet, apparently, the public's appetite for listening at keyholes was immense, as Wharton recognized. Once made public, the letters reveal an undignified tragedy, transforming the accomplished author into the common figure of a pathetic and insufficiently loved woman. The letters appear, as one reader asserts, as "unloved letters," exposing a profoundly unequal romance (*Touchstone* 68).

Wharton discovered the negative effects of publicity in her early adulthood when her first engagement to a Mr. Harry Stevens was broken in 1882; gossip columnists wondered aloud if her literary aspirations were the cause of the breakup. *Town Topics* reported that "the only reason for the breaking of the engagement hitherto existing between Harry Stevens and Miss Edith Jones is an alleged preponderance of intellectuality on the part of the intended bride. Miss Jones is an ambitious authoress, and it is said that, in the eyes of Mr. Stevens, ambition is a grievous fault" (Benstock 46). This would not be the last time Wharton would encounter public criticism leveled at her supposedly unfeminine intellectualism; similar critiques would be voiced when she sought a divorce from her husband in 1913.

While, from all accounts, the intimate aspects of the Wharton union were disastrous, the couple enjoyed traveling together early in their marriage, beginning with a cruise in the Aegean islands in 1888, which Wharton describes in glowing terms in *A Backward Glance*. Although expensive, costing nearly a year's income, the cruise affirmed a lifelong interest in travel, including the beauties of the scenery, access to cultural customs, and removal from an insular milieu (Lee 82). Additionally, however, the journey predicted some of the trouble that would emerge in the marriage, with Wharton embracing the aesthetics and cultures of exotic locales and Teddy preferring the adventure of travel, then a return to American living. Journeys through Italy and France would follow for them, but they were not enough on which to maintain a satisfying marriage, particularly when Wharton's preference for the European intellectual and artistic climate became clear. Furthermore, by 1909, Teddy increasingly exhibited signs of mental disturbance, originally diagnosed as gout, neurasthenia, and melancholy.[6] His family publicly criticized her during the divorce, their stance being that "'Teddy is a homeless martyr, victimized by my frivolous tastes for an effete society,'" Wharton wrote, particularly after she made it clear that she intended to pursue her career rather than serve as Teddy's caretaker (Lee 398). Other published criticisms surrounded the Whartons' plan to sell their Massachusetts home, The Mount in Lenox, under the suspicion that Wharton preferred life in Europe to the charms of the American countryside. She was, incidentally, equally criticized when an early attempt at a sale fell through because of supposed feminine capriciousness (Lee 392).

Given such reactions to her intellectualism, and such public discussions of her decision making, it is little wonder that Wharton valued her privacy so greatly. While she sought to place her fiction prominently (frequently corresponding with publishers about marketing strategies), she also desired the personal freedoms she associated with anonymity. Her first widely circulating poems, which appeared in *The Atlantic Monthly* in 1880, were published anonymously (Benstock 38). More than thirty years later, when anticipating her divorce and potentially unpleasant exposures, Wharton sought a different level of privacy as she gathered and destroyed all correspondence from her lover of 1908–10, Morton Fullerton. She also attempted, without success, to regain her letters to Fullerton, requesting their return repeatedly, even before the cessation of the romance. The remains of this relationship, rediscovered in the form of a "love diary" dating from 1907–1908, have formed a view of the writer as a passionate, intellectually demanding, and intensely romantic lover – a view never meant for more than two readers' eyes. The letters, which reveal the combination of passion and discretion that governed Wharton's management of the affair, also suggest that great affection could inspire the considerable labors of discretion. Biographers find these documents unusually revelatory, for few other communications to close associates remain; Wharton destroyed most letters to and from Teddy as well as most involving close relatives (Lee 11).

Wharton's acts of self-insulation are echoed by her fictional characters for whom privacy is crucial, but often difficult to maintain. These figures struggle to control perceptions of their behaviors and degrees of access to their lives, particularly in light of the capacity of publicity to diminish an individual's value. In *A Son at the Front*, an artist won't "cheapen his art" by taking too many sitters, or by becoming too available,[7] while New York's high society retreats from Lily Bart when she appears insufficiently exclusive in *The House of Mirth*. Other women's reputations are compromised by their public circulation, as in Charity Royall's movements about town in *Summer* and Sophy Viner's appearances in Paris in *The Reef*; in

The Age of Innocence, May Welland's mother objects to the potential publicity surrounding her daughter's nuptials in the conservative (but also accurate) belief that a woman's conspicuousness too easily overlaps with notoriety. For Mrs. Welland, as for other figures in Wharton's fiction, shielding another from public view constitutes an act of great affection.[8]

Although Wharton had begun publishing by the time of her marriage in 1885, she adapted to the expectations facing a woman of her milieu, at least outwardly, although she would be preoccupied by ill health for more than a decade after marrying. Writing to Sara (Sally) Norton, Wharton reflected on this period, describing twelve years filled with an "intense feeling of nausea, & such unutterable fatigue," or a condition she terms "neurasthenia" (*Letters* 140). Teddy, a friend of the brothers with whom she had little in common, remained aloof from Wharton's writing career, and the distance between them grew with her success, which was established with the 1905 novel, *The House of Mirth*, which met with critical and popular acclaim. As her interests continued to diverge from Teddy's, Wharton made her home in France, having been exposed to European culture from the ages of four to ten, when her family traveled to avoid the high costs of American living in the post-war years. As a consequence, she absorbed the architecture, languages, and cultures of France and Italy during her formative years and was culturally at home in both countries, frequently traveling in and writing about each.

As a lifelong traveler who wove her journeys into her literary career, both in terms of fictional settings and her non-fiction writing, Wharton developed a characteristic rhythm of life, which alternated steady, grounded work with energetic journeys to exotic and out-of-the-way places across Europe and North Africa. One of her travel companions, Henry James, who favored presentations of himself as timid and deliberate, prosaic and non-demanding, termed her the "Angel of Devastation," or a brazen and energetic force (Lee 252). His various monikers for Wharton, or "our famous and invincible Firebird," the "golden eagle," and the "Maenad" (Lee, 245, 247, 394), suggest the degree to which an energetic Wharton took charge of and organized their journeys, offering diversion but also laying waste to James' daily routine.

Counterbalancing her travel, however, was Wharton's need for aesthetic and social stability, as formed by interests in architecture and design as well as ideals of privacy and ease. Early in her career, she coauthored *The Decoration of Houses* (1897), a guidebook on the history of decorative principles, with architect Ogden Codman who designed the Whartons' home in the Berkshires, The Mount, with Wharton's help. Its building and design preceded the composition of *The House of Mirth*, in which domestic spaces are so important, and this novel laid the groundwork for the many other architecturally and aesthetically conscious fictions to follow. Wharton's aesthetic imagination also led her to rework, restore, and decorate multiple apartments as well as two permanent dwellings in France: one near Paris and the other on the French Riviera.[9] Frequently consumed with the work of reorganizing and modernizing her homes as well as gardens (in which she delighted), she operated in a material moment when, as Bill Brown has asserted, "objects seemed to tyrannize" their owners, in part because of "the sheer proliferation of things" in late-nineteenth-century everyday life.[10] Wharton's life as a designer of spaces suggests the tension between feeling the need to organize her material existence and allowing it to "tyrannize" her. In the 1927 novel, *Twilight Sleep*, for example, a character muses, "Where indeed – she wondered again – did one's own personality end, and that of others, of people, landscapes, chairs or spectacle-cases, begin?" (*TS* 237). It is the kind of question that any number of her characters could raise, for many, like their creator, are homeowners, travelers, decorators, and art lovers. Even when characters do not own or control their environments, such as the servants who are featured in her ghost fictions, they nonetheless confront the material and spatial possibilities of their dwellings.

As an essayist and guidebook author who frequently wrote about material culture (particularly that of France and Italy), Wharton was comfortable with marshaling facts, detailed descriptions, and historical contexts for the substance of her work, for she wrote in a style in which judgments encircling taste and cultural knowledge appear in an impersonal voice, which helped earn Wharton a reputation as a serious literary professional.[11] It is a type of writing that announces the play of consciousness without revealing the personal life of the writer and is comparable to intellectual autobiography (Henry Adams' *The Education of Henry Adams*, 1918), Virginia Woolf's essays explicating critical judgment (as in *The Common Reader*, 1925), and social criticism by Floyd Dell, the Greenwich Village intellectual who wrote in the 1910s through the 1930s. As Barbara Hochman contends, the "impersonal voice had become a sign of authority and value" as authors sought to create a space for themselves in the "newly emergent culture of professionalism," characterizing late-nineteenth-century writing.[12] This intellectual vein appears throughout Wharton's letters to friends, where she frequently references theology, history, and art. In 1919, T. S. Eliot highlighted the importance of a writer's "historical sense"; like Eliot, Wharton, attested to the belief that tradition "cannot be inherited," but must be attained "by great labor."[13] Her intellectual labors included the study of authors such as Darwin, Dante, Homer, Nietzsche, Goethe, Virgil, Whitman, Keats, Ruskin, and George Eliot, among others. As the editors of her selected letters note, "The learning displayed in Edith Wharton's letters – the close acquaintance with texts literary, artistic, scientific, historical, philosophic, religion, in five languages, from medieval to modern, from European to American – is of sometimes awesome proportions" (*Letters* 18). As Claire Preston points out, Wharton read Darwin at the age of twenty-two (alongside a great deal of non-fiction) and was influenced by such topics as natural selection, ethnology, and anthropology, to which she was indebted for her language of tribal behaviors (55).

Even after she chose France for her home – a move made in spirit in 1907, as she divided her time between Paris and Lenox, and further solidified by the 1911 sale of The Mount – Wharton's fiction continued to draw from the site of her young adulthood, New York, with her work and life displaying a cosmopolitanism comparable to that in the works of other modern expatriates, including Eliot, Pound, Dos Passos, Stein, and Hemingway. While Wharton wholeheartedly committed herself to French relief efforts at the outbreak of World War I (see Chapter 27 by Julie Olin-Ammentorp in this volume), and while a character in her novel, *A Son at the Front,* describes the "denationalized modern world" of the war years (*SF* 70), U.S. nationhood continued to figure prominently in her literary work. In fictions such as *Old New York, Summer, The Age of Innocence, The Mother's Recompense, Twilight Sleep,* and *Hudson River Bracketed,* Wharton returned conceptually to a homeland she did not care to inhabit. From the *Old New York* novella sequence set in the 1840–70s, to the contemporary fictions, which cover subjects into the early 1930s, she explored almost a century of U.S. cultural values. Upon visiting the United States on multiple occasions, however, Wharton expressed dismay at the country's ugliness and crudity of expression; for her characters too, U.S. society exerts a dulling effect and renders everyday life as limited and claustrophobic. Widespread across her work is the depiction of a character that chaffs under forms of cultural, familial, and intellectual entrapment within U.S. society, whether in rural New England or high-society New York. The U.S. culture's tendency to inculcate smallness of mind and an inability to deal with difference are her frequent subjects, even as she personally and paradoxically condoned the ideological narrowness of anti-Semitism, classism, eugenics, and a skepticism of the women's movement. Terming herself a "wretched exotic,"

Wharton announced to Sally Norton in 1903 that she felt "out of sympathy with everything" in the United States, whereas in England, "I like it all – institutions, traditions, mannerisms, conservatisms, everything but the women's clothes & the having to go to church every Sunday" (*Letters* 84).

A greater and more troublesome set of tensions encircled Wharton's economic circumstances. Although her lifestyle included the material privileges that afforded her the space in which to order her life (with the aid of various servants), and time in which to work and read, these advantages were counterbalanced by mundane difficulties surrounding personal control of her resources. One vision biographers present of Wharton at work suggests pure luxury: writing each morning in bed, surrounded by small, pampered dogs, "tossing the completed pages over the side of the bed for the secretary to collect and type up" (Lee 670). However, Wharton was also unrelenting in her professional habits, enormously productive, and obsessively concerned with the details of publishing contracts. Although born into wealth and accustomed to a luxurious lifestyle, she continually worried about expenditures and about her ability to support herself, as her letters to friends and publishers reveal. Teddy had only a small income during their marriage, and Wharton's inheritances were not as substantial as anticipated. For much of her life, she lived almost entirely on her earnings. For many years, too, she financially supported and remained close with Minnie and Beatrix Jones, her brother Frederic's ex-wife and daughter, whom he declined to support after his divorce.

In an age when, as Floyd Dell writes, the moderns suffered from a slow shift away from "the paraphernalia of early patriarchal education," Wharton experienced financial anxiety that was traceable to male authority figures.[14] Her father died when she was twenty years old, his condition forcing her to interrupt her society debut and with it, her opportunities for an immediate marriage. After his death, her brothers, whom she had been "taught to treat … with filial deference," exerted notable influence over her life (*BG* 98). They introduced their sister to Teddy, and later, with him, made crucial decisions about her inheritance, effectively excluding her from financial decision-making after the death of her mother in 1901. She was not left any money directly, but was granted a life "trust" in an inheritance that could be used only by her descendants (Benstock 120). Both then and in 1909, when Teddy admitted that he had embezzled money from her trust account under the guise of "managing" it (and then spent it on a home, mistress, and luxury items), Wharton's vulnerability to male management was all too clear.

Given these experiences with the men in her life, it may appear some-what paradoxical that Wharton's social preferences were often for the men of her acquaintance; her women friends were fewer in number and less professionalized, and she wrote about them less frequently, particu-larly in her autobiography. Her lifelong male friends were experts in their fields, reflecting her respect for authentic knowledge and for friendships rooted in intellectual play. Long-term friends included Ogden Codman (architect), Henry Adams (traveler and historian), Morton Fullerton (reporter and author), Bernard Berenson (art critic and historian), Henry James (author), Walter Berry (diplomat and lawyer), Gaillard Lapsley (medievalist and don at Trinity College), and Theodore Roosevelt who, in 1905, hosted the Whartons at a White House luncheon (Benstock 90). Wharton's occasionally vexed relations with James, Fullerton, and Codman, who were known to voice ungenerous opinions of Wharton, as did Percy Lubbock in his biography, *Portrait of Edith Wharton* (1947), echo some of the dimensions of her family dynamic in which a self-willed woman is subject to masculine approval. By contrast, her closest women associates (a somewhat smaller group) were less exalted in the eyes of the world, and included family friend Sally Norton, fellow traveler Daisy Chanler, relief worker Elisina Tyler, Mary Berenson, and niece and land-scape architect Beatrix Jones Farrand. All were well educated, outspoken, and, in most cases, of cosmopolitan upbringings. If these relationships remain shrouded from public view, Wharton's relations to other pro-fessional women writers are even more infrequently discussed, in part because she was far removed from the social circuits of the women writers with whom she could most easily be compared by literary historians such as Willa Cather, Gertrude Atherton, Anita Loos, Katherine Anne Porter, Dorothy Parker, and Lillian Hellman.

Wharton wrote until just before her death in August of 1937 (aged seventy-five) at her home, the Pavillon Colombe, and left a novel about U.S. women who marry British aristocrats, *The Buccaneers*, unfinished. She chose to be buried outside of Versailles, near Walter Berry's grave. As she pursued the steady, capacious gathering of knowledge and beauty (much of it classical), Wharton led an exacting life, often pushing herself to exhaustion to meet deadlines and complete revisions. Her passions for gardening, decorating, and traveling were formidable and served as out-lets for her energies when she was not writing. As with her compositions, these projects demanded long-term commitments and a broad, compre-hensive vision, or the exercise of what she described as her "irresistible ten-dency to improve and organize" (*BG* 103). As Wharton decorated rooms and gardens, testing out compositional theories, she also actively revised, weeded out unsuccessful arrangements and tightened her vision. In everyday life, as with her writing, Wharton lived according to the advice she offered Morton Fullerton as she urged him to "Mow down every old cliché, uproot all the dragging circumlocutions, compress, diversify, clarify, vivify" (Benstock 268). Her patience for a methodology of trial and error highlights her ability to balance detail and the broad strokes of her vision. For the society intellectual, decorator, traveler, novelist, reader, daughter, wife, aesthete, horticulturalist, editor, poet, organizer, American, Frenchwoman, preserver of tradition, innovator, and cosmopolitan, it was advice that suggested the vividness not only of each sentence, but of each of life's facets.

NOTES

1. C. Preston, *Edith Wharton's Social Register* (New York: St. Martin's, 2000), 2. Subsequent references to this work are included in the text.
2. Benstock writes that despite wealth, the Jones family was "forced" to economize in the post-war depression and thus traveled to Europe (12) and that "By the standards of the later Gilded Age, the Joneses lived a simple life centered on social and church activities" and typically "entertained at small dinners and luncheons with close friends and relatives" (14).
3. N. Bentley, "Edith Wharton and the Science of Manners" in M. Bell (ed.), *The Cambridge Companion to Edith Wharton* (Cambridge: Cambridge University Press, 1995), 47–67; 50.
4. E. Wharton, "A Little Girl's New York" in F. Wegener (ed.), *Edith Wharton: The Uncollected Critical Writings* (Princeton: Princeton University Press, 1996), 274–88; 276.
5. E. Wharton, *The Touchstone* (New York: Charles Scribner's Sons, 1900), 90–91. Subsequent references to this work are included in the text.
6. Just before the divorce papers were served, Wharton wrote to Morton Fullerton that Teddy's family "will say he has had neuralgia, as they did before. Nothing will enlighten them, because they don't want to be enlightened – but they may get very weary of trying to look after him" (*Letters* 324).
7. E. Wharton, *A Son at the Front* (New York: Charles Scribner's Sons, 1923), 130. Subsequent references to this work are included in the text (*SF*).
8. See M. E. Montgomery, *Displaying Women: Spectacles of Leisure in Edith Wharton's New York* (New York: Routledge, 1998), where Montgomery links Mrs. Welland's objections to the spectacle of Consuelo Vanderbilt's marriage in 1895 (59).
9. See J. Fryer, *Felicitous Space: The Imaginative Structures of Edith Wharton and Willa Cather* (Raleigh-Durham: University of North Carolina Press, 1986) on the alignment of fiction writing and building in Wharton's career.

10. B. Brown, *Things* (Chicago: University of Chicago Press, 2004), 24, 34.

11. Early in her career, when asked by her editor to "introduce into the next number a few anecdotes, and a touch of human interest" into her essays about Italian gardens, Wharton refused, holding fast to the integrity of facts and rejecting "sentimental and anecdotic commentaries" (*BG* 138).

12. B. Hochman, *Getting at the Author: Reimagining Books and Readers in the Age of American Realism* (Amherst: University of Massachusetts Press, 2001), 28.

13. T. S. Eliot, "Tradition and the Individual Talent" in *Selected Essays 1917–1932* (London: Faber and Faber, 1932), 13–22; 14.

14. F. Dell, *Love in the Machine Age* (New York: Octagon Books, 1973), 53.

CHAPTER 4

Composition and Publication

Sharon Kehl Califano

In biographical lore, the adolescent Edith Newbold Jones gained attention and praise from her family and friends through writing entertaining juvenilia, which included elegies, carols, and ballads (Lee 42). Her first published work (although not under her name) was a translation of a German poem by Heinrich Brugsch, completed with the help of Reverend Washburn,[1] a family friend for whom the young Edith harbored a girlish crush. At the age of fourteen, in 1876, she began a narrative titled *Fast and Loose* – a work of 30,000 words that she finished in January 1877. Later, the adult Wharton described her first attempt at writing a novel, abandoned and later lost, which became notable because of her mother's infamous response to its opening lines. In *A Backward Glance*, Wharton recounted the "icy" comment, her mother's only feedback, as "so crushing to a would-be novelist of manners that it shook me rudely out of my dream of writing fiction, and I took to poetry instead" (*BG* 73). Thus, Wharton shifted her attention to verse for the next several years.

Wharton's first published book was *Verses* – a volume her parents had privately printed in Newport, Rhode Island in 1878, when she was only sixteen. According to R. W. B. Lewis, the volume garnered the attention of Henry Wadsworth Longfellow, who passed along the work to William Dean Howells at *The Atlantic Monthly* (Lewis 32), and Howells decided to publish one of the young author's poems. During the year that followed, Wharton's "Only a Child," based on a newspaper article about an orphaned child who committed suicide while in prison, was published in the *New York World* on May 30, 1879 under the pseudonym "Eadgyth" (Benstock 37), and, in 1880, Wharton crafted five poems ("Aeropagus," "A Failure," "The Parting Day," "Patience," and "Wants") that were published in *The Atlantic Monthly*, anonymously. After these publications, nine years passed until she ventured into the publishing world once more, with two pieces in *Scribner's Magazine* ("The Last Giustiniani," in

October and "Happiness," in December) and one piece in *The Atlantic Monthly* ("Euryalus," in December).

Between 1880 and 1889, Wharton experienced numerous important life changes, including two engagements and an eventual marriage with Edward "Teddy" Wharton – their wedding taking place on April 29, 1885. The marriage occurred after two failed romances: one with Harry Leyden Stevens, whom Edith agreed to marry in 1882, only to find their engagement cut short by outside family pressure and issues relating to his inheritance (local papers suggested her literary ambitions were the cause); and the other with Walter Berry, who never proposed despite gossip from friends that he might, during the summer of 1883 (Singley 25–26). Adjusting to the new challenges of married life, Wharton traveled with her husband and began a number of visits to Italy and Europe. Notably, in 1887, she first saw, but failed to meet, Henry James at the Paris home of Howard Sturgis' cousin, Edward Boit (*BG* 171). In 1888, Wharton kept a travel journal, recording her experiences during a four-month cruise of the Aegean – the journal unexpectedly discovered and published as *The Cruise of the Vanadis*, more than fifty years after the writer's death.

Around 1899, Wharton's publications started to re-emerge. Hermione Lee records the poem, "The Last Giustiniani," as her first credited, published work "in *Scribner's Magazine* in October 1889" (Lee 105), while Shari Benstock writes that three poems that were accepted for publication in 1889 "announced the emergence of 'Edith Wharton,' the professional writer" (Benstock 68) at twenty-seven years old. Shortly afterward, in 1890, *Scribner's Magazine* accepted the story, "Mrs. Manstey's View," for publication, the first of her short fiction pieces and, in 1891, several works by Wharton were published, including "Botticelli's Madonna in the Louvre," "The Tomb of Ilaria Giunigi," and "The Sonnet." In 1892, Wharton wrote the *Bunner Sisters*, which was put aside (after Charles Scribner had rejected it, twice). She published the poem, "Two Backgrounds" in *Scribner's Magazine* in November and, during the following two years, the magazine continued to publish her verse. Yet, in 1894, Wharton started another kind of writing that garnered her much popularity as an author: travel writing.

During 1894, Wharton passed through Tuscany, during a period when she traveled Italy extensively, and her time there and its effect on her imagination led to a significant number of publications (see Robin Peel's Chapter 26 in this volume). With Ogden Codman, Jr., she discussed architecture and classical design, which largely influenced their collaborative work later – in 1897. Lee dates the composition of *The Valley of Childish Things and Other Emblems* to between 1894 and 1895, citing the appearance of an architect at the gate of heaven in one of the fables as connected to Wharton's work with Codman.[2] With Codman, one of many queer men-of-letters with whom the author developed a close friendship and established a literary exchange, she cowrote and published *The Decoration of Houses*, which appeared in December 1897. The book sold quite well, influenced home design in the years that followed and was popular enough to warrant reprinting.

In 1898, Wharton wrote a number of short stories, including "Souls Belated," "A Coward," and "The House of the Dead Hand"; the former two works appeared in her short story collection *The Greater Inclination*, published by Scribner's in March of 1899, but the latter story was later published separately in *The Atlantic Monthly*, in 1904.[3] Wharton steadily wrote at Land's End during 1898, reworking "The Twilight of the God," and polishing a longer piece, "A Cup of Cold Water," which "Burlingame had rejected in 1894 as 'wildly improbable'" (Lewis 81). *Scribner's Magazine* also published "The One Grief" and "Phaedra," and she wrote one of her finest short stories, "The Muse's Tragedy." *The Greater Inclination*, her first collection of stories, sold very well and garnered notable literary success on both sides of the Atlantic.

Early in 1900, Wharton worked on *The Touchstone*, which was serialized in *Scribner's Magazine* from March to April and released by Scribner's in book form at the end of April. The book was considered a minor success, and Wharton spent the summer of that year traveling through northern Italy, gathering inspiration for her next project, *The Valley of Decision*, and a book of travel writing,[4] later published as *Italian Backgrounds* in 1904. The discipline of playwriting also formed a very significant part of her prolific output during this period, with the years 1899 to 1902 witnessing her at work on at least four plays, including the original social comedies *The Tight-Rope*, and *The Man of Genius*. Wharton returned to novel writing with her Italianate work, *The Valley of Decision*, from August to October while working on short stories. Eventually, she set aside *The Valley of Decision* and focused on her short story collection, which Scribner's published as *Crucial Instances* in April 1901, and which critics considered rather "inferior" to *The Greater Inclination* (Lewis 98).

During 1901, while Wharton's iconic home, The Mount, was being built in the Berkshires, the author resumed writing the novel *The Valley of Decision*. She juggled two writing projects at the time, reading proofs for the novel's publication while composing "Sub Umbra Liliorum," one of her essays for *Italian Backgrounds*. She also saw her poem "Mould and Vase" published in *The Atlantic Monthly* in September of 1901, but shifted her focus back to her novel; Scribner's published *The Valley of Decision* in February 1902, and volumes were available in both New York and London. Wharton published a poem in *Harper's Monthly* and also sent "The Lady's Maid's Bell" along to her editor at Scribner's, the first of many ghost stories she would write (Lewis 107). As spring unfolded, she diligently developed a new novel, set in New York and Long Island, under the title "Disintegration," but abandoned the manuscript after having completed more than eighty pages. Lewis called "Disintegration" an "invaluable rehearsal for *The House of Mirth*," which Wharton wrote only three years later (Lewis 107).

In 1902, Wharton had a number of shorter works published in *Harper's Monthly* (including "The Mission of Jane," "The Reckoning," "The Quicksand," and "The Bread of Angels"), while others appeared in *Scribner's Magazine* ("The Lady's Maid's Bell," "Artemis to Actaeon," and "Uses"), and one in the *North American Review* ("Vesalius in Zante"). Other periodicals, such as *The Bookman* and the New York *Commercial Advertiser*, published her work during that year. *The Joy of Living* reinforced her interest in playwriting, which she completed in September. In 1903, she published the novel *Sanctuary*, and worked on her volume of essays *Italian Villas and Their Gardens*, which was illustrated by Maxfield Parrish. She also published shorter pieces like "A Venetian Night's Entertainment" and "A Torchbearer" in *Scribner's Magazine*, and "The Dilettante" in *Harper's Monthly*. This mode of writing continued into 1904, when Wharton focused on short stories for the collection *The Descent of Man and Other Stories*, published by Scribner's in April, and for periodicals: "The Other Two" (*Collier's Weekly*), "Expiation" (*Cosmopolitan*), "The Letter" (*Harper's Monthly*), "The Last Asset" and "The Pot-Boiler" (*Scribner's Magazine*). In the second half of 1904, Wharton set to work for an intense period of writing that lasted through March of 1905, composing one of her most famous novels – *The House of Mirth*.

Beginning in January 1905, *The House of Mirth* was first published serially, during an eleven-month run in *Scribner's Magazine*, and later published in book form in October, to great success; by December, "140,000 copies had been printed" to meet public demand (Benstock 150). While her novel was being serialized, Wharton published the nonfiction work *Italian Backgrounds*, a series of essays about regions of Italy. Her short story, "The Best Man," was then selected and published by *Collier's* as a finalist in a short story contest, favored by Henry Cabot Lodge, one of the judges. Harnessing the public fervor for her New York novel, which remained on the bestseller list well into 1906, Wharton collaborated with Clyde Fitch on a stage adaptation of *The House of Mirth*. In August, she published her successful novella *Madame de Treymes* in *Scribner's Magazine* (published in book form in 1907). Her short stories "The Hermit and the Wild Woman" (*Scribner's Magazine*) and "In Trust" (*Appleton's Booklovers Magazine*) also appeared during 1906, showing the year to be an extremely productive and lucrative one.

An important period in Wharton's life and writing career began in 1907. During the summer, she and Henry James embarked on a "motor-tour" of France that inspired continued travel writing, and, by the fall, James arranged for her to meet the dashing W. Morton Fullerton. With James' letter in hand, Fullerton appeared at The Mount during October of that year, the same month during which *The Fruit of the Tree* was published by Scribner's, and she soon recorded her feelings for Fullerton in a "love diary." While new romance inspired Wharton, she kept up a productive writing schedule during the following year. In 1908, several new stories appeared in *Scribner's Magazine*, including "The Verdict" and "The Pretext," and she penned "Les Metteurs en Scene" for the *Revue des Deux Mondes*. By September, the collection of stories *The Hermit and the Wild Woman* was published, followed by the travel book, *A Motor-Flight through France*. As her works populated the pages of the *Century Magazine*, *The Atlantic Monthly*, and *Scribner's Magazine*, Wharton became "the famous, best-selling, well-connected American novelist, to whom doors opened" (Lee 232).

The years 1908–10 ushered in a number of changes in Wharton's life that influenced her writing, as her relationship with Fullerton found both physical consummation and emotional complication. In 1909, she published a collection of poems, *From Artemis to Actaeon and Other Verse*, through Scribner's, while a passionate night in London with Fullerton culminated in the writing of "Terminus," a poem written very much in the style of Walt Whitman. By the end of the year, Wharton faced her husband's psychological collapse, infidelity, misappropriation of her money, and financial losses. To cope with events during this period, she turned to writing, once again, to ride out the oceanic changes in her life and began *Ethan Frome*.

During 1910, Wharton watched James suffer a psychological decline as a result of his depression, which included thoughts of suicide. Turning to Fullerton for support of their mutual friend, she became disillusioned as Fullerton proved fickle. "The Eyes" – a tale about the pederastic figure of

Andrew Culwin and his haunting, disembodied eyes – acted as a creative outlet. Photographs of James from this period reinforce Wharton's description of his "tragic eyes" that had "looked upon the Medusa," peering from a "stony stricken face" (Benstock 245). Her ghost story appeared in *Scribner's Magazine* in June, and became a part of her collection *Tales of Ghosts and Men*, published that October. Wharton, betrayed by Fullerton's abandonment when needed most, began to distance herself. She ended their affair in July, and invested her energy into her close friendship with Walter Berry, who moved into her Paris home. During the following year, 1911, she published the bleak *Ethan Frome*, sold The Mount, and tried to cope with her husband's worsening "neurasthenia."

Wharton found respite in her travels during the next year, visiting Italy, Switzerland, and England, her friends a great source of comfort and mirth. In March 1912, her long poem "Pomegranate Seed" appeared in *Scribner's Magazine*, and, by November, she completed and published her most "Jamesian" of novels, *The Reef*. Facing the end of her marriage, after learning of her husband's continued, blatant indiscretions, she resigned herself to divorce, which was finalized by April 1913. In January, her novel *The Custom of the Country*, which featured the ugliness of divorce, had already begun serialization in *Scribner's Magazine* and by October, the entire work appeared in book form with Scribner's. During 1913, Wharton had also begun the novel "Literature," periodically returning to the work over the years, but leaving it an unpublished manuscript – one of her largest – in the end.[5]

By August 1914, Wharton found a new calling with the outbreak of World War I. Her residence in Europe, particularly France, made her keenly aware of the unforgiving realities of human destruction. Having once traveled the countryside for pleasure, she and Berry journeyed through once familiar, now devastated landscapes of favored French provinces, recording the harsh results of warfare during 1915, gathering material for a series of articles that were published in *Scribner's Magazine*, with accompanying photographs. Wharton and Berry visited the Argonne, Ypres, and Verdun, and toured hospitals. She also headed a fundraising effort, soliciting submissions from poets, artists, essayists, and other works from well-known figures (among them, James, Paul Bourget, W. D. Howells, Thomas Hardy, Joseph Conrad, and Theodore Roosevelt) for *The Book of the Homeless*. By October, her travel essays were collected in *Fighting France, from Dunkerque to Belfort* and her poems inspired by the war appeared in periodicals. *The Book of the Homeless* was published in January 1916 to disappointing sales.

That October, Wharton's volume *Xingu and Other Stories*, which included *Bunner Sisters* and "Kerfol," was published, and, during the spring of 1917, she started and completed *Summer* – a work she referred to as "the Hot Ethan" – which was fittingly published in July. After beginning the novel *The Glimpses of the Moon*, she took a month-long trip to Morocco in the fall and this inspired her travel book, *In Morocco*, later published in 1920. Her friendship with André Gide, a happy byproduct of her volunteer work in France during the war, had led to a literary exchange that had influenced her vision of the African desert; Gide had sent her a copy of *The Immoralist*, her reading of which had awakened her "nostalgia" and had provided a glimpse of what was "awaiting" (Lewis 404). In 1918, Wharton refocused on World War I in her writing, setting to work on *A Son at the Front*, and writing and publishing *The Marne*, in December. Her written work on France continued with *French Ways and Their Meaning*, which appeared in 1919.

The year 1919 was a year of remembrance, when Wharton started work on *The Age of Innocence* in September. Published by Appleton in October 1920, the novel won the author the Pulitzer Prize in May of 1921, making her the first female recipient. The following spring, in 1922, she resumed work on *The Glimpses of the Moon*, which became a huge success when published in July, and was comparable to *The House of Mirth*, selling 100,000 copies in only a few months. Consistently writing, Wharton produced novel after novel during the 1920s. In 1923, she completed the shorter works "The Young Gentleman" and *The Spark*, began writing *The Mother's Recompense*, and published *A Son at the Front* in September (Lewis 456). By 1924, Wharton published *The Spark* in her collection, *Old New York*, printed by Appleton in May, and the serial publication of *The Mother's Recompense* began; yet, her novel was not made available in full book form until April 1925.

As the literary world shifted during the 1920s, Wharton found a younger generation of modernist writers eager to replace her, many of whom considered the author a relic from a rejected age. Hurt by such dismissal, her frustration colored *The Writing of Fiction*, published in October 1925, and her critical essays of the early 1930s, as she rallied against being perceived as irrelevant. Nonplussed, she forged ahead, shifting back to the short story and poetry genres after publishing her writing guide. Her collection of stories *Here and Beyond*, which came out in April, was shortly followed by a volume of verse, *Twelve Poems*, in October 1926, demonstrating her versatility as an author. Her next novel, *Twilight Sleep*, published in 1927, tellingly addressed a contemporary, social idolatry of youth, and even featured rejuvenation treatments. This focus on very young women as desirable came to the fore in Wharton's *The Children*, on which she worked from October 1927 through the beginning of 1928. The book was a huge success, becoming a "Book of the Month" Club selection in September, the same month her new novel *Hudson River Bracketed* began serialization in *The Delineator*. That year became her best in earnings, as she earned $95,387.08 in royalties and advances (Lewis 484).

Wharton's writing ideology permeated her novel *Hudson River Bracketed* and its sequel, *The Gods Arrive*, which appeared in 1929 and 1932, respectively. Yet 1930 became a difficult year financially as "Wharton's royalties plummeted from $95,000 in 1929 to $5,000 in 1930" (Lee 691). By October, she published a collection of six stories, *Certain People*, but all pieces had been previously published in magazines. In April 1931, her story "Pomegranate Seed" appeared in *The Saturday Evening Post*, and was considered one of "her best two tales" (Benstock 424). Wharton continued her writing of *The Gods Arrive* through the next year, until its completion in January 1932 (published September). She also wrote the story, "Joy in the House," which many editors rejected because of "the ugliness of its theme" (Lewis 506). Her volume of short stories, *Human Nature*, came out in March 1933 to mixed reviews, before she began her unfinished novel, *The Buccaneers,* that year.

In 1934, Wharton completed her autobiography, *A Backward Glance*, and saw it published in entirety in April by Appleton-Century; only the year before, she had haggled a deal with the *Ladies' Home Journal* for her memoir's serialization, earning $25,000 (Lewis 507). During the same year, she wrote important critical essays about writing, which voiced her theoretical approach to composing fiction, in pieces like "Tendencies in Modern Fiction" and "Permanent Values in Fiction" in the *Saturday Review of Literature*. By the fall of 1934, Wharton hit the "low point of her literary income," only earning 70 percent of what she had been yielding only a few years earlier (Benstock 441). During 1935, Wharton started to write the play *Kate Spain*, but stopped when she experienced a stroke that April; she later used the unfinished draft to inspire her story, "Confession," written a year later. By April 1936, she published her last book before her death, *The World Over*, a collection of short stories, which included literary fare like "Roman Fever" and "The Looking-Glass."

The year of Wharton's death, 1937, found her health rapidly declining, which affected her writing at the end of a long and prodigious career. Early in the year, she had worked on *The Buccaneers* and written a short story, "Weekend," an autobiographical article "A Little-Girl's New York," and a "postscript" for *A Backward Glance* that *Harper's* published posthumously (Benstock 451). By February, Wharton had sent her agent her last story, "All Souls'," one of her finest pieces, which was published after her death. Her collection of stories, *Ghosts*, appeared in October 1937, while her incomplete novel *The Buccaneers* was published in September 1938. With an impressive publishing career that spanned almost sixty years, Wharton, at her death, left behind a remarkably vast and complex legacy of work – both published and unpublished, inclusive of multiple genres; her canon continues to fascinate and challenge her literary critics, scholars, and biographers, as works are rediscovered and reexamined through the kaleidoscopic lenses of historical, theoretical, and cultural contexts.

NOTES

1. C. J. Singley, *A Historical Guide to Edith Wharton* (Oxford: Oxford University Press, 2003), 23. Subsequent references to this work are included in the text.
2. R. W. B. Lewis writes that Wharton even "spoofed the size of Codman's bills for the work on Land's End" in this collection (Lewis 100).
3. S. B. Wright, *Edith Wharton A to Z: The Essential Guide to the Life and Work* (New York: Facts on File, Inc., 1998), 114.
4. Benstock dates the opening essay for *Italian Backgrounds* to the summer of 1900 (114).
5. M. Bell (ed.), *The Cambridge Companion to Edith Wharton* (Cambridge: Cambridge University Press, 1995), 6.

CHAPTER 5

Portraits of Wharton

Susan Goodman

Edith Wharton understood the art of biography from the perspectives of reader, memoirist, and subject. "When I get glimpses, in books & reviews, of the things people are going to assert about me after I am dead," she wrote in her diary, "I feel I must have the courage & perseverance, some day, to forestall them."[1] Stories such as "The Portrait" (1899) and "The Daunt Diana" (1909), which obliquely comment on the relationship between biographer and subject, focus, as Wharton's lament might suggest, on varying degrees of violation. In "The Daunt Diana," an obsessed collector tries to extract the mysterious, secreted essence of his most prized if never quite possessed treasure. In "The Portrait," a character would prefer to sit for a Kenyon Cox than see herself through the eyes of a John Singer Sargent: "Your other painters do the surface – he does the depths; they paint the ripples on the pond, he drags the bottom ... My advice is, don't let George Lillo paint you if you don't want to be found out – or to find yourself out."[2]

Ambivalent about the writing of her own biography, yet determined to dictate the outlines of her story, Wharton trumped would-be biographers with *A Backward Glance* (1934), a memoir whose opening chapter she coyly titled "A First Word." She also constructed an archive, including a draft of her autobiography titled "Life and I," as well as documents pertaining to the deterioration of her husband's emotional health and their 1913 divorce, marked specifically "For My Biographer." More sensationally, she preserved "The Life Apart: L'Âme Close" – or what has become commonly known as the Love Diary – whose entries from October 29, 1907 to June 12, 1908 offer glimpses of her relationship with the U.S. journalist, William Morton Fullerton. The diary includes her poem "Terminus," beginning "Wonderful was the long secret night you gave me, my Lover / Palm to palm, breast to breast in the gloom ... " (*Poems* 160). Considering that Wharton composed her archive as assiduously as *The Custom of the Country*'s Elmer Moffatt assembled his collections, her efforts to thwart biographers appear to have been more teasing than serious.

Wharton understood that successive generations of readers would judge her life by different standards than her own, and she tried her best to guide – if not ghostwrite – the various ways her story could be told. As her friend, the Renaissance art historian Bernard Berenson explained, readers respond to artists who seem the embodiment of a particular historical moment, ideal, or type, or what he called an "assimilable and inspiring ideated personality."[3] If nothing else, Wharton wanted, through her own autobiography, to direct readers interested in her life to the many books which made that life exceptional.

Published three years before her death, *A Backward Glance* tells a familiar story, albeit with a twist: a misunderstood child escapes her captors, pleases the equivalent of a prince – in this case, readers of her novels – and succeeds to a kingdom of her own. The book, which begins with the author's stirring first to the "conscious" and then to the "feminine *me* in the little girl's vague soul" (*BG* 2), might best be compared to a *Künstlerroman*. Wharton's ordering of the twin elements of her awakening indicates the value she attached to perception or "consciousness." Refusing to pander to others' definitions of "self," she emphasized the growth of intellect and creative power over trials and tribulations of the heart. Most readers find *A Backward Glance* unsatisfying because it fails – as she allows in her Forward – to expose "every defect and absurdity in others" and resentment in herself (viii). Its power and passion lie elsewhere. Describing an almost demonic state of creative reverie, she writes: "Experience, observation, the looks and ways and words of 'real people,' all melted and fused in the white heat of the creative fires – such is the mingled stuff which the novelist pours into the firm mould of his narrative" (*BG* 211–12). As the force of this quotation implies, Wharton defined "intimacy" differently from readers eager for more banal confessions: "no picture of myself would be more than a profile if it failed to give some account of the teeming visions which, ever since my small-childhood, and even at the busiest and most agitated periods of my outward life, have incessantly peopled my inner world" (*BG* 197). Successive generations of readers, who resist the idea of a world where "the soul sits alone" – as Wharton writes in "The Fulness of Life" (1893) – "and waits for a footstep that never comes," have faulted her autobiography for its reticence (*CSI* 14).

Inevitably, *A Backward Glance* raised more questions than it answered, and no doubt intentionally. A full decade passed before the next portrait appeared, which was a variation on the typical "life in letters" usually edited by a relative or close friend of the author. For Wharton, the friend became friends who sent her literary editor, Gaillard Lapsley, ruminations on her character, which Percy Lubbock then pieced together with his narrative. A novelist, critic, and editor, Lubbock appeared from one perspective to be the perfect candidate to oversee a commemoration. From another, the choice could not have been more misguided or, as it turned out, vindictive. Although Lapsley knew that Wharton no longer considered Lubbock a confidant after his marriage to Sybil Cutting Scott, he still placed her reputation in his hands. The resulting memoir, titled *Portrait of Edith Wharton* (1947), seemed, in the words of one reader who questioned Lubbock's motives, as if it were edited by someone who hated her. An astonished but perhaps self-deceiving Lubbock evidently responded to the accusation by striking his forehead and exclaiming, "But I *adored* her!"[4]

Portrait of Edith Wharton dictated subsequent portraits for the simple reason that it came first, and because its contributors actually knew Wharton. The front book jacket guaranteed "[a]n intimate first-hand portrait of a distinguished lady who was also a novelist of enduring importance." Other biographers repeated Lubbock's mistakes as well as his judgment that Wharton's "pretty literary talent" paled beside Henry James' genius.[5] Wharton emerges from its pages as a consummate if fussy hostess, a snob, and a misogynist. The long apprenticeship she recounted in *A Backward Glance* receives, as do her many books, short shrift. "She dressed, she furnished her house, she fed her guests, she laid out her garden, all better than anyone else. I never heard of such an apprenticeship for a writer," Lubbock concedes, "but it served in this case" (25).

Lubbock saw no problem with the book's almost exclusive focus on the personal since it supplied what Wharton's *A Backward Glance* lacked. As he wrote to Lapsley in a letter included in the book's preface: "any critical handling of her own books would be out of place; they would only appear, so to speak, as her own, in association with her, and there would be no attempt to take them from her and deal with them as ours, the possession of us all" (v). Lubbock's division between "hers" and "ours" raises the larger question of whose narrative a biographer actually tells, especially in a book that features the biographer as a character. Recounting his introduction to Wharton within the text, Lubbock writes: "she wasn't in the habit of delving into shyness, she was accustomed to see gifts laid before her, and this poor creature's gifts, if he had any, were seldom to hand at the right moment ... The young man was interesting when you knew him – but would she see it? ... my place was in the shade" (9).

Managing simultaneously to inflate Wharton's sense of her importance while asserting his own, Lubbock asks the reader to adopt his perspective. However much *Portrait of Edith Wharton* can be read as a settling of old scores, especially in anecdotes unattributed to the editor's wife, it is in fact a document of the social forces that served to discourage a woman of Wharton's era from becoming a novelist. Those forces include a prejudice against female "genius" and deviations from traits that might fall under the category of "feminine," notably flattering the ego of a young man with literary aspirations. Lubbock's "tribute" raises an issue that might be described as the ethics of biography. James' biographer, Leon Edel, argued that a biographer "must apprise the life of another by becoming that other person; and he must be scrupulously careful that in the process the other person is not refashioned in his image."[6] *Portrait of Edith Wharton* begins from a different premise by actively engaging with a subject, who, in the end, resists analysis. Little in Wharton's background, notwithstanding her formidable intelligence, can explain to those who knew her best the fact of the books themselves.

R. W. B. Lewis approached the writing of Wharton's life through the lens of Lubbock's *Portrait*. He expected to find "an aloof and fashionable woman of the world . . . abrasive in her outward relationships, and puritanically repressed within," and instead discovered someone "hardly recognizable": a woman of endless energy, creative daring, and deep affections (Lewis xii). Most importantly, he focused in *Edith Wharton: A Biography* (1975) on her dedication to her craft and her place in U.S. letters, and wondered "whether her reputation might today stand even higher if she had been a man" (xiii). The significance of her life to Lewis grows from its being representative of a large swath of history – the post-bellum world of old New York, Edwardian London, and Paris from *la belle époque* through World War I – and her friendships with public figures, among them Vernon Lee, Theodore Roosevelt, William Dean Howells, Isabella Gardner, Aldous Huxley, and Kenneth Clark. For Lewis, whose approach to literary history tips the scale more toward the historical than the literary, "[her] writings find their larger human implications out of a vast imaginative report on one segment of American social history and on Americans glimpsed . . . amid the international community" (xiii).

Lewis' story begins with Wharton at the height of her career celebrating her sixtieth birthday and ends with her body entombed "behind the closed blinds of her bedroom" (531). Published in 1975, during a dynamic period of feminist scholarship, it acknowledges "modes of entrapment, betrayal, and exclusion devised for women in the first decades of the American and

European twentieth century" (xiii). Reviewers of the book focused less on Wharton's contribution to U.S. letters than on the revelation of her affair with Fullerton and an exotic sketch for a longer piece, describing sex between a father and daughter titled the "Beatrice Palmato" fragment. Late in life, Bernard Berenson observed that people were now "sleuthing Henry James' sexual condition and Edith Wharton's legitimacy as if those questions would solve the mystery of their careers as novelists," but it took the revelation of the Love Diary and "Beatrice Palmato" fragment to rejuvenate Wharton studies.[7] If her books suddenly appeared to have been written by a more sympathetic person, they also appeared to be new books, redolent with frustrated passion.

Lewis' Pulitzer Prize–winning biography generated its own controversy. To some extent, this was inevitable. The first major biography, it provided a road map for subsequent biographers, who then drew alternative routes, correcting false signs and highlighting different landmarks. The controversy over Lewis' book centered on his interpretation of information given him by two researchers: Marion Mainwaring, who reconstructed Wharton's life in Paris, and Mary Pitlick, who followed her life in the United States. Both researchers accused Lewis of misrepresenting their research in his biography and subsequent edition of Wharton's letters. In 2007, Mainwaring told the story of her relentless search for details about Wharton's paramour in *Mysteries of Paris: The Quest for Morton Fullerton*. Her most serious charges against Lewis concern his confused account of Fullerton's employment, the chronology of his affair with Wharton and their financial dealings, and the mistranslation of his divorce decree from Camille Chabbert, which damagingly skews images of Fullerton. Mary Pitlick disputed Lewis' contention that Wharton had a prolonged breakdown in late summer 1894 lasting approximately two years (Lewis 74).[8] The quarrel over facts and interpretation underscores how the misreading of a single detail can distort the reading of an entire life. While it brings to the fore the often mutable border between biography and fiction, it also exposes the personal investment in writing biography, which James presciently captured in his 1888 novella, *The Aspern Papers*.

Whereas Lewis' biography largely presents the many facets of Wharton's exterior life, Cynthia Griffin Wolff's *A Feast of Words* (1977) furnishes its interior. Focusing on Wharton's psychological development and its impact on her writing, Wolff divides Wharton's life into four parts: "A Portrait of the Artist as a Young Woman"; "Landscapes of Desolation: The Fiction, 1889–1911"; "Studies of Salamanders: The Fiction, 1912–1920"; and "Diptych – Youth and Age: The Fiction, 1921–1937." "How could she have written so well?" Wolff asks. "Indeed, why did she write at all?" (5). Despite Wolff's claim that her ultimate concern is the fictions, "not the life," the two cannot be separated in a book that relies on one to argue the other. Wharton's affair with Fullerton, for example, provides the context for Wolff's readings of "The Letters" and *The Reef*. Similarly the "Beatrice Palmato" fragment links her reading of *In Morocco* to *The Age of Innocence* and *The Age of Innocence* to *Summer*, a story that ends with an adopted daughter marrying her father.

For Wolff, who incorporates the theories of feminist critics such as Nancy Chodorow and Carol Gilligan, gender remains central to Wharton's artistry. Although Lewis takes gender into account, he places Wharton more squarely in the tradition of male counterparts. He sees her primarily as an artist as opposed to a woman artist. Structuring her story around the metaphors of feast and starvation, Wolff argues that Wharton's "lifelong love of words sprang from her early emotional impoverishment" (27). Subtitled "The Triumph of Edith Wharton," her narrative follows Wharton as she works out personal conundrums in her fiction. *A Feast of Words* stands out among Wharton biographies for its concentrated analysis of the work that made Wharton – in Wolff's words – "[o]ne of the half-dozen greatest novelists that America has produced" (5), but that said, it does not differ appreciably in its basic plot from Wharton's autobiography or, for that matter, Lewis' biography. In all three, Wharton finds her voice as a woman and artist through her writing.

Shari Benstock's *No Gifts from Chance* (1994) also chronicles the transformation of the author from shy tomboy to unparalleled artist and woman of the world; and like Wolff, she stresses the role gender played in Wharton's process of "self-transformation ... through the act of writing" (Benstock viii). Her biography, which utilized newspaper repositories in France, emphasizes the business of writing by detailing Wharton's finances and the difficulties in providing for herself, her sister-in-law Minnie Cadwalader Jones, and her staff. More deeply than Lewis and more broadly than Wolff, *No Gifts from Chance* examines Wharton's construction of a surrogate family and her many friendships. Intentionally revisionist, it corrects errors in Lewis' biography, including the mistranslation of Fullerton's divorce decree from Camille Chabbert and his dating of letters in *The Letters of Edith Wharton* that adjust the chronology of the Wharton-Fullerton liaison.

Agreeing with Mary Pitlick, Benstock objects to Lewis' claim that Wharton suffered an extended nervous collapse. She offers as contrary evidence Wharton's ebullient correspondence, written after recovering from recurrent bouts of flu, and her maintenance of a rigorous travel schedule. She supports Pitlick's sense that Wharton used her various illnesses as a pretext to buy time when feeling pressed or flailing creatively. Embedded in the structure of Benstock's biography is the idea that every choice has a direct consequence, that individuals are indeed captains of their fate. Both the book's title – taken from a phrase Wharton particularly liked in Matthew Arnold's 1853 poem "Resignation" – and the titles of individual sections ("The Old Order," "Choices," and "Rewards") reinforce the idea of free will.

Eleanor Dwight's 1994 biography, *Edith Wharton: An Extraordinary Life*, is a handsome, oversized book full of black-and-white photographs that allow the reader to visualize the material circumstances of Wharton's life. Organized primarily around places – New York, Newport, Italy, Lenox, Paris, and Hyères – it traces Wharton's developing aesthetics through her love of gardening, travel, architecture, and decoration, and depicts in the spirit of Louis Auchincloss' *Edith Wharton: A Woman in Her Time* (1971) the social milieu of her novels. In Dwight's biography, Wharton's personality results from her keen visual imagination and visceral response to spaces. Departing from her predecessors, Dwight sees the non-fiction books on decoration and architecture as being as important as the novels, with which they are in conversation. Her book draws on previously unpublished material to highlight the importance of Wharton's friendships with Bernard Berenson, Ogden Codman, Jr. – the architect with whom she wrote her first book, *The Decoration of Houses* (1897) – and her niece Beatrix Farrand, who was one of the era's most respected landscape architects.

Despite following Wharton from birth to death, *An Extraordinary Life* might be seen as one of a number of books that concern themselves with a particular aspect of Wharton's personality and life, ranging from social and psychological studies to literature, culture, and aesthetics. Millicent Bell's *Edith Wharton and Henry James: The Story of Their Friendship* (1965) corrects Lubbock's portrait of their literary relationship by showing an exchange between equals. In *Edith Wharton's Women* (1990), Susan Goodman examines Wharton's friendships with women like Sara Norton while she focuses in *Edith Wharton's Inner Circle* (1994) on Wharton's relationships with male friends, including Gaillard Lapsley and Percy Lubbock. Gloria Erlich looks at the impact of Wharton's family constellation and erotic development in *Sexual Education of Edith Wharton* (1992). Highlighting Wharton's social and political views, Dale Bauer's *Edith Wharton's Brave New Politics* (1994) was the first book to concentrate on

Wharton's later fiction. Alan Price offers a biography of Wharton during World War I in *The End of the Age of Innocence* (1996), and Sarah Bird Wright, who detailed "the making of a connoisseur" in *Edith Wharton's Travel Writing*, provides a guide to Wharton's life and work in *Edith Wharton, A–Z* (1998). Biographical in their mode of inquiry, these "partial portraits" – to borrow James' phrase – augment the standard biographies, which proceed from a few obvious premises and which writers of fiction can ignore or reimagine more easily than biographers: that the key to an author's life lies buried in the work (and vice versa); that the past informs the present; and that life has a largely logical, cause-and-effect trajectory. Any portrait of Wharton materializes from a process of selection and arrangement that reflects the biographer's interests as well as those aspects of the life that have received little attention, have recently come to light, or support new interpretation. A writer foremost, but also a critic, gardener, householder, designer, war correspondent, and businesswoman, Wharton particularly lends herself to multiple studies.

By 2007, Wharton's name had become familiar enough to readers and movie-goers for Hermione Lee to title her book simply *Edith Wharton*. Apart from drawing on Wharton's unpublished letters to people such as Lily Norton, Walter Berry, and Charles and Zézette Du Bos, she had access to part of Wharton's library, which The Mount purchased in 2006. The importance of the library to scholars cannot be overestimated, for Wharton's underlinings and marginalia reveal her developing thinking about topics in history, philosophy, and religion, and constitute, as Lee notes, "a form of autobiography" (Lee 675). She also sees Wharton's life and work evolving in tandem, but pays special attention to the intersecting social spheres that made Wharton a Europeanized American. Her detailed accounts of Wharton's professional obligations and financial dealings, including her real estate holdings in France, make palpable the unexpected burdens of wealth and fame and the ways in which publishers, reviewers, readers, and economics influenced the course of Wharton's career. Iconoclastic and conventional, ambitious and paralyzed, Lee's Wharton embodies the contending forces that make her work seem obsessed with "double lives, repression, sexual hypocrisy, hidden longings" (589). Lee, who poignantly ends her biography beside Wharton's neglected grave in the *Cimetière des Gonards*, provides an overview of the work still to be done on Wharton, not least an edition of her collected letters. The omission of ugly references to Jews and African Americans in *The Letters of Edith Wharton*, for example, potentially skews interpretations of her fiction. The strength of Lee's biography rests on its transparency. Rather like Henry James in *The American Scene*, she draws attention both to her own process of weighing evidence and to gaps in the record, which the recent discovery of Wharton's correspondence with her friend and teacher Anna Bahlmann may partly close. More than other Wharton biographers, with the exception of course of Lubbock, Lee figures self-consciously in the narrative.

Beginning with Lubbock's *Portrait of Edith Wharton* and ending, for the moment, with Lee's *Edith Wharton*, the biographies and biographical studies of Wharton follow a pattern from memoir to "official" literary biography to revisionist studies, which reflect their era's values, politics, social practices, and theoretical understandings about the self. Lubbock envisioned Wharton, shortly after World War II, as an antiquated *grande dame*. Subsequent biographers have ably amended that portrait to show – along with her great intellect – her vulnerabilities, engagements, and commitments in order to make her more contemporary and accessible.

What, we might ask, with Wharton's biographies in mind, are the attractions and pitfalls of biography? Why did a writer like John Updike disdain the form? Was it a fear of being posthumously "cannibalized" (to borrow Rudyard Kipling's description), a distaste for the daily barrage of celebrity scandals passing for biography, or a belief in fiction offering the "truest" biography? His and Wharton's objections notwithstanding, biography continues to be a viable form partly because it offers a measure of our own lives, partly because its form reassuringly imposes order on life's inconsistencies, and more importantly because it offers testimony that individual lives do matter. Edith Wharton's life has mattered to successive generations of readers for reasons, though sometimes titillating, that primarily center on her artistic achievement. In 1977, Cynthia Griffin Wolff felt the need to defend her assessment that Wharton ranked among her country's best half-dozen novelists. Today that statement needs no defending.

NOTES

1. Diary note, 1924; diary reprinted in L. Rattray (ed.), *The Unpublished Writings of Edith Wharton*, 2 vols. (London: Pickering and Chatto, 2009), vol. II, 205–15; 211.
2. "The Portrait," *The Greater Inclination* (New York: Charles Scribner's Sons, 1899), 230–31.
3. B. Berenson, *The Bernard Berenson Treasury*, ed. H. Kiel (New York: Simon and Schuster, 1962), 138.

4. See R. W. B. Lewis, "Edith Wharton, The Beckoning Quarry," *American Heritage Magazine*, 26 (October 1975), 56.

5. P. Lubbock, *Portrait of Edith Wharton* (New York: D. Appleton-Century-Crofts, 1947), 6. Subsequent references to this work are included in the text.

6. L. Edel, *Literary Biography* (Bloomington: Indiana University Press, 1973), 11.

7. B. Berenson, *Sunset and Twilight: From the Diaries of 1947–1958*, ed. N. Mariano (New York: Harcourt, Brace & World, 1963), 219. Cynthia Griffin Wolff shared her discovery of the Beatrice Palmato fragment with Lewis.

8. See M. Mainwaring, "The Shock of Non-Recognition," *Times Literary Supplement*, December 16, 1988, 1394, 1405; M. Pitlick, "Edith Wharton," *Times Literary Supplement*, December 30, 1988, 1443; and R. W. B. Lewis, "Edith Wharton," *Times Literary Supplement*, February 17, 1989, 165. Also see H. Lee, "Gatsby of the Boulevards," *London Review of Books*, 23 (March 8, 2001), 3–6.

PART II

Critical Receptions

CHAPTER 6

Contemporary Reviews, 1877–1938

Heidi M. Kunz

Among Edith Wharton's many distinctions is the charming fact that she was the first reviewer of her own work. Her earliest known novel, *Fast and Loose* (1877), did not appear in print until a century after she wrote it, but it elicited critical commentary nevertheless – from the author herself, who appended three parodic reviews to the manuscript before sharing it with her first known reader.[1] Impersonating an unnamed critic from *The Nation*, she pronounces that "... in such a case, it is false charity to reader & writer to mince matters. The English of it is that every character is a failure, the plot a vacuum, the style spiritless, the dialogue vague, the sentiments weak, & the whole thing a fiasco."[2] Her first literary checklist is understandably immature; after all, she completed *Fast and Loose* when she was but fourteen. By the time she commenced professional authorship two decades later, her more writerly comprehension of the elements of fiction included the more abstract concept of form. Yet for all its immaturity, her adolescent autocriticism predicts the criteria – character, action, manner, theme – by which so many bonafide reviewers eventually would attempt to critique her writing. Frustrated throughout her long and prolific career by critics' relative inattention to her artistic priorities, she elucidated her literary values and took her own measure in expositions such as her introduction to the 1922 edition of *Ethan Frome* (1911), her artistic manifesto *The Writing of Fiction* (1925), and her memoir *A Backward Glance* (1934). In this way, Wharton contributed deliberately and significantly to the print conversation about her work in her time. That print conversation spanned the five decades of her professional writing, from the collaborative nonfiction *The Decoration of Houses* (1897) to the unfinished final novel *The Buccaneers* (1938).

The range, quality, and popularity of Wharton's oeuvre evoked an abundant critical response. Scholars who concentrate on the reviews accept Edmund Wilson's 1938 notion that her first bestseller, *The House of Mirth* (1905), and her Pulitzer Prize-winner *The Age of Innocence* (1920), bracket a period of sustained artistic achievement that effectively subdivides her literary career into three tidy "phases," and organize the commentary accordingly.[3] The first phase encompasses responses to her belletristic writing from *The Greater Inclination* (1899) through *The Descent of Man and Other Stories* (1904). This earliest cohort of reviewers undertook to identify Wharton's preoccupations and techniques in order to place her on the map of *fin de siècle* U.S. literature. "She isolates one or two men and women, and studies them," explains one. Summarizes another, her tales "deal with character, with its development through circumstance, the simple delineation of it, or the play of one personality upon another." She characterizes with deft economy: "In a moment, in the twinkling of an eye, you are able to place ... characters. Pages and pages of description and repetition would not have served so well." However, her sure touch for character does not extend to her handling of action. "What Mrs. Wharton lacks, and we feel the shortcoming to be grave, is a sense of the dramatic," complains an anonymous reviewer. Another says more plainly, "Every character feels and thinks, and reflects and feels again. But nothing happens ... The revolver never goes off." A number concur that her strengths and weaknesses find expression in "some of the most skilful and finished writing which has appeared in recent years," except when she appears to imitate "some of [Henry] James' worst faults of style ... notably his trick of repeating words ... and his habit of spoiling the formation of his sentences by inserting parenthetical clauses." In theme as well as manner, reviewer after reviewer located her in James territory. A scattered few note that Wharton traverses the realm of Naturalism when "She accepts the law of environment literally and invariably squeezes the right people out of a situation," but many hold that "She is clearly of the school of Henry James. Her subjects are chosen similarly to his – dramas of sentiment, of the soul; excursions into the obscure recesses of psychology." Only seldom, at wide intervals, appear references to form. "Her genius consists in a delicate perception of forms and color," says one reviewer, by way of compliment, sans further elaboration. Another begins promisingly, "Every one of [these stories] has the external shape and coloring of the world in which we mingle day by day," but veers immediately into critical incoherence by continuing, "and every one of them is at heart a poignant and spiritual tragedy." Only one reviewer, who sees that "the small compass in which Mrs. Wharton succeeds in turning round is amazing," seems to look beyond the conventional obvious to recognize her efforts at narrative design.[4] Wharton may have intended her mock reviews of *Fast and Loose* facetiously, but her parody of the genteel tastes and limited technical apprehension of Gilded Age reviewers was truer than perhaps she knew.

The contemporary critical response to *The House of Mirth* abruptly resituated Wharton in a broader literary map and an expanded literary tradition. Her preferred focus on the apex of New York "society," eyed with a realist's love of documentary detail combined with a naturalist's skepticism about the morality of social Darwinism, coincided neatly with the waxing of the Progressive Era. General disillusionment with the financially most fit of the Gilded Age – encouraged by the work of photojournalist Jacob Riis, particularly *How the Other Half Lives* (1890) and *Children of the Poor* (1892), and the widely-discussed theses of multidisciplinary academic Thorstein Veblen, especially *The Theory of the Leisure Class* (1899) – pervaded a turbulent half-century that cultural historian Lisa Rado deems "a period of revolutionary change."[5] Wharton's painful and painstaking study of downward mobility, personified in an intelligent woman fatally entrapped by the marriage imperative of her class, tapped the spirit of a cultural moment; in the words of one reviewer, "No tract for the times could have been more scathing and opportune … it describes with merciless veracity." As a result, *The House of Mirth* urged Wharton's critical reputation into a transatlantic frame of reference as well as an extended historical one. Reviewers ranked it with *Père Goriot, Madame Bovary, Anna Karénina, Vanity Fair, Adam Bede, The Scarlet Letter*; they did not shrink from drawing comparisons to Aeschylus or Shakespeare, or from deeming its author a twentieth-century Ecclesiastes (from whose Book Wharton derived her novel's title).[6]

Meteoric improvement in Wharton's critical stature notwithstanding, the contemporary reviews continued to measure her accomplishment according to erstwhile criteria. The characterization of the novel's heroine often makes the assessment: "… the central figure of the book, [is] a portrait on which Mrs. Wharton has lavished all her skill and insight," writes the reviewer who concludes, "It is hardly possible to praise too highly the way in which Mrs. Wharton has followed out this history." The reviewer who praises the collection of "trifling indiscretions, careless compromises, minor infidelities" that comprise its plot declares the novel an "achievement, which lies within the reach of the novelist of genius and of no other." Somehow the reviewers find her a dispassionate naturalist and a satiric moralist at once: "The force and value of *The House of Mirth* lie in the pitiless psychological dissection of … Lily Bart, and of the forces and tendencies of 'Society,'" and yet the "relentless arraignment" of her portrayal portends "ethical significance" that proves "Mrs. Wharton's remarkable and distinguished powers as a writer." As in the first phase, an occasional reviewer attempted to praise Wharton's formal craftsmanship, but knew not quite whereof he spoke. "The thoroughness of the structure which binds the chapters by the logic of life not less firmly than by the order of events..." begins one well-intended but uselessly tangled sentence about narrative design. Ultimately, Wharton won acclaim as an artist of the first order for her depiction of "the present state of our democracy, where the higher ideals and spiritual needs of humanity are lowered and diverted from the channels of aspiration by the materialistic environment of social ambition, and the aesthetic craving for a comfortable compla- cency and elegance of life engendered by the sudden rise of the country to great wealth." And, of course, for her "salutary pessimism" that resonated with Progressive pushback. [7]

Having demonstrated her capacity for excellence with *The House of Mirth,* Wharton warranted such high praise repeatedly during the next fifteen years as she brought out such novels destined for the canon as *Ethan Frome, The Custom of the Country* (1913), *Summer* (1917), and *The Age of Innocence.* Critical responses of the second phase suggest that her success secured her place on the map, but also established a concomitant set of expectations through an evolutionary process. "Mrs. Wharton ... may be counted upon to record with automatic minuteness certain lesser vibrations of the social ether," begins a review of *Madame de Treymes* (1907). A commentary on *Tales of Men and Ghosts* (1910) concludes that "Mrs. Wharton ... in spite of her subtle gift for analysis, never forgets the power of pure human love." Expectations easily become entrenched: sighs a reviewer of *Xingu and Other Stories* (1916), "We confess to approach- ing the novels and stories of Mrs. Wharton with mingled emotions, in which a reverent admiration for her ability, her subtlety, and her artistic skill is tempered by apprehensions ... that we must put away all expecta- tions of happy endings." Delineation shades almost imperceptibly into delimitation. There comes a problematic point in the process when devi- ation from perceived norms provokes negativity: "It is to be hoped that when Mrs. Wharton writes again she will bring her great talent to bear on normal people and situations," sniffs a reviewer of *Ethan Frome.* And a point at least as problematic, when adherence to certain precedents reaps rewards: a review that praises her "immaculate art" declares that "*The Age of Innocence* is perfect Wharton."[8] Style, theme, plot, and character – the perennial criteria – dominate the reviews of the second phase, threatening as much as did her reputation to ossify the terms of her achievement. The general omission of form from the reviewers' criteria during the earliest decades of the twentieth century proved inauspicious, given that modernism, an aesthetic movement that prized formal experimentation, was already on the ascendant. Wharton was perceived to have perfected her art, so attuned to the tone of an era, just as that era was giving way to a fresh revolution.

Its preeminent spokesman, F. Scott Fitzgerald, writes of the Jazz Age that "It was an age of miracles, it was an age of art, it was an age of excess, and it was an age of satire," fueled by "great filling stations full of money."[9] Wharton would seem to have been well prepared to write the new *Zeitgeist*, given her socioeconomically-inflected interests and her signal talent for documenting the passage of one era into another. Her star had never been higher; *The Age of Innocence* would secure for her the Pulitzer Prize for Fiction in 1921, and would predicate the honorary doctorate she was destined to accept from Yale in 1923. However, the reviewers of the third phase often deemed her gifts less than perfectly suited to the new times. Indeed, some of the ways in which her novel of 1920 won approval were the very ways for which her novel of 1922 would be found wanting. The inane major characters in *The Age of Innocence*, for instance, are construed as ingenious: "The formal routine and hinting gossip wrap themselves like a boa constrictor about the characters and squeeze the naturalness out of them." The jejune figures populating *The Glimpses of the Moon*, on the other hand, are "puppet[s] ... their attitudes are necessarily limited, and it seems to us that they are also quite unnecessarily stale." The vacuity of the era itself may have been to blame. To Fitzgerald's mind, the Jazz Age "eventually overreached itself less through lack of morals than through lack of taste" (15). Rebecca West observes that the contemporary action of *The Glimpses of the Moon* is a "situation of crude primary colors Mrs. Wharton writes with an air of discussing fine shades in neutral tints."[10] (Another reviewer dates Wharton's tasteful manner as "the agreeable suavity of the fin de siècle.") West sounds the common generational note in her review, speaking of "the America into which Mrs. Wharton was born" and suggesting the insufficiency of Wharton's "method ... that of William Dean Howells and Henry James," to the Jazz Age "truth that novelty is a test of the authenticity of art" (314). The cultivated expectations of one set of readers, those for whom "the publication of a full-length novel by Edith Wharton is probably the most important thing that can happen in any current year of American fiction," thus collided with the standards of another set, those who are "not amused. Nor interested. Nor tolerant. Merely bored."[11]

Among Wharton's many distinctions is the curious fact that the period during which her critical reputation declined was also her period of greatest commercial success.[12] *The Glimpses of the Moon* garnered a strongly positive market response without a correspondingly strong critical one. Third-phase reviewers pounded the old drum of Wharton's affinities with James and other novelists among the honored dead in U.S. letters. Thenceforth, many reviewers would find her themes "belated," out of touch with "the American point of view," and tired, with "not much in them which had not already been done more effectively in *The Age of Innocence*." Yet her books – not only novels but also collections of short stories, travelogues, *The Writing of Fiction* – continued to sell, overall better than ever, often on both sides of the Atlantic, not infrequently with popularity that would justify translation into stage plays, for example, *Ethan Frome* and *The Old Maid* (1922), or films, for example, *The Glimpses of the Moon* and *Twilight Sleep* (1927). Reviewers into the 1930s might opine that "Despite a practiced stirring of bobbed hair, synthetic gin and cocktails and modern ideas into a 100 percent American background [in her novels], Mrs. Wharton must remain forever of that generation that saw *The Age of Innocence*." However, when she treats the privileged class that, in the baleful years of the Great Depression, was more anathema to readers than ever, even a jaded reviewer must admit that "From behind its worn-out forms, its self-imposed seriousness, importance, and virtue Mrs. Wharton draws whatever humanity it has." Her abiding popularity could not be gainsaid: "To the last, Mrs. Wharton kept faith with her public, even in the novel for whose completion she could not stay," writes a reviewer of posthumously-published *The Buccaneers*.[13]

Only a small minority of the reviewers in any phase failed to extol or at least to acknowledge Wharton's literary craftsmanship. Indeed, for some commentators, her "technique" was the redeeming feature of works they could not countenance otherwise. Compliments to her vivid phrasing appear in the earliest reviews, and appear regularly and often, to the end. On the very few occasions when reviewers essayed technique on a higher plane of abstraction, namely form, the commentaries usually floundered for want of information or adequate critical language or both. The reviewers who did speak intelligibly of Wharton's form (for example, Gilbert Seldes, V. S. Pritchett) happened to be novelists and/or short-story writers themselves, and consequently shared her understanding of *form* as narrative design. Yet such informed criticism was rare in the contemporary response, and Wharton felt the scarcity keenly. When the Jazz Age critics began redrawing the lines of the literary map, she entered the fray herself in order to educate her readers about what she considered the essential element of fiction.

Wharton's introduction to the 1922 edition of *Ethan Frome* emphatically articulates form as the animating impulse of her art. "I have written this brief analysis – the first I have ever published of any of my books – because, as an author's introduction to his work, I can imagine nothing of any value to his readers except a statement as to why he decided to attempt the work in question, and why he selected one form rather than another for its embodiment," she declares.[14] The first part of her authorial "statement" is desultory, and ends "there is nothing else of interest to say about [*Ethan Frome*], except as concerns its *construction*" (*Novellas and Other Writings* 1125). Her prose bursts into dramatic life with the second part:

> The problem before me, as I saw in the first flash, was this: I had to deal with a subject of which the dramatic climax, or rather the anti-climax, occurs a generation later than the first acts of the tragedy. This enforced lapse of time would seem to anyone persuaded – as I have always been – that every subject (in the novelist's sense of the term) implicitly *contains its own form and dimensions*, to mark *Ethan Frome* as the subject for a novel. (*Novellas and Other Writings* 1124)

Narrative design not only inspires Wharton's creativity, but also serves as her operative criterion for identifying the novel-worthy among myriad tantalizing "good situations" (*Novellas and Other Writings* 1124). Wharton's chief joy in writing lies in crafting the solution to the "problem," in designing a narrative exquisitely proportionate to the inherent aesthetic potential of the situation. Character, action, manner, theme are predetermined by the "scheme of construction," and thus subordinate; these are less interesting because they are not elements "on which many variations could be played" once the structure has suggested itself to her imagination (*Novellas and Other Writings* 1125, 1124). Having claimed the artistic high ground, she condescends to her detractors: "But all this is self-evident, and needs explaining only to those who have never thought of fiction as an art of composition" (*Novellas and Other Writings* 1125). She maintains the primacy of form in *The Writing of Fiction*, where she reiterates that "every subject contains its own dimensions, so its conclusion *ab ovo*," and conceptualizes the novel as an edifice "in which every stone has its particular weight and thrust to carry and of which the foundations must be laid with a view to the proportions of the highest tower" (*WF* 51, 50). She thrusts back at the critical proponents of modernism, "The distrust of technique and the fear of being unoriginal – both symptoms of a certain lack of creative abundance – are in truth leading to pure anarchy in fiction" (*WF* 14). The elemental preeminence of form had ever been Wharton's artistic credo. The thesis of *The Decoration of Houses*, which designates as definitive "those architectural features which are part of the organism of every house, inside as well as out," and argues the importance of "*architectural proportion*" over "*superficial application of ornament*" or furnishings, evinces an early version of her conviction.[15] She would develop similar principles for the architecture and style of her literary constructions by 1911, and profess them to the end of her career. As late as *A Backward Glance,* she posits that the art of fiction requires "constructive power" to make it ideally "compact and centripetal" (*Novellas and Other Writings* 939). For all the stalwart consistency – or perhaps defensive rigidity – with which she maintained them, however, Wharton's ideas were overwritten by the inexorable course of the general print conversation about her art.

The contemporary reviews of her fiction provide a useful context for Wharton's writing. Apprehended collectively as a corollary text in themselves, the reviews chronicle directly (that is, in their historical references) and indirectly (that is, in their interpretive premises) the development of U.S. culture during a half-century of extraordinary change, for example, in the matter of gender. A critic of the 1890s considers that "the work, strong, quiet, and dignified, does not need a signature to show that it is a woman's work after all, the work of a woman who, to use her own phrase, 'reasons her emotions' and understands other women better than the keenest analyst among the men." The year of the ratification of the Nineteenth Amendment, William Lyon Phelps observes, "In this present year of emancipation it is pleasant to record that in the front rank of American living novelists we find four women," and yet he still praises Wharton volubly for giving readers "so vivid an idea of the furnishing and illuminating of rooms in fashionable houses" and details of "elaborate dinner parties in New York in the [eighteen] seventies" before he offers tempered enthusiasm for the substance of the novel at hand. A dozen years of women's political empowerment later, reviewer R. Ellis Roberts explains "why a man should study women's novels: he will get an idea of what a woman thinks women have to, and can, tolerate, and he may revise his own naturally high opinion of himself."[16] The reviews, in seeking to evaluate Wharton's writing for their own readerships, present a rich longitudinal study of the multiple dialogic relation among artist, art, and several kinds of audience. As one of the contemporary reviewers, Wharton both complicates and sophisticates the print conversation about her work with her formulation of her own literary priorities, which she maintained resolutely – or perhaps obstinately – from the last years of the lingering Gilded Age to the throes of the Great Depression. It should be noted that in her (re)view, Wharton saw her career divided into two phases, not the three that later scholars would see axiomatically. In the judgment of the author herself, "It was not until I wrote 'Ethan Frome' that I suddenly felt the artisan's full control of his implements" (*Novellas and Other Writings* 941). Form, for her, was pivotal. Twenty-first-century readers would do well to attend to Wharton's autocriticism. Having had the prescient first word, she may yet guide our current critical conversation toward the last.

NOTES

1. L. Rattray, "Introduction: Novels and Life Writings" in L. Rattray (ed.), *The Unpublished Writings of Edith Wharton*, 2 vols. (London: Pickering and Chatto, 2009), vol. II, vii–xxvi; ix–xi.

2. E. Jones, "From *The Nation*" reprinted in L. Rattray (ed.), *The Unpublished Writings of Edith Wharton*, 2 vols. (London: Pickering and Chatto, 2009), vol. II, 63.

3. E. Jones, "From *The Nation*," reprinted in L. Rattray (ed.), *The Unpublished Writings of Edith Wharton*, 2 vols. (London: Pickering and Chatto, 2009), vol. II, 63. J. W. Tuttleton, K. Lauer, and M. Murray, *Edith Wharton: The Contemporary Reviews* (Cambridge and New York: Cambridge University Press, 1992), x. All reviews cited in this essay appear in this indispensable collection; all citations reference it, denoted *CR*. For more nuanced versions of the tripartite scheme, see Millicent Bell's "Introduction: A Critical History," in M. Bell, ed. *The Cambridge Companion to Edith Wharton* (Cambridge and New York: Cambridge University Press, 1995), and H. Killoran, *The Critical Reception of Edith Wharton* (Rochester, NY: Camden House of Boydell & Brewer, 2001).

4. A. Gorren, "Studies in Souls," *CR* 35; M. Earle, "Some New Short Stories," *CR* 16; F. J. G., "Mrs. Wharton and Her Use of the Epigram," *CR* 15; Anonymous untitled review of *The Greater Inclination*, *CR* 22; "Recent Fiction," *CR* 24; "The Rambler," *CR* 17; Anonymous untitled review of *The Greater Inclination*, 21; "Literature," *CR* 43; Anonymous untitled review of *The Greater Inclination*, 21; "Literature," 43; W. Payne, "Recent Fiction," *CR* 22; F. J. G., 16.

5. L. Rado, *Modernism, Gender, and Culture: A Cultural Studies Approach* (New York and London: Garland, 1997), 8.

6. "A Notable Novel," *CR* 111; "A Notable Novel," 111; "The Abode of the Fool's Heart," *CR* 121; "*The House of Mirth*, and Other Novels," *CR* 114–15.

7. "Fiction: *The House of Mirth*," *CR* 117; "A Notable Novel," 112; "The Abode of the Fool's Heart," 120; J. MacArthur, "Books and Bookmen," *CR* 118, 119; "A Notable Novel," 110; MacArthur, 118, 118.

8. "Current Fiction," *CR* 137; Anonymous untitled review of *Tales of Men and Ghosts*, *CR* 176; "Fiction," *CR* 233; "*Ethan Frome*," *CR* 182; V. Parrington, Jr., "Our Literary Aristocrat," *CR* 294.

9. F. Fitzgerald, "Echoes of the Jazz Age," *The Crack-Up* (New York: New Directions, 1931), 14, 18. Subsequent references to this work will be noted in the text.

10. V. Parrington, Jr., 294; R. Hale, "Two Lady Authors," *CR* 318; R. West, "Notes on Novels," *CR* 314. Subsequent references to West's work will be noted in the text.

11. C. Morley, "Edith Wharton's Unfinished Novel," *CR* 549; K. Gerould, "Mrs. Wharton's New *House of Mirth*," *CR* 307; A. Leovy, "*The Glimpses of the Moon*," *CR* 316.

12. See M. Bell, "Introduction: A Critical History," 1.

13. R. Lovett, "*A Son at the Front*," *CR* 331; W. Phelps, "Dr. Edith Wharton Makes a Diagnosis," *CR* 344; E. Wilson, "*Old New York*," *CR* 364; D. Gilman, "Some Distinguished Stories," *CR* 480; [F. Codman], "Short Stories By Novelists," *CR* 485; M. Becker, "Last of Edith Wharton: Wherein She Reverted to the Secure Mood and Period of Her Greatest Books," *CR* 546.

14. E. Wharton, *Novellas and Other Writings* (New York: Literary Classics of the United States, 1990), 1125. Subsequent references to this work will be noted in the text.

15. E. Wharton and O. Codman, Jr., *The Decoration of Houses* (New York: W. W. Norton, 1978), n.p.

16. M. Earle, 17; W. Phelps, "As Mrs. Wharton Sees Us," *CR* 283–86; R. Roberts, "The Woman Novelist," *CR* 496.

CHAPTER 7

Obituaries

Linda De Roche

When Edith Wharton died at her villa, Pavillon Colombe, near Saint-Brice-sous-Forêt outside Paris, on August 11, 1937, the seventy-five-year-old Pulitzer Prize-winning writer was lauded by critics on both sides of the Atlantic Ocean as one of the United States' most distinguished novelists. The *New York Herald*, for instance, headlined her death notice with the phrase "foremost woman novelist,"[1] while the London *Times* used the phrase "a great American novelist" in the title of its obituary.[2] In France, where Wharton had made her home for more than thirty years, headlines announced the death of "la première romancière,"[3] the "célèbre romancière américaine,"[4] and "un très grand romancier,"[5] while Louis Gillet, of *l'Academie français*, prefaced his official tribute with the phrase "grand écrivain américain."[6] Wharton's reputation since the publication of her Pulitzer-winning novel *The Age of Innocence* (1920) may have diminished: none of the seventeen works of fiction, short story collections, reminiscences, travel, and criticism published in the intervening years had achieved its success. She may have been regarded at her death as a remnant of a previous literary age, her fiction an anachronism in an era of modernism, but critics, nevertheless, were uniformly convinced of her stature in the literary world (although some doubted her lasting reputation). The basis for their judgments rested at least in part on different attributes of her work. U.S. critics, for example, emphasized her role as social historian, finding in it both her greatest strength and her most serious weakness. European critics, in contrast, appreciated her treatment of her subject, her prose style, her tone, and admired especially her cosmopolitanism. Indeed, in some ways, they valued the art of Wharton's fiction more than her countrymen did.

In the newspapers of Wharton's native New York, the writer's death naturally prompted much interest. She was, after all, a product of the city's aristocracy, descended from Colonial and Revolutionary ancestors including the Schermerhorns, Pendletons, Stevenses, Ledyards, and

Gallatins as well as her father's Joneses, and her mother's Rhinelanders. She had, moreover, achieved her literary fame by exploiting those connections. Indeed, for the New York newspapers, her life was the central fact of her art. "The New York background in which her genius flowered and which she was to picture in many of her novels," reported the *New York Herald*, "was that of the brownstone front and the Victorian drawing room, an aristocracy of wealthy merchants, shipowners, bankers and lawyers" (*NYH* Aug. 13). For the *New York Times*, the "reputation" of a writer who had "as a child ... lived within the inner circle of the New York society that always thought of itself as spelled with a capital S" was built primarily "upon her achievement as the chronicler of Fifth Avenue when the brownstone front hid wealth and dignity at its ease upon the antimacassar-covered plush chairs of the Brown Decade."[7] All of the New York obituaries emphasized Wharton's privileged childhood and adolescence and frequently noted, as the *New York World-Telegram* did, that she had "moved in the most select group of New Yorkers who brought their children up with French, Italian and German governesses, and who believed in giving them a background of continental culture before they had reached the toddling stage."[8] They also noted her society marriage to Edward Wharton, with one newspaper, the *New York Sun*, including the fact that it followed her coming out as a debutante in the "approved fashion" of the day, and the many residences in the United States and abroad that she called home.[9] In this accumulation of personal details, the New York press clearly documented and thereby reinforced the primary judgment of Wharton's place in literary history. She was, above all, a novelist of manners, recording the attitudes and habits, the manners and mores of a specific social class during a particular era.

Having firmly fixed Wharton's literary place, the New York obituaries then subtly undermined it. As a social realist, Wharton was unsurpassed, they acknowledged. Her works, according to the *New York Herald*, were "historical and sociological documents";[10] "future historians will go to her novels for authentic social background," asserted the *New York Sun*.[11] Yet implied in such praise was the criticism leveled in the *New York World-Telegram*: "The world she knew and the silk-lined emotions she recorded were those of the best Knickerbocker society. That was her strength and her limitation."[12] Her subject, in other words, was too narrow, limited by her own very limited experience of the world. She had led a "sheltered life," noted the *New York Times*, growing up in old New York, and knew little of "real life" and "real people" (*NYT* Aug. 12). In fact, the *New York Herald* asserted that "her only sustained contact with the sterner world outside the salon and the study" occurred during World War I, when she worked tirelessly for the benefit of refugees and orphans in her adopted homeland and "visited the front-line trenches and hospitals to tell their story to American readers," work for which the French government awarded her the Cross of the Legion of Honor and Belgium made her a Chevalier of the Order of Leopold (*NYH* Aug. 13). For these critics, little of Wharton's world was "real." That life was lived outside the drawing room, and was a world neither Wharton nor her fictional characters understood. Even *The Age of Innocence*, claimed the *New York Times*, which "showed Mrs. Wharton at her best, understanding the cramped society of her youth, unaware of the world beyond it," suffered this limitation (*NYT* Aug. 12). The U.S. upper classes provided "thin soil for novels," noted the *New York Herald*, quoting an observation by Wharton's biographer Robert Morss Lovett that had been endorsed by other critics, a criticism that clearly had the effect of diminishing the writer's achievement (*NYH* Aug. 13).

The reason for this criticism, however, as the obituaries also imply, may have had less to do with Wharton's recreation of her social milieu than with changing literary fashion. In 1920, when Wharton dramatized the manners and mores of late-Victorian society in *The Age of Innocence*, F. Scott Fitzgerald was documenting the exploits of a contemporary generation in *This Side of Paradise*, and *Ulysses*, James Joyce's modern masterpiece, was in serialization. (It would be published privately by Sylvia Beach in 1922, the same year T. S. Eliot would publish *The Waste Land*.) Responding to the poet Ezra Pound's call to "Make It New," a younger generation of writers was recording the modern moment in prose and verse that were frequently experimental, often controversial, and always provocative. Literary modernism, in other words, was in the ascendency, and Wharton's social realism had fallen out of favor with critics.

Wharton's U.S. obituaries noted this shift and found in it further reason to fault her fiction. The *New York Times*, for instance, concluded a brief review of her oeuvre and a listing of her honors with a one-sentence judgment – "But that was many years ago" – that implied that her relevance to contemporary readers had passed, a view that was reinforced by its assertion that "the generation which knew her best for *The Age of Innocence*" had driven the theatrical success of adaptations of that novel as well as *Ethan Frome* and *The Old Maid* (*NYT* Aug. 12). The *New York World-Telegram* noted that in the midst of literary change, "as hard-boiled novelists have crowded into the field of fiction," Wharton remained ever and only herself, refusing to "follow any alien pattern" (*NYWT* n.d.), while *The New York Sun* concluded that she had "lived to see American fiction develop in ways that, compared to hers, seem bizarre." Wharton may once have been considered a "revolutionary writer," noted the *New York Herald*, her subject and themes may once have been "audacious," but literary fashion had moved beyond her (*NYH* Aug. 16). To the writers of her U.S. obituaries, she was distinctly not modern.

This status, which made Wharton a literary anachronism in her homeland, did not prevent her European critics from acknowledging her achievement and praising her artistry in the obituaries printed in the British and French newspapers at her death. Like their U.S. counterparts, European critics recognized Wharton's stature "as the social historian of a New York that has long since gone with the wind," as the London *Times* reported (*LT* Aug. 14). Indeed, Louis Gillet, of *l'Academie française*, asserted that the "twelve great novels starting with *The House of Mirth* ... remain a major document in the history of New York society and the transformation of the lifestyles that had been taking place for sixty years" (*L'Epoque* Aug. 16). He as well as John Charpentier, writing in the *Mercure de France*, even compared her favorably to British novelist George Eliot, another social realist, and both mentioned her in connection to the French writer George Sand, whose novels explored some of the same themes of class and convention that were central to Wharton's work. To her European critics, however, just as important to her stature and substance was her style, and they did not count it a fault that Wharton was not modern.

Few of Wharton's U.S. obituaries, including the *New York Herald*'s, gave more than passing mention to what it called her "consummate artistry" (*NYH* Aug. 16). In fact, only the New York *Herald-Tribune* wrote more than a phrase or a sentence about a writer whose artistry went beyond the "pursuit of the 'mot juste'" because she sought to fuse substance and form.[13] The London *Times*, in contrast, devoted a full paragraph at the beginning of its death notice to an analysis of Wharton's "technical equipment," which it pronounced "faultless" from the beginning of her career and judged more favorably than contemporary scaffolding: "She learned her craft at a time when mastery was appreciated more than it is to-day [sic], and she continued to the end to show to the world what finish and lightness meant in fiction." Wharton's style, the writer observed, was "admirably lucid," demonstrated "a keen instinct for the *mot propre*," and lacked "superfluities," "undue compressions," or "affectations in her use of language." Moreover, it achieved even "greater perfection" in her later works, which were "told with an ease and dexterity, a smoothness and control, which could only be compared with the playing of a long-experienced virtuoso" (*LT* Aug. 14). In its praise of Wharton's style, the London *Times* made clear that changing literary fashion should and could not diminish appreciation for the art of her prose.

Equally admired as Wharton's prose style among her European critics, but especially the French, was her tone. They recognized and praised her gift for satire and irony in ways that her U.S. critics entirely ignored. Citing a short list of her most important works, J. A., writing in *Les Débats*, for example, noted the "irony, the essential bitterness" in their titles,[14] while Andre Chaumeix noted in his tribute to Wharton published in *L'Echo de Paris* that in *The House of Mirth*, the writer "demonstrated with perspicacity that was not without irony or even sarcasm, the great socialites" in the United States, presenting a "true and terrible image of an egalitarian society where moneyed royalty created all sorts of abuse."[15] Louis Gillet echoed his colleague's judgment of Wharton's tone in *L'Epoque*, claiming that her Pulitzer-winning novel *The Age of Innocence* was "a satire of conventions, where the nothingness of the rich society was no more than the frame where the bright author put, with creative ingenuity, the tragedies of the heart and the tortures of love" (*L'Epoque* Aug. 16). It was clearly this tension between appearance and reality, this disjunction between what was and what could be, that distinguished Wharton from other writers for European critics and contributed to her greatness.

Another attribute that Wharton's European critics valued, perhaps not surprisingly, was her cosmopolitanism. It, too, was a quality largely ignored in the U.S. obituaries. As a member of the United States' social elite, Wharton had lived a peripatetic life. She followed the seasons, as many of her obituaries noted, between family homes in New York and Newport, Rhode Island, throughout her childhood. She traveled frequently to Europe during her youth and adolescence, where she could achieve the finish required of her fashionable education, and divided much of her adult life (when she was not entertaining her friends from the worlds of art and literature at The Mount) between London and Paris. She broadened her perspectives on life in travel to Spain, Italy, Morocco, and other foreign lands, eventually shifting home between a villa in the south of France, near Hyères, and one near Versailles, where she died. While "her early impressions," as the *New York Times* asserted, were indeed "international" (*NYT* Aug. 12), so, too, were her adult sensibilities; her experience of and engagement with other cultures, however limited, made her, as the London *Times* tribute claimed, "a citizen of the world," but not, as the writer clarified, in any pejorative way. Wharton, he explained, was "a cosmopolite not in the shallow, surface-touching way of those men and women whose souls she searched with her satire, but in the way of one who early learned to cross the international boundaries of character and custom, and to fathom the springs of human action abroad and at home."[16] Wharton's cosmopolitanism, in other words, manifested itself in far more than fluency in French, Italian, and German. Rather, it shaped her worldview and imbued her fiction with a breadth and depth of understanding that may have been limited without it.

For the French, Wharton's cosmopolitanism was also essential to her Americanism. According to Gillet, in fact, "this tower of cosmopolitan spirit did not stop her from being American to the marrow" (*L'Epoque* Aug. 16). For Jaloux, this Americanism manifested itself in the writer's exploration of international themes. Comparing her to Henry James, whose influence is mentioned in nearly every obituary, Jaloux asserted that Wharton "loved painting the image of the evolution of Americans, the history of their indecisive and conscientious connection with old Europe, that Europe that troubled them until 1920" (*Le Jour* Aug. 17). Like James, Wharton was, in effect, a more profound writer because her cosmopolitanism gave her the ability to view her U.S. world from outside its confinements and conventions, through the lens of a different value system and moral code.

Yet Jaloux went on to locate Wharton's Americanism in her Puritanism. "She was," he claimed, "a true puritan (in the most noble sense of the word), an absolute American, for whom the domestic life was a reality of the tragic orders" (*Le Jour* Aug. 17). For all her cosmopolitanism, in other words, Wharton remained American in spirit. The nation's values were an inheritance from those Colonial and Revolutionary ancestors. Wharton's fiction, consequently, reflected a distinctively American ethical sensibility, emanating from what John Charpentier identified as the "moral gravity of very refined Puritanism" that animated the writer, despite – or perhaps more accurately as a consequence of – her long contact with European society.[17] Her contact with Europe helped her to know her American self.

In their emphasis on Wharton's Puritanism, French critics articulated an appreciation for the deep moral center of her work that they shared with the British. Indeed, this attribute of Wharton's fiction, far more than her "mere veracity" as a social historian, elicited the highest praise for her literary achievement in the tribute published in the London *Times*. Unlike many contemporary writers, the *Times* critic explained, Wharton understood that "art, to be important, must use important material" and that such material was not a matter of time or place. Rather, it lay "beneath the surface of those places," in the "things that twist the hearts and minds of men and women." For the *Times* critic, any "reading of human character" depended on "ethics," and "tragedy" could not exist "without conflict between things that matter." Wharton, he concluded, "knew and never forgot" these requirements of high art (*LT* n.d.). Her fiction, he implied, mattered and would continue to matter, however unfashionable her subject and style had become, because it examined these conflicts and applied to them standards of behavior by which to judge thought and action.

For the French, of course, beneficiaries of her love for her adopted home, Wharton lived as well as wrote her deep moral conviction. During World War I, she dedicated herself tirelessly to relief efforts. She cared for thousands of Flemish orphans; she opened a sewing workshop for the production of medical supplies and other military needs that also employed women left without work when the fashion industry collapsed. She edited *The Book of the Homeless*, with literary contributions from illustrious writers, to raise funds for charitable work and established rest homes where soldiers and refugees battling the outbreak of war-induced tuberculosis could continue their recuperation following release from hospital. "Whenever the opportunity arose," notes Hermione Lee, "she was an interpreter of France to America and an advocate of American intervention" in the war (462). By the armistice, Wharton was a hero to the French and had been properly honored by the nation, so it is not surprising that many of her French obituaries were decidedly personal.

French writers, the majority of whom signed their tributes, unlike the anonymous reports and retrospectives printed in U.S. and British newspapers, naturally emphasized Wharton's war efforts and her love of France, but they also provided glimpses of the woman they had known. Gillet, for instance, recalled a morning ten years before when Wharton had opened a terrace window to bid him welcome to her home at Hyères and had glimpsed in the sunlight a vision of what her younger self must have been because she was still "capable, in her extreme autonomy, to astonish us by these returns of her radiant flame and rebelliousness" (*L'Epoque* Aug. 16). In the *Mercure de France*, Charpentier shared with readers a remembrance of his first meeting with the writer, at the home of the art critic Bernard Berenson, during the war. "She was knitting for our soldiers," he recalled, "all while talking, and I admired hearing her wonderful knowledge" (*MF* Sept. 15). For Raymond Recouly, in the *Gringoire*, and Philomène Lévis-Mirepoix, writing under her pen name Claude Silve, in *Le Figaro*, Wharton would be forever associated with her gardens, their beauty an expression of her being. Their heartfelt reminiscences left no doubt that Wharton's love of France had been reciprocated by the French.

Despite their deep and long acquaintance with Wharton, her French compatriots failed to appreciate fully one of the writer's chief personal – and perhaps even cultural – attributes, her drive and ambition, especially to become a writer. The French, of course, had witnessed the quality in action during the war years, but only her fellow Americans recognized and appreciated its importance to overcoming the barriers of gender and class that Wharton had faced to become a writer. Her "position," asserted the *New York World-Telegram*, "was a personal achievement" because Wharton, who "was born into the aristocracy of old New York," had "made herself a novelist by her own drive and self-discipline" (*NYWT* n.d.) Forced as a child to scavenge brown paper wrappings on which to write, related the *New York Times*, "she was not encouraged" in her literary efforts (*NYT* Aug. 12). Indeed, "her determination to write novels," noted the *New York Herald*, "constituted a defiance of tradition difficult to comprehend today" (*NYH* Aug. 16). Members of Wharton's class, these writers recognized, simply did not become writers, for "authorship," as the *New York Times* quoted Wharton explaining, "was still regarded as something between a black art and a form of manual labor" (*NYT* Aug. 12).Women of her class, moreover, who were expected to devote themselves to social and domestic responsibilities and were permitted few opportunities to venture outside the drawing room or rose garden, risked ostracism if they stepped beyond the bounds of propriety to pursue a writing career, and Wharton's "scribbling," observed the *New York Herald*, had indeed "made her an outsider" in her world (*NYH* Aug. 16). That she prevailed against such attitudes was without doubt testament to her force of character. A woman of lesser drive and determination would have been defeated. There may have been, as ever, some condescension in their tribute to Wharton the woman. "Seldom in her writing," asserted the *New York World-Telegram*, "could she forget that she herself was a lady," implying that her fiction had been limited by that status (*NYWT* n.d.). Nevertheless, at a time when Harriet Beecher Stowe remained one of the few women writers included in the nation's literary pantheon, her critics could not deny her accomplishment.

No matter their nationality, the authors of Wharton's obituaries almost universally agreed on the work they considered her masterpiece, *Ethan Frome*, and were equally convinced of the merits of *The House of Mirth* and *The Age of Innocence*. They were, without doubt, the works on which her reputation would rest. They were also united in their view that Wharton had learned the lessons of her mentor Henry James. Jaloux, for instance, asserted that "Like Henry James, she too wrote psychological novels ... where the intensity of moral drama produced mysterious conflicts" (*Le Jour* Aug. 17), and the *New York World-Telegram* reported that "her work showed the influence of James, and that was a source of great pride to her" (*NYWT* Aug 12). Yet they were certain as well that she placed on her fiction the stamp of her own intellect, that her voice was her own.

Ten years after Wharton's death, the U.S. critic Edmund Wilson began an essay that promised "Justice to Edith Wharton" with the assertion that "the notices elicited by her death did her, in general, something less than justice."[18] His evaluation, however, was not entirely accurate (just as his analysis did not quite do justice to the writer). The authors of Wharton's obituaries and death notices expressed genuine appreciation for her literary achievements. They clearly acknowledged the veracity with which she created the social milieu of her novels and the penetrating ironies that she turned on it. Yet without doubt, Wharton's U.S. critics were far more ambivalent about her literary stature than their European counterparts. Unlike the Europeans, who focused their analysis on the work only, the Americans conveyed the idea that her art was the relic of another age, with the implication that what she had to say no longer mattered to the contemporary generation. Their criticism was often a matter of tone, which was frequently dismissive and occasionally cutting. The *New York Times*, for instance, concluded a paragraph about Wharton's early career and her acknowledgment that she had never forgotten the advice of her editors and mentors by quoting the reply of a "well-known critic": "One well believes it" (*NYT* Aug. 12). More often, however, their criticism arose from her failure to be modern. At a time of revolutionary change in literary fashion, Wharton, as the *New York World-Telegram* stated, "merely showed the continuing vitality" of her style and subjects, that "merely" subtly undermining the writer's praise by suggesting that she was incapable of change (*NYWT* n.d.). The tendency of her U.S. critics to evaluate Wharton not for what she did but for what she failed to do effectively created the impression that her achievement was limited, her reputation already in eclipse, and perhaps deservedly so. Their prejudice may indeed have prevented them from doing justice to her art. In fact, it was her European critics, such as the writer for the London *Times*, rather than her U.S. compatriots, who claimed unequivocally that at her death Wharton went "securely to her place among the great artists of fiction" (*LT* n.d.).

NOTES

1. "Edith Wharton Dies in France," *New York Herald*, August 13, 1937, n.p. Subsequent references to this work are included in the text (*NYH* Aug. 13). All obituaries cited in this essay have been obtained from the Edith Wharton collection at, and are published courtesy of, The Lilly Library, Indiana University, Bloomington, Indiana.

2. "Edith Wharton. A Great American Novelist," the London *Times*, August 14, 1937, n.p. Subsequent references to this work are included in the text (*LT* Aug. 14).

3. "Les obsèques d'Edith Wharton la première romancière américain ont eu lieu ce matin à Versailles," *Paris-Soir*, August 14, 1937, n.p. I am grateful to Stéphane De Roche for all French translations.

4. "Edith Wharthon [sic] la célèbre romancière américaine repose dans la terre de France qu'elle a tant aimée," *L'Excelsior*, August 15, 1937, n.p.

5. E. Jaloux, "Edith Wharton, un très grand romancier," *Le Jour*, August 17, 1937, n.p. Subsequent references to this work are included in the text.

6. L. Gillet, "Edith Wharton, grand écrivain américain repose dans la terre de France qu'elle a aimée," *L'Epoque*, August 16, 1937, n.p. Subsequent references to this work are included in the text.

7. "Edith Wharton, 75, is Dead in France," *New York Times*, August 12, 1937, n.p. Subsequent references to this work are included in the text (*NYT* Aug. 12).

8. "Edith Wharton, Novelist, Dies Abroad at 75," *New York World-Telegram*, August 12, 1937, n.p.

9. "Edith Wharton Dies in France," *New York Sun*, August 12, 1937, n.p.

10. "Edith Wharton," *New York Herald*, August 16, 1937, n.p. Subsequent references to this work are included in the text (*NYH* Aug. 16).

11. "An American Novelist," *New York Sun*, August 13, 1937, n.p. Subsequent references to this work are included in the text (*NYS* Aug. 13).

12. "Edith Wharton," *New York World-Telegram*, n.d., n.p. Subsequent references to this work are included in the text (*NYWT* n.d.).

13. "Edith Wharton," *Herald-Tribune*, n.d., n.p.

14. J. A., "Edith Wharton," *Les Débats*, n.d., n.p.

15. A. Chaumeix, "Mrs. Edith Wharton," *L'Echo de Paris*, August 14, 1937, n.p.

16. "Edith Wharton," the London *Times*, n.d., n.p. Subsequent references to this work are included in the text (*LT* n.d.).

17. J. Charpentier, "Edith Wharton," *Mercure de France*, September 15, 1937, n.p. Subsequent references to this work are included in the text (*MF* Sept. 15).

18. E. Wilson, "Justice to Edith Wharton," *Edmund Wilson: Literary Essays and Reviews of the 1930s and 40s* (New York: Library of America, 2007), 405–17; 405.

CHAPTER 8

"Justice" to Edith Wharton? The Early Critical Responses

Melissa M. Pennell

A survey of the critical writings on Edith Wharton and her work from the time of her death in 1937 to 1980 reveals the process by which an author popular during her own lifetime becomes part of the literary canon. The criticism written in this period includes considerations of Wharton's stature as an author, appraisals of the themes and issues that dominate her fiction, and discussions of specific novels and stories. Although Helen Killoran labels 1938 to 1975 "The Lull" in Wharton scholarship, a time in which Wharton critics and scholars "mostly speculated, repeating much of what had previously been written" about her and her work,[1] a number of monographs and articles did appear, establishing a foundation for critical discussion and identifying those works that would, over the years, receive the most attention. When he wrote "Justice to Edith Wharton" in 1937 – first published in 1938 and later revised for his collection *The Wound and the Bow* (1941) – Edmund Wilson suggested that not enough attention had been paid to the writer's achievements, especially those that occurred during the first two decades of the twentieth century.[2] One assumes he would have been pleased by the attention Wharton's work was receiving by the 1970s, even if scholars did not adhere to his prescription regarding the novels most worthy of consideration.

Prior to the publication of Wilson's essay, little critical material that focused solely on Wharton's work, other than contemporary reviews, had appeared. A number of texts that survey the development of the U.S. novel or the shaping of U.S. fiction include discussions of the writer and her work, but few explored her work in great depth. In many of these discussions, critics suggested that because her fiction focused primarily on the elite in the United States, it lacked relevance to the mainstream of U.S. culture.[3] Of the books or monographs on Wharton to appear prior to 1937, two were bibliographies of her writings and two were theses, one of which, by E. K. Brown, was then published as *Edith Wharton: Étude Critique* (1935).[4] This volume, written in French, is divided into two sections: the first offers comment on Wharton's fiction and the second explores her relationship to other writers, including those who influenced her work, as well as an analysis of her style and the structure of her fiction.

Brown argues that in her best short stories, Wharton remains behind the scenes, allowing the tales to develop without authorial commentary. He discusses each collection of stories, occasionally highlighting a story that he finds particularly effective, such as "Souls Belated" or "The Lady's Maid's Bell." Brown offers an analysis of the "novellas," including *Ethan Frome* and *Summer*, which he sees as narratives that demonstrate the writer's force and power in conveying the natural scene. He divides the novels into groups: those set in New York, those that explore the *"scène internationale,"* and those that are historical – the category into which he places *The Age of Innocence*. In light of Wharton's subjects and method, Brown argues that she is indebted to Henry James, but he also explores the relationships between her work and that of Ellen Glasgow, George Eliot, and Honoré de Balzac. In 1938, Brown published an essay entitled "Edith Wharton" that appeared in *Études Anglaises*; written in English, this essay provides in brief his analysis of the significant themes and conflicts in her fiction, especially her concern for enduring values, both aesthetic and moral. Brown's view that her "creative power was not that of the masters of fiction" and that even though her work has a "special tone," it is "not the tone of the highest art indeed, but a tone ... unfailingly interesting and stimulating" [5] seemed to provide evidence for Wilson's belief that the writer's accomplishments were not fully appreciated.

Having Wilson as a champion may have been a mixed blessing for Wharton. One of the most influential of U.S. critics in the first half of the twentieth century, Wilson was known for exercising vigorous and opinionated judgments on the work of writers, both historical and contemporary, through his essays and reviews. While he argued for Wharton's stature as an author and for the place of her work in the U.S. canon, his remarks also set limitations on which of her works merited attention. He claimed that 1905 to 1917 marked the period of her best work, identifying among her later novels only *The Age of Innocence* (1920) as being worthwhile. Wilson asserted that with *The House of Mirth* (1905), Wharton "emerged as a historian of the American society of her time" and praised it and the novels written during the ensuing fifteen years for their "realism and intensity" (Wilson 405). He dismissed the references to her as a disciple of Henry James, stating that her work "very soon took a direction totally different" from that of James (406). Wilson identified the conflict between an individual and his or her social milieu as a driving force in Wharton's narratives, a conflict that many later critics would explore in detail. He also pointed to the problematic nature of many of her male characters, that "the typical masculine figure" in her fiction was "a man set apart from his neighbors by education, intellect, and feeling, but lacking the force or the courage either to impose himself or to get away" (Wilson 412).

Disappointed by Percy Lubbock's *Edith Wharton: A Memoir by an English Friend* (1947) for its failure to address what Wilson saw as the crucial questions one needs to answer to understand her career, Wilson commented, in the course of reviewing Lubbock's text, on the importance of the Wharton papers at Yale that would be available to scholars in 1968.[6] He believed that access to this material would make a significant difference to the understanding and appreciation of her work. While he was critical of Lubbock's failure to address Wharton's U.S. background as a defining element in her work and of his attempts to see the influence of her friend Walter Berry in the qualities of her male characters, Wilson had engaged in some biographical interpretations of his own. In "Justice" he suggested that the unhappiness in Wharton's marriage prompted her best writing. He offered this observation: "It is sometimes true of women writers – less often, I believe of men – that a manifestation of something like genius may be stimulated by some exceptional emotional strain, but will disappear when the stimulus has passed" (Wilson 413). Wilson claimed that after Wharton divorced her husband and settled permanently in France, she became "comfortably adjusted" and this adjustment caused "the real intellectual force" behind her work to evaporate "almost completely" (414). Given the way his own understanding was shaped by the gender expectations of his time, Wilson could not foresee that along with the opening of the Wharton archive, the changes in literary scholarship inspired by second-wave feminism beginning in the late 1960s would also have a profound influence on Wharton scholarship.

The first major text on Wharton's work to be published in the United States after her death appeared in 1953, *Edith Wharton: A Study of Her Fiction* by Blake Nevius. Nevius acknowledged the neglect the author had suffered, but he, like Brown before him, found it necessary to qualify and defend the choice of Wharton as a subject for extended study, in light of the view that she did not display the "intellectual force [of] George Eliot and Henry James."[7] Nevius places her work in the novel of manners tradition, seeing in her fiction the exploration of the "deterioration of Old World ideals under the impact of industrial democracy" (65). According

to Nevius, much of her fiction focuses on a central problem: a main character commits a "sentimental error" in believing that another character
shares his or her sensibilities and views of the world; this "error" results
in an unequal partnership. Once this relationship is established, the main
character is forced to wrestle with the "question … of [his or her] moral
obligation" or loyalty to that partner (Nevius 110). In his analysis, Nevius
reflects on this thematic development in those works identified by Wilson
and others as warranting discussion, but he also considers novels that
had not been emphasized in earlier commentary, especially *The Fruit of
the Tree*. At times, Nevius finds fault with Wharton's views, especially
what he sees as her inability to sympathize with the plight of some of
her female characters, including Sophy Viner of *The Reef* and Charity
Royall of *Summer*, which he links to her class sensibilities. Ultimately,
he sees Wharton as a writer separated from the mainstream of the U.S.
tradition by her embrace of classicism, her inability to accept "the doctrine of inevitable progress," and her distrust of "romantic individualism"
(Nevius 246). Because Nevius' text remained the only extended study
of Wharton's fiction for nearly a decade, it often served as a touchstone
against which other critics measured their readings, including Marilyn
Jones Lyde in her *Edith Wharton: Convention and Morality in the Work of
a Novelist* (1959).

Although the archive of Wharton's papers would not be open to scholars until the late 1960s, Nancy R. Leach published two articles in the
1950s that must have piqued scholars' interest as to what might be waiting
in this treasure trove. The first, "Edith Wharton's Unpublished Novel,"
discussed the manuscript of a projected novel entitled "Literature" found
in a small writer's notebook in the Yale Library collection. Leach asserted
that this manuscript is of interest primarily for "the light it casts on Edith
Wharton's methods of writing and suggested that it formed a basis for
what fifteen years later became *Hudson River Bracketed* and *The Gods
Arrive*."[8] The second, "New England in the Stories of Edith Wharton,"
summarized the content of three fragmentary novels in the unpublished
papers and indicated that the manuscripts "emphasize the virtues and
defects of [Wharton's] understanding and interpretation of the region."[9]
Because letters that Wharton had exchanged with her publishers were
held in collections that were open to scholars, analysis of her professional
life as an author and businesswoman was to some degree possible, as evidenced by Millicent Bell's essay "Lady into Author" (1957) that examined
letters held in the Scribner archive. This correspondence revealed, as Bell

noted, that the writer "developed an effective grasp of the commercial values that govern a literary career."[10]

Throughout the 1950s and into the 1960s, articles and book chapters on Wharton's work began to appear more frequently. The approach followed in many of these reflected the tenets of New Criticism, in which close reading of a text and analysis of its formal structure governed the commentary while biographical and social considerations were downplayed or omitted altogether. Those who practiced New Criticism examined the structure of a narrative and explored the ways in which an author made use of irony, satire, and ambiguity as well as character, setting, and imagery to convey meaning. The use of this approach allowed critics to shift their focus away from Wharton's elite background and the limitations it may have imposed and instead examine the interrelationship between thematic development and narrative technique that operated within her work. A number of these articles continued to explore the relationship between Wharton's work and the novel of manners tradition, such as Viola Hopkins' "The Ordering Style of *The Age of Innocence*"; others, such as Larry Rubin's "Aspects of Naturalism in Four Novels by Edith Wharton" and Christof Wegelin's "The Rise of the International Novel," explored the writer's connections to important literary movements of her day.[11] Even though the number of critical discussions on Wharton continued to increase, Diana Trilling asserted in her essay "*The House of Mirth Revisited*" that "it still remains for criticism to show Mrs. Wharton in her proper place in the mainstream of American literature."[12]

During the 1960s, critical texts appeared that began to suggest that Wharton's "proper place" might be as a canonical author. In 1962, *Edith Wharton: A Collection of Critical Essays*, edited by Irving Howe, was published in Prentice-Hall's Twentieth Century Views series. The volumes in this series presented collections of essays, some previously published and some written specifically for the volume. All of the volumes treated authors who were viewed as significant voices in the U.S. tradition. When the volume on Wharton appeared, the U.S. series of Twentieth Century Views featured only one other woman writer, poet Emily Dickinson. In his introduction, Howe argued eloquently for the significance of the work: "To read these books is to discover how the novel of manners can register both the surface of social life and the inner vibrations of spirit that surface reveals, suppresses, and distorts."[13] Identification of Wharton and her work as a subject for serious academic study was also evident in the twelve doctoral dissertations written on her in the 1960s. Some compared her to other writers, including Dreiser and Crane, while others began to treat her later novels in greater depth. All of these provided a foundation for the expansion of Wharton scholarship that occurred in the late 1960s and throughout the 1970s. Surprisingly, even though many indications revealed that she was becoming an accepted figure in the canon, critics continued to offer qualifications for their interest in her writing. As late as 1970, Geoffrey Walton in *Edith Wharton: A Critical Interpretation* felt the need to do so, when he admitted that there had "been a serious attempt at a revival of interest in Edith Wharton on both sides of the Atlantic during the past few years," but noted that "appreciation of her work in England [had] been patchy."[14]

Among those who had focused on Wharton in their doctoral work, James Tuttleton became a frequent contributor of articles to Wharton studies, addressing a wide range of topics from her friendships with Henry James and Theodore Roosevelt to her ideas about the value of tradition and culture. Tuttleton argued that she saw culture and tradition as elements that provided individuals with a sense of identity, of connectedness, and of morality. In analyzing the work that Wharton wrote after World War I, Tuttleton claimed that her postwar novels "vividly portray the plight of rootless and ephemeral people in the postwar world, cut adrift from their moral moorings."[15] One of Tuttleton's major contributions was his "Edith Wharton: An Essay in Bibliography" published in *Resources for American Literary Study*.[16] This journal, founded in 1971, provides scholars and graduate students with access to information related to holdings in archival collections, forecasts of new directions in the critical study of certain authors, and overviews of the state of scholarly work on particular figures. Tuttleton's bibliographical review runs to thirty-nine pages and offers an extensive survey of the work that had been done to date on Wharton. Tuttleton argues that the "thirty-year ban imposed on the examination of her private papers have stifled rather than encouraged critical and biographical interest in Mrs. Wharton and her work" (166). He speaks of the anticipation with which he and other Wharton scholars of the era look forward to the publication of the biography then underway by R. W. B. Lewis.

In many ways, the 1970s marked the decade during which Wharton was fully accepted as a canonical author in the U.S. tradition. In 1968, her papers, housed in Yale's Beinecke Library, were opened. However, as was customary at the time, exclusive access to the papers was granted to R. W. B. Lewis, a Yale professor of English, who was at work on a biography of the writer. His book, *Edith Wharton: A Biography*, was published in 1975. It received much praise and won numerous awards, including the Pulitzer

Prize, the Bancroft Prize, and the National Book Critics' Circle Award. Many Wharton scholars and enthusiasts welcomed the volume as a major resource for understanding her life and for revealing details that necessitated reassessment of her relationships with certain figures, especially Walter Berry, and earlier biographical texts, including Percy Lubbock's. Not everyone, however, was pleased with Lewis' treatment of Wharton. In a review essay, Mary Ellmann criticized Lewis for placing too much emphasis on her social life and not enough on her writing life.[17] Cynthia Ozick, recalling the title of Edmund Wilson's essay in her own "Justice (Again) to Edith Wharton," expressed her frustration with the way Lewis presents the "life," but not the "writer."[18] Despite these objections, this successful biography brought to an end the need for scholars and critics to justify why they had chosen to address Wharton and her work.

In addition to Lewis' biography of Wharton, other volumes appeared in the mid-1970s that reinforced Wharton's position as a canonical author. In 1976, *Edith Wharton* by Margaret McDowell was published in Twayne's United States Authors series.[19] Like the earlier Twentieth Century Views text, this volume was designed as a resource for students and teachers, including college faculty. Rather than offering reprints of critical essays, the volumes in this series contained chapters that present the major critical approaches to an author's work and discussions of works that are frequently included on high school and college reading lists. McDowell's volume included individual chapters on *The House of Mirth*, *The Custom of the Country*, and *The Age of Innocence*, along with a chapter that discussed the novellas and short stories, and two chapters that looked at the novels written after *The Age of Innocence*. A similar volume by Richard Lawson was published in Ungar's Modern Literature Monographs series in 1977.[20] This volume contained separate chapters on *The Age of Innocence*, *The House of Mirth*, *The Custom of the Country*, *The Reef*, and *Ethan Frome*. It also offered a chapter that surveyed the short stories, but omitted discussion of "Roman Fever," which has become one of Wharton's most anthologized works.

Throughout the 1970s, scholars continued to explore the ways in which Wharton's fiction was shaped by and contributed to the novel of manners tradition. James Tuttleton included her work in *The Novel of Manners in America* and Gary Lindberg devoted an entire volume to an exploration of what constitutes the novel of manners and Wharton's relationship to this tradition in his *Edith Wharton and the Novel of Manners*.[21] Others extended the debate over moral issues in her fiction, many asserting, as do David Eggenschwiler and James Gargano, that greater complexities

underlie the human relationships in Wharton's fiction than earlier readings acknowledged.[22] Scholars also began to argue for the significance
of lesser-known works in the oeuvre, as Viola H. Winner does for *Fast
and Loose*, a product of Wharton's teenage literary endeavors.[23] Wharton's
suitability as a subject for graduate-level study was clearly established as
well, as dissertations written during the 1970s that focused on Wharton
exclusively or included her in comparison with the work of other authors
more than tripled compared to the output of the 1960s.

The effects of the women's movement and the rise of feminist scholarship influenced the topics addressed in dissertations and articles written
on Wharton in the 1970s. Many of the readings offered in these texts
reflect what Elaine Showalter labeled "revisionary" feminist criticism,
an approach that "offers feminist readings of texts which consider the
images and stereotypes of women in literature, [and] the omissions and
misconceptions about women in criticism."[24] Examples of such essays
include Margaret McDowell's "Viewing the Custom of Her Country:
Edith Wharton's Feminism" that highlights the "social criticism implicit
in [Wharton's] preoccupation with the problems of women in a changing
society"; Elizabeth Ammons' "Fairy-Tale Love and the Reef" in which
Ammons identifies the "false romantic visions generated and perpetu-
ated by limitations imposed on women"; and Judith Saunders' "Ironic
Reversal in Edith Wharton's *Bunner Sisters*" that posits how the narrative
"implicitly links the dangers of self-sacrifice to woman's chattel-like place
on the marriage market."[25] As the decade progressed, Showalter noted an
evolution in feminist scholarship toward an approach that explored "the
psychodynamics of female creativity" (Showalter 185), one that shaped
another major text on Wharton, Cynthia Griffin Wolff's *A Feast of Words:
The Triumph of Edith Wharton* (1977). Like the Lewis biography, this volume received much attention and although Wolff's interpretation of the
writer was not without controversy, it was praised by critics such as Blake
Nevius for its "shrewd and challenging integration of the inner life with
its fictive expression."[26]

Although the word *triumph* in Wolff's title has multiple meanings,
it provided a measure of the change that occurred in Wharton scholarship and in the writer's place in the U.S. canon from the publication of
Wilson's essay forty years earlier. By the late 1970s, questions of Wharton's
relevance to the mainstream of U.S. fiction, her overshadowing by Henry
James, and her lack of sympathy toward characters outside her own social
class had been laid to rest. Instead, new questions were being formulated,
shaped by the continuing development of feminist criticism and the growing influence of post-structuralist literary theory, as well as wider access

to the writer's papers, all of which propelled the direction of Wharton scholarship over the coming decades.

NOTES

1. H. Killoran, *The Critical Reception of Edith Wharton* (Rochester, NY: Camden House, 2001), 6.
2. E. Wilson, "Justice to Edith Wharton," *Edmund Wilson: Literary Essays and Reviews of the 1930s and 1940s* (New York: Library of America, 2007), 405–17. Subsequent references to this work are included in the text. "Justice" was first published in *New Republic*, 95 (June 29, 1938), 209–13, and reprinted with revisions in *The Wound and the Bow* (Boston: Houghton Mifflin, 1941), 195–213.
3. See, for example, V. Parrington, *Main-currents in American Thought* (New York: Harcourt Brace, 1927); P. H. Boynton, "American Authors of Today: V. Edith Wharton," *The English Journal*, 12 (1923), 24–32; J. W. Beach, *The Twentieth Century Novel* (New York: Century, 1932); and H. Hartwick, *The Foreground of American Fiction* (New York: American, 1934).
4. E. K. Brown, *Edith Wharton: Étude Critique* (Paris : E. Droz, 1935). See also L. Melish, *A Bibliography of the Collected Writings of Edith Wharton* (New York: Brick Row Book Shop, 1927); L. Davis, *A Bibliography of the Writings of Edith Wharton* (Portland, ME: Southworth Press, 1933); a biographical pamphlet by W. L. Cross, *Edith Wharton* (New York: Appleton, 1926); and the primarily biographical monograph by R. M. Lovett, *Edith Wharton* (New York: McBride & Co., 1925). The other thesis written on Wharton was by J. van Klooster, "Modern Amerikaansche Letterkunde: Edith Wharton," University of Gronnigen, 1924.
5. E. K. Brown, "Edith Wharton" in I. Howe (ed.), *Edith Wharton: A Collection of Critical Essays* (Englewood Cliffs, NJ: Prentice-Hall, 1962), 62–72; 71. First published in *Études Anglaises* (Jan–Mar 1938), 16–26.
6. E. Wilson, "Edith Wharton: A Memoir by an English Friend," *Edmund Wilson: Literary Essays and Reviews of the 1930s and 1940s*, (New York: Library of America, 2007), 799–803; 803. First published in *New Yorker*, 23 (October 4, 1947), 101–04.
7. B. Nevius, *Edith Wharton: A Study of Her Fiction* (Berkeley: University of California Press, 1953), 10. Subsequent references to this work are included in the text.
8. N. Leach, "Edith Wharton's Unpublished Novel," *American Literature*, 25 (1953), 334–54; 334. Although Leach implies that a single manuscript version of "Literature" is extant in the notebook she describes, Laura Rattray explains that "[T]he material evidence for *Literature* is the most expansive and complex of the archival manuscript sources, comprising notebook, miscellaneous notes, manuscript, and multiple, non-sequential typescript and carbon drafts" (II: 119). For additional information on the manuscript and to read the text of "Literature," see L. Rattray (ed.), *The Unpublished Writings of Edith Wharton*, vol. II (London: Pickering and Chatto: 2009), vii–xxvi; 119–82.

9. N. Leach, "New England in the Stories of Edith Wharton," *New England Quarterly*, 30 (1957), 90–98; 95.

10. M. Bell, "Lady into Author," *American Quarterly*, 9 (1957), 295–315; 295–96.

11. V. Hopkins, "The Ordering Style of *The Age of Innocence*," *American Literature*, 30 (1958), 345–57; L. Rubin, "Aspects of Naturalism in Four Novels by Edith Wharton," *Twentieth Century Literature*, 2 (1957), 182–92; C. Wegelin, "The Rise of the International Novel," *PMLA*, 77 (1962), 305–10.

12. D. Trilling, "The House of Mirth Revisited," in I. Howe (ed.), *Edith Wharton: A Collection of Critical Essays* (Englewood Cliffs, NJ: Prentice-Hall, 1962), 103–18; 103. First published in *American Scholar*, 32 (1962–63), 113–28.

13. I. Howe, "Introduction: The Achievement of Edith Wharton" in I. Howe (ed.), *Edith Wharton: A Collection of Critical Essays* (Englewood Cliffs, NJ: Prentice-Hall, 1962), 1–18; 12.

14. G. Walton, *Edith Wharton: A Critical Interpretation* (Rutherford, NJ: Fairleigh Dickinson University Press, 1970), 7.

15. J. Tuttleton, "Edith Wharton: The Archeological Motive," *Yale Review*, 61 (1972), 568.

16. J. Tuttleton, "Edith Wharton: An Essay in Bibliography," *Resources for American Literary Study*, 3 (1973), 163–202. Subsequent references to this work are included in the text.

17. M. Ellman, "Manners, Morals, and Mrs. Wharton," *Sewanee Review*, 84 (1976), 528–32.

18. C. Ozick, "Justice (Again) to Edith Wharton," *Commentary* (October 1976), 48–57.

19. M. McDowell, *Edith Wharton* (Boston: Twayne, 1976).

20. R. Lawson, *Edith Wharton* (New York: Ungar Publishing, 1977).

21. J. Tuttleton, *The Novel of Manners in America* (Chapel Hill: University of North Carolina Press, 1972); G. Lindberg, *Edith Wharton and the Novel of Manners* (Charlottesville: University of Virginia Press, 1975).

22. D. Eggenschwiler, "The Ordered Disorder of *Ethan Frome*," *Studies in the Novel*, 9 (1977), 237–46; J. Gargano, "Edith Wharton's *The Reef*," *Novel: A Forum on Fiction*, 10 (1976), 40–48.

23. V. H. Winner, "Convention and Prediction in Edith Wharton's *Fast and Loose*," *American Literature*, 42 (1970), 50–69.

24. E. Showalter, "Feminist Criticism in the Wilderness," *Critical Inquiry*, 8 (1981), 179–205; 182. Subsequent references to this work are included in the text.

25. M. McDowell, "Viewing the Custom of Her Country: Edith Wharton's Feminism" *Contemporary Literature* 15 (1974), 521–38; 523; E. Ammons, "Fairy-Tale Love and the Reef," *American Literature* 47 (1976), 615–28; 616; J. Saunders, "Ironic Reversal in Edith Wharton's *Bunner Sisters*," *Studies in Short Fiction*, 14 (1977), 241–45; 244.

26. B. Nevius, Untitled Review, *Modern Philology*, 77 (1979), 249.

CHAPTER 9

Modern Critical Receptions

Jessica Schubert McCarthy

Edith Wharton's writings continue to capture the imaginations of both readers and critics for a number of reasons, the most significant being her exquisitely detailed rendering of the early-twentieth-century's complex social and historical milieux. However, many themes and issues explored by Wharton speak to readers in the late-twentieth and early-twenty-first centuries as well. The result of continued interest in Wharton has been a vast body of scholarship on a wide range of topics. Feminist critics, for example, have found many rich veins to mine in her reflections of the challenges facing women writers, and scholars of race and transatlanticism have found much to discuss in her war writings. Even more recently, historical events such as the United States' billion-dollar banking bailout remind us of Wharton's relevance, as evidenced by renewed interest in *The Custom of the Country*, her novel of social and financial climbing.

Although a great deal has been written about Wharton since Yale University's Beinecke Library unsealed her papers in 1968, this essay is structured to provide readers with a broad overview of modern critical trends and to highlight publications that have most affected scholars' understanding of her life and work in the past three decades.

THE 1980S

For Wharton scholars, one of the 1980s' most exciting publications was *The Letters of Edith Wharton* (1988), edited by R. W. B. Lewis and Nancy Lewis. Containing approximately 400 letters written over the course of sixty years, this collection proved invaluable to readers interested in the writer, her circle of correspondents, and the historical period at large.

The momentum behind feminist literary criticism continued into the 1980s and with it came two significant examinations of Wharton's views on women's roles. In *Edith Wharton's Argument with America* (1980), Elizabeth Ammons traces her engagement with "the woman question."

Ammons' influential book suggests Wharton sought to argue that, despite the appearance of progress, women still faced great oppression – both socially and economically. Although the 1890s produced many examples of bold female heroines, Wharton's writing from that time tends to portray womanhood as a state of suffering and sacrifice. Ammons, however, has to account for the priority given to maternity in Wharton's later writings and does so by suggesting that the author's age, combined with the tragedy and violence of World War I, had given her a new appreciation for protecting society's most vulnerable members.[1] Carol Wershoven's *The Female Intruder in the Novels of Edith Wharton* (1982), considered the writer's inclusion of "the woman who is in some way outside of her society," a character who forces men to reexamine their society, demonstrates the confinement of other women, teaches alternative ways of thinking about gender roles, and encourages readers to reconsider society on the intruder's terms.[2]

In addition to the longer studies, the 1980s included a swell of scholarly essays. In a 1987 issue of *College Literature* dedicated to Wharton, scholars such as Katherine Joslin weighed in on critical attitudes toward the writer on what would have been the year of her 125th birthday.[3] Many other essays demonstrate scholars' continued interest in feminist criticism and the unique challenges facing women writers. Joan Lidoff's "Another Sleeping Beauty" provides a psychological analysis of Lily Bart, diagnoses her as narcissistic, and suggests that Wharton's fictive world is limited by her harsh portrayal of practical action. In "'The Blank Page' and the Issues of Female Creativity," Susan Gubar uses the Isak Dinesen story of that title as a point of departure from which to consider the difficulties facing creative women who are themselves seen as an aesthetic object, specifically examining Lily Bart's treatment as a work of art rather than as a fully actualized individual. "The Death of the Lady (Novelist)," by Elaine Showalter, interprets Lily Bart's death as symbolic of Wharton's transformation from a lady novelist to an artist and draws attention to the degree that both men and women are limited by social conventions. Marilyn French's "Muzzled Women" locates Wharton alongside other major women writers such as Cather, Eliot, Sand, and Woolf and highlights the common problem in women's literature that female characters are rarely granted the same opportunities and advantages afforded the authors. "Cool Diana and the Blood-Red Muse," by Elizabeth Ammons, argues for the significance of *The Age of Innocence* because it allowed Wharton to explore disparities between the U.S. woman and the woman artist.[4]

Perhaps because the 1980s proved to be a time of great financial growth in the United States, *The House of Mirth* was of particular focus as critics sought to understand the economy of Lily Bart's social scene. In an essay that remains frequently cited by other scholars, Wai-chee Dimock explains that *The House of Mirth* employs the language of the marketplace to validate the prices of social exchanges. Other scholars emphasized formal elements of Wharton's writing. Michael O'Neal's essay, "Point of View and the Narrative Technique in the Fiction of Edith Wharton," is an analysis of her style and an examination of how language creates characterization and judgment in *The House of Mirth*. In "'Natural Magic'," Carol Miller defends Wharton's use of irony by suggesting that it forges a connection between reader and author. James Tuttleton's "Mocking Fate" suggests that *The Reef*'s departure from Wharton's typically episodic structure resulted from the author's emotional turmoil during and after her affair with Morton Fullerton.[5]

THE 1990S

In the 1990s, Wharton scholarship began to broaden its scope. The 1995 publication of the *Cambridge Companion to Edith Wharton*, edited by Millicent Bell and including essays written by a range of established Wharton scholars, might be seen as Wharton scholarship's coming of age. As the first volume in this well-known series to focus on a woman writer, this collection signaled that Wharton had taken her place amongst highly-regarded canonical authors.[6] She was also included in Cambridge University Press' American Critical Archives series, which led to the publication of a volume of contemporary critical responses to the writer's work.[7] The annotated bibliography of Wharton's primary works and scholars' criticism, edited by Kristin O. Lauer and Margaret P. Murray, also proved a useful resource and put in evidence the large body of work produced on Wharton's writings.[8] *A Forward Glance* (1999), a collection of essays on Wharton's work, provided new insights into topics ranging from the author's clothing to race and *The Age of Innocence*.[9]

As Wharton's visibility increased, many feminist interpretations still appeared but attention was also turned to the cultural climate and literary circles in which she moved. Two new biographies of the writer appeared in 1994: *No Gifts from Chance* by Shari Benstock and *Edith Wharton: An Extraordinary Life* by Eleanor Dwight. (See Susan Goodman, Chapter 5 in this volume, for a study focused on biographies and memoirs of Wharton.) Dwight's study, however, was notable for organizing the details of her life around places, rather than time, and relies on a vast array of images to reconstruct the sphere in which the author lived.[10] This volume's photographs and illustrations provide a glimpse into Wharton's luxurious but, as suggested by so many empty interiors, sometimes lonely world. Dwight's biography remains a useful resource for scholars of the early-twentieth century interested in visual culture. In *Displaying Women* (1998), Maureen Montgomery examines the formation of upper-class identity at the turn of the century by exploring how "women's appearance and activities signified leisure with the express intention of laying claim to high social status."[11]

Other studies that used biographical information as a means to access new aspects of her writing include *Edith Wharton's Women* (1990) by Susan Goodman, a text that examines Wharton's own relationships with women and the female friendships created in her novels. For Goodman, Wharton and her characters demonstrate the complex task of balancing social expectations with one's own personal and intellectual desires. Gloria Erlich studies the intersection between Wharton's life and writing, relying on literary criticism and biography to trace "the filial, the sexual, and the creative" aspects of her identity. Dale Bauer seeks to depart from other Wharton studies by focusing entirely on the last twenty years of the author's life and career. These later years, Bauer argues, illuminate her political engagement with the culture surrounding her and reveal the author as an active public intellectual. Carol Singley's work, which is also interested in the philosophical Wharton, suggests that she used writing to engage spiritual and metaphysical questions. Her study, *Edith Wharton: Matters of Mind and Spirit* (1995), contemplates Wharton's attitudes toward Anglicanism, Calvinism, Transcendentalism, and Catholicism, coming to the conclusion that the author was not so much a novelist of manners as morals.[12]

While many scholarly studies emphasize biography, *Edith Wharton's Inner Circle* (1994) looks at the author's small, very selective circle of close friends, including Henry James, and examines their influence on the author, each other, and the period's literature and culture. In *Resisting Regionalism* (1997), Donna Campbell examines Wharton's relationship to the women writers of local color fiction by placing the author in the transitional period from that genre to literary naturalism. For Campbell, Wharton's desire to move away from local color fiction demonstrates her desire to avoid the pitfalls of being associated with the conventions of female authorship. Adeline Tintner's *Edith Wharton in Context* (1999) maps the intersections between Wharton's work and that of writers including Henry James and Paul Bourget. In addition to highlighting ways that Wharton's texts respond to and inspire others, Tintner also identifies works in which the author is depicted as a fictional character and concludes with a study of recent reinterpretations of her writings. In the same year, Linda Costanzo Cahir published a study that pairs Wharton with Herman Melville and examines intersections between the authors' understanding of solitude and society in U.S. culture.[13]

In the 1990s, the longer studies of Wharton's work were complemented by a host of insightful essays. The "Edith Wharton in Paris" conference of 1991 led to a special issue of the *Edith Wharton Review* that examines aspects of the writer's life in Europe and her reception abroad. The tradition of feminist approaches to Wharton continued and a range of new theoretical lenses was applied. Debra MacComb's 1996 essay considers early-twentieth-century attitudes toward dissolving marriages and how Wharton's own divorce from her husband of twenty-eight years intersects with her portrayal of marriage in *The Custom of the Country*. Richard Kaye's "Edith Wharton and the 'New Gomorrahs' of Paris: Homosexuality, Flirtation, and Incestuous Desire in *The Reef*," grapples with the writer's views on gender by considering the "breakdown of customary sexual categories evinced by Wharton's male coterie."[14]

Perhaps owing to the 1990s' continued economic prosperity, there also remained consistent interest in Wharton's novels of materialism, particularly *The House of Mirth*. Ruth Bernard Yeazell's "The Conspicuous Wasting of Lily Bart" discusses the critique of conspicuous consumption in *The House of Mirth*. "From Tea to Chloral: Raising the Dead Lily Bart," by Bonnie Lynn Gerard, studies materialistic influences in *The House of Mirth* and illuminates the paradox of Wharton's social determinism – what Lily consumes also causes her to be consumed. In "The Naturalism of Edith Wharton's *The House of Mirth*," Donald Pizer agrees that the novel can be read as an example of literary naturalism but argues that it does not necessarily participate in conventional assumptions about that genre.[15]

In addition to her major novels, Wharton's war writings were subjected to scholarly scrutiny. Annette Benert appraises the novel, *A Son at the Front*, for its depiction of French culture via descriptions of the physical structures threatened by World War I and Claire Tylee's 1997 essay historicizes Wharton's feminism by considering three of her war stories in light of feminist writings published by her contemporaries.[16]

The appearance of four movie adaptations of Wharton's work, and a television miniseries based on *The Buccaneers* accounts for the 1990s' heightened interest regarding the writer and film. Scott Marshall's essays in the *Edith Wharton Review* provide a thorough history of Wharton on both the big and small screens.[17]

THE 2000S

In the 2000s, lesser-read texts such as *Summer* and *The Fruit of the Tree* received increased critical attention. Dianne Chambers' *Feminist Readings of Edith Wharton* (2009) engages with the previous work done by earlier feminist critics and provides readings of texts including *The Reef*, *Summer*, and *Glimpses of the Moon*.[18] *Edith Wharton's Writings from the Great War* (2004), by Julie Olin-Ammentorp, considers the writing during and about World War I to provide an understanding of how the author's work presented the war to her readers while being simultaneously shaped by her wartime experiences.[19]

As critical eyes were focusing on previously known peripheral texts, the 2000s also saw the printing of never before published Wharton writings. Wharton's negotiations of the literary marketplace can be traced in *The Correspondence of Edith Wharton and Macmillan* (2007), three decades of letters, edited by Shafquat Towheed and illuminating Wharton's relationship with the publisher. Laura Rattray's two-volume collection, *The Unpublished Writings of Edith Wharton* (2009), contains five plays, three novels, and two pieces of life writing, a body of work that also offers new insights on the development of Wharton's career and her writing processes. Another useful resource is *The Cambridge Introduction to Edith Wharton* (2009), by Pamela Knights, which provides readers with a helpful overview of the writer's life, works, and critical reception.[20]

Critical trends in post-colonialism and race also influenced Wharton criticism. Although published in 1993, Irene Goldman's "The 'Perfect' Jew and *The House of Mirth*: A Study in Point of View," foreshadowed this trend. In her essay, Goldman points to a letter from Wharton to F. Scott Fitzgerald, complimenting the latter on his depiction of the *"perfect* Jew" (emphasis Wharton's) in an equally famous depiction of wealth, *The Great Gatsby*, and examines the portrayal of Simon Rosedale. A decade later, Jennie Kassanoff's *Edith Wharton and the Politics of Race* (2004) broaches the subject of Wharton's conservative political views by suggesting that scholars' tendency to overlook this subject is indicative of critical assumptions about Wharton made on the basis of her class, as well as "a limited conception of gender and class" that continues to pervade modern thought.[21] Several article-length essays published from

2000–10 also placed an emphasis on race and imperialism. Kassanoff's "Extinction, Taxidermy, Tableaux Vivants: Staging Race and Class in *The House of Mirth*" argues that Wharton employs Lily Bart as an example of racial resistance to cultural shifts brought about by phenomena such as increased class mobility and immigration. Frederick Wegener's 2000 essay highlights a letter in which Wharton refers to herself as a "rabid imperialist" as a starting point from which to examine the author's views on imperialism and national expansion, and how those beliefs are made evident in her writings. In "Race, Culture, Nation: Edith Wharton and Ernest Renan," Carol Singley discusses her reading of Renan and suggests that his rational positivism had the effect of encouraging her religious skepticism and affirming her expatriation. Lori Harris' 2004 essay engages with portrayals of race and gender in *The House of Mirth*, and suggests that Lily's feminine identity is intertwined with her whiteness, an observation supported by Lily's unwillingness to forge a future with either a New Woman, Gerty Farish, or a Jew, Simon Rosedale.[22]

In the wake of the 1990s' Wharton film surge, and continuing critical trends pertaining to visual culture and media, the relationship to material culture and media was also of great interest to scholars. *Edith Wharton on Film* (2007), by Parley Ann Boswell, examines the author's relationship to popular films, both as they are alluded to in her fictional writings and as her writings have been translated by Hollywood.[23] Emily Orlando's *Edith Wharton and the Visual Arts* (2007) provides a study of Wharton's frequent invocation of artwork, particularly the paintings of the Pre-Raphaelite Brotherhood, and demonstrates how the author critiques artistic misrepresentations of women, not as complete individuals but as reflections of male desire and idealization. *Memorial Boxes and Guarded Interiors* (2007), edited by Gary Totten, is a collection of essays that examine Wharton's relationship with material culture in both her life and writing. Another material-culture study, Katherine Joslin's *Edith Wharton and the Making of Fashion* (2009), provides an historical overview of fashion during Wharton's day and examines the central role played by clothing in the author's life and writing.[24]

The most recent Wharton biography, Hermione Lee's *Edith Wharton* (2007), distinguishes itself by providing an episodic treatment of the writer's life in which Lee mixes literary criticism with biographical and historical context. In fact, much of her life is revealed and examined through the lens of her own writing. Rather than creating an image of Wharton for the reader, Lee uncovers an image of Wharton as the author herself crafted it (Lee 184–88).

In the 2000s, critics continued to build upon the well-established foundations of feminist scholarship, placing particular emphasis on how genre could inform and be informed by Wharton's novels. Mary Marchand argues that a feminist message in *The Fruit of the Tree* can be clarified if the work is read as an industrial reform novel, in which there is a place for romantic subplots, rather than as participating in the muckraking tradition. "Marriage and Modernism in Edith Wharton's *Twilight Sleep*," by Jennifer Haytock, argues that this novel uses divorce as both a symptom and signifier of the isolation and fragmentation traditionally associated with definitions of modernism, thereby addressing modern issues such as the breakdown of identity and communication. Although Haytock approaches the writer's relationship to modernism via attitudes toward marriage, many aspects of Wharton's modernism engage scholars interested in understanding the evolution of her work and ideas. Jennifer Fleissner's 2006 essay, "The Biological Clock: Edith Wharton, Naturalism, and the Temporality of Womanhood," suggests that femininity is defined largely by biological time constraints, such as childbearing, and argues that the natural element of a typically mechanized system, such as time, allows for a feminist dimension to literary naturalism.[25]

Critics also reconsidered Wharton's portrayal of gender with regard to social class. In her 2005 essay, Teresa Tavares suggests that the contradictions contained within *The Fruit of the Tree* are meant to illuminate the conflicting options facing New Women who were both limited and supported by social convention. "Between the Town and the Mountain: Abortion and the Politics of Life in Edith Wharton's *Summer*," by Karen Weingarten, examines Charity Royall's choices by considering both the regulation of women's reproductive bodies and the normative power of legislation. Meredith Goldsmith's "'Other People's Clothes': Homosociality, Consumer Culture, and Affective Reading in Edith Wharton's *Summer*" examines class tensions evidenced by Charity's interactions with other women as she struggles to adopt a middle-class identity through the acquisition of goods.[26] As the first decade of the new century came to a close, economic crisis plunged the United States and many other countries into recession – a trend made manifest in Wharton criticism, primarily through increased interest in the maneuverings of Undine Spragg and in *The Custom of the Country* generally, the author's most blatantly economic novel, and one of her most currently relevant pieces of fiction.[27]

Since 1969, much has been written about Edith Wharton's life and work, and in the past four decades, she has secured her place as a seminal

U.S. author and an important figure in U.S. history. In 1971, her estate, the Mount, was added to the National Register of Historic Places and deemed a National Historic Landmark. In December 1983, the Edith Wharton Society was founded at the MLA convention in New York City and the society's publication, the *Edith Wharton Review*, is currently sent to 300 subscribers. These accomplishments are certainly promising ones for Wharton studies, and the work already performed by enthusiastic scholars suggests many fruitful avenues for future study. If the past forty years are any indication, no matter what the coming decades hold, Wharton's writing will continue to spark important critical conversations.

NOTES

1. E. Ammons, *Edith Wharton's Argument with America* (Athens: University of Georgia Press, 1980), 5, 173–87.
2. C. Wershoven, *The Female Intruder in the Novels of Edith Wharton* (Rutherford, NJ: Fairleigh Dickinson University Press, 1982), 14.
3. K. Joslin, "Edith Wharton at 125," *College Literature*, Edith Wharton Special Issue, 14.3 (1987), 193–206.
4. J. Lidoff, "Another Sleeping Beauty: Narcissism in *The House of Mirth*," *American Quarterly*, 32 (1980), 519–30; S. Gubar, "'The Blank Page' and the Issues of Female Creativity," *Critical Inquiry*, 8 (Winter 1981); E. Showalter, "The Death of the Lady (Novelist): Wharton's *House of Mirth*," *Representations*, 9 (Winter 1985), 133–49; M. French, "Muzzled Women," *College Literature*, Edith Wharton Special Issue, 14.3 (1987), 219–29; E. Ammons, "Cool Diana and the Blood-Red Muse: Edith Wharton on Innocence and Art" in F. Fleischmann (ed.), *American Novelists Revisited: Essays in Feminist Criticism* (Boston: G. K. Hall, 1982), 209–24.
5. W. C. Dimock, "Debasing Exchange: Edith Wharton's *The House of Mirth*," *PMLA*, 100 (October 1985), 783–92; M. O'Neal, "Point of View and the Narrative Technique in the Fiction of Edith Wharton," *Style* (Spring 1983), 270–89; C. Miller, "'Natural Magic': Irony as Unifying Strategy in *The House of Mirth*," *South Central Review*, 4.1 (Spring 1987), 82–91; J. Tuttleton, "Mocking Fate: Romantic Idealism in Edith Wharton's *The Reef*," *Studies in the Novel*, 19.4 (Winter 1987), 459–74.
6. M. Bell (ed.), *The Cambridge Companion to Edith Wharton* (Cambridge: Cambridge University Press, 1995).
7. J. Tuttleton, K. Lauer, and M. Murray (eds.), *Edith Wharton: The Contemporary Reviews* (Cambridge: Cambridge University Press, 1992).
8. K. Lauer and M. Murray (eds.) *Edith Wharton: An Annotated Secondary Bibliography* (New York: Garland Publishing, Inc., 1990).
9. C. Colquitt, S. Goodman, and C. Waid (eds.), *A Forward Glance: New Essays on Edith Wharton* (Newark: University of Delaware Press, 1999).

10. S. Benstock, *No Gifts from Chance* (New York: Charles Scribner's Sons, 1994); E. Dwight, *Edith Wharton: An Extraordinary Life* (New York: Harry N. Abrams, 1994).

11. M. Montgomery, *Displaying Women: Spectacles of Leisure in Edith Wharton's New York* (New York: Routledge, 1998), 6.

12. S. Goodman, *Edith Wharton's Women: Friends and Rivals* (Hanover, NH: University Press of New England, 1990); G. Erlich, *The Sexual Education of Edith Wharton* (Berkeley: University of California Press, 1992), x; D. Bauer, *Edith Wharton's Brave New Politics* (Madison: University of Wisconsin Press, 1994); C. Singley, *Edith Wharton: Matters of Mind and Spirit* (Cambridge: Cambridge University Press, 1995).

13. S. Goodman, *Edith Wharton's Inner Circle* (Austin: University of Texas Press, 1994); D. Campbell, *Resisting Regionalism: Gender and Naturalism in American Fiction, 1885–1915* (Athens: Ohio University Press, 1997); A. Tintner, *Edith Wharton in Context: Essays on Intertextuality* (Tuscaloosa: University of Alabama Press, 1999); L. Cahir, *Solitude and Society in the Works of Herman Melville and Edith Wharton* (Westport, CT: Greenwood Press, 1999).

14. D. MacComb, "New Wives for Old: Divorce and the Leisure-Class Marriage Market in Edith Wharton's *The Custom of the Country*," *American Literature*, 68.4 (Dec. 1996), 765–97; R. Kaye, "Edith Wharton and the 'New Gomorrahs' of Paris: Homosexuality, Flirtation, and Incestuous Desire in *The Reef*," *MFS: Modern Fiction Studies*, 43.4 (Winter 1997), 860–97; 861.

15. R. Yeazell, "The Conspicuous Wasting of Lily Bart," *ELH*, 59.3 (Autumn 1992), 713–34; B. Gerard, "From Tea to Chloral: Raising the Dead Lily Bart," *Twentieth Century Literature*, 44.4 (Winter 1998), 409–27; D. Pizer, "The Naturalism of Edith Wharton's *The House of Mirth*," *Twentieth Century Literature*, 41.2 (Summer 1995), 241–48.

16. A. Benert, "Edith Wharton at War: Civilized Space in Troubled Times," *Twentieth Century Literature*, 42.3 (Autumn 1996), 322–43; C. Tylee, "Imagining Women at War: Feminist Strategies in Edith Wharton's War Writing," *Tulsa Studies in Women's Literature*, 16.2 (Autumn 1997), 327–43.

17. S. Marshall, "Edith Wharton on Film and Television," *Edith Wharton Review*, 7.1 (1990), 15–17, and "Edith Wharton on Film and Television: A History and Filmography," *Edith Wharton Review*, 13.2 (1996), 15–26.

18. D. Chambers, *Feminist Readings of Edith Wharton: From Silence to Speech* (New York: Palgrave Macmillan, 2009).

19. J. Olin-Ammentorp, *Edith Wharton's Writings from the Great War* (Gainesville: University Press of Florida, 2004).

20. S. Towheed (ed.), *The Correspondence of Edith Wharton and Macmillan, 1901–1930* (New York: Palgrave Macmillan, 2007); L. Rattray (ed.), *The Unpublished Writings of Edith Wharton*, 2 vols. (London: Pickering & Chatto, 2009); P. Knights, *The Cambridge Introduction to Edith Wharton* (Cambridge: Cambridge University Press, 2009).

21. I. Goldman, "The 'Perfect' Jew and *The House of Mirth*: A Study in Point of View," *Modern Language Studies*, 23.2 (Spring 1993), 25–36; J. Kassanoff,

Edith Wharton and the Politics of Race (Cambridge: Cambridge University Press, 2004).

22. J. Kassanoff, "Extinction, Taxidermy, Tableaux Vivants: Staging Race and Class in *The House of Mirth*," *PMLA*, 115.1 (Jan. 2000), 60–74; F. Wegener, "'Rabid Imperialist': Edith Wharton and the Obligations of Empire in Modern American Fiction," *American Literature*, 72.4 (Dec. 2000), 783–812; C. Singley, "Race, Culture, Nation: Edith Wharton and Ernest Renan," *Twentieth Century Literature*, 49.1 (Spring 2003), 32–45; L. Harrison-Kahan, "'Queer myself for good and all': *The House of Mirth* and the Fictions of Lily's Whiteness," *Legacy: A Journal of American Women Writers*, 21.1 (2004), 34–39.

23. P. Boswell, *Edith Wharton on Film* (Carbondale: Southern Illinois University Press, 2007).

24. E. Orlando, *Edith Wharton and the Visual Arts* (Tuscaloosa: University of Alabama Press, 2007); G. Totten (ed.), *Memorial Boxes and Guarded Interiors: Edith Wharton and Material Culture* (Tuscaloosa: University of Alabama Press, 2007); K. Joslin, *Edith Wharton and the Making of Fashion* (Durham: University of New Hampshire Press, 2009).

25. M. Marchand, "Death to Lady Bountiful: Women and Reform in Edith Wharton's *The Fruit of the Tree*," *Legacy: A Journal of American Women Writers*, 18.1 (2001), 65–78; J. Haytock, "Marriage and Modernism in Edith Wharton's *Twilight Sleep*," *Legacy*, 19.2 (2002), 216–29; J. Fleissner, "The Biological Clock: Edith Wharton, Naturalism, and the Temporality of Womanhood," *American Literature*, 78.3 (Sept. 2006), 519–48.

26. T. Tavares, "New Women, New Men, or What You Will in Edith Wharton's *The Fruit of the Tree*," *Edith Wharton Review*, 21.1 (Spring 2005), 1–15; K. Weingarten, "Between the Town and the Mountain: Abortion and the Politics of Life in Edith Wharton's *Summer*," *Canadian Review of American Studies*, 40.3 (2010), 351–72; M. Goldsmith, "'Other People's Clothes': Homosociality, Consumer Culture, and Affective Reading in Edith Wharton's *Summer*," *Legacy: A Journal of American Women Writers*, 27.1 (2010), 109–27.

27. See L. Rattray (ed.), *Edith Wharton's* The Custom of the County: *A Reassessment* (London: Pickering & Chatto, 2010).

PART III

Book and Publishing History

CHAPTER 10

Wharton and Her Editors

Sharon Shaloo

Edith Wharton wrote during a period of rapid change in the publishing industry, and her relations with editors throughout her half-century career reflect major shifts in market forces during the late nineteenth and early twentieth centuries. An engaged businesswoman and accomplished literary artist, Wharton intended from the outset not only to write but also to manage the design and production of her books, their English and foreign editions, their serializations, and their adaptations for the stage and screen. As her career developed, Wharton's ideas about the role of the author and editor/publisher developed as well. She absented herself from most decisions about the physical form of her books and she agreed, in a limited way, to participate in the promotion of her role as author/celebrity in the marketing of her work. The arc of her engagement can be best understood through an examination of Wharton's relationships with her two U.S. publishing houses, Charles Scribner's Sons and, later, D. Appleton and Company.

John Tebbel calls the fifty years between the American Civil War and World War I "the period of expansion" in U.S. publishing.[1] It was also a chaotic period of industrial identity formation and market definition inflected by a search for sustainable business models. This was the first generation to inherit the mantle of "publisher" from those who earlier in the century first embraced the entrepreneurial role of middleman between authors and the trades of bookmaking and bookselling.[2] Although the emergence of the role of publisher was understandable in an increasingly complex industry, the business practices these budding entrepreneurs adopted often were not and, by 1876, publishers would meet on the occasion of the country's centennial celebration to resolve problems of irrational price-cutting and small profit margins, attempting to save themselves from practices of their own instigation.[3]

These first-generation publishers also sought to profit from the magazine market, which had come into full flowering in the decade preceding the Civil War (Tebbel 86–87).[4] Harper & Bros. launched *Harper's Monthly* and *Harper's Weekly* in 1850 and 1857, respectively. *Putnam's Monthly Magazine of Literature, Science and Art* first appeared in 1853, and in 1859, Ticknor & Fields purchased *The Atlantic Monthly*, which began publication in 1857 as a competitor to *North American Review*. Scribner's entered the market with *Hours at Home* in 1865, replacing that early attempt in 1870 with *Scribner's Monthly*, a magazine issued in partnership with Josiah Holland and Roswell Smith two years after *Lippincott's Monthly* appeared in 1868.

The magazine market was volatile. *Putnam's Monthly*, among others, faltered during the economic downturn of 1857, reviving in 1868 only to be folded into *Scribner's Monthly* in 1870. In 1881, the *Scribner's Monthly* partnership disbanded: Holland and Smith took the magazine, renamed *Century Magazine*, and Scribner's agreed to absent itself from the market for five years. In 1887, it issued *Scribner's Magazine*, a "fully-illustrated" monthly, with Edward L. Burlingame as the founding editor. At this time, Scribner's also named William Crary Brownell its "Literary Advisor." Brownell, at that time writing for *The Nation* and earlier associated with the *New York World*, was tasked with being the point person for book publication in a publishing house that would soon be driven by the requirements of its magazine.

Publishers looked to other, post-publication profit possibilities in authors' work as well. Gift editions of books were issued for the holiday market, often produced with special bindings featuring substantial gilt decoration. As U.S. books became popular abroad, publishers sought to insert themselves into agreements for foreign rights, either as a party to negotiations or as publisher of its own English edition through a London office. When novels were adapted for the stage and, later, screen, publishers sought a share in those negotiations as well. From our current perspective, the many and varied market possibilities, especially for a work of fiction, elicit no surprise. Yet in Wharton's time, the developments were new, and authors and publishers had to devise models for interaction and for allocation of earnings that would balance market opportunities against their beliefs in the cultural importance of the book and its author.

The reconciliation of art and business became an important subject for both editors and authors. *Scribner's Magazine* discussed the subject often, primarily in its monthly "The Point of View" column, with short considerations of "The Author and His Works," "The Author on Exhibition" (about the author tour), and "The Critical Value of Popularity." It argued for an "honest commercialism" in another number, and in yet another proclaimed "bohemia," predicated on the antagonism of art and commerce, to be an exhausted concept.[5] Taken together, these columns seek to justify the commercialized aspects of the publishing enterprise by presenting their outlet as a genial literary–commercial venture that could bring authors to market without adversely affecting their art. Publishing was a business, yes, but it was also something "more." In a 1913 *Saturday Evening Post* article, "Publisher, Author and the Devil," Robert Sterling Yard recalls a conversation with Charles Scribner on the subject. Probing Scribner about the business and professional aspects of publishing, Yard reports that "[Scribner] thought a moment and said, smiling: 'Publishing is neither a business nor a profession. It is a career.'" (Tebbel 79). Although the distinctions among those terms are less sharp today, what remains clear is Scribner's sense that he occupied liminal space between business and a calling.

Authors also joined the debate. In 1888, Robert Louis Stevenson published a "Letter to a Young Gentleman Who Proposes to Embrace the Career of Art," arguing that the aspiring writer must be able to distinguish between a temptation to shirk a more mundane line of work and a true calling to art as work.[6] In 1893, William Dean Howells elaborated on the idea of art as work in "The Man of Letters as a Man of Business," reviewing the concerns of both authors and publishers as he developed a satisfactory model for authorship in a marketplace founded on serial publication fees. Howells entertained the question, *is the man of letters a man of business?* He dismissed the notion, however, because authors were not bringing their "goods" to market, a business function he assigned to the publisher. Howells argued instead that the writer was a kind of worker who created a marketable product through his labor. He admitted that the literary artist had little in common with the vast majority of workers, however, and thus concluded that authorship was in a "transition state," another liminal space, between art and commerce.[7]

Interestingly, when young Edith Newbold Jones first came to print, it was at a distance from this evolving marketplace. Her 1878 collection of poems, *Verses*, was privately printed in Newport and distributed among friends and acquaintances. While the young author must have had some satisfaction in seeing her poems in print, even in a limited and privately distributed edition, she had her eye on the larger marketplace, as Gary Totten demonstrates in his reading of the paratextual frame of the unpublished *Fast and Loose* in "Selling Wharton," Chapter 11 in this volume. She therefore likely experienced a great deal more satisfaction in what followed from *Verses*. In 1879, she published a poem pseudonymously in the *New York World* (with which William Crary Brownell was then associated), followed in 1880 by five poems published in *The Atlantic Monthly*. Many years later, when they had developed a professional friendship, Wharton wrote to Howells, who as editor of *The Atlantic Monthly* had published her 1880 poems, saying, "It must be nearly thirty years ago that a very shy young woman sent you a handful of worthless verse, and received the kindest of letters in reply."[8] In fact, it had been forty years earlier, and Wharton's path to Howells was rather more circuitous. Her poems were recommended to Howells by Henry Wadsworth Longfellow, who had been sent the poems by A. Thorndike Rice, a Newport acquaintance who was then editor of *North American Review*. This multi-stage route to publication demonstrates the ways in which private friendships provided access to public acknowledgment for a young writer who had been, in Rice's words from his covering letter, "brought up in fashionable surroundings little calculated to feed her taste for the muses." Yet with poems able to travel from Rice to Longfellow and then on to Howells, this young writer was clearly exploring the margins of her "fashionable surroundings" for the connections that would aid her in achieving success.[9]

After the activity of 1880, nearly a decade passed before the now-married Wharton would publish again. In 1889, poetry was again her calling card, although by 1891 she would publish her first story, "Mrs. Manstey's View," in *Scribner's Magazine*. Wharton's fiction was well received in the magazine, and Edward L. Burlingame soon proposed a collection of her stories (Benstock 70). The collection was a long time in the making, owing, in part, to Burlingame's reluctance to accept certain of the author's first offerings and, in part, to the reverence in which Wharton held book publication. This was a milestone she wished to pass masterfully and not with the unevenness of the novice writer. While magazine publication was exciting and gratifying, it was also temporal. For Wharton, book publication represented an achievement of a different order, one that opened an entirely new audience for her work.

In the five years that intervened between Burlingame's proposal and the publication of *The Greater Inclination* (1899), Wharton immersed herself in the writing and production of a work of nonfiction, *The Decoration of Houses*, co-written with Ogden Codman. Her involvement with all aspects of the design and production of this volume has been detailed by others. Certainly, Wharton demonstrated in this concern with the form as well as the content of her book the extent to which she wanted the volume to reflect the tenets of design and taste contained within its pages, yet it seems also likely that she brought to her task some memories from her first experience with book publication in Newport, when she would have been involved in discussions about the physical form of the volume. Admittedly, Wharton was not entirely successful with her design for *The Decoration of Houses*. Codman was particularly unhappy with the marbled covers, a criticism with which Wharton eventually concurs.[10] Nevertheless, the experience exerted few inhibiting effects on Wharton, who would again insert herself into the production process when another milestone in her writing life was produced, *The Valley of Decision*, her first full-length fiction.

The Valley of Decision grew by pages and chapters during its writing into the full-length work we know, but its design, most particularly its page size and margins, was set before its completion and seemed better suited to a work like *The Touchstone,* the novella Wharton had published with Scribner's in 1900. The result was that *The Valley of Decision* would have to be published in two volumes, a decision that Wharton initially professed to be delighted about, although she was concerned the ensuing increased price might prove a deterrent to prospective buyers. Within two weeks, Wharton was "more and more regretful" about the two-volume format, and challenged Brownell's statement that he assumed the work would be no longer than 120,000 words by asking in a letter of January 1902 if it still were not a mistake to choose "so small a page." She felt she should have been consulted and that the "make up" of the book and the form seemed inappropriate to its style and its length (*Letters* 47–48).

A reading of the correspondence from this time shows that several factors contributed to the mistaken design of *The Valley of Decision*. When Wharton first presented a portion of the manuscript to Brownell for comment, Scribner's told her it could not make room for the work in its magazine until 1903. The house counseled Wharton to dispense with serialization, perhaps realizing that the alternative was to see the work published in another outlet. Wharton hesitated, for she did not want to lose the serial fee, and professed a willingness to delay publication if another magazine could begin its serialization within six months. Eventually, she yielded to Scribner's desire, communicated through Brownell, that she forego serialization, and then met with Berkeley Updike independently to discuss the book design, a conversation that may or may not have been communicated accurately to Scribner's. A further complication was that as a still-inexperienced writer, Wharton asked to have galleys of the first part of her book sent along to help her see the book coherently, a request with which Scribner's complied. This was likely to the company's later regret, for the early printing determined a design in advance of reckoning the scope of the work. The resulting two-volume edition was not what either author or publisher would have wished. Hermione Lee reports that it sold strongly (Lee 111). Yet profits were undoubtedly compromised by the cost of two-volume publication.

In these two early experiences in book production with an author who could not quite retreat from the business endeavor, as Howells would have counseled, Scribner's must have realized that its publishing practice would have to be regularized so that it could better control outcomes. Part of the regularization was to move the printing of most of Wharton's books to Scribner's customary printing shop, although Updike's Merrymount Press would remain involved for some years to come. Another was to attempt to expand its control over Wharton's various markets – for example, with Brownell's 1903 offer for Scribner's to arrange for the English edition of *Sanctuary*. This was an offer Wharton declined, and she negotiated directly with Macmillan for those editions, before eventually rebelling against Scribner's exclusive control over her U.S. rights as well.

In response to the favorable reactions to her early publications, Wharton produced a stream of work that exceeded by a considerable degree the space Scribner's could devote to her in its magazine. Burlingame at first tried to stem the tide by suggesting that Wharton avoid becoming a "magazine bore" (Lee 168). Although she took his caution against overexposure to heart, Wharton chose to address the problem not, as Burlingame preferred, by publishing less but, instead, by expanding her market. Her fictions appeared in *Harper's Monthly* in 1902. In 1903, *Collier's Weekly* and *Cosmopolitan* were added to her list. Burlingame's letters betrayed a note of anxiety in his joviality when, during 1904, he wrote to assure Wharton that he most definitely wanted "The Hermit and the Wild Woman" whenever she could finish it, and to say how pleased he was to have secured "The Last Asset" and "The Potboiler." Burlingame was responding to a situation for which Scribner's was unprepared: the volume of stories Wharton brought out in 1904, *The Descent of Man and Other Stories*, contained only three stories published in *Scribner's Magazine*. The six other stories in the U.S. edition were published in competing magazines against which Burlingame now attempted a defense. Wharton further compounded the problems by agreeing to publish a tenth story, moreover, in the English edition published by Macmillan, much to the consternation of her Scribner's editors.

The misunderstandings surrounding *The Descent of Man and Other Stories* were no sooner overcome when another difficulty arose. As Elsa Nettels notes in Chapter 12 in this volume, Wharton was prevailed on by Burlingame to begin serializing *The House of Mirth* before she had completed the manuscript. During the course of its production, Burlingame would become something of a cheerleader in his response to the installments he read, while Brownell retreated from the field, declining to offer his reactions to the manuscript-in-progress once Burlingame's schedule determined its course. In *A Backward Glance*, Wharton said that during the writing of *The House of Mirth* she became a professional writer. She also learned, however, that all magazine publications brought with them certain irrevocable deadlines, even in the genial literary–commercial venue of *Scribner's Magazine*.

Often, she was more than ready to meet those deadlines. In fact, Wharton offered Burlingame a 20,000-word fiction, nearly ready for print (the novella *Madame de Treymes*), she reported, before she completed the manuscript of *The House of Mirth*. Burlingame, who had just allocated nearly a year of space to the serial in progress, accepted the manuscript, having learned his lesson about competing outlets in 1904, but one can see that space was becoming a serious issue, one that reached its climax in the next decade. Shari Benstock summarizes the crisis well. As she explains, the issues were a continuation of the frictions that had been present from the earliest days at Charles Scribner's Sons. Wharton was disappointed in the sales of *Ethan Frome*, and laid some of the blame for that disappointment on Scribner's promotional efforts. She had long been dissatisfied with these, and was stymied in her desire to begin a new serial, *The Custom of the Country*, owing to space constraints in *Scribner's Magazine*. Wharton had also lost patience with the modest advances she was receiving and wanted to test the waters in the market beyond her house magazine (Benstock 248–50).

Moving houses was not an everyday occurrence. Publishers, constrained by a consideration in the trade, did not actively pursue writers at other firms. Nevertheless, as Walter Hines Page reported, publishers employed agents, or "drummers," who approached authors indirectly to test whether they might be considering a move (Tebbel 87). Evidence suggests that Morton Fullerton, who was for a time Wharton's well-documented romantic intimate, was acting in this capacity for D. Appleton and Co.[11] Fullerton was a Harvard graduate and classmate of Joseph H. Sears, the latter having come to Appleton from Harper's in 1900 during a reorganization of the firm after its near bankruptcy. Initially, Sears focused on raising money quickly by producing "libraries," or collected sets of books, but began to rebuild Appleton's stable of authors once financial stability returned.[12] In 1906, Wharton had published a story in *Appleton's Booklovers Magazine*, and one can assume Sears held her in his sights from then on.

Wharton's first publication with Appleton would be *The Reef*, a book that was initially produced in the burgundy covers that had become the standard for Wharton's publications at Scribner's. Charles Scribner's Sons complained. The house felt that they had an exclusive claim on that form for Wharton volumes, and Appleton acceded to their demand, establishing from then on their own branding of Wharton volumes, in dark blue covers. Thus, what must have been an attempt to maintain a seamless look and feel for the Wharton oeuvre gave way to a consideration in the trade for honoring claims among competitors who also still felt themselves fellow travelers in their business-calling of publishing. Appleton varied from the standard format in one notable case when it experimented with an innovative format for Wharton's four-novella collection, *Old New York*. Wharton betrayed some skepticism, and tried to argue for a single-volume format for the publication, but ultimately acceded to her publisher's wishes, indicating the distance she had traveled away from her earliest demands about book design.[13]

Book publication was not the driving force in the Wharton-Appleton relationship, however; magazine rights were. Because Appleton had discontinued its house magazine in 1909, Wharton could explore a full complement of periodical opportunities. In the coming decade, as Nettels illustrates in Chapter 12, Wharton appeared in a number of mass-circulation magazines, garnering ever-increasing fees for her serials. Indeed, after the institution of the U.S. income tax, Wharton was in the enviable position at the end of more than one year of asking Jewett to hold money for her until January 1. Because Jewett was involved in transmitting these generous offers to Wharton, Appleton's was able to move away from guaranteed advances on royalties, paying on publication only those royalties owing to Wharton for advance sales of each book. This change had obvious attractions for the firm, which carried throughout the author's lifetime negative balances on its advances for *The Reef*, *The Marne*, and *Summer*. The shift of financial risk carried with it, however, a dramatic shift in editorial power. Multiple magazine editors, their timetables, and their subject requirements had to be factored into the publishing equation; and as payments grew, the influence of these outside editors increased. In many ways, their priorities became Jewett's priorities. He encouraged Wharton to meet increasingly difficult deadlines coming from multiple sources, to tailor her work to the requirements editors felt would best serve their readership, and to understand the delicacy in treatment of subject required in this mass marketplace.

Shifts in taste, constraints on subject, conflicting or unreasonable scheduling demands, a publishing model that had settled down with the editor-publisher aligned with other market forces – these were the pressures with which a now aging, expatriate author contended. Eventually, Wharton considered the need for a U.S. literary agent. At the prompting of her neighbor, Louis Bromfield, Wharton contacted Eric Pinker and contracted with him in March of 1935. Wharton's turn to literary agency is noteworthy. The general line on agents at the time was that they were disruptive intruders, insinuating themselves into the mutually beneficial relationship between authors and editors. Yet in Wharton's case, the relationship of author to editor, from its beginnings at Charles Scribner's Sons to its concluding days at D. Appleton and Co., had always needed some adjustment. Ultimately, the publishing house could not be the middleman between authors and the marketplace because it was part of the marketplace, and the literary agent emerged, in the early twentieth century, as the author's new mediator between art and commerce.

NOTES

1. J. Tebbel, *Between Covers: The Rise and Transformation of Book Publishing in America* (New York: Oxford University Press, 1987), 79 ff. Subsequent references to this work are included in the text.
2. S. S. Williams, "Authors and Literary Authorship" in S. Casper, J. Groves, S. W. Nissenbaum, and M. Winship (eds.) *History of the Book in America, Vol. III: The Industrial Book, 1840–1880* (Chapel Hill: University of North Carolina Press, 2007), 90–116.
3. S. Casper, "Introduction" in S. Casper, J. Groves, S. W. Nissenbaum, and M. Winship (eds.) *History of the Book in America, Vol. III: The Industrial Book, 1840–1880* (Chapel Hill: University of North Carolina Press, 2007), 1–39 *passim*.
4. For a full discussion of the magazine market at this time, see F. L. Mott, *A History of American Magazines*, vols. II, III, IV (Cambridge, MA: Harvard University Press, 1938 [vol. iv, 1957]).
5. See *Scribner's Magazine* (New York: Charles Scribner's Sons), 12 (March 1892), 393–98; 14 (September 1893), 394–98; 16 (October 1894), 525–30; 19 (February 1896) 253–57.
6. *Scribner's Magazine*, 4 (September 1888), 377–81.
7. W. D. Howells, "The Man of Letters as a Man of Business," *Scribner's Magazine*, 14 (October 1893), 429–46; 430.
8. Letter dated November 5, 1919, quoted in William Dean Howells, *Selected Letters, Volume 6: 1912–1920*, eds. W. M. Gibson and C. K. Lohmann (New York: Twayne, 1983), 8.
9. "Obituary: A. Thorndike Rice," *New York Times*, May 17, 1889, 27.

10. See letter to William Crary Brownell, September 18, 1898, Scribner's Archives, Firestone Library, Princeton University.

11. The evidence for Fullerton's connection to D. Appleton and Co. merits further investigation, but it is strongly suggestive. Benstock reports that Fullerton became Appleton's agent in Europe in 1911 and helped negotiate the contract for *The Reef* (250). She sent him sections of the novel for comment during its writing, as well (Benstock 266). Yet Wharton had established a business aspect of their relationship much earlier, involving him in the placement of the French rights in *The House of Mirth* very soon after they met, for example. It seems likely that Fullerton would have helped set that tone in their relations if he approached her with a goal of testing the waters for his friend's firm.

12. G. R. Wolfe, *The House of Appleton* (Metuchen, NJ: Scarecrow Press, 1981), 295–333.

13. See letters dated January 3 through January 30, 1924, Appleton folders, Wharton Archives, Beinecke Rare Book and Manuscript Library, Yale University.

CHAPTER 11

Selling Wharton

Gary Totten

Wharton recognized her work's consumer contexts from an early age. In a mock review for her teenage novel, *Fast and Loose* (written in 1876–77), Wharton emphasizes factors that contribute to a novel's success in the contemporary marketplace, including strong characters and plot, a distinctive style, clear dialogue, and convincing sentiment. She also identified the critical gatekeepers of a novelist's success, imagining her reviews appearing in the *Nation* and the *Saturday Review of Literature*. Her *Nation* review implies how gender norms and social class expectations might restrict her free expression as a writer, realities she likely absorbed from her mother, Lucretia Jones, who criticized the opening scene of Wharton's first novel, in which a woman apologizes for her unkempt drawing room. Lucretia's response, that drawing rooms are never untidy, implies that young society women do not expose upper-class lives and drawing rooms to public scrutiny, and, perhaps more importantly, do not write novels in the first place. After Lucretia's reaction to her first fictional effort, Wharton only shared *Fast and Loose* with her friend, Emelyn Washburn, but she had sufficient cultural conditioning to sign the male pseudonym "David Olivieri" to the novel. In her mock review, she accuses Olivieri of possessing the fictional sensibility of a schoolgirl (this and other self-criticism seems to echo Lucretia's opinion), which she recognized as a liability to the work's success (Wolff 45–46). When Lucretia privately published a selection of her daughter's poems in 1878, they, too, were unsigned, and five of these poems were published anonymously in *The Atlantic Monthly* in 1880. Yet, as her career makes clear, gender and class restrictions would not hamper Wharton's desire or ability to understand and control consumer forces; indeed, she was more involved in the business of selling her work than many other writers of her time.

Wharton's first experience of producing and marketing her writing occurred with *The Decoration of Houses* (1897), coauthored with Ogden Codman, Jr. Wharton did not regard the book as related to her literary pursuits (*BG* 112), but in the process of writing and organizing it, locating visual materials, interacting with editors and publishers, and ensuring that it was adequately reviewed and advertised, she gained valuable insights that would assist her in directing and promoting her career (Benstock 84). Of Scribner's editors, William C. Brownell and Edward Burlingame, Wharton noted that Burlingame offered precise verbal counsel, while Brownell, often without speaking, imparted advice about how to most successfully navigate the writing business,[1] and, as was his approach with many authors, he generally avoided being too prescriptive about changes in her work (Lewis 133).

Wharton obviously found such mentoring valuable, but she also possessed strong instincts for managing the commercial aspects of her career, acting largely as "her own agent, manager, administrator and negotiator" (Lee 422). Her efforts were complicated by the fact that her writing career began when attitudes in the United States toward the profession of authorship were in flux. In 1893, William Dean Howells argued that artists should not live by their art and deemed business "the opprobrium of Literature." While publishers, agents, and printers became increasingly successful at organizing and professionalizing, authors were not considered either professionals or tradespeople but common laborers, as Howells concluded.[2] Frank Norris similarly observed that writing required considerably less training or initial expense than architecture, painting, or music.[3] Authors in the United States did not benefit from organizations such as the Society of Authors in England, and although Howells advocated for the organization of U.S. publishers and authors in 1904, this never materialized, and already existing groups such as the Association of American Authors (later the Authors League of America) did not offer much by way of professional solidarity or security.[4]

Furthermore, while many large nineteenth-century publishing houses did their own printing and owned retail bookstores, when Wharton began publishing her work, much of the production and marketing had been outsourced to other firms or divided into separate departments within firms. Publishers began to consider themselves as professionals who mediated the relationship between authors and production workers and, increasingly, the editor's role was to protect other departments from authors' demands (West 17), which were sometimes viewed as unreasonable; however, some publishers themselves, such as Henry Holt, still questioned the status of publishing as a *bona fide* profession.[5] By the early twentieth century, the value of a text was judged not only in relation to the author's work and talent, but also in the context of its promotional campaign, explaining the concerns about marketing shared by Wharton and other authors.[6] These changes in the publishing industry contributed to authors' alienation from the processes of production and promotion and sometimes increased their paranoia about a publisher's handling of their work. Wharton, however, refused to be insulated from the processes by which her writing became a marketable product.

Despite publishers' preference that authors concede "to their publishing friends the business interests connected with their literary work," as George Putnam argued,[7] Wharton's involvement in selling her work is apparent even in her early correspondence. In letters to Ogden Codman, Jr. about *The Decoration of Houses,* she asked him to leave publishing negotiations to her (after a failed deal with Macmillan) and criticized his lack of participation in the project (Benstock 84, 85). Discussing the marketing of *The Greater Inclination* (1899) in a letter to Brownell, Wharton criticized Scribner's promotional strategy, complaining that her book had received inadequate promotion in comparison to that of Scribner's competitors. Wharton is specific about these differences, noting the frequency, size, content, and venue of competitors' advertisements (*Letters* 37–38). Although not necessarily demanding changes in Scribner's advertising practices, which relied on the firm's name recognition and were less aggressive than other publishers (Benstock 99), she notes that "in these days of energetic & emphatic advertising, Mr. Scribner's methods do not tempt one to offer him one's wares a second time" (*Letters* 38). Her desire for more energetic advertising did not mean that she would settle for sensationalism, either, and she later disapproved of a Scribner's wrapper advertisement emphasizing *The House of Mirth*'s exposé of polite society and insisted they remove it (Lee 202). Roger Burlingame, who witnessed the reactions of many authors to their newly published books during this period, notes that concerns about the marketing or look of the final product were not unusual among authors, male or female.[8] Although Wharton's concerns may have exceeded those normally expected from beginning authors, given the positive reviews for *The Greater Inclination,* she seems justified in her criticism of Scribner's tepid marketing (Lewis 88). This book was significant to her writing career both psychologically and economically: she viewed it as an indication of her arrival as a writer and citizen in the "Land of Letters" (*BG* 119), and it was also a financial success, selling 3,000 copies by the end of the year, impressive sales, Brownell informed her, for a short-story collection (Lee 163).

Wharton developed into an "astute businesswoman" and "the shrewdest of professionals" (Wolff 223, 224) in matters of selling and marketing.

Between 1893 and 1937, Wharton wrote at least 776 letters to Scribner's regarding her work.[9] Soon after *The Greater Inclination* was published, she informed Brownell that another publisher had offered 15 percent royalty on her next book, and she did not want to enter into a contract with someone else before consulting with Scribner's, who agreed to a 15 percent royalty for *The Touchstone* (1900) and gave her a $500 advance. During negotiations with Scribner's over *The House of Mirth* (1905), Wharton also emphasized her options for serialization at either *Harper's* or *Century Magazine*.[10] With Macmillan, her English publisher, she was similarly insistent about the need for better advertising and advances, questioning aspects of the finished product from paper quality to binding and implying defection to other publishers,[11] and she later complained to her Appleton editor, Rutger Jewett, that the firm had not properly advertised her in the English press (Lee 695). Wharton consistently confronted the conservatism and paternalism at both Scribner's and Macmillan and progressed well beyond such strictures (Lee 165–66). She seemed to challenge the complicity between the genteel man of letters and the sentimental woman artist that she had dramatized in "The Pelican" (1898) and, ultimately, defined herself against such an unflattering portrait.[12]

Scribner's agreed to 15 percent royalties on *The House of Mirth* while Macmillan offered 20 percent in the United Kingdom. Alluding to her belief that she could do better at *Harper's* or *Century Magazine*, she requested an $8,000 advance from Scribner's on her next novel (*The Fruit of the Tree*) and 20 percent royalties (Macmillan offered their top rate of 25 percent for this and four of her following books). Scribner's agreed to 20 percent after sales exceeded 10,000 (Benstock 146; Towheed 23, 24). Frank Norris imagined much more modest gains when he insisted that novelists could count on making $250 on a novel that had sold 2,500 copies and been an "extraordinary success" (Norris 159). Scribner's rates seemed to remain steady even two decades after Wharton's 1905 bestseller when F. Scott Fitzgerald agreed to royalties of 15 percent up to 40,000 copies and 20 percent thereafter for *The Great Gatsby*.[13] From 1905 to 1908, Wharton earned $65,000 from advances, serialization, royalties, and other income connected with her writing (Lewis 180). *The House of Mirth* sold 30,000 copies in its first three weeks (a rate exceeding any other Scribner novel to date) and 140,000 copies in its first year (Lee 159). Of Wharton's early successes, Brownell observed that if *The Greater Inclination* sold any more vigorously, one might question its quality (Lee 167), reflecting a tendency during the period (which persists even today) to be suspicious of the literary quality of a "seller" (Holt 598).

Wharton's interest in the marketing of her work persisted beyond her best-selling first novel. When *Ethan Frome* (1911) was a critical success, Wharton questioned Scribner's sales reports and, given the demand and lack of availability (anecdotally reported to her by friends), asked why Scribner did not mention a second edition. Scribner reminded her that the statements of authors' friends and bookstore clerks were unreliable, and he sent her sales figures from four Boston stores and Brentano's in New York as proof that the novel was available and selling (*Letters* 262–64). Wharton's asking price steadily increased, and Appleton offered a $15,000 advance, the highest she had received to date, for *The Reef* (1912) (Lewis 327). Wharton continued to play Scribner's against Appleton and other offers, informing Scribner that a New York magazine was offering $12,500 for serial rights to her next novel (*The Custom of the Country*), an offer which Scribner agreed to match (Lewis 345–46). She informed Scribner that she would expect an advance on her next novel larger than the $5,000 they had given for *The Custom of the Country*, and he offered $10,000, noting that it was the largest advance in the firm's history; however, Scribner's would publish no more novels by Wharton until *A Son at the Front* in 1923. When Wharton began publishing with Appleton, Scribner regarded the loss as the most painful blow of his professional career.[14]

Wharton's success continued into the 1920s, which, after a slump during the war, was her most profitable period (Lee 526). By 1921, *The Age of Innocence* had sold 66,000 copies (eventually reaching 115,000) and by 1922, she had earned $70,000 on the novel, including $15,000 for film rights from Warner Brothers (Lewis 429–30). Wharton's celebrity capital steadily increased; in fact, she was earning so much literary income (about $250,000 from 1920 to 1924) that she worried about tax rates (Lewis 459). In comparison, Fitzgerald's income from his magazine fiction and novels over a much longer period from 1919 to 1936 was a little more than $290,000.[15]

By 1934, Wharton experienced a 70 percent drop in income as compared to the late 1920s, largely because of the Depression and waning popularity owing to the perception, right or wrong, that her work was out of step with modern culture (Lee 691). Critics both then and now posit that Wharton wrote too quickly during the latter part of her career and her art suffered because of it. Earlier in her career, Burlingame had suggested that she pace her fiction output so as not to "risk ... becoming *a magazine bore*" ("William C. Brownell" 601), and Gorham Munson's contemporary review in *The Bookman* seems to corroborate this advice;

he considers *The Children* (1928) as decidedly inferior to a masterpiece
such as *Ethan Frome* and clearly written for a less discerning magazine
(and female) audience (*CR* 462). R. W. B. Lewis suggests that sometimes
Wharton wrote to magazine editors' and the mass public's expectations
rather than to her capacity, but Rutger Jewett insisted that she was probably one of the few magazine authors writing what could be considered literature while pulling in the high salary usually reserved for "tosh" (Lewis
446–47). Indeed, despite the tenuous economic climate, she was still able
to garner a high price for some of her work. When Wharton asked Jewett
how popular magazines were able to keep paying top dollar for work in
which she suspected readers were not interested, Jewett noted that advertisers would pay "top-notch rates" to have their ads *"enclosed in an Edith
Wharton … story"* (Lewis 484). Even in the 1930s, Wharton received a
high rate of $5,000 for her story "Bread Upon the Water" (1934) (later reti-
tled "Charm Incorporated") in Hearst's *Cosmopolitan* (Lewis 507), during
a time when highly paid writers such as Fitzgerald and Booth Tarkington
were receiving top prices of $4,000 per story at *The Saturday Evening
Post*.[16] Notwithstanding the give and take between Wharton's work and
the consumerist and aesthetic pressures exerted by advertising messages
and reader expectations within the magazine context, she benefitted
financially while also managing to retain a measure of control over her
content and voice.[17]

Wharton was sometimes surprised by magazine editors' dismissal of
her work or concerns about her asking price, given her reputation. After
she revised her short story "Duration" per the editor's request for *Women's
Home Companion*, the magazine's editor, Gertrude Lane, wrote to Jewett
refusing to publish it although it was bought and paid for. Wharton
wrote to Jewett, "When I think of my position as a writer I am really
staggered at the insolence of her letter" (Lewis 507; *Letters* 571). She also
expressed surprise to Jewett when Loring Schuyler of the *Ladies' Home
Journal* reduced the payment for her memoirs from $25,000 to $20,000
and asked her to cut 40,000 words. Wharton cabled Jewett: "Absolutely
decline reducing price and will sue him unless agreement kept." The magazine eventually met her price (Lewis 507).

In addition to revenue from advances, royalties, and serialization,
Wharton also made considerable amounts from dramatic and film adaptations of her work. Income from theatrical adaptations of her works
appears to have been at least $130,000 (Lewis 529), and she made more
from theatrical and film adaptations during the last decade of her life
than from her fiction (Towheed 2). Equally important, her work on such

adaptations allowed her to collaborate in significant ways with other female artists and professionals.[18] Wharton's understanding of herself and her image as a publicly and visually consumed commodity also became more sophisticated as her career progressed. She did not like to be photographed (*Letters* 57), but her clothing choices, as seen in photographs, reveal how she carefully managed her public image and negotiated her "dual strivings for beauty and accomplishment" as a female artist.[19] Wharton would examine these costs and benefits of public celebrity and how it exposes private lives in works such as *The Touchstone* and "Copy: A Dialogue" (1900) (Kaplan 81–84; Glass 13–17).

Wharton's ability and desire to command top prices for her work, which might be seen as an admirable trait in a male author, continues to be debated by critics. Charles Madison characterizes Wharton as an extravagant rich woman hawking her wares to the "highest bidder" and willing to abandon her obligations to Scribner's when Appleton or other publishers offered more money. He contends that Wharton did not need the extra money and concludes that any supposed financial problems stemmed from the fact that "she lived like an extravagant society woman ... rather than as the gifted author dedicated primarily to her art." In comparison, Madison's representation of Sherwood Anderson's sometimes acrimonious negotiations with B. W. Huebsch over contracts, royalties, and advertising, and his eventual defection to Liveright, is decidedly softer in tone and Madison does not attribute a failure to reach agreement to Anderson's gender or class (Madison 133, 143, 198–204). Wharton negotiated the contradictory positions of famous female author and society woman throughout her career, not without her own misgivings and insecurities about her professional status and social position (Lewis 297–98), and the notion that she squandered her talent because of society obligations seems a reductive appraisal of the complex relationship between her art and the marketplace. Lee characterizes Wharton's break with Scribner's (and again with Macmillan when Appleton set up London offices in the 1920s) as a "divorce" worthy of Undine Spragg, and, given the writer's business decisions, notes the irony of Appleton's tag line for their *Age of Innocence* advertising campaign: "Was She Justified In Seeking A Divorce?" (Lee 427). Cynthia Griffin Wolff, however, notes that Wharton's decision to sell *The Reef* to Appleton for more money indicates her "growing confidence" in commercial matters and views her decisions to seek the most money for her work as "shrewd" rather than mercenary (Wolff 429 n38).

Wharton's fiction dramatizes some of her own desires for acceptance and success in the literary marketplace. Jennifer Shepherd observes that through her characterization of Simon Rosedale in *The House of Mirth* as a "social *arriviste*" who "make[s] good through the exploitation of commodity aesthetics," Wharton may be "scripting the possibility of success for herself [as a sort of *arriviste* in the literary-critical world] in the increasingly commercialized and competitive sphere of turn-of-the-century American letters."[20] Jacqueline Wilson-Jordan argues that the characterization of the woman writer in "Mr. Jones" reveals Wharton's conviction that women's attempts to wield authority and control over narratives do not come without challenge and cost.[21]

Contrary to her youthful acquiescence to critical opinion in her mock reviews of *Fast and Loose*, Wharton later in her career spoke out against what she saw as contradictions in critical appraisals of fiction in the consumerist context of the early twentieth century. She believed that anyone offering "wares for sale in the open market should accept rose wreaths or rotten eggs with an equal heart," but she was critical of the fickle patterns of modern reviewing and of critics' application of "ready-made" criticism to artistic forms that "shape themselves in obedience to their inner organism." Wharton claimed that since she did not significantly revise her fictional method over the course of her career, critics' changing attitudes toward her work revealed more about the waxing and waning of critical fads than about perceived changes or deficiencies in her approach, implying that the criticism rather than her fiction was more influenced by cultural and market forces. [22]

Of course, a fidelity to her inner artistic vision did not keep Wharton from worrying about the marketability of her work, and through to the end of her career she was aware of the importance of having staying power in the literary marketplace, as evidenced by her own appraisal of *The House of Mirth* thirty years after its publication. Although a place on the backlist, upon which publishers relied for steady income and as protection from slow sales or economic upheaval (West 23), might be more or less advantageous for an author depending on her specific circumstances, Wharton seemed to appreciate the advantages to her reputation and economic position in remaining on the backlist at Oxford University Press, and she emphasizes in her 1936 preface to the Oxford edition of *The House of Mirth* that the novel "still lives" on Oxford's backlist thirty-one years after publication.[23] Wharton's commercial and critical staying power is probably best indicated by ongoing scholarship on her life and writing, the frequent inclusion of her work in literary anthologies and on course syllabi, and continued film and theatrical adaptations of her works, all of which emphasize the various ways in which she continues to "sell."

NOTES

1. E. Wharton, "William C. Brownell," *Scribner's Magazine*, 84 (1928), 596–602; 601. Subsequent references to this work are included in the text.
2. W. D. Howells, "The Man of Letters as a Man of Business," *Scribner's Magazine*, 14 (1893), 429–45; 429, 430, 445.
3. F. Norris, "Fiction Writing as a Business" in *The Responsibilities of the Novelist and Other Literary Essays* (New York: Doubleday, Page, and Company, 1903), 157–65; 161–62. Subsequent references to this work are included in the text.
4. J. L. W. West III, *American Authors and the Literary Marketplace Since 1900* (Philadelphia: University of Pennsylvania Press, 1988), 13–14. Subsequent references to this work are included in the text. W. D. Howells, "A Painful Subject," *Harper's Weekly* 48 (1904), 48.
5. H. Holt, "The Commercialization of Literature," *The Atlantic Monthly*, 96 (1905), 577–600; 577, 600. Subsequent references to this work are included in the text.
6. L. Glass, *Authors Inc.: Literary Celebrity in the Modern United States, 1880–1980* (New York: New York University Press, 2004), 12–13. Subsequent references to this work are included in the text.
7. G. H. Putnam and J. B. Putnam, *Author and Publisher: A Manual of Suggestions for Beginners in Literature*, 7th ed. (New York: G. P. Putnam's Sons, 1897), 142.
8. R. Burlingame, *Of Making Many Books: A Hundred Years of Reading, Writing and Publishing* (New York: Scribner's, 1946), 109–11.
9. J. Tebbell, *A History of Book Publishing in the United States*, 4 vols. (New York: R. R. Bowker Company, 1978), vol. III, 85.
10. C. A. Madison, *Irving to Irving: Author-Publisher Relations 1800–1974* (New York: R. R. Bowker Company, 1974), 135. Subsequent references to this work are included in the text.
11. S. Towheed (ed.), *The Correspondence of Edith Wharton and Macmillan, 1901–1930* (New York: Palgrave Macmillan, 2007), 92, 94, 122, 138–39, 156. Subsequent references to this work are included in the text.
12. A. Kaplan, *The Social Construction of American Realism* (Chicago: University of Chicago Press, 1988), 73. Subsequent references to this work are included in the text.
13. M. J. Bruccoli with J. S. Baughman (eds.), *The Sons of Maxwell Perkins: Letters of F. Scott Fitzgerald, Ernest Hemingway, Thomas Wolfe, and Their Editor* (Columbia: University of South Carolina Press, 2004), 31.
14. M. Bell, "Lady into Author: Edith Wharton and the House of Scribner," *American Quarterly*, 9 (1957), 295–315; 304–05, 315.
15. M. J. Bruccoli and J. M. Atkinson (eds.), *As Ever, Scott Fitz – Letters between F. Scott Fitzgerald and His Literary Agent, Harold Ober, 1919–1940* (Philadelphia: Lippincott, 1972), xviii.
16. M. J. Bruccoli, *Some Sort of Epic Grandeur: The Life of F. Scott Fitzgerald*, 2nd rev. edn. (Columbia: University of South Carolina Press, 2002), 278; West, 105.

17. E. Thornton, "Selling Edith Wharton: Illustration, Advertising, and *Pictorial Review*, 1924–1925," *Arizona Quarterly*, 57 (2001), 29–59; S. Whitehead, "Breaking the Frame: How Edith Wharton's Short Stories Subvert Their Magazine Context," *European Journal of American Culture*, 27 (2008), 43–56.
18. J. Barlowe, "No Innocence in This Age: Edith Wharton's Commercialization and Commodification" in G. Totten (ed.), *Memorial Boxes and Guarded Interiors: Edith Wharton and Material Culture* (Tuscaloosa: University of Alabama Press, 2007), 44–62.
19. K. Joslin, *Edith Wharton and the Making of Fashion* (Lebanon, NH: University Press of New England, 2009), 44–45.
20. J. Shepherd, "Fashioning an Aesthetics of Consumption in *The House of Mirth*" in G. Totten (ed.), *Memorial Boxes and Guarded Interiors: Edith Wharton and Material Culture* (Tuscaloosa: University of Alabama Press, 2007), 135–58; 157.
21. J. Wilson-Jordan, "Materializing the Word: The Woman Writer and the Struggle for Authority in 'Mr. Jones'" in G. Totten (ed.), *Memorial Boxes and Guarded Interiors: Edith Wharton and Material Culture* (Tuscaloosa: University of Alabama Press, 2007), 63–79; 78–79.
22. E. Wharton, "A Cycle of Reviewing," *The Spectator* [London], 141 (1928), 44–45.
23. E. Wharton, Introduction to *The House of Mirth* (London: Oxford University Press, 1936), v–xi; vii.

CHAPTER 12

Serialization

Elsa Nettels

In his essay "Criticism" (1891), Henry James defined "Periodical literature" as a "huge open mouth which has to be fed – a vessel of immense capacity which has to be filled."[1] He was writing of reviewing, but he could have chosen serialized fiction as the food to fill the great maw of the magazines. During the nineteenth century, countless pages in hundreds of newspapers and magazines were filled with fiction in installments by practically every writer of fiction, from the most famous – Dickens, Thackeray, Hardy, George Eliot, and Trollope in England; James, Hawthorne, Howells, and Mark Twain in the United States – to the obscure and long forgotten.

Serialization did not begin and end in the nineteenth century. By the middle of the eighteenth century in England, installments of original novels or reprints "totalled several hundred."[2] The first novel to be serialized in the United States, Jeremy Belknap's *The Foresters,* appeared in the *Columbian Magazine* in the 1780s.[3] Serialization continued well into the twentieth century (*Esquire* published Norman Mailer's *An American Dream,* January–August 1964; *Rolling Stone* published Tom Wolfe's *The Bonfire of the Vanities,* July 1984–August 1985).[4] However, the nineteenth century, when literacy increased and printing costs declined, was the golden age of serialization. Michael Lund's *America's Continuing Story* illustrates "the centrality of the serial form to America's literary history in the nineteenth century."[5] According to Patricia Okker, in England the serial "reached its zenith in the late 1880s and early 1890s" (134).

In Victorian England, it was standard practice to publish a novel, first as a serial in installments, then as a three-volume novel. Authors might follow the practice set by Dickens with *The Pickwick Papers* of publishing in "numbers" – installments of novels published as separate issues, to be sold for a shilling apiece. By the 1860s, most novels were serialized in magazines such as *Macmillan's Magazine* and the *Cornhill,* which owed their "explosive growth" mainly to serials.[6] Philip Quilibet, in an essay on "magazine novels" in the U.S. *Galaxy* (1869), claimed that "many magazines live, move and have their being through serial novels."[7] As the serial novel was "a prime necessity to the popular magazine" (Quilibet 128), so serialization, followed by book publication, enabled many writers – some 200 by 1900 – to support themselves by writing fiction (Sutherland 152).

When Wharton published *The Touchstone* as a two-part serial in *Scribner's Magazine* in March and April 1900, she joined those writers who had made serial novel writing "a regular branch of the literary calling" (Quilibet 133). From that point on, Wharton published fifteen more novels and novellas as serials. Until the outbreak of World War I, *Scribner's Magazine* serialized three of her long novels – *The House of Mirth* (January–November 1905), *The Fruit of the Tree* (January–November 1907), and *The Custom of the Country* (January–November 1913) – and the shorter work *Ethan Frome* (August, September, and October 1911).

Wharton had turned to Charles Scribner's Sons after several English publishers had refused her first book, *The Decoration of Houses*, written with Ogden Codman, Jr. Scribner's published it in 1897. (Later it was published in England by B. T. Batsford.) Scribner's editor, Edward Burlingame, Wharton's friend and adviser, offered $750 for the serial rights of *The Touchstone* (Lewis 95). *Scribner's Magazine* continued to publish Wharton's short stories, along with the serial installments.

When Wharton accepted D. Appleton and Company's offer to publish *The Reef* (1912, not serialized), the decline of the venerable literary journals had begun. *Scribner's Magazine, Century, The Atlantic Monthly,* and *Harper's Magazine* were all losing subscribers and advertisers.[8] During the war years, *Scribner's Magazine* serialized *Bunner Sisters* (October and November 1916), but *Summer* was serialized by *McClure's Magazine* (February–August 1917) and published by Appleton (1917).

By 1919, Rutger B. Jewett of Appleton had become Wharton's editor and also her agent who negotiated the serial rights of her novels with Arthur Vance, editor of the *Pictorial Review,* which was one of the most popular of the mass-circulating women's magazines. Vance paid $18,000 for the serial rights to *The Age of Innocence* (1920) (Lewis 423) and subsequently paid thousands to serialize in the *Pictorial Review* Wharton's next four novels: *The Glimpses of the Moon* (1922), *The Mother's Recompense* (1925), *Twilight Sleep* (1927), and *The Children* (1928). Compared to the $750 offered for *The Touchstone,* the $40,000 Vance offered for *The Children* (Lewis 473) attests not only to Wharton's stature as a novelist, but also to Vance's enormous resources. Jewett negotiated the serial rights with the *Ladies' Home Journal* for *A Backward Glance* (1934). Wharton returned to Scribner's for publication of *A Son at the Front* (1923), as a serial in *Scribner's Magazine*, after Jewett advised against trying to publish it when readers were tired of the war (Lewis 423), and Scribner's was eager to get Wharton back on its list.

Scribner's Magazine was a dignified periodical, backed by an old established firm and addressed to the well-educated and the affluent. The majority of its advertisers were private schools and manufacturers of motor cars. In *Scribner's Magazine*, Wharton was in the company of Henry James, George Meredith, and Robert Louis Stevenson. In the *Pictorial Review*, *The Age of Innocence* was followed by Kathleen Norris' *The Beloved Woman* (1922), and Wharton's text appeared alongside advertisements for deodorant and corsets. She accepted these indignities for the sake of the income needed to maintain her wartime charities and her houses in St. Brice and Hyères.

In becoming a writer of serials, Wharton subjected herself to the requests and needs of magazine editors. As a writer for *Scribner's Magazine*, she was called on to produce copy for *The House of Mirth* and *The Custom of the Country* before she had completed either novel (Lewis 144, 209). Years later, she wrote that the request of Burlingame to have *The House of Mirth* ready to begin serialization in January 1905 had transformed her from a "drifting amateur, into a professional" who embraced "the discipline of the daily task" (quoted in Benstock 149).

Most of her complaints to Scribner's concerned their failure, as she saw it, to advertise her books sufficiently. The proposals and acts that most outraged her came from the editors who offered her enormous sums for serial rights. When she learned that the *Pictorial Review* "proposed cutting some installments [of *The Age of Innocence*] since space was needed for illustrations and other displays," she wrote angrily to Jewett: "I cannot consent to have my work treated as prose by the yard" (quoted in Lewis 429). She reminded Jewett of the agreement that "the novel furnished to the *Pictorial Review* should not be less than 100,000 words long" (*Letters* 428), but she was powerless to change the copy advertising her forthcoming novel. Edie Thornton, the best critic of Wharton's 1920s serializations, notes how the advertising distorted the novel by inviting readers to identify with May Welland, making the novel about a "wronged wife," the unfaithful husband, and the "other woman." "Does your husband really love you?" the copy asks, playing on the reader's anxieties. "You may be in young Mrs. Archer's position without knowing it!" As Thornton observes, the *Pictorial Review* promoted sympathy for May as the heroine because as a model of "traditional women's magazines' virtues and quandaries," she was "the most likely link between fiction and intended reader."[9]

Wharton considered *Hudson River Bracketed* (1929) all but ruined by the high-handed editor of the *Delineator*, who "without warning or permission" began serializing the novel "ahead of the agreed schedule" (*Letters* 521 n. 1). However, she had to return to the *Delineator* to serialize *The Gods Arrive* (1932) after several magazines turned it down. When the editor of the *Ladies' Home Journal* proposed that Wharton cut the manuscript of *A Backward Glance* by 40,000 words and accept a fee reduced from $25,000 to $20,000, she wrote to Jewett, "certainly not"; "he is at liberty to cut out everything he wishes but not of course to back out of his price" (*Letters* 559).

Wharton's first objection to the practice of editors came over the matter of illustrations. A. B. Wenzell, who illustrated the serial of *The House of Mirth*, was one of the most popular illustrators of the time, but may now be remembered for Wharton's dislike of his illustrations and her strong objection to having them in the book. To her editor at Scribner's, William Crary Brownell, she expressed keen regret at having "[sunk] to the depth of letting the illustrations be put in the book – & oh, I wish I hadn't now!" (*Letters* 94). In her copy of the novel, now in the library at the Mount, she crossed out Wenzell's name on the title page and cut out his illustrations.

Wharton apparently made no objections to Wenzell's illustrations of *Madame de Treymes*, to Alonzo Kimball's illustrations of *The Fruit of the Tree*, or to Walter Clark's illustrations of *Sanctuary*. Perhaps she realized that protest was futile. Illustrations were often regarded as vital to the success of a serial novel as a pianist's accompaniment was to a singer. Popular illustrators could command more than the highest-paid novelists. "Publishers vied for the best illustrators, paying them yearly salaries of up to $100,000 and establishing them as media stars."[10] Charles Scribner urged Wharton to yield to reality. "Illustrations are expected," he wrote to her, "and their absence may be unfavorably noticed [by booksellers]. [I] do not wish to importune you but it seems only right to … ask you to decide. It might be added that illustrations are useful for sales purposes."[11] As Jason Williams has noted, the January 1905 edition of *Scribner's Magazine* promoted illustrator over author by its frontispiece, "a full-color reproduction of Wenzell's illustration of Lily Bart descending Selden's staircase – many pages before Wharton's text appears."[12]

Jewett had advised Wharton against giving anything to the *Delineator* when the magazine offered her more money than the *Pictorial Review*.

"Work of high literary quality," he wrote, "is not so good for these popular magazines [for example, the *Delineator*] as [is] the typical lowbrow serial publication. Mary Roberts Rinehart and Kathleen Norris grind out ideal stuff – for serialization. You write novels without a thought for the magazine" (quoted in Lewis 472).

This was not entirely true. Thornton claims that Wharton in *The Mother's Recompense* made a "serious challenge" to the *Pictorial Review*'s ruling idea that "youth, slimness and fashionable attire are the prerequisites for sexuality" by giving her middle-aged protagonist Kate Clephane a youthful appearance, slim body, and sexual passion but emphasizing her age, forty-five ("Selling" 32). However, the staff of the *Pictorial Review* who wrote the synopses of the installments, "The Story of the Story," did all they could to transform Kate into a youthful figure, a "brilliant butterfly" who had "flitted about Europe for many years," in the words of the second synopsis ("Selling" 38).

Although Wharton resisted the proposal relayed by Jewett from Arthur Vance, editor of *Pictorial Review*, that the serialized novel after *The Age of Innocence* be divided into four parts, each one leading to an "interesting situation that will leave the reader in suspense and eager to get to the next issue of the magazine" (quoted in Lee 598), she did compose her novels in short chapters easily grouped in serial installments. Occasionally, even her characters think in terms of chapters. Moreover, her novels accommodated themselves well to serialization. Dramatizing in chronological sequences the stages in a character's life or in the unfolding of a relationship among several characters, they exemplified the linear concept of time, fostered by the serial, "a gradual developing story and pattern of significance" (Hughes and Lund 7). Without claiming pleasure as James did in making a "small compositional law" out of the "recurrent breaks and resumptions in the serial,"[13] Wharton often used the enforced interruption to effect a change of time or place. For instance, between the sixth and seventh installments of *The House of Mirth*, at least a month passes and the scene shifts to Monte Carlo, where Selden views Lily as she arrives on the Dorsets' yacht.

The chief effect of the serial's enforced break is to create suspense, exciting the reader's desire to know what will come next. Sometimes novelists interrupt conversations, as Howells does in *The Rise of Silas Lapham* at the end of chapter 14, when Silas asks Tom Corey after the fateful dinner at the Coreys, "Was I drunk last night?" and the reader must wait a month before reading Tom's honest but diplomatic answer. Sometimes, but not always, a critical point of potential suspense is buried in the middle of a

Wharton installment. This happens in the June installment of *The Fruit of the Tree*, when a chapter in the middle ends as Justine "turned about to rebuke [Wyant] for his insistence, and found herself face to face with John Amherst."[14] However, that installment ends with the promise of more to come. As Bessie leaves the room, Amherst feels that the door has closed on his marriage. "But nothing in life ever ends, and the next moment a new question confronted him – how was the next chapter to open?" (XLI: 734).

Justine – and the reader – knows that she faces the crisis of her marriage to John Amherst at the end of the September installment, when she comes upon Dr. Wyant with her husband. She has refused to let Wyant continue to blackmail her, despite his threat to tell her husband of her deliberate ending of his first wife's suffering by a fatal dose of morphine. The installment concludes, "She opened the drawing room door, and saw her husband talking with Wyant" (XLII: 378).

The month dividing the installments also allowed readers to reflect on past events. Moved by the novelist's art, one might, at the moment of reading, applaud a character's controversial action (such as euthanasia), then on reflection see it differently. Such was the experience of the reviewer of *The Fruit of the Tree* for the *Kansas City Star*:

> Never did a story gain more in power than this one in the slow reading ... Almost one feels justified in the suspicion that the author wrote this story primarily for the effect it would have on the reader as a serial ... Readers ... will still remember the day ... they laid down the August Scribner's after an hour or so in the atmosphere of whirling anguish ... by Bessie's bedside; even the sternest moralist of them, almost convinced that the drop of poison which had released the suffering body was mercy, imperatively demanded a common humanity. And during the ensuing weeks the mind turning the problem over and over began to feel that the author had not really justified her heroine, began to feel that the fruit of this tree must be bitter.[15]

The reviewer was right. As readers of the October installment of the novel learned, Justine never doubts the moral rightness of her act, but when her husband and father-in-law are repelled by what she has done, she realizes that they will always take "the traditional view of the act" (XLII: 453) that she has violated emotions "rooted far below reason and judgment, in the dark primal depths of inherited feeling" (XLII:453). The novel ends with Justine and Amherst still together but their marriage is blighted by the "tenuous impenetrable barrier between them" (XLII: 465).

Quilibet in his 1869 *Galaxy* essay observed that "in the English magazine, the serial plays a far more important role than in the American"

(133). Yet rarely a month passed when a serial was not running in one of the leading U.S. literary magazines – *Harper's*, *Century*, and *The Atlantic Monthly*. Between 1850 and 1900, twenty-eight novels by Dickens, George Eliot, Hardy, Charles Reade, Thackeray, and Trollope were serialized in U.S. magazines, twenty-one of them in *Harper's Magazine* (Lund 153–228). Sometimes serials ran concurrently. One could read in the February 1885 issue of *Century* the first installment of James' *The Bostonians*, the fourth installment of *The Rise of Silas Lapham,* and three chapters, "Royalty on the Mississippi," from *Adventures of Huckleberry Finn.*

In the United States, as in England, serial installments that people were reading at the same time created a community of readers, drawing together "thousands of widely dispersed readers."[16] Serials became part of daily life: according to the *Kansas City Star* reviewer, *The Fruit of the Tree* generated "endless discussions this summer." Howells recalled in *Years of My Youth* that serial installments provided topics of conversation during courtship. "*The Newcomes* was passing as a serial through *Harper's Magazine,* and we were reading that with perhaps more pleasure than any of the other novels ... We went about trying to think who in the story was like whom in life."[17] The death of a protagonist was newsworthy. After the final installment of *The House of Mirth*, a reader telegraphed a friend: "Lily Bart is dead" (Lewis 152).

Serials also promoted a close relationship between author and reader, as readers "could convey their opinion to authors as novels unfolded, on occasion actively shaping the direction that particular novel took" (Mays 18). If Wharton received letters begging her to let Lily Bart live and marry Selden, she was not persuaded by them; she made clear at the beginning of *The House of Mirth* that Lily is doomed. She recalled in *A Backward Glance* that early chapters of the novel were published before she had reached the climax. "What that climax was to be, I had known before I began" (*BG* 208).

She did, however, revise the serial version of *The Fruit of the Tree* for the published volume after receiving "several letters from literate mill workers kindly pointing out various inaccuracies" (Lewis 181). Most of the corrections in the first two installments required changing the word "loom" to "card." "Loom-room" becomes "carding-room." "Revolving carders" becomes "revolving cards." "Superintendent" becomes "manager."[18] Wharton was always aware of the response of readers to the serialized novel, using favorable responses to argue for greater advances on the book publication. She wrote to Frederick Macmillan, her English publisher, to request and justify an advance of £400 for *The Custom of the Country* (the book): "The success in the magazine has been so great that Mr. Scribner has reprinted the first numbers in a pamphlet for new subscribers."[19]

Although Wharton left Scribner's and turned to Appleton's, she did not forget the importance of her first publisher. In *A Backward Glance*, she paid tribute to her editors at Scribner's, William Crary Brownell and Edward Burlingame; she dated the beginning of her literary career to the publication of her earliest stories in *Scribner's Magazine* (*BG* 112). At the end of her professional life, Wharton wrote to Gaillard Lapsley that she was "sustained ... by the regular click of coin in [her] savings-box as ... *three* plays (2 Old Maids & one Ethan) continue their fruitful rounds" (*Letters* 592). Wharton always valued the "click of coin" for her labors, and three decades previously, serializations had begun their fruitful rounds in her career. They would go on to play a consistent and consistently profitable role, ensuring that the majority of Wharton's most notable writings were first available to the reading public in serial form.

NOTES

1. H. James, "Criticism" in W. Veeder and S. M. Griffin (eds.), *The Art of Criticism: Henry James on the Theory and Practice of Criticism* (Chicago: University of Chicago Press, 1986), 232–41; 232.

2. G. Law, *Serialization Fiction in the Victorian Press* (New York: Palgrave, 2000), 3.

3. P. Okker, *Social Stories: The Magazine Novel in Nineteenth-Century America* (Charlottesville: University of Virginia Press, 2003), 31. Subsequent references to this work are included in the text.

4. L. Hughes and M. Lund, *The Victorian Serial* (Charlottesville: University Press of Virginia, 1991), 275–78. Subsequent references to this work are included in the text.

5. M. Lund, *America's Continuing Story: An Introduction to Serial Fiction, 1850–1900* (Detroit, MI: Wayne State University Press, 1993), 21. Subsequent references to this work are included in the text.

6. J. Sutherland, *Victorian Fiction: Writers, Publishers, Readers* (New York: St. Martin's Press, 1995), 55. Subsequent references to this work are included in the text.

7. P. Quilibet, "Magazine Novels," from *The Galaxy* (January 1869), in M. Lund, *America's Continuing Story* (Detroit, MI: Wayne State University Press, 1993), 128–34; 130. Subsequent references to this work are included in the text.

8. R. E. Spiller et al. (eds.), *Literary History of the United States,* 3rd rev. edn. (London: Macmillan and Company, 1969), 1125.

9. E. Thornton, "'Elegance Is Refusal': Style and Consumer Culture in American Women's Magazine Fiction, 1910–1930," unpublished PhD thesis, University of Wisconsin, Madison (1998), 321–27.

10. E. Thornton, "Selling Edith Wharton: Illustration, Advertising, and *Pictorial Review, 1924–1925*," *Arizona Quarterly* 57.3 (2001): 29–59; 30. Subsequent references to this work are included in the text.

11. Quoted with the ellipses in E. Thornton, "Beyond the Page: Visual Literacy and the Interpretation of Lily Bart," unpublished essay, 10.

12. J. Williams, "Competing Visions: Edith Wharton and A. B. Wenzell in *The House of Mirth*," *Edith Wharton Review* 36.1 (2010): 1–9; 2. Subsequent references to this work are included in the text.

13. H. James, *The Art of the Novel: Critical Prefaces by Henry James* (New York: Charles Scribner's Sons, 1934), 340.

14. E. Wharton, *The Fruit of the Tree*, Scribner's Magazine, 41, 720. Subsequent references to the serialization are included in the text.

15. "Fine High Standards," *Kansas City Star*, October 26, 1907.

16. K. J. Mays, "The Publishing World" in P. Brantlinger and W. B. Thesing (eds.), *A Companion to the Victorian Novel* (Oxford: Blackwell, 2002), 11–30; 18.

17. W. D. Howells, *Years of My Youth, and Three Essays* (Bloomington: Indiana University Press, 1975), 142.

18. See also Donna Campbell, introduction and notes to *The Fruit of the Tree* (Boston: Northeastern University Press, 2000).

19. S. Towheed (ed.), *The Correspondence of Edith Wharton and Macmillan, 1901–1930* (New York: Palgrave, 2007), 148–49.

CHAPTER 13

Short Story Markets

Bonnie Shannon McMullen

Edith Wharton's first published fiction was a short story. So was her last. Her first volume of fiction was a collection of stories. Her last completed book of fiction was also a collection of stories. Between 1891 and 1937 she would publish eighty-six stories, a major part of her total output. Her career coincided with a flourishing U.S. magazine publishing market in the late nineteenth and early twentieth centuries, which both stimulated and catered to the public appetite for short stories.

Several factors contributed to this favorable climate for short story publication. Technological advances in publishing enabled mass-circulation magazines to increase their profits while lowering their costs, and these developments forced the "quality" magazines, with which Wharton started her career, to lower their own subscription costs and widen their circulation. It is estimated that about 7,500 magazines were added, between 1885 and 1905, to the 3,300 that already existed in the United States, although not all would survive long.[1] Circulations rose steeply. By 1906, ten U.S. magazines, including the *Saturday Evening Post* and the *Ladies' Home Journal*, were selling more than 500,000 copies per issue whereas, before 1891, none could boast of such circulation numbers. The line between elite and popular periodicals gradually became blurred.[2]

The prospects for U.S. short story writers were greatly improved by a change in international copyright law in 1891, the Chace Act, which protected foreign authors in the United States and U.S. authors abroad. With royalties payable to foreign authors, publishers no longer had any incentive to publish pirated British fiction, opening the field to U.S. talent. Competition among magazines for the best U.S. stories resulted in higher fees to authors, which in turn encouraged novelists to put more energy into story writing.

In addition, the widely accepted critical theory of Edgar Allan Poe concerning the unity of the short story, as set out in his review of Hawthorne's *Twice-Told Tales*, raised the status of this genre. Poe's precepts were later canonized by Brander Matthews in "The Philosophy of the Short Story" of 1885, in which he argued that the short story as a genre was not only superior to the novel, but that it was a peculiarly U.S. phenomenon. Whether true or not, these assumptions may have contributed to a trend, after 1885, for magazines in both the United States and Britain to show a marginal preference for short stories over serialized novels (Levy, n. 45, 137–38). The short story was the perfect form for the magazine, and founding an elitist literary magazine was Poe's greatest ambition. He died before he could realize his goal, but the elite magazines of Wharton's time could be seen as a latter-day materialization of Poe's dream. People on the move could best respond to short works with a single strong effect, Poe had argued. That was even truer by the 1890s and early twentieth century. All of these factors made 1891 an auspicious moment for a novice author to launch into magazine story writing.

BEGINNINGS

Scribner's Magazine was, like Wharton, at the start of its career when its editor, Edward Burlingame, accepted what would be her first piece of published fiction, "Mrs. Manstey's View," which appeared in July 1891. *Scribner's Magazine* had joined the already established *Century Magazine*, *Harper's Magazine*, and *The Atlantic Monthly* in 1887 as an organ for fiction, criticism, and articles on art and travel. Reducing the length, but not the quality, of its contents, it maintained its sales by selling for twenty-five cents a copy instead of the thirty-five cents charged by its rivals. The audience it sought and, in turn, helped to create, was the educated and leisured well-to-do middle class.

This class, Wharton's own, inseparably associated with her place in literature, was, nevertheless, not the subject of her first published story. Mrs. Manstey is a widow living at the back of a boarding house, her solitude relieved by her intense enjoyment of the view from her window, her "coign of vantage" (*CSI* 3). The window through which Mrs. Manstey experiences her world is like the opening the short story form afforded the story's author, a "coign of vantage" for attack and defence. Whether Wharton intended the pun or not, the short story was the coin with which she negotiated her way into the fiction markets of her day.

After this propitious start, several more stories appeared in *Scribner's Magazine* during the nineties, with others in *Century*, edited by the reformer and poet Richard Watson Gilder, and the Philadelphia magazine *Lippincott's*. Wharton's stories had an edge that sometimes seemed at odds with the prevailing tone of these genteel publications, and it is even possible that her sex gave her a certain latitude that would be denied to male story contributors. Sentimental illustrations of some stories by Maxfield Parrish or Walter Appleton Clark were oddly incongruous with the darkness of their contents. Burlingame rejected *Bunner Sisters*, one of her strongest works of this period, and instead proposed publication of a volume of short stories. This volume, consisting mainly of new stories, was *The Greater Inclination*, and was published by Scribner's in New York in March 1899, and by John Lane at Bodley Head in England two weeks later. Sales of more than 3,000 copies exceeded expectations, and the ground for this triumph was prepared by Wharton's earlier success with magazine stories.

The reviews that greeted this volume illustrate the expectations of the short story market and set the trend for approaches to her work that are still current, such as her indirection, economy, female insight, irony, and similarity to James. Wharton's more muted success with the British short story market, where the genre enjoyed less popularity and prestige, is illustrated by a mix of praise with condescension, touching both on her sex and nationality. The *Academy* of July 8, 1899 followed a discussion of Wharton's "skilled" craftsmanship with the remark that "Such a phenomenon is rare, especially among women writers" (*CR* 21). The *Athenaeum* of August 5 noted that, for an American, "she yet has a command of good English . . ." (*CR* 23).

It is clear that these reviews, and others, were read carefully by Wharton and played a part in the future direction of her career. Unlike George Eliot, for example, who never read reviews until they had been filtered by George Henry Lewes, and depended on Lewes for all business correspondence with her publishers, Wharton, until almost the end of her life, conducted, with little help, her own negotiations concerning publishing details and contracts, and saw her talent as a commodity to be marketed in the most advantageous way possible. Good reviews were an important bargaining counter in her interactions with the market. She quickly learned how to deal with the publishing gatekeepers. In her correspondence with Burlingame in the 1890s, Wharton is self-deprecating, thanking him for his criticism ("I always recognize its justice"), which she didn't necessarily follow, and admitting to needing "more assurance (the quality I feel I most lack)" (*Letters* 32–33). Self-effacement disappears in her correspondence with Scribner's William Crary Brownell, however, as she upbraids the publisher on April 25, 1899 for not giving *The Greater Inclination* sufficient publicity, in spite of its "unusually favourable reception" (*Letters* 37).

She proved herself a competent and far from bashful business manager, alive to marketing opportunities, mentioning to Brownell in December 1899 that a later printing with a white and gold binding might appeal to Christmas shoppers.[3] The same assertiveness would characterize her correspondence with Frederick Macmillan, her London publisher from 1903 to 1923. While she repeatedly blamed disappointing sales on inadequate advertising, Macmillan would counter defensively that the British market for volumes of short stories was not so healthy as in the United States.[4]

In 1901, Scribner's and Murray brought out her second volume of short stories, *Crucial Instances*, which included stories previously published in *Scribner's Magazine, Harper's*, and the less prestigious but broader *Cosmopolitan*, publisher of stories by the well-established Kipling, Stevenson, Twain, London, and others. Reviewers of this second volume were more guarded in their praise. The critic in the *Independent* writes alarmingly of the reader's need for "mental endurance." *Munsey's Magazine* complains that "Her men are subtle and complex ladies wearing mustaches. This may lead one to wonder whether the fault is with Mrs. Wharton's power of characterization, or in the material that she has for study" (*CR* 43–44). These reactions suggest that Wharton, although she had clearly already mastered the short story form and gauged the market, was pushing against its confines, dealing with subject matter that could benefit from a more extended development, something that she was already doing.

For the first eleven years of Wharton's career in fiction, she was known, primarily, as a short story writer. Her first novel, *The Valley of Decision*, was not published until 1902, but even before that, her authorial career was speeding ahead faster than the motor car the Whartons were soon enabled to buy. In 1904, certain of a market, Scribner's brought out a third collection, *The Descent of Man*, published in London by Macmillan. This volume, in particular, shows Wharton's willingness to cater to the interests of her audience without compromising her aesthetic standard, realizing the importance of satisfying a market and, inseparable in her mind, earning what she thought her stories were worth. In stories such as "The Other Two," first published in *Collier's* in 1904, featuring the thrice-married, twice-divorced Alice Waythorne, and "The Mission of Jane," first published in *Harper's* in 1902, where an incompatible couple belatedly find connubial harmony in marrying off a difficult adopted daughter, Wharton explores, with humor and irony, changing social attitudes to family life. She satisfied the markets, but remained true to her own vision by visiting the subject matter, but avoiding the authorial stance, of the popular sentimental fiction of her day. The volume also contains her first ghost story, "The Lady's Maid's Bell," a sought-after genre she would develop and exploit throughout the rest of her career.

After the publication of *The House of Mirth* in 1905, Wharton's position was unassailable. She continued to explore themes and situations in the short story form, finding this activity a relief from the longer-term commitment of novel composition. It was also important for maintaining her income between novels and keeping her name constantly in the public eye. In addition, the short story genre enabled her to experiment with form and subject matter in a way that would be riskier in a novel, given the greater financial implications of failure with a longer work. One such example is her story, "The Hermit and the Wild Woman," first published in 1906 – a radical departure from her earlier stories and the title story in her next volume of 1908.

Reviews of this collection presented a salutary warning. The *New York Times Saturday Review* of October 1908 was, possibly, the first to discuss her writing specifically in relation to "the difficult art of short-story writing" (*CR* 157), but "difficult art" did not necessarily make for easy reading. Some of her audience wanted to be entertained, and the *Spectator* complained that the stories "do not minister in any way to the gaiety of the reader." The reviewer expresses concern at the negative picture of Americans conveyed by the stories, which are, "if not hostile, at any rate by no means flattering to their strength of purpose or altitude of aim" (*CR* 157, 159–60). Wharton was, by now, spending more and more time abroad, and even while in the United States, associating with visiting expatriates such as Henry James and other members of his circle. Her view of U.S. life was, indeed, somewhat jaundiced and detached. These reviews show that she still needed to balance the tastes and sensitivities of her audiences on both sides of the Atlantic against her sense of artistic integrity. Reviewers were the middlemen between publisher and author, on one side, and audiences on the other, and influenced the fickle markets with their praise or censure. Wharton could not push them too far. Competitive magazine editors, with their fingers on the pulse of authors' fluctuating reputations, took such views into consideration when deciding whether to accept stories or not. It was the author's name and reputation that could sell a magazine, as Zelda Fitzgerald found out some years later when she was forced to allow some of her stories to be published under her more famous husband's name.

Continuing the same frantic pace, amid increasing complexities in her personal life, Wharton brought out a collection of stories in French,

Les Metteurs en Scene in 1909, and by 1910, *Tales of Men and Ghosts* was published by Scribner's and Macmillan's. U.S. reviews were lukewarm, *The Nation* referring to "the enervating influence upon our popular story-writers of American magazine policy," which allegedly caused Wharton to churn out ten stories to fulfill "an announcement of the previous year" (*CR* 175). This complaint says much about the publishing industry, but is unfair with respect to Wharton. English reviewers were more positive. The volume contains much strong work, including two of her best-known ghost stories, "The Eyes" and "Afterward," both of which depict uprooted and morally compromised Americans. The *Athenaeum* reviewer was right in detecting a raw quality in these stories that indicated a new emotional depth and complexity (*CR* 176). While Wharton was achieving a more sensitive reception in England, Americans were distancing themselves from a writer whose insight into their foibles was too close to the bone.

WAR AND ITS AFTERMATH

The war only briefly interrupted Wharton's story writing and was her subject in "Coming Home," first published in *Scribner's Magazine* in December 1915, a story that exploits what turned out to be a short-lived market interest in the European conflict. Partly intended to heighten U.S. awareness of French suffering, it traces the relationship between a wounded French aristocrat, Réchamp, who is worried about the fate of his home and family, and an American ambulance driver, dramatizing the displacements of war and the difficulties of maintaining personal integrity in times of crisis. It was included in *Xingu and Other Stories*, published by Scribner's and Macmillan in 1916, although most of these stories were pre-war. Reviewing the volume, Edward E. Hale places Wharton within the tradition of Irving, Hawthorne, and Poe, stating that "supplying the demand has become a trade which anyone can learn, according to the advertisements of the trade schools of the craft," but, for books of short stories, "publishers are likely to decline the latter without thanks" (*CR* 234).

This remark shows the change in publishing in the twenty-five years since Wharton's career began, as she had been a novice when invited by Scribner's to bring out a collection of stories. With more magazines publishing stories and more writers writing them, a further editorial process resulting in book publication, would, in theory, separate the wheat from the chaff. Paradoxically, however, placing stories in a more permanent format than the magazine contradicted the prevailing canonical view of the inherent timeliness and disposability of short stories. It blurred the line between stories and novels, as Faulkner would do in *Go Down, Moses*, implicitly suggesting the interrelatedness of stories within a collection. Considering the profits, however, no publisher, and few authors, worried about this breach of orthodoxy.

In discussions of the U.S. short story from the nineteenth century to today, the genre is often identified as a peculiarly democratic form in that anyone, in theory, with a little time, can read or even write one. In Wharton's stories, however, reviewers on both sides of the Atlantic began to note an anti-democratic trend; the *Spectator*, for example, remarking that "'triumphant democracy' … finds no panegyrist in this fastidious critical writer …" (*CR* 235). Francis Hackett in the *New Republic* remarked that her characters "are not the kind of people with whom you share cracker-jack in a day-coach," and her U.S. scene was limited to the Atlantic seaboard, "using the Alleghenies as a sort of privet hedge" (*CR* 237). In spite of her established reputation, Wharton may have worried about these reviews, for, owing to U.S. tax and the expense of her relief work during the war, she was more dependent on her literary earnings. Although she also published in Britain and France, her main income came from U.S. sales, so she could not afford to alienate that audience.

Wharton continued to divide her time between writing short stories and novels, with many, but not all, of her stories collected in book form every few years. Her rate of story writing abated after the war to about one or two per year, as she put more energy into the broader canvasses of her novels. Between *Xingu* in 1916 and her death in 1937, Wharton would publish four more collections of stories, *Here and Beyond* (1926), *Certain People* (1930), *Human Nature* (1933), and *The World Over* (1936). In 1918, she made Appleton her publisher, although she still placed stories with *Scribner's Magazine*. With lower earnings from stories after the war, she was attracted by the higher fees paid by a wide range of publications. Her stories began appearing in the *Woman's Home Companion*, *Pictorial Review*, *Red Book*, *Ladies' Home Journal*, *Saturday Evening Post*, *Story-Teller*, and *Liberty*. These "popular" organs had a much broader circulation than the elite magazines with which she launched her story-writing career. Many of them also had a predominantly female readership and contained other features on what were thought to be exclusively women's interests. The *Pictorial Review*, for example, which published several Wharton stories in the 1920s, including the ghost stories "Miss Mary Pask" and "Bewitched," began its life as the off-shoot of a dress pattern business.[5]

Some editors were fearful of the moral sensibilities of their readers, and, perhaps more pertinently, their advertisers, particularly with regard to sexual content, and attempted to prescribe story content. Wharton had more trust in her readers than she did in nervous, profit-conscious editors. She knew that formulaic stories that failed to address real concerns would never satisfy for long. She did not, on the whole, write down to her less-elite audiences, and it would be hard to tell, in most cases, from the style or content, whether any particular story first appeared in the prestigious *The Atlantic Monthly* or one of the mass-circulation organs. In *A Backward Glance*, she writes of the opinion of Edwin Godkin, former editor of the New York *Evening Post*, that the choice of articles in U.S. magazines was "determined by the fear of scandalizing a non-existent clergyman in the Mississippi Valley." She resolved, early on, to ignore this "ghostly censor," as much for the sake of other writers less capable of asserting artistic independence as for the sake of her own integrity (*BG* 139–40). The passage of years has demonstrated that her sense of what was marketable surpassed that of many magazine editors, who, in attempting to bend too much to the perceived demands of a particular social and moral authority, endangered the long-term viability of their own periodicals.

THE HOME STRETCH

Shortly before her death in 1937, Wharton finished her last story, "All Souls.'" Published posthumously by Appleton in *Ghosts*, it revisits a theme that Poe made inseparable from the short story: premature burial. It concerns, as did Wharton's first story, an elderly woman whose beloved home is suddenly threatened. Ultimately, Sara Clayburn flees in terror, breaking her widow's pledge: "Here I belong, and here I stay" (*CSII* 799). "All Souls'" is the culmination of the treatment in short story form of a subject that had preoccupied Wharton, and engaged her audiences, from the beginning. "Home" can take many forms, and all the stories about troubled marriages, divorce, ungrateful children, parental tyranny, and vocational crises could be read as variations on this theme. "All Souls'" shows that, right to the end, Wharton was unable to let the subject rest.

Indeed, in the 1930s, the subject took on a new urgency, as troubling political and economic developments meant that few could feel "at home." The markets had also changed, with more demand for writers who were addressing immediate problems, and Wharton, whose stories were subtle and indirect, could no longer be so confident of her place in this new scheme. Even *Scribner's Magazine*, which had ushered Wharton into her career of story writing, was under pressure and would cease publication in 1939, two years after Wharton's death. Politically, artistically, and, even physically, Wharton felt under siege. "I feel about my houses as a crab must about its carapace," she noted in her diary as European politics took a troubling turn in 1934 (Lee 739).

Wharton's last novel, *The Buccaneers*, remained unfinished at her death, and, as she faced failing health and an increasingly alienating international situation, it is possible her world was no longer conducive to novel writing. As Raymond Carver asserted, "a writer should be living in a world that makes sense" to write a novel (Levy 25). The U.S. short story, from its alleged beginning in Poe's anguished life, thrives on instability, and from her late-life troubles, Wharton created in "All Souls'" a triumphant finale to her career that addressed personal, aesthetic, and global concerns. A ghost story in more senses than one, it is proof that Wharton's versatile command could hold sway over the market for stories from beyond the grave, unlike *Scribner's Magazine*, which perished from its inability to adapt. Although Mrs. Manstey, Réchamp, and Sara Clayburn lose their "coigns of vantage," Wharton did not. The much-anthologized "All Souls'" shows that, when other supports fail, the story audience that enabled the start of Wharton's fiction-writing career endures. With the prescience that characterized her professional life, Wharton played, not only the short story markets of her own day, but those of posterity.

NOTES

1. F. L. Mott, *A History of American Magazines, III, 1865–1885* (Cambridge, MA: Harvard University Press, 1938), 5; F. L. Mott, *A History of American Magazines IV, 1885–1905* (Cambridge, MA: Harvard University Press, 1957), 11.
2. A. Levy, *The Culture and Commerce of the American Short Story* (Cambridge: Cambridge University Press: 1993), 32. Subsequent references to this work are included in the text.
3. S. Garrison, *Edith Wharton: A Descriptive Bibliography* (Pittsburgh: University of Pittsburgh Press: 1990), 17.
4. S. Towheed, *The Correspondence of Edith Wharton and Macmillan, 1901–1930* (New York: Palgrave Macmillan, 2007), 1–57.
5. T. Peterson, *Magazines in the Twentieth Century* (Urbana: University of Illinois Press, 1964), 166–67.

PART IV

Arts and Aesthetics

CHAPTER 14

Stage Adaptations of Wharton's Fiction

John Dennis Anderson

Edith Wharton's fiction was adapted for the stage in her lifetime and beyond in the shifting context of a U.S. theater in transition. In 1906, when she collaborated with the playwright Clyde Fitch to adapt *The House of Mirth*, Fitch and the play's producer Charles Frohman were among the ruling elite who controlled the commercial U.S. stage by providing popular stars in often effective but ephemeral plays. Fitch was among a group of successful playwrights who had absorbed the tenets of literary realism espoused by such writers with theatrical aspirations as Henry James and William Dean Howells, as well as playwrights such as James A. Herne and William Gillette.[1] The result was a growing emphasis on realism in commercial theater, even in the context of an audience that demanded laughter, tears, and spectacle – or, in Howells' lapidary phrase to Wharton on the opening night of *The House of Mirth*, "a tragedy with a happy ending" (*BG* 147).

With the rise of the bestseller made possible by advances in book publishing and marketing, theatrical producers turned to popular novels as sources for drama, promising ready-made audiences. Theater historian Glenn Loney identifies 1900 to 1906 as "probably the high-water mark in popularity of dramatized novels," noting that seventy-one were adapted for the New York stage during that time.[2] Canny authors such as Wharton also kept an eye on the bottom line. She earned $15,000 in box office receipts on the New York run of *The Age of Innocence* in 1929, for example, and monitored carefully the $130,000 earned in royalties and box office returns on the dramatizations of *The Old Maid* in 1935 and *Ethan Frome* in 1936.[3]

Stage adaptations of novels are interpretations of the source material. Faithfulness is only one possible criterion to apply in evaluating the results. Stage and performance conventions of the time provide a context in which to view such adaptations. Wharton commented in her foreword to the dramatization of *Ethan Frome* that it was "always a curious, and sometimes a painful, revelation" to see her books "as they have taken shape in other minds," and she imagined "few have had the luck to see the characters they had imagined in fiction transported to the stage without loss or alteration of any sort, without even that grimacing enlargement of gesture and language supposed to be necessary to 'carry' over the footlights."[4]

In spite of Wharton's comment in her memoir that she derived little pleasure from theater, she wrote various plays and fragments, including translating a play at the request of Mrs. Patrick Campbell that was produced in 1902 (Hermann Sudermann's *Es Lebe das Leben* as *The Joy of Living*) and adapting Abbé Prévost's novel *Manon Lescaut* as a stage vehicle for Marie Tempest, later planned for Julia Marlowe, although it was never staged with either actress (Rattray xxix–xxxiii). This essay explores, in addition to the Wharton–Fitch version of *The House of Mirth*, other notable commercial stage adaptations of *The Age of Innocence* (1928), *The Old Maid* (1935), and *Ethan Frome* (1936) in the context of the evolving stage and performance conventions of their times.

Several important figures in the world of professional theater were instrumental in getting Wharton's work to Broadway. Elisabeth Marbury, a pioneering theatrical agent, had represented Wharton in negotiations related to the adaptation of *Manon Lescaut* in 1900–01 and also in those with Fitch, another of Marbury's clients, to adapt *The House of Mirth*. Much later, in February 1921, Marbury worked to negotiate a stage adaptation by the playwright Zoë Akins of *The Age of Innocence*, which never materialized, although Akins would later win the 1935 Pulitzer Prize for drama for her adaptation of Wharton's *The Old Maid*. Wharton had been enthusiastic in 1921 about the prospect of Ellen Olenska in *The Age of Innocence* being played by Doris Keane, an actress mostly known for playing the lead role in Edward Sheldon's long-running hit play *Romance* from 1913 to 1918. Sheldon was a long-time friend of Wharton's former sister-in-law, Mary Cadwalader Jones,[5] and through her, Wharton met Sheldon in 1923 and they became close friends in spite of his severe invalidism. He encouraged a Chicago childhood friend of his, Margaret Ayer Barnes, to adapt *The Age of Innocence* for the stage when they reconnected in 1926. The play was directed in 1928 by Guthrie McClintic as a starring vehicle for his wife Katharine Cornell. McClintic also directed the Akins adaptation of *The Old Maid* in 1935, and it was Edward Sheldon who recommended Ruth Gordon to play Mattie Silver in the 1936 adaptation of *Ethan Frome*.

After Wharton worked to no avail with Frohman and Marbury to have her play adaptation of *Manon Lescaut* produced professionally in 1900–01, Frohman produced Wharton's translation of Sudermann's *Es Lebe das Leben* on Broadway in 1902. In November 1905, Wharton met with Marbury to discuss dramatizing *The House of Mirth*. These connections led to Frohman suggesting to Wharton and Fitch that they should collaborate on a stage adaptation of the novel. Frohman apparently told each that the idea had originated with the other (Loney 28). Wharton acquiesced, flattered that the wildly successful "playwright of the hour" should see the potential in her novel as a play.

Wharton described the division of labor in their collaborative process: Fitch structured the scenario and Wharton wrote all of the dialogue. Fitch was ingenious in condensing and compressing the novel to fit the stage conventions of the period, although he insisted that he was merely "*staging* the *book* so far as was possible," given that the book's "whole drama was *wholly* psychological." He claimed their "one hope" was "to make it as *real* as possible, and as like its source as the two and a half stage hours' traffic would allow."[6]

Cynthia Griffin Wolff points out that the novel itself references contemporary stage conventions, noting the affinities of several characters to recognizable stage types. These include Gus Trenor's links to the low villain of traditional melodrama, Simon Rosedale's origins in the stage Jew, and Lawrence Selden as the *raisonneur* (or voice of reason), "the on-stage apologist for conventional wisdom."[7] More telling, according to Wolff, is the centrality to the plot of a bundle of letters. "Comedy, tragedy, farce, historical pageant, even burlesque: in 1905, the one element that all of these forms were most likely to have in common was a plot that turned upon the concealment, discovery, interception, destruction, or revelation of a letter" ("Masquerade" 266). Thus, in the Wharton–Fitch adaptation, Lily Bart obtains the incriminating love letters of Bertha Dorset to Lawrence Selden in Act One, takes them out of a locked box in Act Three, and burns them in a climactic moment of Act Four. The physical presence of the letters in the play adds visual and dramatic action to a narrative plot device that was stagy even in the novel.

Although Wharton wrote the dialogue, Fitch's sense of theatricality is often evident in the stage "business" (incidental activity performed by an actor for dramatic effect) and the shaping of scenes, creating visual effects as important as the dialogue in conveying subtext. Thus, Fitch's scenario deftly compresses the first ten chapters of the novel into an act that occurs in the single setting of the Trenors' country home, Bellomont. At the end of the act, Fitch has Lily buying Bertha Dorset's letters from a housemaid (who, as in the novel, obtains them while working at Selden's apartment building where she had seen Lily leaving his rooms) when Bertha's cuckolded husband George Dorset interrupts the transaction. Building the act to a suspenseful close, Fitch has Lily invent a lie to explain Dorset recognizing his wife's handwriting on an envelope addressed to Selden. Fitch further heightens the theatricality of Wharton's already stagy plot device.

In her memoir, Wharton noted that in writing the novel she was aware that "a frivolous society can acquire dramatic significance only through what its frivolity destroys. Its tragic implication lies in its power of debasing people and ideals" (*BG* 207). Society's destruction of Lily Bart was thus essential to the drama at the heart of both the novel and the play. Fitch endeavored to do justice to the theme while still providing theatrical touches, especially in Act Two, which includes the *tableaux vivants* at the Wellington Bly home and Gus Trenor tricking Lily into coming to his house afterward. The former scene is cleverly structured so as to provide a backstage view of the action as the *tableaux* are presented upstage. Fitch then adds a significant prop in the form of an expensive fan Gus Trenor has given to Lily and which various characters notice as a visual clue to Lily's compromised connection to Trenor. In the second scene, Fitch also has Selden interrupt Trenor's attempted seduction of Lily to end the act dramatically. Through touches such as these, Fitch heightened the melodramatic aspects of Wharton's plot.

Yet, in a postmortem interview about the play in the *New York Times*, Fitch acknowledged that *The House of Mirth* was a "negative story," as opposed to "book plays" that present thrilling romances or stories of action and adventure and that the experiment had not found an audience (Loney 176). Although the play was well received in an out-of-town tryout in Detroit, when it opened in New York on October 22, 1906, critics pronounced it a failure and it closed after fourteen performances, confirming Howells' opening-night comment that the American public wanted a tragedy with a happy ending.

Wolff notes that the theater of Wharton's day was "remarkably heroine-focused" ("Masquerade" 263), and the next stage adaptation of a Wharton novel largely succeeded on the basis of the leading lady's performance and her costumes. In the spring of 1924, Sheldon suggested Wharton adapt her 1920 novel *The Age of Innocence* as a play, and he made some suggestions as to how she might approach it. Sheldon was a key figure in the transition from romantic melodrama to social realism in the

U.S. theater, realistically depicting slum life in *Salvation Nell* (1908) and treating racial injustice in *The Nigger* (1909) and muckraking politics in *The Boss* (1911). In August 1924, Wharton responded enthusiastically to Sheldon's "admirable scenario" for *The Age of Innocence*: "It is most interesting to me to see how your stage technique remodels mine of the novel, contracting here and pulling out there. ... How I wish you felt like dramatizing the book yourself."[8] Two years later, Sheldon encouraged Barnes to adapt the novel, and when she had drafted a first act, he asked Wharton for dramatic rights and urged Barnes to write the second act. The fledgling playwright was daunted by the prospect, but under Sheldon's sturdy mentorship she proceeded, and even before the play was completely written, Katharine Cornell agreed to play Ellen Olenska.

The Age of Innocence, set in the 1870s Old New York of Wharton's youth, was a period piece that required attention to detail in its *mise en scène*. The intense romanticism of the story is embedded in a highly realistic historical, social, and material milieu. Earlier, in 1921, when Zoë Akins was negotiating to adapt *The Age of Innocence*, Wharton expressed concerns to Minnie Jones about the accuracy of "staging & dressing," insisting on details of the men's moustaches, frock coats, hats, buttonholes, and waistcoats, and, "above all," the avoidance of slang and Americanisms: "If she does not know this ... she will never get the right atmosphere" (*Letters* 439).

Even more problematic for Wharton than such details of costume and dialogue, however, were Barnes and Sheldon's changes in the character of Newland Archer. They felt that to appeal to modern audiences, Archer needed to be more dynamic and less passive. Taking their cue from Teddy Roosevelt (for whom Barnes had campaigned in 1912) and Barnes' grandfather who had fought Boss Tweed and Tammany Hall in New York, they created a new background for Wharton's exemplary Old New Yorker of the 1870s. The new dramatic Newland became, with Custer, a veteran of the Indian Wars in the West who had then returned to New York to fight Tammany Hall as a reform-minded politician and later became a Senator. Barnes reported to Sheldon a conversation with Minnie Jones, who was representing Wharton, in which Jones and Wharton objected to Archer dabbling in "vulgar" political squabbles and "common" Indian fights: "They feel a U.S. Senator is 'very distinguished' so the political career can be left in – just the mud and sweat toned down a bit. Mrs. Jones asked very sweetly, 'Why would Archer have gone to a fireman's ball? It makes him seem very provincial, my dear, to be a crusader. One of the points of the book was that he was very conventional'" (Barnes 154).

According to the unpublished manuscript of the play in the Barnes papers at Bryn Mawr College, Wharton's views did not prevail. In Act One, set at a party where Archer's engagement to May van der Luyden (changed from Welland in the novel) is to be announced, Archer professes to his fiancée's exotic cousin Ellen Olenska his progressive political views before he departs for a political commitment at an Irish firemen's ball. Not knowing about the impending wedding announcement, Ellen warns him to choose a wife who will support him. She teases him about being overdressed for a firemen's ball and about the lilies of the valley earlier placed in his buttonhole by May. Ellen throws away May's flowers and provides him with a gardenia from her corsage just as May enters and reveals to Ellen that she and Archer are engaged.[9]

In addition, Wharton's original Archer and Ellen only veer close to an adulterous sexual liaison, a course abandoned when his wife May reveals to Ellen that she is pregnant in a scene not directly shown. In the play adaptation, however, Archer and Ellen spend a night of passion together in Act Two and – after a curtain drop to suggest the passage of a night – May's conversation with Ellen is enacted. Barnes noted to Sheldon her surprise that Wharton did not comment on Ellen's fall from virtue: "It is apparently immaterial whether or no Archer spends the night with Ellen so long as he doesn't go to the fireman's ball" (Barnes 155).

Barnes felt strongly that she should share playwriting credit with Sheldon, but he insisted that he go unacknowledged. However, Barnes made a point of crediting his contributions in interviews. The play opened on November 27, 1928 in New York and ran for twenty-six weeks, followed by a four-month road tour. Barnes and Sheldon went on to coauthor two subsequent plays, and Barnes won the Pulitzer Prize for fiction in 1931 for her first novel. In her memoir, Katharine Cornell noted that for the role (which was only her third appearance with above-the-title star billing) "Worth made me divine clothes which Barbier designed – my favorite being a gray velvet dress with a bustle and train with which I used a tiny muff covered with Parma violets."[10] The actress-manager's appearance and stellar performance were the most noteworthy aspects of *The Age of Innocence*'s mixture of romance and realism, an unstable combination often noted as a characteristic weakness of Sheldon's body of work.[11]

Wharton had serialized the novella *The Old Maid* in 1922, just two years after *The Age of Innocence*. She spent the first section of the novella setting the scene in Gramercy Park in the 1850s, a generation before the 1870s New York setting of the previous novel. In *The Old Maid*, however, Wharton continues to focus on how a rigid society constrains and silences individuals – in this case resulting in an unwed mother, Charlotte Lovell, masquerading as the old-maid cousin of her illegitimate daughter.

Zoë Akins, who embraced the label of a professional "Broadway playwright," in 1935 made the muted novella into a sentimental melodrama aimed directly at a female audience. According to Alan Kreizenbeck, "The liberties she took created dramatic action out of contemplation and clarity out of ambiguity," giving the adaptation greater emotional power.[12] Writing the play in the middle of the Depression, Akins resisted the trend toward social relevance, declaring in her unpublished memoir that "realism and I have never been friends" (Kreizenbeck 158). The result was a popular success, lasting on Broadway for 205 performances and controversially winning the 1935 Pulitzer Prize over such contenders as Lillian Hellman's *The Children's Hour*, Robert Sherwood's *The Petrified Forest*, and Clifford Odets' *Awake and Sing*. It was an ironic reversal of Wharton's experience with publishing the novella, which several magazines had rejected because the subject of illegitimate children was too unpleasant (Lee 596). Little more than a decade later, critic Brooks Atkinson objected to the play's Pulitzer Prize because it portrayed antiquated social manners and was like "old letters that have been stored in a garret, in the same chest that contains a pair of baby shoes" (Kreizenbeck 181).

In her adaptation, Akins spends the first two of five "episodes" or scenes in the play dramatizing the background Wharton presented through early narrative exposition. Akins shows rather than explains the preparations for Delia Lovell's wedding and the operations of her cousin Charlotte Lovell's day nursery. These episodes simplify the complexity of the main characters and portray Delia as more selfish and Charlotte as more noble than in the novella, making the conflict between the cousins more overt and emotionally charged. The reviews were mixed, although even when making negative judgments the critics tended to couch them in terms that would appeal to Akins' target audience of women seeking "to be put into an emotional state or merely amused" (Kreizenbeck 161–62, 176–77, 156).

The 1936 Broadway production of Wharton's somber 1911 work *Ethan Frome* was also successful, running for 120 performances, and suggesting that by the middle of the Depression, the U.S. public was finally ready for a tragedy without a happy ending. Adapted by the father-son team of Owen and Donald Davis, the play benefited from the senior Davis honing his craft in a long string of successful cheap melodramas leading to two highly praised dramas, *The Detour* (1921) and *Icebound* (1923), the latter of which won the Pulitzer Prize. These two realistic plays, and even more so *Ethan Frome*, as Brenda Murphy notes, demonstrate Owen

Davis' "special gift for showing the relationship between character and milieu" (143).

The *mise en scène* of the play consisted of five sets designed by Jo Mielziner that included the exterior and two interiors of the decrepit farmhouse of Ethan Frome (played by Raymond Massey), a church exterior, and the top of a hill. The stage directions include meticulous details of setting and costume, such as the "Fancy Hero" wood-burning heating stove in the kitchen and the shapeless, nondescript calico dress, high black shoes, and brown stockings of Ethan's wife Zeena (played by Pauline Lord). Murphy points out that the setting provides not just regional local color but reflects "the bleakness, the dreariness, the poverty of [the characters'] existence in clear, objective detail, suggesting a social and economic context for their lives and for the people they have become" (145).

As in Wharton's original, Zeena's red glass pickle dish stands out as a sign of vibrant life against the unrelieved gloom of the setting. When it is accidentally broken as Zeena's young cousin Mattie Silver jerks her hand away from Ethan's touch, the small action takes on the dimension of a catastrophe as vivid as the failed suicides in the sledding incident that climaxes the play. The barely off-stage sledding crash would seem to test the limits of realism in the theater and the stage conventions of Wharton's day, but the Davises' adaptation apparently made it work. In a contemporary theatrical context that has moved beyond such literal-minded realism, it is telling that no major revivals of the Davises' adaptation have been mounted. However, other versions of *Ethan Frome* have been adapted and staged. One that brings into relief changes in theatrical conventions and contexts from those in Wharton's lifetime was by Laura Eason at Chicago's Lookingglass Theatre in spring 2011. The company, which was recognized with the 2011 Regional Theatre Tony Award, often stages literary adaptations. Eason, who adapted and directed *Ethan Frome*, described in an interview how she centered her adaptation on the idea that the play's view of Ethan Frome is the empathetic vision of the narrator. Rather than stripping the story of all narration as in the conventional fourth-wall realism of Wharton's day, Eason kept the narrator on stage throughout the play to make transitions and to reflect Ethan's consciousness as the play moves toward a climax. Also, rather than attempting realistic sets, the production, designed by Dan Ostling, consisted of a skeletal, sculptural suggestion of the Frome house, while the sledding was staged in a stylized rather than realistic way, with Ethan and Mattie leaning toward each other on a spinning platform, turning ever faster, as a film of the bleak landscape played over them.[13]

This brief description of a recent, non-realistic narrative Wharton adaptation highlights by contrast the theatrical conventions that provided the context of the Broadway productions during Wharton's lifetime. Over the thirty-year course of the four adaptations from 1906 to 1936 considered here, the balance gradually shifted from melodramatic to relatively more realistic styles of acting and staging, in spite of some backsliding. Of these adaptations, none has been given a major revival except *The House of Mirth*, perhaps symptomatic of how bound by their original context these adaptations remain and inviting new theatrical idioms in future adaptations.[14]

NOTES

1. B. Murphy, *American Realism and American Drama, 1880–1940* (Cambridge: Cambridge University Press, 1987), 86. Subsequent references to this work are included in the text.

2. G. Loney, "Edith Wharton and *The House of Mirth*: The Novelist Writes for the Theatre," in G. Loney (ed.), *The House of Mirth: The Play of the Novel, Dramatized by Edith Wharton and Clyde Fitch, 1906* (Toronto: Associated University Presses, 1981), 19. Subsequent references to this work are included in the text.

3. Lee 595–96; L. Rattray, "Edith Wharton as Playwright" in L. Rattray (ed.), *The Unpublished Writings of Edith Wharton, Vol. 1: Plays* (London: Pickering & Chatto, 2009), xxvii–l; xlv. Subsequent references to Rattray's work are included in the text.

4. O. Davis and D. Davis, *Ethan Frome: A Dramatization of Edith Wharton's Novel* (New York: Scribner's, 1936), viii.

5. In February 1921, Wharton appointed Jones (known to Wharton as Minnie) in New York as her representative in "theatrical and cinematographic matters" (Lee 594).

6. M. J. Moses and V. Gerson, *Clyde Fitch and His Letters* (Boston: Little Brown, 1924), p. 323.

7. C. G. Wolff, "Lily Bart and Masquerade Inscribed in the Female Mode" in K. Joslin and A. Price (eds.), *Wretched Exotic: Essays on Edith Wharton in Europe* (New York: Peter Lang, 1993), 259–94; 265–66. Subsequent references to this work are included in the text.

8. E. W. Barnes, *The Man Who Lived Twice: The Biography of Edward Sheldon* (New York: Scribner's, 1956), 149.

9. M. A. Barnes, "*The Age of Innocence*: Dramatized from Edith Wharton's Novel," Margaret Ayer Barnes Collection, Bryn Mawr College, n.d. See I-26–27.

10. K. Cornell as told to R. W. Sedgwick, *I Wanted to Be an Actress: The Autobiography of Katharine Cornell* (New York: Random House, 1939), 84–85.

11. L. Jasper, "Edward Sheldon (1886–1946)" in W. W. Demastes (ed.), *American Playwrights 1880–1945: A Research and Production Sourcebook* (Westport, CT: Greenwood, 1995), 388.

12. A. Kreizenbeck, *Zoë Akins: Broadway Playwright* (Westport, CT: Praeger, 2004), 162. Subsequent references to this work are included in the text.

13. L. Eason, "Ethan Frome: Stageplay Adapted from the Novel by Edith Wharton," Draft March 6, 2011, Lookingglass Theatre Company, Chicago, IL, 3; 70–71.

14. The Wharton–Fitch version of *The House of Mirth* was revived with some modifications by dramaturge John Tillinger at the Long Wharf Theatre in New Haven, CT, in 1976, and again with other modifications by Jonathan Bank at the Mint Theater Company in New York in 1998 and published in J. Bank (ed.), *Worthy But Neglected: Plays of the Mint Theater Company* (New York: Granville Press, 2002), 49–95.

CHAPTER 15

Wharton's Writings on Screen

Anne-Marie Evans

On April 23, 1896, just a week before Edith Wharton would mark her eleventh wedding anniversary, the first public screening of a motion picture took place in New York City. Masterminded by Thomas Edison, the event was held at Koster and Bial's Music Hall, and today is marked by a plaque next to Macy's Department Store in Herald Square, which now occupies the original site.[1]

Wharton was witness to many technological and aesthetic developments in the film industry during her lifetime. The popularity of film, however, made her deeply uneasy. Her suspicion that film as a medium was to blame for what she perceived as a general decline in U.S. culture was never as well-articulated as in the much-quoted passage from her 1937 introduction to *Ghosts*, where film is brought to account for its effect on the modern imagination:

[D]eep within us as the ghost instinct lurks, I seem to see it being gradually atrophied by those two world-wide enemies of the imagination, the wireless and the cinema. To a generation for whom everything which used to nourish the imagination because it had to be won by an effort, and then slowly assimilated, is now served up cooked, seasoned, and chopped into little bits, the creative faculty (for reading should be a creative act as well as writing) is rapidly withering, together with the power of sustained attention.[2]

Wharton's enthusiasm for the stage contrasts with her disdain for the screen. She was clearly interested in the aesthetic politics of the public spectacle (think of Lily Bart's trip to the theater in *The House of Mirth*, where seeing and being seen are paramount) but this did not apply to film. Considering Wharton's interests in art and design, both essentially visual mediums, her perception of film as in opposition to the imagination is remarkable. Early films were also often associated with vaudeville (Mintz and Roberts 10), a relationship that might have influenced Wharton's disapproval.[3] Although her letters reveal that she did watch a silent film in 1914 when in Spain with Walter Berry (*Letters* 325), there is no evidence that she ever attended a screening of an adaptation of her work (Lewis 7).

By 1896, when the first public screening of a motion picture took place, Wharton had bought a house in New York at 884 Park Avenue and was working on *The Decoration of Houses* with Ogden Codman, Jr., inspired by her refurbishment of Land's End, her house in Newport. At the same time as Wharton was considering space, color and the niceties of good taste, the motion picture industry was developing at an accelerated rate, and began to develop business regulations and a more organized structure. By 1909, the success of motion pictures was such that Edison and other moviemakers collaborated to form the Motion Picture Patents Company, marking the beginning of distribution legislation (Mintz and Roberts 10).

Despite her misgivings, Wharton acted on her Appleton editor Rutger Jewett's advice and sold the rights to three of her works in 1918, earning her $22,000.[4] The film industry at this time, led by Jewish New Yorker Adolph Zukor, who became one of the founding members of Paramount Pictures, was beginning to increase its power and influence (Mintz and Roberts 11). Throughout the 1920s and 1930s, the "Big Five" of film companies emerged: Paramount, Warner Brothers, RKO, 20th Century-Fox, and (MGM) Loews (Mintz and Roberts 12). Of the five leading companies, three would produce film versions of Wharton's novels over the next twenty-year period.

The results of the 1918 deal are the three "lost" silent films based on Wharton's writings: *The House of Mirth* (1918) released by Metro, *The Glimpses of the Moon* (1923) produced by Paramount, and *The Age of Innocence* (1924) released through Warner Brothers. It is, sadly, no great surprise that these early features are no longer available for viewing in the twenty-first century. Martin Scorsese's nonprofit organization The Film Foundation, established in 1990 to help preserve and restore early film, estimates that more than 90 percent of films made before 1929 have been lost.[5] The only information retained about these lost films is the basic details of cast and crew, but even these minor details can reveal much about the developing film culture of the early part of the twentieth century.

The 1918 version of *The House of Mirth* was directed by Albert Capellani, an established director and screenwriter. He cowrote the film's script with June Mathias, and cast Katherine Harris Barrymore in the lead role. Wharton's story of Lily Bart, an aging society beauty whose awakening moral awareness parallels her social downfall, is a rich text for filmmakers, laden with what would become Wharton's customary attention to detailed observation and psychological insight. William Larsen's discovery of a synopsis of the film in the magazine *Picture Play* reveals a major change in the story's ending, with Lawrence Selden arriving at Lily's boarding house with a doctor in time to save her life.[6] This new, happy ending entirely subverts Wharton's deliberately bleak finale; R. W. B. Lewis famously recounts that when the final installment was published, one woman immediately telegraphed her friend with the news, "Lily Bart is dead" (Lewis 152). The timely arrival of Selden in the 1918 film version can surely only have infuriated Wharton, who had insisted that Lily die at the end of the earlier stage version she wrote in collaboration with Clyde Fitch.

The Glimpses of the Moon in 1923 had a script written by F. Scott Fitzgerald that was never actually used, and starred Bebe Daniels, Nita Naldi and Maurice Costello, who were all well-established silent movie stars of the period (Marshall 17). As with *The House of Mirth*, *The Glimpses of the Moon* was a serious production with an experienced and popular cast. It ran to seven reels, one more than Capellani's, and had a respectable budget and a high-profile image. In 1924, the third lost film was released, *The Age of Innocence*. Only four years after the novel's publication, this production demonstrates Wharton's popularity and the public impact of her Pulitzer Prize for literature in 1921. The film starred Beverly Bayne as Ellen Olenska and Elliot Dexter as Newland Archer, and was directed by Wesley Ruggles.

The production of these three films within a six-year period when the film industry was still relatively young demonstrates Wharton's reputation as a bestselling author. Mintz and Roberts estimate that during the 1920s, 50 million people went to see a film every week. The technical development that allowed a pre-recorded soundtrack to be added to the moving image more than doubled this figure, with a probable 110 million people going to the movies every week by 1929 (Mintz and Roberts 16). Producers recognized that there was an audience for Wharton's work on screen, and this was particularly significant in a period when her fiction was considered by some to be old-fashioned; and film rights offered substantial financial returns for Wharton and many of her contemporaries. It must have been a shock for Wharton when Edith M. Hull's desert romance *The Sheik*, which famously sports a heroine that falls in love with her rapist-hero (one cannot imagine that Wharton would have had much time for this story), knocked *The Age of Innocence* from the top of the bestseller list (Boswell 65–66). Hull's novel, quickly translated into a film with

Rudolph Valentino cast in the title role, and a rape scene that is implied but not depicted, went on to become one of Paramount Pictures' most successful screen ventures. Hull produced the sequel, *Son of the Sheik*, in 1925, which followed almost exactly the same capture and rape plot as the first, and United Artists made the novel into another hugely successful silent film, *Sons of the Sheik* (1926). The release of the sequel unexpectedly coincided with Valentino's sudden death, and the subsequent publicity made the film even more popular with audiences eager to see his final performance, resulting in the displacement of Archer and Olenska's delicate love affair by dubious shenanigans in Hull's fictional desert.

In 1929, Wharton's novel *The Children* (1928) was reimagined on film as *The Marriage Playground*, produced by Paramount and directed by Lothar Mendes. Ignoring the dark complexities of the original novel, in which middle-aged Martin Boyne falls for attractive teenager, Judith Wheater, the film version dramatically shortens the age gap between the two leads. Linda Costanzo Cahir notes that when the film was released, the two lead actors, Fredric March and Mary Brian, were only two years apart in age.[7] In Wharton's novel, which explores issues of abandonment and loneliness, the ever-cautious Boyne is unable to admit his feelings for the lovely Judy, who is determined to keep her younger step-brothers and step-sisters together. Boyne, in a bittersweet ending to the novel, realizes that he must allow Judy to meet a man closer to her own age. This was clearly too nuanced an ending for Paramount, and Wharton's finale is rewritten as a conventional fairy tale of love through the eventual marriage of Judy and Boyne. Even the change in title from *The Children* to *The Marriage Playground* reveals the distinct shift from Wharton's character-driven piece to the film version's dependence on romantic plot.[8]

The 1934 adaptation of *The Age of Innocence* boasted a popular and well-known cast, including John Boles as Newland Archer, and Irene Dunn as Ellen Olenska. The pair had previously starred together two years earlier in the film adaptation of Fannie Hurst's rather scandalous 1931 bestseller, *Back Street*. Hurst's tragic story of Ray Schmidt, who falls in love with a married man, Walter Saxel, offers an intriguing counterpoint to *The Age of Innocence*. In Hurst's melodrama, Ray chooses to become Walter's mistress rather than marry a man whom she does not love and live a "respectable" life, and the novel charts the consequences of her decision over the next twenty years, until she is eventually left penniless and alone. Hurst rewrites the "fallen woman" stereotype, just as Wharton did in *The House of Mirth* twenty-six years previously. Ray's choice of love and independence outside the confines of marriage highlights Walter's innate selfishness; she can only ever be a "back street" wife, as children and respectability are unobtainable. The choice, therefore, to repeat the winning combination of Boles and Dunn (who had played Walter and Ray in *Back Street*) in *The Age of Innocence* represents a clever casting choice. As Archer and Olenska, they once again play romantic partners, but the emphasis is instead on non-consummation and renunciation. It is Newland's relationship with Ellen that teaches him the world he lives in is emotionally artificial, just as Ray gradually realizes that Walter's affections can never translate beyond the parameters of their secret relationship. The original 1934 poster for *The Age of Innocence* advertises the names of the stars well above the film's title, and reveals that the repeated screen pairing of Boles and Dunn meant another respectable box office return for RKO Radio Pictures. Directed by Philip Moeller, it was an expensive production, as the rare stills of the film reveal, although Cahir describes it as "void of any genuine emotion" (219).

After the success of *The Age of Innocence*, Bette Davis starred in *The Old Maid* in 1939, which was based on Wharton's novella from 1924. *The Old Maid* had been translated into a Pulitzer Prize-winning play of the same name by Zoe Akins in 1935, and the screenplay is based on Akins' script. Released two years after Wharton's death, this was the last major adaptation of her work for more than fifty years. By the time she starred as Charlotte Lovell in *The Old Maid*, Davis had already won two Academy Awards for *Dangerous* (1935) and *Jezebel* (1938). Throughout the 1930s, Davis was one of Warner Brothers' most bankable stars, and the decision to cast her as the lead in *The Old Maid* is unsurprising. The film, however, takes liberties with the original text, moving the action from the 1850s to the 1860s, which Marshall has suggested was done to capitalize on the popularity of the same year's big release, *Gone With the Wind* (Marshall 18), and allows for Clem Spender to be rewritten as a war hero. As the storyline involves illegitimacy, Wharton had faced initial opposition from her publishers, and Warner Brothers faced a similar predicament with the film version (Cahir 217). The Board of Censorship of Motion Pictures was established in 1909 and sought to review any potential on-screen immorality and impropriety. There was a history of lobbying from religious groups throughout the rise of the film industry and by 1934 the "Breen Office" had been created to read every script and decide on its moral values. In *The Old Maid*, this meant that a kiss between Clem and Charlotte had to be carefully orchestrated so as not to condone pre-marital relations (Cahir 218). This constraint on the film contributes to Lisa Weckerle's argument that what was subversive in Wharton's text is entirely lost in the film version that "reinterprets and reinvents the story as a cautionary tale, one that warns against the perils of unmarried women."[9]

Despite the success of *The Old Maid* in 1939, and perhaps because of the decline in Wharton's literary reputation after her death in 1937, there were no more film adaptations of Wharton's work until the 1990s. *The Children* (1990), with a screenplay cowritten by playwright Timberlake Wertenbaker, is a dark, art house version of Wharton's text and stars Ben Kingsley as John Boyne. One of the criticisms of the film is that it is too literal and too faithful an adaptation with no allowances for imaginative cinematic flair, "a movie that is frozen in fatigue" (Cahir 215). Three years later, *Ethan Frome* (1993) was directed and adapted by John Madden. Frome is played by Liam Neeson, Zeena by Joan Allen, and Mattie by Patricia Arquette. Although largely faithful to Wharton's text, this adaptation includes the consummation of Ethan and Mattie's relationship, adding an incongruous and unnecessary sex scene.

However, it was Martin Scorsese's adaptation of *The Age of Innocence* (1993) that brought Wharton's fiction most publicity. The film was an unusual choice for Scorsese, as he is best known for his dark, violent, and gritty portrayals of U.S. life in films such as *Taxi Driver* (1976), *Raging Bull* (1980) and *Goodfellas* (1990). The drawing rooms and social soirees of Old New York seem a world away from the tales of organized crime and poverty that traditionally feature in his films; Roger Ebert has commented that the very titles of Scorsese's earlier films "are a rebuke to the age of innocence."[10] Vincent Canby's review of the film for the *New York Times* stated that the film was "gorgeously uncharacteristic" for Scorsese, who also cowrote the screenplay.[11] The film is a stylish adaptation with impressive production values that bring 1870s New York startlingly to life, and has a high caliber cast, elegant costumes and sumptuous sets. Scene setting proved crucial for the success of the overall look of the film, and the artwork of John Singer Sargent and James Tissot were used as sources for the set design. The production designer, Dante Fernetti, stated to Scorsese that three elements were vital for the film's sets (of which there were sixty-five): color, artwork and food, but this attention to surfaces and finery does not eclipse the performances.[12] Interestingly, Scorsese reverses Wharton's physical descriptions of May Welland and Ellen Olenska by casting blonde Michelle Pfeiffer as Olenska and dark-haired Winona Ryder as May. Daniel Day-Lewis excels as Archer, and is surrounded by an imposing supporting cast including Richard E. Grant, Miriam Margolyes, Jonathan Pryce and Robert Sean Leonard. This adaptation also uses a narrator (played by Joanne Woodward) to propel the narrative, which lends a sense of gravitas to the occasion while simultaneously neatly underscoring the importance of the narrative voice in Wharton's novels.

The screenplay utilizes much of Wharton's language, and Jay Cocks, who cowrote the screenplay with Scorsese, relates that there were early concerns about this decision. There was an anxiety that Wharton's complex language and rich dialogue would not translate to the screen (perhaps another reason for the use of a narrator) and that it would be a problem for the actors to learn. However, as Cocks reveals, "The actors … cherished the language; the confidence they drew from the rhythm and shading of the novel's dialogue seemed to anchor them" (Scorsese and Cocks xv). The film was almost universally praised and went on to win several awards. Miriam Margolyes won a British Academy Award for best Supporting Actress for her performance as matriarch Mrs. Manson Mingott, and the film also won an Academy Award for Gabriella Pescucci for Best Costume Design. The film won eleven international awards in total, and was nominated for a further seventeen (including an Oscar nomination for Best Supporting Actress for Winona Ryder, who lost out to the eleven year old Anna Paquin for *The Piano*).

In 2000, Terence Davies released his version of *The House of Mirth*, starring Gillian Anderson, who was at the time best known from her role as Agent Scully in the cult TV show, *The X Files*. The film was a coproduction between the United States and the United Kingdom and has generated considerable interest among Wharton scholars.[13] Augusta Rohrbach argues that the casting of Anderson is pivotal to Lily's central and increasingly isolated role. By continuously emphasizing Lily's sensuality and innate sexiness, Davies' intent is to show how none of Lily's potential husbands are worthy of her.[14] This is a film that places Lily's body at the center of the narrative. In contrast to the inadequate men, the female characters are all more than worthy foes. Laura Linney plays *femme fatale* Bertha Dorset with spiteful relish; she is jealous of Lily's beauty and calculates her rival's public downfall with a smile. Controversially, Davies conflates two female characters, Gerty Farish and Grace Stepney (played by Jodhi May). In Davies' version, Grace, like Gerty in the novel, is in love with Selden. In the film, this directly relates to Grace's refusal to financially support Lily, and makes her, as Rohrbach suggests, "the most repugnant character in the film" (23). Davies' use of framing and art (similar to Scorsese's in *The Age of Innocence* but on a much more modest budget) is particularly insightful, and the opening of the film, where the viewer sees Lily's curvaceous silhouette amid the bustle and smoke of Grand Central Station, is perhaps the film's most striking image. As Boswell suggests,

"Before we hear a word of dialogue or see any other character on screen, we have been given enough visual signs to anticipate Lily's fate: the clock is ticking, the schedules are set, and Lily Bart, pinned alone under a massive structure, has been framed" (Boswell 135). The final scene of Selden's discovery of the dead Lily forms a still-life image that deliberately echoes the earlier *tableau vivant* centerpiece, where Davies replaced Wharton's detail that Lily appears as Joshua Reynolds' *Mrs. Lloyd* – a portrait that resonates with the novel's themes of ownership and female identity – with Watteau's *Summer*, which Rohrbach suggests is a more sexually explicit choice (24). The film was nominated for thirteen international awards and won seven, including a Best Actress prize for Gillian Anderson at the British Independent Film Awards.

Adaptations of Wharton's work have also been successful on the small screen. *Ethan Frome* was filmed for U.S. television in 1960, and starred Sterling Hayden, Julie Harris and Clarice Blackburn (Marshall 19). There was a series of three Wharton dramas produced by the Public Broadcasting System in 1981. The first offered a biographical retelling of Wharton's life, starring Kathleen Widdoes. There was a televised version of *The House of Mirth*, with Geraldine Chaplin as Lily and William Atherton as Selden. Finally, a version of *Summer*, directed by Dezso Magyar, completed the trio of films, starring a sixteen-year-old Diane Lane as Charity Royall. Two years later, Granada Television filmed three of Wharton's ghost stories, "The Lady's Maid's Bell," "Afterward," and "Bewitched," and all three were later broadcast in the United States. Wharton's unfinished novel *The Buccaneers* was filmed by the BBC in 1995, with screenwriter Maggie Wadey using Wharton's plot outline as a guideline for finishing the story (Marshall 20). In 1999, there was a made for television version of *The Reef* (1912), and this starred Sela Ward as Anna Leath, Timothy Dalton as Charles Darrow, and Alicia Witt as Sophy Viner. Repackaged with the title of *Passion's Way*, the film employs a voiceover from Anna throughout, adding her imaginings of Sophy and Darrow's affair, and rewrites the ending to avoid Wharton's original ambiguity by clearly showing Anna's decision to reunite with Darrow.

Considering that she once cited cinema as one of the "two world-wide enemies of the imagination," it is noticeable that in Wharton's later fiction she references film more frequently. Sophy Viner wants to be an actress (there is also, of course, more than a hint from Wharton linking acting to prostitution); in *Summer* (1917), Charity Royall goes to watch a silent film in Nettleton, and in *Twilight Sleep* (1927) the "movies" are referred to several times, and Rudolph Valentino is mentioned by name. Despite her misgivings about film as a medium, Wharton recognized film's power as a metaphor and contemporary reference for her readers. The politics of sight, of looking, observing, and watching, which film naturally engages with, continued to interest Wharton throughout her career. This is perhaps best illustrated by a scene from one of her earlier novels; Lily Bart's participation in the *tableau vivant* allows Wharton to explore the crucial gap between how Lily perceives herself (as triumphant), and how she is perceived by society (as scandalous). Sight, spectatorship and performance all occupy central roles in the narrative; Wharton may not have liked the movies, but she frequently explored the concept of the visual in her fiction. The cinematic versions of her work have been many and varied. From the early silents to opulent Hollywood productions and new, intertextual reimaginings of her work, all offer new ways of exploring, reconsidering and engaging with Wharton's fiction. Recent reports suggest that Ben Stiller is soon to direct a horror film called *The Mountain* based on *Summer* (one presumes this must be very loosely based).[15] Wharton, it seems, still has a place in Hollywood.

NOTES

1. S. Mintz and R. Roberts, *Hollywood's America: Twentieth-Century America Through Film* (New York: Brandywine Press, 2001), 8. Subsequent references to this work are included in the text.
2. E. Wharton, "Preface," *The Ghost Stories of Edith Wharton* (New York: Charles Scribner's Sons, 1937), 7–11; 8–9.
3. It was not until the 1910s that the middle classes started to frequent picture houses; previously it had been a predominantly working-class activity (Mintz and Roberts 15).
4. P. A. Boswell, *Edith Wharton on Film* (Carbondale: Southern Illinois University Press, 2007), 85. Subsequent references to this work are included in the text.
5. The Film Foundation, 1990, www.film-foundation.org.
6. W. B. Larsen, "A New Lease on Life: Cinematic Adaptations of Five Edith Wharton Novels," unpublished dissertation, University of Tennessee (1995), 59. Quoted in S. Marshall, "Edith Wharton on Film and Television: A History and Filmography," *Edith Wharton Review*, 13.2 (Spring 1996), 15–26; 17. Subsequent references to Marshall's essay are included in the text.
7. L. Costanzo Cahir, "Wharton and the Age of Film" in C. J. Singley (ed.) *A Historical Guide to Edith Wharton* (Oxford: Oxford University Press, 2003), 211–28; 214. Subsequent references to this work are included in the text.
8. There was also a film version of Wharton's short story "Bread Upon the Waters" released as *Strange Wives* in 1935. Sadly, this film is also lost and very little is known beyond some of the production details.

9. L. Weckerle, "Taming the Transgressive: A Feminist Analysis of the Film Adaptation of *The Old Maid*," *Edith Wharton Review*, 20.1 (Spring 2004), 13–19; 14.

10. R. Ebert, *The Age of Innocence* (September 17, 1993), www.rogerebert.suntimes. com/apps/pbcs.dll/article?AID=/19930917/REVIEWS/309170301/1023.

11. V. Canby, "*The Age of Innocence*; Grand Passions and Good Manners," *New York Times* (September 17, 1993), www.nytimes.com/1993/09/17/movies/review-film-the-age-of-innocence-grand-passions-and-good-manners. html?pagewanted=all.

12. M. Scorsese and J. Cocks, *The Age of Innocence, A Portrait of the Film*, ed. Robin Standefer (New York: Newmarket Press, 1993), xii. Subsequent references to this work are included in the text.

13. A. Higson, *English Heritage, English Cinema: Costume Drama since 1980* (Oxford: Oxford University Press, 2003), 4.

14. A. Rohrbach, "Sexing the Lily: Shadows and Darkness in Terence Davies' *House of Mirth*," *Edith Wharton Review*, 20.1 (Spring 2004), 19–25; 21. Subsequent references to this work are included in the text.

15. O. Williams, "Ben Still Ascends *The Mountain*, Directing a Literary Horror Story," *Empire* (October 21, 2011), www.empireonline.com/news/story. asp?NID=32281.

CHAPTER 16

Visual Arts

Emily J. Orlando

As Undine Spragg of *The Custom of the Country* uses her French husband's connections to grant her next spouse a private viewing of an Ingres painting, Wharton's narrator discloses that "a year ago she had never heard of the painter, and did not, even now, remember whether he was an Old Master or one of the very new ones whose names one hadn't had time to learn" (*CC* 561). Ascending the social ladder, Undine "acquire[s] as much of the jargon as a pretty woman needs to produce the impression of being well-informed" (*CC* 561). A dilettante-ish, acquisitive interest in art, from which not even the well-read Newland Archer of *The Age of Innocence* is exempt, evidently was typical of Wharton's age and leisure class. Wharton knew well the difference between an Old Master and a nineteenth-century French painter. Her writings reveal a life-long interest in and remarkably vast knowledge of the visual arts, and art history provides one of the richest contexts for appreciating her work. In the gentleman's library of her father, she read art historians and critics Anna Jameson, Franz Kugler, and John Ruskin. As a young woman she studied Sir Joshua Reynolds' *Discourses on Art* and carried the books of Vernon Lee with her on trips to Italy. Wharton's close friendships with Lee, Charles Eliot Norton, Bernard and Mary Berenson, Kenneth Clark, Egerton Winthrop, and Royal Cortissoz afforded her access to the visual arts by way of their conversations and collections. As Hermione Lee notes, "Three of her pall-bearers, Metman, Gillet and Clark, would be museum directors" (Lee 702). In her travel writings, she refers with dexterity to such Italian Renaissance artists as Bellini, Carpaccio, Botticelli, Botticini, Piero di Cosimo, Signorelli, and Romanino. She admired the Carracci and revered Tiepolo, Longhi, and Guardi.[1] While it might be said that Wharton's heart was with Italian painting and sculpture, a close examination of her career suggests an engagement with visual culture extending well beyond Italian art in general and the Renaissance in particular.

Reflecting on her early years viewing art across Italy, Spain, France, Germany, and England, Wharton speaks of her tendency to see "the visible world as a series of pictures, more or less harmoniously composed" and of her desire "to make the picture prettier" (*LI* 185). As a teenager, she spent "rapturous hours" making the "memorable acquaintance" of several paintings at London's National Gallery (*LI* 202). Viewing Titian, Leonardo, and Giorgione at the Louvre, Wharton was overtaken by "all the great waves of the sea of Beauty" (*LI* 202). She relishes the happy memories of spending hours at San Giorgio dei Schiavoni in Venice, dwelling for the first time on the tomb of Ilaria del Carretto at Lucca, and deciphering the frescoes at Santa Maria Novella in Florence (*LI* 203). Having lived a number of her childhood years in Rome and Florence, she was engulfed in and absorbed by European art, architecture, and landscapes.

The writings of Ruskin – the preeminent Victorian art critic whose influence is felt in the works of William Morris, William Holman Hunt, Walter Pater, Oscar Wilde, and W. B. Yeats – helped Wharton process her early exposure to the European scene. Describing her discovery of the formidable art historian in her father's library, Wharton notes that Ruskin's prose restored to her "the image of the beautiful Europe [she] had lost" and awakened in her "the habit of precise visual observation" (*LI* 195). She acknowledges the "incomparable service" his work did for her developing aesthetic (*LI* 195). Ruskin's *Stones of Venice* and *Mornings in Florence* endowed Wharton with what she called "a sense of organic relation, which no other books attainable by me at the time could possibly have conveyed" (*LI* 203). His *Modern Painters* gave Wharton the language with which to analyze and critique visual culture.

Wharton did not, however, always agree with Ruskin's teachings. In *The Decoration of Houses*, she and Ogden Codman, Jr. criticize the great master for compromising symmetry and balance in design. Although conceding that Ruskin's value as "a guide through the byways of art" is unparalleled, they note that "as a logical exponent of the causes and effects of the beauty he discovers, his authority is certainly open to question" (*DH* 33). In *Italian Backgrounds*, Wharton takes issue with Ruskin for steering travelers away from eighteenth-century European art. This was an oversight she could not forgive (*IB* 110). Wharton herself harbored a "secret weakness" for the very traditions Ruskin and other art historians had summarily dismissed (*IB* 110).

Wharton, for example, validates the sculptor Gian Lorenzo Bernini as the "genius" of the Baroque style (*IB* 185). She argues that thoughtful students who consider Bernini's historical context will identify him as "the natural interpreter of that sumptuous *bravura* period" that witnessed the blending of ecclesiasticism and a growing esteem for nature and country life (*IB* 185). Wharton was unusual in her enthusiasm and respect for art of the eighteenth century. In fact, she locates in Michelangelo's Sistine Chapel frescoes and his statue of Moses in San Pietro in Vincoli the seeds of both Bernini and Tiepolo, "however much the devotees of Michael Angelo may resent the tracing of such a lineage" (*IB* 182). Wharton had little patience for critics who failed to recognize the extent to which the grandeur of the Renaissance paved the way for the drama of the Baroque. In suggesting a shared pedigree between Bernini, whose work figures prominently in the short story "The Duchess at Prayer," and the larger-than-life Michelangelo, Wharton not only was working against the grain, but was also ahead of her time.

For Giambattista Tiepolo, eighteenth-century painter of the Venetian Baroque, Wharton reserved particularly high praise. She describes with reverence Tiepolo's ceiling frescoes in Venice, notwithstanding that the guidebooks disapprove of "an undue admiration of Tiepolo" (*IB* 195) – if they even mention him at all – and that Ruskin had relegated the artist to the "Grotesque Renaissance." Reynolds, whose *Discourses* were profoundly important to Wharton, also dismissed Tiepolo when he denigrated Venetian art as something that overly appealed to the senses and was thus morally suspect. Quoting Shakespeare's Macbeth, Sir Joshua suggested the art of Venice ultimately signified nothing.[2] As art historian Rosella Mamoli Zorzi notes, because of the influence of Reynolds and later Ruskin, and in light of a general disregard for eighteenth-century works, Tiepolo had few fans in the nineteenth century (Zorzi 213). It was only after the *fin-de-siècle* attitude of "art for art's sake" and the eventual reassessment of Ruskin that eighteenth-century art in general, and Tiepolo in particular, received their due. Wharton, greatly inspired by Vernon Lee's *Studies of the Eighteenth Century in Italy*, admired Tiepolo at a time when Henry James and Berenson could only express a limited appreciation of the artist's contributions. She recognizes Tiepolo – whose name, she asserts, "is familiar to the cultivated minority of travelers" (*IB* 199) – as a logical descendant of Titian and Veronese, a claim that to many would have sounded blasphemous. She suggests that while Tiepolo's use of color may pale in comparison with the brilliant golds of the Renaissance, his work restores the lines, the types, and the majesty of the Venetian sixteenth century. Paolo Veronese's "Venice Enthroned" in the Palazzo Ducale is, to her mind, the "direct forbear" of Tiepolo's paintings of the Virgin Mary and of Cleopatra (*IB* 199). (Readers of *The*

House of Mirth will recall Gerty Farish's dismissal, in the *tableaux vivants* scene, of Veronese's "dreadfully fat" women.) In *Italian Backgrounds*, Wharton mentions Tiepolo more than a dozen times, extolling especially the virtues of his frescoes in Venice's Church of the Gesuati, which depict Saint Dominic receiving the rosary (Figure 1). Tiepolo's ceiling at the Scalzi church, later decimated by a bomb in 1915, is featured prominently in *The Glimpses of the Moon*, while in *The House of Mirth* Lily Bart considers modeling her *tableau vivant* on Tiepolo's Cleopatra in the home of the moneyed but unrefined Wellington Brys who boast a ballroom ceiling fashioned after Veronese.[3] Tactful allusions to Italian art appear throughout Wharton's fiction.

After marrying in 1885, the Whartons made annual pilgrimages to Italy and Edith's command of art led her to a major discovery concerning Italian sculpture. During a visit to Florence, she trekked to the country to investigate a group of large terra-cottas depicting Christ's passion at the San Vivaldo Monastery (*IB* 86). Originally, Berenson and others had ascribed the figures to the seventeenth-century sculptor Gonnelli, but the attribution was out of step with Wharton's understanding of Italian art. Studying the design of the hands, arrangement of figures, draperies, and facial expressions, Wharton detected the influence of the fifteenth century. Further, the glazed moldings and the colors adorning the chapel ceilings seemed to suggest a compelling link to the later school of the della Robbias (*IB* 100–01). Wharton was particularly taken with "Lo Spasimo," which depicts the Virgin Mary swooning at the sight of Christ bearing the cross (Figure 2). Wharton locates clues in the composition of "Lo Spasimo" that confirm her suspicion of the faulty attribution. She explains that inaccurately ascribing the sculptures to a later period effectively relegated them to obscurity, in light of prevailing tastes for early Italian art. With the help of the director of the Royal Museums in Florence, she correctly identified the figures as the work of Giovanni della Robbia (1469–1529). Wharton basked in "the rare sensation of an artistic discovery" (*IB* 105).

For Wharton, a love of Italian art is interchangeable with a love of Italy. She conceived of Italy as art in itself – as a kind of "great illuminated book" that never ceases to enlighten and reward its "real lovers" (*IB* 179). Describing a Romanino painting in a church in Brescia, she contemplates, with a pang in her heart, the countless beautiful objects ripped from their native soil simply to adorn the overcrowded walls of the moneyed art collector (*IB* 37). Here, Wharton expresses her disdain at the U.S. leisure-class habit of assembling works of the Old Masters as

Figure 1: Giambattista Tiepolo (1696–1770). Saint Dominic institutes the Rosary.
Chiesa dei Gesuati, Venice, Italy. Photo credit: Scala/Art Resource, NY.

Figure 2: della Robbia (school) (15th–16th CE), The Swooning of Mary. Painted terra-cotta group. S. Vivaldo, Montaione, Italy. Photo credit: Alinari/Art Resource, NY.

signifiers of status. Consumption so conspicuous is critiqued in the *nouveau riche* examples of Undine Spragg and Elmer Moffatt, who, Wharton suggests, are incapable of appreciating the sublime in art.

Wharton's distaste for the art of her native country, and for much of the art displayed in the homes of wealthy Americans, was as strong as her esteem for that of Italy. The prevailing taste among the Americans of Wharton's class, at the time of her youth, was for copies of didactic

European masterpieces. She discloses, rather tongue-in-cheek, that the society whose company her parents kept "did not, perhaps, profit much by the artistic and intellectual advantages of European travel" (*BG* 62). As a product of her class, time, and Europeanized upbringing, Wharton was unable to appreciate or even respect U.S. art. She derided the U.S. art in the homes of her parents' friends. On seeing John Trumbull's paintings in the Capitol Rotunda, which depict her great-grandfather, Wharton observed, evidently with a cringe, "I was vaguely sorry to have any one belonging to me represented in those still old-fashioned pictures, so visibly inferior to the battle scenes of Horace Vernet and Detaille" (*BG* 8–9). She wrote in a 1903 letter to Sally Norton of her difficulty acclimating to the U.S. scene after having been in Italy: "The tastes I am cursed with are all of a kind that cannot be gratified here, & I am not enough in sympathy with our 'gros public' to make up for the lack on the aesthetic side" (*Letters* 84). As Katherine Joslin and Alan Price have noted, "In Europe, American exotics could gratify their glass-house refinements by placing themselves in close proximity to aesthetically satisfying art, architecture, even urban and rural landscapes pruned into tasteful designs."[4] In the United States, Wharton found herself "an exile," disconnected from everything (*LI* 192).

Wharton's work evidences a close acquaintance and tacit displeasure with nineteenth-century visual art and particularly the paintings of the Pre-Raphaelites. This short-lived, profoundly influential British collective enjoyed a renaissance in the years when Wharton was writing fiction. From its inception in 1848, the Pre-Raphaelite Brotherhood (PRB) was united as a reaction against the teaching of the Royal Academy, which advocated an imitation of the Old Masters. Rejecting the art of Raphael, the Pre-Raphaelites sought to reinvigorate painting by locating a more authentic origin, which they found in medieval art and the art of the early Italian Renaissance (pre-Raphael). The movement was led in its first generation by Dante Gabriel Rossetti, Hunt, and John Everett Millais, and, a decade later, by Edward Burne-Jones and Morris, artists who applied the tenets of the PRB to illustrated books and interior design. Ruskin was an early champion and he and Rossetti appear as characters in Wharton's *False Dawn*, which, set in the 1840s, documents the PRB's preference for the early Renaissance.[5] Although the original Brotherhood lasted only until 1853, its influence on art was felt through the 1920s and was particularly embraced by Wilde and the Aesthetic movement of the 1890s.

Notwithstanding the Pre-Raphaelite objective of subverting convention, the movement proved to be backward looking rather than forward

thinking. Indeed, the painters ultimately committed the artistic sins
they had vehemently protested, as Pre-Raphaelite work increasingly replicated formulaic, artificial representations of women. Wharton's writings are peppered with overt references to Rossetti and subtle allusions
to his best-known model-lovers Elizabeth (Lizzie) Siddall and Jane
Morris. Wharton repeatedly illuminates the extent to which PRB paintings depict women as expiring muses, drowning tragediennes, martyred
saints, reclining dreamers, or otherwise disempowered damsels. Millais'
"Ophelia" and Rossetti's "Beata Beatrix," for which Lizzie Siddall posed,
offer two illustrative examples. Scores of paintings by such Victorian artists as Albert Moore, Lord Leighton, Homer Watson, Edward Robert
Hughes, John Atkinson Grimshaw, and John William Waterhouse suggest the popularity of this theme.

   In her fiction, Wharton engages the politics of nineteenth-century
visual culture by letting her female subject manage the project of her own
representation, and Lily Bart is a case in point. Wharton's Lily empowers
herself in a triumphant *tableau vivant* of a Sir Joshua Reynolds painting.[6]
Lily fashions her living picture after a portrait of a lady by Reynolds, first
President of the Royal Academy of Art and the artist who dominated the
late eighteenth-century British art scene (Figure 3). Reynolds, as an icon
of the establishment, is the painter the Pre-Raphaelites most despised;
they found his technique artificial and academic. Lily's embodiment of
Reynolds' portrait of (the affianced) Joanna Lloyd is far removed from
the sort of melancholy maiden memorialized by the PRB, who were quite
fashionable at Lily's historical moment, given the turn-of-the-century
opening and immediate success of London's Tate Gallery, which show-
cased British art and became known for its expansive collection of
Pre-Raphaelite paintings. (In fact, the unseemly Gus Trenor calls Lily
a "stunner" – Rossetti's term for a woman so beautiful she ought to be
painted.) Nor does Lily's tableau emulate J. M. Whistler's nameless wan,
waxen women depicted reclining, resting, or reading. Lily as Mrs Lloyd –
with her free-flowing dress, ample bosom, and natural surroundings – is
the picture of health, poise, and liberation.

   Undine Spragg typifies the women of Wharton's later fiction who manage to draw pleasure and power from a culture of display by overseeing
their own representation and making compromises that ensure their survival. Wharton admits us to the artist's studio to see Undine's reincarna-
tion at the hands of the society portraitist named Popple – a veiled John
Singer Sargent, whose friendship Wharton shared with James. Although
Undine's admirer might envision her looking "dead white ... in the cold

Figure 3: Sir Joshua Reynolds (1723–1792) (after) *Portrait of Joanna Lloyd of Maryland*. Musée Cognacq-Jay, Paris, France. Photo credit: Bridgeman-Giraudon/Art Resource, NY.

light," with "the long curves of her neck," and hair "a shadowless rosy gold" (*CC* 118), and thus imagine her as a sort of Pre-Raphaelite stunner, the portrait Undine commissions is closer to the kind of full length for which Sargent was known. Wharton may have had in mind Sargent's "Mrs. Ralph Curtis" when she unveiled Undine's full-length portrait. Like Undine, Mrs. Curtis, a striking beauty with hair "rosy gold," similarly costumed in a "shimmering dress," "faint and shining" and exposing an exquisitely proportioned neck and shoulders, is captured in glistening whites and reds (*CC* 189). Like Sargent's painting of Lisa Colt Curtis, an expatriated U.S. heiress who moved in Wharton's circle, "the full-length portrait of Mrs. Ralph Marvell ... from her lofty easel and her heavily garlanded frame," presents the subject as a formidable hostess ready to "receive" guests into the home (*CC* 188). Both portraits suggest the subject's self-possession as well as her confidence in the power her beauty might purchase.

Throughout the later years of Wharton's career, which coincide with the Jazz Age, art tastes were again transforming and Wharton's fundamental distrust of modern art – and of modernist literature – was no secret. Hermione Lee notes that while Wharton was living at Ste-Claire, she "had wary relations with her most avant-garde neighbours" like Charles de Noailles and his wife who "hung Picasso, Ernst, Braque, Gris, Chagall and Miro on their walls" and screened films by Cocteau and Man Ray (Lee 541). References in Wharton's work to modern art are infrequent and ungenerous. Wharton did, perhaps surprisingly, include a few works of the moderns in her private art collection. She owned two paintings by the French artist Odilon Redon, a floral still life by Renoir, and a lush landscape by Cézanne (bequeathed by Walter Berry).[7] These pieces, however, were not what would be called "modern"; her Redon "flower pictures," for example, were products of the late nineteenth century rather than the whimsical paintings of smiling spiders and happy flowers for which the artist was known.[8] Wharton also owned two watercolors by Brabazon, celebrated for his exquisite renderings of Venice, two flower paintings by Jacques-Emile Blanche, who painted a famous portrait of Henry James, a portrait of Lord Elcho by Allan Ramsay, and a seascape by an English painter of the Norwich School. Perhaps because of the problematic ways in which women's bodies had been depicted in nineteenth-century visual art – as passive, sexualized, infantilized, sickly, dying, dead – Wharton's collection was comprised of considerably more landscapes and floral pictures than portraits. Lee observes that when Kenneth Clark visited Wharton in France, "he admired her few good paintings": "Clark would say that he liked looking at paintings with her, not because she was good on the 'purely pictorial qualities of paintings' but because of her 'highly civilized non-specialist point of view'" (Lee 702).

One might say Clark undersold Wharton by calling her a non-specialist. After all, in *The Decoration of Houses* Wharton and her coauthor articulate their criteria for those who would collect art in their homes. The would-be collector who wishes to acquire *objets d'art* must not only possess the means but also, of course, "the skill to choose them – a skill made up of cultivation and judgment, combined with that feeling for beauty that no amount of study can give, but that study alone can quicken and render profitable" (*DH* 187). This kind of knowledge, to be sure, is gained only at the expense of great effort and considerable error. The successful collector must be able to discern the difference between "old and new Saxe, ... an old Italian and a modern French bronze, or ... Chinese peach-bloom porcelain of the Khang-hi period and the Japanese imitations..." (*DH* 187). As we have seen, Wharton cultivated a knowledge of the visual arts that allowed her to appreciate the nuances of old and new Saxe, of Italian master and modern French, of Baroque and Rococo, and of Pre-Raphaelite and impressionist. Indeed, French writer Paul Bourget, her friend and peer, aptly said of Wharton that there was "not a painter or sculptor of whose work she could not compile a catalogue" (Lewis 69). Her respect for and command of visual art permeates not only her prose but also her poetry: she wrote ekphrastic poems inspired by Botticelli's Madonna, Leonardo's Mona Lisa, and Rossetti's Beata Beatrix. Months before her death she spoke in a letter to Berenson of yearning to see the Tintorettos in Venice (*Letters* 604). At the close of *A Backward Glance*, Wharton writes of sharing a visit with a treasured friend, "wandering from one picture gallery to another in happy talk – the happiest I ever had with him" (378). To voyage through her pages of fiction, poetry, and prose seasoned with carefully-placed allusions to the visual arts – for example, Newland Archer equating Ellen Olenska with a Carolus-Duran, Undine Spragg commissioning a gown after a Prud'hon – is to wander through such a picture gallery. Edith Wharton, who was gifted with the means, the skill, and "that feeling for beauty that no amount of study can give," relished in the art of putting her own theories into practice.

NOTES

1. A. Tintner, *Edith Wharton in Context: Essays on Intertextuality* (Tuscaloosa: University of Alabama Press, 1999), 158.

2. R. M. Zorzi, "Tiepolo, Henry James, and Edith Wharton," *Metropolitan Museum Journal*, 33 (1998), 211–29; 213. Subsequent references to this work are included in the text.

3. Although Wharton could not accept Ruskin's dismissal of Tiepolo and other painters of the Baroque style, the critic appears in *False Dawn* as an enlightened seer, and in *A Backward Glance*, she pays him tribute as a genuine connoisseur of Italy.

4. K. Joslin and A. Price (eds.), *Wretched Exotic: Essays on Edith Wharton in Europe* (New York: Peter Lang, 1993), 2.

5. Of Ruskin, John Hale notes: "He wrote six works entirely devoted to pre-Raphaelite art.... He wrote so much, so wildly and so urgently, he lectured so willingly to undergraduates and workmen's institutions, because he thought this sort of art could save civilization." See J. Hale, *England and the Italian Renaissance*. Fourth edition, (Malden, MA: Blackwell, 2005), 127.

6. Wharton's admiration of Reynolds seems to have inspired her to name *The Age of Innocence* after one of his paintings.

7. Details on Wharton's private art collection are drawn from Erica Donnis of The Mount, unpublished document titled "Works of Art Owned by Edith Wharton," dated February 3, 2006. Special thanks to David Dashiell, Publications Director of The Mount, for sharing this document in our June 30, 2008 e-mail correspondence.

8. The Cézanne, displayed in Wharton's library at Pavillon Colombe, is titled *L'Allée au Jas de Bouffan* (1874–75, now at the Tate Gallery, London).

CHAPTER 17

Architecture

Cecilia Macheski

In 1896, Edith Wharton was working with the architect Ogden Codman, Jr. on *The Decoration of Houses*. Three years earlier, the World's Columbian Exposition had opened in Chicago, a gleaming "White City" advocating a renaissance of architecture and city planning based on the training of the Ecole des Beaux-Arts in Paris: Venetian canals, monumental statues draped in togas with uplifted torches, soaring columns and domes referencing the classical landmarks of ancient Greece and Rome. The architects and artists who participated had trained largely in Paris, as the United States had no school of architecture. They would shape U.S. cities in the generation to come, among them Charles McKim of McKim, Mead and White; Louis Sullivan; Daniel H. Burnham; Daniel Chester French; Richard Hunt; Augustus St. Gaudens and Candace Wheeler, a self-taught textile designer working with Tiffany and Company, who established herself with her work on the Women's Pavilion in Chicago. She returned to New York inspired by the "City Beautiful" to advocate for a reproduction of Rome's Trevi Fountain in a muddy triangle of urban space near Madison Square, a short walk from the home at 14 West 23rd Street in which Wharton was born in 1862. Wheeler makes the case for "Beauty," arguing for its necessity to both moral and commercial success. She asserts that "the first purely intellectual human sensation is the enjoyment of beauty, for after hunger is satisfied and warmth attained, and our eyes awaken to consciousness of pleasure, that is the answer to the awakening."[1] Her speech addresses the need to make New York a beautiful city if it is to become "one of the world's attractions" (23) and adds "cleanness and healthfulness, freedom from danger and pestilence" to the requirements. Her evidence that a perfect city is possible is the "waking dream" of the fair in Chicago, where "every white palace which stood like a materialization of symmetry between the earth and the sky – the streets and the bridges and the wonderful water-ways – were all material facts; answering the same purposes as if they had been ugly and squalid; and

189

answering to a thousand spiritual demands which they never could have done except for their ideal beauty" (24).

Instead of the soaring Neptune, swirling horses and rocky waterfalls of the Roman landmark, however, by 1902 that muddy triangle sported the shockingly modern "Flatiron" building. This was an early skyscraper designed by Daniel H. Burnham, who was now a national celebrity as a result of the success of the 1893 exposition. Striving to present a carefully planned and unified city at a time when urban centers were "eclectic and straggling," the Exposition offered an ideal that was viewed by critics as mere "stage decoration; a diamond shirt-stud; a paper collar."[2] Louis Sullivan, whose skyscrapers in Chicago and other U.S. cities soon defined the modern appreciation of an urban skyline, lamented that the backward-looking European copies set U.S. architecture back "for half a century from its date, if not longer."[3]

In this tension between the traditional Beaux-Arts and the emerging modern styles that was brought into the public eye through the Exposition, the American Century was launched, just as Wharton came of age as a novelist and an architectural and landscape critic. In 1902, as the Flatiron was completed, Wharton launched her own architectural project: her home in Lenox, The Mount. Working first with coauthor Ogden Codman, Jr., and later with architect Francis L. V. Hoppin, Wharton created what her friend Henry James called "a delicate French chateau mirrored in a Massachusetts pond" (quoted in Benstock 129–30). Her choice of English, French and Italian elements for her house and grounds at The Mount demonstrates her alignment with European taste, as her fiction reflects her dissatisfaction with the skyscrapers and oversized mansions that were replacing the row houses of Old New York. However, her preference for the elegance and scale of French and Italian houses was defeated as New York's familiar skyline continued to grow; the Woolworth Building, the Singer tower and the Metropolitan Life campanile in Madison Square Garden were already rooted in the granite of the city, and by 1931 the Empire State Building defined U.S. style. James said of the early skyline, "You see the pin-cushion in profile ... on passing between Jersey City and Twenty-Third Street." He decried the new buildings for reflecting the business-driven and temporary condition of life even in 1904: "Crowned not only with no history, but with no credible possibility of time for history and consecrated to no uses save the commercial at any cost, they are simply the most piercing notes in that concert of the expensively provisional into which your supreme sense of New York resolves itself."[4]

As an antidote to this modern architectural "pin-cushion" in the fiction she wrote in the late 1920s, Wharton would reference the work of A. J. Downing, the romantic architect and landscape gardener whose publications in the early nineteenth century were among the first to present cohesively a vision for U.S. rural homes and gardens. By the Jazz Age, Downing had become a relic of a bygone era, his roots in rural and republican values overshadowed by the urban skyline, but before World War I, European-inspired architecture, monumental design for public buildings, and palatial homes for the Robber Barons defined New York style.

The reader familiar with this architectural context soon recognizes that when Wharton opens *The House of Mirth* with Lily Bart at Grand Central Terminal, she is positioning the protagonist for dramatic change. In 1905, when the book was published, this railway station did not sport the exuberant façade that has since become a New York landmark. The station Lily uses is a functional, flat-fronted stone building in the Second Empire style that was being expanded to remove the train tracks from the Park Avenue side. The new Beaux-Arts façade unveiled in 1913 would employ the monumental scale of the Chicago-inspired City Beautiful and replace the severe front of the earlier building with columns and classical arches designed by the firm of Warren and Wetmore. The blocks surrounding the station were likewise undergoing architectural revision. J. P. Morgan's mansion on East 36th Street and Madison Avenue was under construction a few blocks south; the wealthy Morgan was striving to showcase the United States' emerging place as a world power and, ironically, he scavenged the Old World for artifacts of wealth and power. Tapestries, rare books, antique furniture, and Old Masters were displayed in the palace he was building, suggesting that the New World had conquered the Old. The Croton reservoir at 42nd Street and Fifth Avenue, New York's main source of drinking water, was drained and transformed into labyrinths of underground book storage for the New York Public Library. This was a design by Carrère and Hastings that incorporated the Lenox, Astor and Tilden collections into another monumental Beaux-Art design that has become a landmark, but that Vance Weston, in *Hudson River Bracketed* sees as sporting "its rhetorical façade, so unlike a haunt of studious peace."[5]

As *The House of Mirth* opens, Lily has missed her train, but is spotted by Lawrence Selden, who invites her to his nearby apartment in a building called The Benedick, a name taken from an 1879 apartment building designed for bachelors by Stanford White. The "commission was for a cheap, quickly built residence of six stories in red brick, intended to

provide living and working spaces exclusively for bachelors…."[6] White's
biographer David Garrard Lowe identifies the building as the Benedict,
and locates it "on the east side of Washington Square" and notes that it
"even achieved literary immortality when, in *The House of Mirth*, Edith
Wharton gave a similar name to Lawrence Selden's apartment house…."[7]
However, Wharton has moved the building uptown; if Selden and Lily
stroll to the street within a few blocks of Grand Central Terminal, they
are far from Washington Square. Moreover, Wharton has revised the
design of the building as well as the location in keeping with the changing patterns of New York life by 1905. The block she describes suggests
an antidote to the ugly brownstones Wharton dislikes; Lily glances "with
interest along the new brick and limestone house-fronts, fantastically varied in obedience to the American craving for novelty, but fresh and inviting with their awnings and flower-boxes." She adds: "Ah, yes – to be sure:
The Benedick. What a nice-looking building!" and she "looked across at
the flat-house with its marble porch and pseudo-Georgian façade" (*HM*
8). Wharton's design is updated, favoring the English models she preferred to the heavier arched bricks with bow windows of White's original. This refreshing block will contrast strongly with Lily's final home,
a boarding house "along the street through the squalor" with its "blistered house-front" and "paintless railings" below her "darkened window"
(*HM* 523).

    Wharton reveals much about her characters through precise descrip-
tions of the houses they inhabit or build, as when Van Alstyne comments
on Simon Rosedale's newly acquired Fifth Avenue mansion:

The Greiner house, now – a typical rung in the social ladder! The man who
built it came from a milieu where all the dishes are put on the table at once.
His façade is a complete architectural meal; if he had omitted a style his friends
might have thought the money had given out. Not a bad purchase for Rosedale,
though; attracts attention, and awes the Western sight-seer. By and bye he'll get
out of that phase, and want something that the crowd will pass and the few
pause before (*HM* 257).

Nearby is the Wellington Brys' mansion, more sedate, with a "wide white
façade, with its rich restraint of line." Van Alstyne continues his critique:

That's the next stage; the desire to imply that one has been to Europe, and has
a standard. I'm sure Mrs. Brys thinks her house a copy of the *Trianon*. What a
clever chap that architect is, though – his use of composite order. Now, for the
Trenors … he chose the Corinthian: exuberant, but based on the best precedent.
The Trenor house is one of the best things – doesn't look like a banqueting hall
turned inside out (*HM* 258).

The New York Wharton thus satirizes in *The House of Mirth* is one emerging from the 1870s portrayed in *The Age of Innocence*. This is the "Old" New York Wharton revisited in her autobiography, *A Backward Glance*: brownstone architecture, resulting in the Archers' house "cursed with its universal chocolate-coloured coating of the most hideous stone ever quarried" (*BG* 55). Wharton, writing from Europe in the 1930s, wonders that New Yorkers who "had seen Rome and Seville, Paris and London" could tolerate "this cramped horizontal gridiron of a town without towers, porticoes, fountains or perspectives, hide-bound in its deadly uniformity of mean ugliness" (*BG* 55). "Old Mrs. Mingott," Archer's aunt, provides an antidote. She has built "a visible proof of her moral courage" in a "large house of cream-colored stone (when brown sandstone seemed as much the only wear as a frockcoat in the afternoon) in an inaccessible wilderness near the Central Park" (*AI* 10). This house alerts the reader to Wharton's sympathy for the feisty, oversized matriarch, while the newly rich "invader" Julius Beaufort, like the Brys and Rosedale, owns a mansion "that New Yorkers were proud to show to foreigners ... The Beauforts had been among the first people in New York to own their own red velvet carpet and have it rolled down the steps by their own footmen, under their own awning, instead of hiring it with the supper and the ballroom chairs" for their annual ball. The interior likewise reflects the owners' use of architectural elements to display their new wealth: "Then the house had been boldly planned with a ballroom ... one marched solemnly down a vista of enfiladed drawing rooms (the sea-green, the crimson and the *bouton d'or*), seeing from afar the many-candled lusters reflected in the polished parquetry" and finally to a conservatory "where camellias and tree ferns arched their costly foliage over seats of black and gold bamboo" (*AI* 18–19). While Mrs. Mingott's house may be unconventional, she has made it comfortable, and designed the rooms for practical and personal use. Beaufort's mansion, in contrast, is a showplace of consumerism, designed to display his excessive wealth rather than offer comfort.

When May and Archer marry, they travel north along the Hudson River to Rhinebeck for their honeymoon, having been offered a house by the van Luydens that was once inhabited by the Dutch settlers from whom Wharton's society claims descent. To Archer's dismay, the modern house they planned to enjoy has developed a leak in the water tank, necessitating a move to the intimate Patroon's house. This is the very place he had visited earlier with Ellen, and where the cozy domestic intimacy leads Archer to imagine Ellen "stealing up behind him to throw her light arms about his neck" (*AI* 133). When Beaufort suddenly arrives,

Archer's jealousy is evident. By returning Archer to this historic building with his new bride, Wharton reinforces his predicament with the very Dutch bricks and mortar that imprison him. Returning to married life in New York, to a "newly built house on East Thirty-Ninth Street" he faces "a ghastly greenish-yellow stone that the younger architects were beginning to employ as a protest against the brownstone of which the uniform hue coated New York like a cold chocolate sauce" (*AI* 69). The architectural context, then, leaves the reader with no doubt that Archer cannot escape his "tribe."

The architectural changes with which Wharton framed her New York City novels were also altering rural life. Two short texts, *Ethan Frome* and *Summer*, illustrate the writer's continuing attention to architecture in the fiction she set in countryside near The Mount. Drawing on scenes she observed as she motored through the hill towns in one of the first automobiles to compete with horses on the Berkshire County roads, Wharton surrounds her characters with the impoverished and decaying colonial buildings that had been abandoned by Yankees moving West as the railroad promised greater economic opportunity than the rocky hillside farms of New England.

Ethan Frome (1911), which is among Wharton's best-known tales, is staged in Starkfield, a small town with a nearby railway junction, Corbury Flats, the rural equivalent of Grand Central Station. Through the eyes of the narrator, who is an engineer temporarily living in town, the reader sees Frome's house, "one of those lonely New England farm-houses that make the landscape lonelier."[8] In contrast to Van Alystyne's description of the Fifth Avenue mansions in *The House of Mirth*, the engineer sees "plaintive ugliness" and images of decay as a "black wraith of a deciduous creeper flapped from the porch, and the thin wooden walls, under the worn coat of paint, seemed to shiver in the wind that had risen with the ceasing of the snow" (*EF* 22). Frome comments that the house had been bigger in his father's day, noting that he had to "take down the 'L,' a while back." The engineer observes that the "L" rather than the house itself seems to be the center, the actual hearth-stone, of the New England farm (*EF* 22). If the Frome farm is nearly derelict, even the best house in Starkfield, the Varnum house, shows signs of wear. This house, "the most considerable mansion in the village," features a "classic portico and small-paned windows" of the Greek revival style popular during the 1830s and 1840s, a style favored by the early Republic to suggest U.S. roots in Athenian democratic ideals. However, the narrative observes that "the Varnum fortunes were at the ebb, but the two women did what they could to preserve a decent dignity," displaying "a certain wan refinement not out of keeping with her pale old-fashioned house" (*EF* 10).

Wharton's other New England novel, *Summer*, her "Hot Ethan" (Lewis 396), brings another outsider to observe isolated rural life, this one an aspiring young architect. Lucius Harney visits North Dormer in order to research colonial houses for a book he wants to write. He visits the town library, where Charity Royall works, seeking books on local architecture, surprising her with his assertion that old books and old houses might be rather seductive. Charity becomes his guide, driving Harney in lawyer Royall's buggy from one old house site to another so that he might sketch outdoors. In the façades of the crumbling and often abandoned houses, Harney recognizes the beauty of old tracery and pilasters, and also of his pretty young guide. Soon he and Charity meet to make love among simple furniture and wildflowers with which they decorate their playhouse. Yet Charity's beauty is like the delicate windows and columns Harney draws, and is doomed to be abandoned. The pregnant Charity must return to "the red house" in town to marry her guardian as Harney's "social ladder" is soon propped against Annabel Balch's much finer home.

In both novels, then, Wharton decries, like James, the loss of the early U.S. houses in a country that ignored history. In fact, her fiction mirrors growing concern, especially among upper-class New Englanders, at the loss of early buildings like those Harney sketched. An underlying fear of the increasing number of immigrants further fueled the often romanticized impulse to preserve the U.S. past. In 1876, the United States celebrated its centennial with an exposition in Philadelphia. The exhibits fueled a national taste for what became the Colonial Revival movement in design and architecture, with its period rooms featuring spinning wheels, antique kitchens and early textiles. Lucius Harney is a product of this impulse to preserve and codify U.S. culture. In 1905, a million dollars was raised to restore the so-called Betsy Ross House in Philadelphia; the House of Seven Gables in Salem was opened as a museum in 1908. The Society for the Preservation of New England Antiquities, founded in 1910 by William Sumner Appleton, advocated the need to save New England heritage, purchasing and restoring houses like those Wharton describes in *Summer*.

When Wharton moved permanently to France just before World War I, her fiction more frequently compared U.S. and European manners and customs. Architecture continues to be the dress that society wears, but, as characters like Undine Spragg discover, the newest style is not always the most fashionable. In *The Custom of the Country* (1913), Wharton creates in the unsinkable Undine a lens through which readers examine upward mobility achieved through transatlantic marriage. The U.S. craving to grasp the prestige of the Old World while not sacrificing the dynamism of the New World is evident in Undine's willingness to sell the old tapestries that adorn her French husband's chateau regardless of his objections; she will attempt to undress the antique house to acquire cash to adorn herself.

Undine comes from the Midwest, with her willing but naïve parents, planning to take New York Society by storm, supported by wealth from her father's drugstore empire. No sooner have they settled in a hotel with its "Stentorian façade" and "monumental threshold" than Undine realizes her choice is vulgar by Old New York standards (*CC* 116). At first she misreads Ralph Marvell, until her mentor Mrs. Heeny coaches her: "'His mother was a Dagonet. They live with old Urban Dagonet down in Washington Square.'" Mrs. Spragg's response shows her inability to penetrate the codes: "'Why do they live with somebody else? Haven't they got the means to have a home of their own?'" Undine, quicker to grasp the implications, suddenly sees Marvell as "swell." Marvell returns to Washington Square after his visit to Undine and her vulgar family thinking that "society was really just like the houses it lived in: a muddle of misapplied ornament over a thin steel shell of utility. The steel shell was built up in Wall Street, the social trimmings were hastily added in Fifth Avenue; and the union between them was as monstrous and factitious, as unlike the gradual homogeneous growth which flowers into what other countries know as society" (*CC* 73).

His marriage to Undine takes place but eventually ends in divorce, and soon Undine has married a rung higher on the social ladder, French aristocrat Raymond de Chelles. Expecting the glamor of Paris, she finds herself once again isolated in the French countryside, living quite frugally in an "old house which has so long been the custodian of an unbroken tradition: things had happened there in the same way for so many generations that to try to alter them seemed as vain as to contend with the elements" (*CC* 517). When Undine finally suggests that her husband sell the chateau, he is flabbergasted. She continues to argue that he cares "'for all this old stuff more than you do for me.'" He repeats simply, "'You don't understand,'" as his face "hardened into lines she had never seen" (*CC* 527). When an opportunity arises to sell the tapestries, or "chip off an heirloom," to get cash for "a good many Paris seasons," the resulting confrontation with Raymond de Chelles leads to divorce (*CC* 536). Undine, again, misreads the architecture that she inhabits.

After so many novels where architecture evokes the ugliness or constraint of urban life, or the greed and rampant social climbing of characters, Wharton toward the end of her life wrote two novels that offer romantic and sympathetic houses. *Hudson River Bracketed* (1929) and (posthumously published) *The Buccaneers* (1938) incorporate "houses with history."

Vance Weston, like Undine Spragg, comes to New York with a dream, but his is to become a writer. In *Hudson River Bracketed*, Weston visits cousins near Rhinebeck, which is the same town where the Archers had their honeymoon. Coming from the Midwest, he is taken with the notion of "An old house! It occurred to him that he had never seen a really old house in his life" (52). He is not disappointed as he approaches The Willows: "a hint of a steep roof, a jutting balcony, an aspiring turret. The façade, thus seen in trembling glimpses, as if it were as fluid as the trees, suggested vastness, fantasy, and secrecy" (57). Entering the house, Weston asks, "'Why wasn't I ever told about the Past before?'" (62). When he learns that the house was built around 1830, and has always been lived in by the same family, Weston, unlike Undine Spragg, is curious and excited to learn more. So important is the architectural context that Wharton offers her readers explicit information about it as the owner shows him "the epoch-making work of A. J. Downing Esqre on Landscape Gardening in America" (69). Although not an architect, Downing made his name as a landscape designer and nurseryman who published influential books and essays calling for the development of an American aesthetic, where houses and gardens related to the geography and scale of the region. So familiar has Wharton's title become that many readers accept it as Downing's, but Wharton localizes the style by altering Downing's "the bracketed style" as "Hudson River Bracketed."

The magic of "The Past" that enfolds Vance at The Willows is again evident in Wharton's final, unfinished novel, *The Buccaneers*. Wharton brings her protagonist, Nan St. George, to England, where she sees Honourslove, an ancient family home: "warm, cared-for, exquisitely intimate."[9] In its owner, Guy Thwarte, she detects "a latent passion for every tree and stone of the beautiful old place – a sentiment new to her experience, as a dweller in houses without histories" (136). Like Vance, she encounters through the old house a feeling of "beyondness" (155). Although Lily Bart also yearns for "Beyond," she remains, like James' vision of New York, without the possibility of history, and, like the City Beautiful, little more than a stage decoration. For Vance, Nan St. George and Wharton herself, transcendence comes because they finally inhabit houses that have history.

NOTES

1. C. Wheeler, "How to Make New York a Beautiful City" (New York: Nineteenth Century Club, 1895), 21. Subsequent references to this work are included in the text. Wheeler's remarkable production of textiles, wallpaper, and other decorative artifacts was the subject of a 2001–02 exhibit at The Metropolitan Museum of Art in New York. The catalogue, *Candace Wheeler: the Art and Enterprise of American Design 1875–1900* by Amelia Peck and Carol Irish (New York: MMA and Yale University Press, 2001) contains an extensive bibliography but omits Wheeler's address, a copy of which is in the New York Historical Society Library.

2. J. M. Weimann, *The Fair Women: The Story of the Woman's Building, World's Columbian Exposition Chicago 1893* (Chicago: Academy Chicago, 1981), vii.

3. L. Sullivan, *The Autobiography of an Idea* (New York: Dover Books, 1956), 325.

4. H. James, *The American Scene* (New York: Harper and Brothers, 1907), 74, 76.

5. E. Wharton, *Hudson River Bracketed* (New York: Appleton, 1929), 168. Subsequent references to this work are included in the text.

6. M. Broderick, *Triumvirate: McKim, Mead and White, Art, Architecture, Scandal, and Class in America's Gilded Age* (New York: Alfred A. Knopf, 2010), 109.

7. D. G. Lowe, *Stanford White's New York* (New York: Watson-Guptill Publications, 1999), 92.

8. E. Wharton, *Ethan Frome* (New York: Charles Scribner's Sons, 1922), 21. Subsequent references to this work are included in the text.

9. E. Wharton, *The Buccaneers* (New York: Appleton, 1938), 136. Subsequent references to this work are included in the text.

CHAPTER 18

Interior and Garden Design

Helena Chance

For design historians, the discovery of Edith Wharton's novels is one of those productive encounters with literature when the relationship between spaces, objects and people are brought to life. Wharton locates a narrative and shapes her characters in the context of consumption, using objects and spaces to define taste and class and wider social and cultural change. In *The Age of Innocence*, the contrast between May Welland's drawing room with its cold garish furnishings and reproduction furniture and Ellen Olenska's aesthetic and exotic sitting room, intensifies Newland Archer's fascination with and desire for Ellen, whose way of life and taste is outside the norm of respectability for upper-class women of the period. Wharton, writing the novel after World War I, but situating the story in the 1870s, knew with hindsight that in the last decades of the nineteenth century, tastes in interior design were being shaped by reforming movements that became linked to women's bids for independence. Upper and middle-class women were playing more active roles in modernizing taste and practice in design, particularly in the domestic sphere of interiors, gardens and in horticulture. Wharton became a leader of taste in interior and garden design from the turn of the century, and her volumes, *The Decoration of Houses* (1897) and *Italian Villas and Their Gardens* (1904) became handbooks of their day for home and garden-makers, both professional and amateur.

Wharton's life spanned a period of transformative and dramatic change in art, architecture and design that began with the reforming movements and the first breaths of modernism in the second half of the nineteenth century, through to the maturing of the avant-garde following World War I. When she was writing about design and architecture around the turn of the nineteenth century, she would not have predicted the modernist revolution that was to sweep away tradition and historicism in the arts, when artists, designers and architects experimented with new approaches to representing and shaping two and three dimensional form and space.

Wharton was highly influential, however, as a wealthy, intellectual and independent woman in her position as a connoisseur, and her reforming design ideas and practices can be said to be modern in the context of the 1890s and the early 1900s. Hermione Lee records that *The Decoration of Houses* "had a marked influence on house design in America" (Lee 135). However, from the 1910s, and particularly after World War I with the increasing visibility of European and North American avant-gardists, and the emergence of "popular modernism" in design, Wharton resisted the impulses of modernity in designing her houses and gardens. Her response to the trauma of World War I was to retreat into her personal spaces, her homes and gardens, which she chose for their potential to revive an idealized past.

THE DECORATION OF HOUSES AND DESIGN REFORM

Wharton became a connoisseur on the model of the taste leaders of the eighteenth century who established the Grand Tour of Europe as essential to an educated start in life. Inspired by what she saw, Wharton read voraciously and she cultivated friendships with other connoisseurs and writers throughout her life, finding alternatives to conventional Victorian upper and upper-middle-class taste. Sociological studies have provided empirical evidence to establish the theory that taste is a product of class combined with education.[1] Wharton fully understood the power of taste leaders: class, money and knowledge gained from travel and education, along with personal and professional networks, shaped her own taste and criticism of the tastes of others. The aging Anson Warley in her story "After Holbein" appears to be a portrait of her fears for her aging self, but at the same time a wry joke at her own expense, for she shares some of Warley's pleasure in: "The right people – the right setting – the right wines ... He smiled a little over his perennial enjoyment of them" (*CSII* 477).

With the publication of *The Decoration of Houses*, Wharton, and her coauthor, the designer Ogden Codman, Jr., joined a movement for design reform that had its origins in earlier nineteenth-century architectural, design and economic theory.[2] Champions of the Gothic Revival, Augustus Welby Pugin (1812–52) and John Ruskin (1819–1900), challenged the design tastes of the expanding middle classes and called for an end to eclecticism in design and the abuse of historical styles, particularly what they perceived as a vulgar taste for excessive ornamentation derived from classical revival, especially French rococo models. William

Morris (1834–96) and his followers embraced the idea that good design and beauty could shape morality and play a key role in social reform.[3] Their Arts and Crafts Movement promoted the ideal of honest construction in natural materials, and restraint in ornament – authentic forms based on vernacular styles, with their origins in the Middle Ages. The movement was influential in Europe, the United States and further afield, and had an important impact on subsequent design theory and practice.[4] However, Wharton and her fellow taste leaders, while in agreement with the Arts and Crafts doctrines of simplicity and authenticity, avowed classicism, not medievalism, as more appropriate to the national identity of a modern United States, which by the end of the century had overtaken the United Kingdom as the dominant world economic power.[5]

This Beaux-Arts style of classicism was so named because its practitioners (one of the most successful being Wharton's friend and mentor, the architect, Charles Follen McKim) had been trained at the prestigious École des Beaux Arts in Paris. The style, which was exemplified in the plan and architecture of the Columbian World's Fair of 1893, favored the language of French classicism of the seventeenth and eighteenth centuries and was regarded by its followers as the pure expression of classical architecture and design,[6] although in reality it was expressed to varying degrees of excessiveness.[7] Beaux-Arts designers aimed to avoid "inauthentic" collisions of classical language and detail seen in many buildings and interiors of the third quarter of the nineteenth century, with what they regarded as extravagant colors and poorly designed reproductions (of the type that Newland Archer found in May Welland's house) and too much gilt and marble (so beloved of Undine Spragg and her mother in *The Custom of the Country*). Wharton and Codman set out to educate their readers in the doctrine of "good taste" – authenticity and simplicity – and they illustrated *The Decoration of Houses* with photographs of genuine French and Italian (and a few British) interiors and furniture from the sixteenth to the eighteenth centuries. The book advised interior decorators and designers how to avoid the kinds of "incongruous effects" of historical styles of the kind found in the interiors of many hotels, public buildings and millionaires' mansions which had become extravagant in their expressions of conspicuous consumption (Massey 22). Wharton uses contrasting taste in interior styles to define Undine Spragg's social elevation in *The Custom of the Country*. Her parents' choice of the Stentorian Hotel in New York, furnished with "heavy gilt armchairs," "highly-varnished mahogany," "salmon-pink damask" (*CC* 4) and reproduction paintings, marks out their status as nouveaux riches provincials. When she marries

Ralph, Undine becomes aware of the importance of "refined" taste in the social class that she has married into. She almost agrees to allow Popple, her design mentor, to redesign her drawing room in the French "period" style, but in a sly pretence of thrift, she settles for some "fragile gilt chairs" instead (*CC* 229).

The logical purity of classicism was regarded as symbolic of the values and identity of the leading industrial nation that sought to distance itself from the stylistic developments of the Arts and Crafts Movement that had emerged in Europe. The Aesthetic Movement (as it became known), originated from the 1860s in Britain, when an elite group of romantic and revolutionary artists and designers (some of them bohemians) looked for new ways to express beauty in art and design and challenged the boundaries of social acceptability.[8] Aestheticism espoused classical ideals, but also embraced the arts of the Middle and Far East to produce innovative, sensuous forms and patterns. On the Continent, artists, collectors and designers were also enthralled by the arts of the Orient, particularly the Japanese approaches to form and composition ("Japonisme") that were to inspire artists and designers for decades. From the 1890s, new styles were embraced partly as expressions of national identities through design: the Art Nouveau (or Jugendstil) became popular in France, Belgium, Germany, and Czechoslovakia, and the Secession Movement in Austria. Art Nouveau and Secession design borrowed forms from the Orient and from nature: the former is recognizable by an asymmetrical "whip-lash" line and by female sensuality while Secession design, characterized by geometric, rectilinear forms based on grid motifs, was more avant-garde.[9] For a decade, Art Nouveau was a huge commercial success in Europe and to some extent in the United States,[10] attracting *nouveau-riche* consumers seeking to express economic and cultural capital through style.[11] Secession ideas spread to the United States and had some impact on the development of architecture and design into the 1920s (Kaplan 108).

Although the new styles in design were still visible as *The Decoration of Houses* was published, and the influence of Arts and Crafts and Aestheticism endured,[12] classicism was the favored style of Wharton's and Codman's social and political milieu, the Establishment. The Aesthetic style had become associated with decadence, Japonisme was less fashionable by the 1890s and extravagant or surprising approaches to form and decoration were more popular with different social groups. Wharton was not immune, however, from the arts of the East, for photographs of her interiors reveal her collections of Chinese or Japanese vases, screens and other objects, but they were always placed within a structure of classical proportion and detail.[13]

Wharton was a reformer, not an innovator in interior design in the early twentieth century, but she was significant in being one of the few women in Europe and the United States to have a substantial impact on taste at this time.[14] In the United States and in Britain, partly inspired by Wharton and Codman's book, interior decoration became established as a profession for women in the interwar years. *The Decoration of Houses* prompted a more modern approach to space, color and detail in interior design, like Elsie de Wolfe's restrained and "light and airy" interiors that were so sought after in the early years of the twentieth century.[15]

GARDEN WRITING, DESIGN AND HORTICULTURE

In the late nineteenth and early twentieth centuries, women embraced gardening, garden design and horticulture as expressions of identity and independence,[16] but Wharton was one of a relatively few female authors writing about architecture and garden design in this period. Her views on garden design were shaped by theories similar to those in interior design and architecture, which were reactions against inauthentic, eclectic approaches to historicism, with a mixing of styles and "inappropriate" use of materials and plants. Architects, landscape architects, horticulturalists and amateur gardeners influenced by the Arts and Crafts Movement played a prominent role in these debates with their educated knowledge of garden and plant history, horticulture and sensitivity to local culture and environment. The popularity and accessibility of gardening and the availability of a variety of exotic plants in this period was fueled partly by modern techniques in plant sourcing and nurture, and in modern transport systems. Wharton's passion for her gardens at The Mount, Pavillon Colombe and Ste-Claire-le-Château reflected the prevailing gardening ideals of her class, but in the same way that she ignored the avant-garde in interior design, she did not allow modernist garden styles that emerged in the 1920s to intrude on her imagination.

Wharton's interest in Italian gardens, and how they could be adapted in different settings, reflected a broader interest in Renaissance gardens in the late nineteenth century, particularly in how to adapt authentic classical design principles to express national identity. The English architect Reginald Blomfield designed gardens in the early 1900s in the character of the English Renaissance,[17] and the French Duchêne father and son, who were subscribers to the Beaux-Arts School, revived seventeenth-century

French formality from the 1870s.[18] Others, such as Charles Peto (British) and Charles Platt (American), favored an Italianate approach to garden design, with its emphasis on different levels, water, statuary and evergreens, which could be adapted to alternative topographies and climates.[19] Platt published a book on Italian Gardens in 1894, ten years before Wharton, but his was more of a "coffee table" book of beautiful photographs with brief descriptions that emphasized the horticultural beauty of the gardens. Wharton's *Italian Villas and Their Gardens* was the most scholarly analysis of the design principles of Italian gardens from the Renaissance onward published in English at that time.[20]

Although North American landscape designers used European garden designs freely, they were not slaves to historicism. They tended to adopt revivalist approaches combined with the natural elements of indigenous landscapes to create national and local identities in garden design and this was Wharton's aim in planning her garden at The Mount from 1902 to 1908.[21] With the help of her niece, Beatrix Jones (later Farrand), she based the design on a combination of Italian classical principles and English and French planting, but with sensitivity to the New England topography and natural conditions (Benert 38). Wharton understood the importance of genius loci – the necessity to blend, rather than impose European garden designs into the landscape. Beatrix Farrand went on to be one of the most sought after landscape architects of her day. Partly inspired by her aunt's understanding of the relationship between house and garden to the wider landscape, Farrand successfully married Italianate formality with more naturalistic Arts and Crafts planting and enclosed spaces (for example, in her work at Dumbarton Oaks in Georgetown, Washington DC).

The Arts and Crafts Movement inspired one of the most influential schools of garden design and horticulture in the late nineteenth and early twentieth centuries (Waymark 22). The concept of an Arts and Crafts garden is a fairly loose one, ranging from a formal design based on revivalist ideals (Reginald Blomfield), to natural or wild gardens, (William Robinson, 1838–1935 and Gertrude Jekyll, 1842–1932). This also ranged from gardens with grand herbaceous borders to cottage-style flower gardens, but they were all sensitive to history and location, to the importance of a structural relationship between house and garden, and an emphasis on authentic materials and planting. The Victorian parterre that displayed garish and expensive bedding-out schemes of half-hardy plants laid out in geometric patterns was particularly disliked (Ottewill 6–8).

The gardeners and writers Robinson and Jekyll greatly influenced middle and upper-class taste in Britain, the United States and in continental

Europe. (Wharton owned a number of their books.) Jekyll's collaborations with the architect Edwin Lutyens resulted in some of the most talked-about gardens of the period, including Jekyll's own garden at Munstead Wood (from 1895), which combined formal and informal elements. A Jekyll/Lutyens garden was a series of rooms in a structure that mirrored the architecture of the house in scale and materials, but the edges were softened by exuberant herbaceous planting, and wilder woodland areas that provided a gradual transition to the landscape beyond (Waymark 22–30). Jekyll became famous for her planting of herbaceous borders based on "drifts" of color, climbers scrambling over and through old walls and trellises and surprising effects of color in woodland settings.[22] Photographs of Wharton's French gardens in the 1920s and 1930s suggest just these kinds of sensual spaces. An interest in Aesthetic theory also contributed to the sensuous pleasures of her gardens, for she embraced Walter Pater's philosophy of beauty and the power of aesthetic pleasure to assault the emotions, qualities of gardens that she strove to achieve (Lee 103).

Wharton's postwar French gardens, particularly her ambitious and exotic garden at Ste-Claire-le-Chatêau at Hyères in the South of France, expressed her creative and intellectual maturity as a garden designer and plantswoman. She restored her gardens in sympathy with the style and history of her houses and with a sensitive understanding of the natural history and topography of their locations. The garden design and planting at Pavillon Colombe, which was laid out as a series of rooms, was inspired by her friend the U.S. Major Lawrence Johnston, who had made an Arts and Crafts garden in England at Hidcote in Gloucestershire in the 1900s. The design also reflected her knowledge of Italian and French gardens and included water features, statuary, trellises, a rose garden, topiary and roses rambling over vertical frames (Craig 166). Johnston also helped her at Hyères, where the climate made it possible for Wharton to indulge her love of exotic plants from around the world.[23] Refusing to be beaten by droughts and a number of catastrophic frosts that killed her tender plants, she created there an ambitious terraced garden bursting with color and unusual plants (see Lee 557–63).

Retreating from Modernism

In the 1920s and 1930s, good taste for most homemakers in the upper echelons of society meant the classical idiom in interior design (Massey 128–29) (which in Britain came to be known as "country house style"), and interior decorators provided a variety of interpretations of the period

interior (Massey 123–35). Grand and large gardens were mostly designed
on revivalist principles, were influenced by Arts and Crafts theories of
design and planting and inspired by many amateur plantsmen and
women whose passions for horticulture created sumptuous gardens of
mixed plantings from around the world.[24] A more adventurous few chose
avant-garde design for their interiors and gardens (Taylor 7–17). Those
who wanted neither historicist nor avant-garde, but a style to express the
modern age, eagerly adopted a brand new popular modern style, which
the modernists pejoratively labeled "moderne."

While Wharton established her houses and gardens in France in the
interwar years, traditional taste was under assault from young architects
and designers in search of ways to express modernity through design.
These new ideas became visible at the 1925 Paris Exposition Internationale
des Arts Décoratifs et Industriels Modernes, where conventional designs
were combined with contemporary interpretations that borrowed elements from modern painting, non-Western cultures (particularly Egyptian),
and the popular culture and technologies of the modern world such as
electricity, Hollywood films, cars and airplanes. A few exhibits, such
as Le Corbusier's Pavillon de L'Esprit Nouveau, were based on a more
radical stylistic, theoretical and philosophical design avant-garde.[25] One
of the most controversial was presented by the architect Robert Mallet
Stephens, who made a garden with trees cast in concrete. This intrigued
the Vicomte de Noailles, who commissioned Mallet Stephens to design a
"cubist garden" at his villa at Hyères, close to Wharton's house. Wharton,
who knew the de Noailles, and shared a passion for gardening with the
Viscount, had little sympathy for the avant-garde in art and design (Lee
541). She satirized modern decoration styles in 1920s New York in her
novel *Twilight Sleep*, with Lita's black boudoir and Mrs. Manford's "shining" dressing room and white and silver bathroom suggesting an age of
superficial materialism.

Wharton's taste remained firmly historicist, reflecting her scholarly
knowledge and interest in the histories of interior and garden design.
Photographs of Pavillon Colombe suggest light and airy rooms designed
in sympathy with the eighteenth-century house. It was furnished with
both antique and reproduction French and Italian furniture and other
items she had collected over the years, including Chinese or Japanese
vases and screens and Chinese wallpaper. The general effect is one of classical elegance, but also of coziness and femininity. Her gardens too were
skillfully restored and photographs and descriptions of them confirm that
she became an accomplished garden designer and plantswoman.

Through her books on interior and garden design, Wharton became a taste reformer and leader in the early twentieth century, but she remained outside the design avant-garde. After World War I, her design choices reflected the prevailing tastes of her class, but with the arrival of modernist and "moderne" design, her approach appeared increasingly conventional. Wharton was never a recluse from modernity, however, for she wholeheartedly embraced the modern comforts and conveniences of "the machine age," with her dependence on the motorcar and oceangoing liner, the telegraph and the telephone. She even sought out the modern sublime at its most brutal in her pursuit of the tanks and heavy artillery at the front line of World War I. Having done her duty in assisting the war effort, she escaped from the city and channeled her design and horticultural expertise into her romantic retreats.

NOTES

1. P. Bourdieu "Introduction" and "The Sense of Distinction" in G. Lees-Maffei and R. Houze (eds.), *The Design History Reader* (Oxford and New York: Berg, 2010), 402–08.
2. R. Houze, Introduction to "Design Reform, 1820–1910" in Lees-Maffei and Houze (eds.), *The Design History Reader*, 3–4.
3. L. Federle Orr, "The Cult of Beauty: The Victorian Avant-Garde in Context" in S. Calloway and L. Federle Orr (eds.) *The Cult of Beauty: The Aesthetic Movement 1869–1900* (London: V & A, 2011), 24–37; 27.
4. K. Livingstone and L. Parry (eds.), *International Arts and Crafts* (London: V & A, 2005), 7.
5. G. Jeansonne and D. Luhrssen. *"A Time of Paradox": America since 1890* (Rowman and Littlefield, 2006), xxi.
6. A. Benert, *The Architectural Imagination of Edith Wharton: Gender, Class and Power in the Progressive Era* (Madison, NJ: Fairleigh Dickinson University Press, 2006), 29. Subsequent references to this work are included in the text.
7. A. Massey, *Interior Design since 1900*, 3rd edition (London: Thames & Hudson, 2008), 22. Subsequent references to this work are included in the text.
8. The trial and conviction of Oscar Wilde in 1895 was a contributory factor in the demise of Aestheticism from the 1890s. See S. Calloway "'Tired Hedonists': The Decadence of the Aesthetic Movement" in S. Calloway and L. Federle Orr (eds.), *The Cult of Beauty: The Aesthetic Movement 1869–1900* (London: V & A, 2011), 224–35; 235.
9. C. McDermott, *Essential Design* (London: Bloomsbury, 1992), 47.
10. The entrepreneur Louis Comfort Tiffany was one of the most brilliant and successful exponents of Art Nouveau in the United States. See W. Kaplan, *"The Art that is Life": The Arts & Crafts Movement in America, 1875–1920* (Boston: Museum of Fine Arts, 1987), 152–53. Subsequent references to this work are included in the text.

11. D. Silverman, "The 1900 Paris Exposition, from *Art Nouveau in Fin-de-Siècle France*" in G. Lees-Maffei and R. Houze (eds.), *The Design History Reader* (Oxford and New York: Berg, 2010), 75–80.

12. Frank Lloyd-Wright, a pioneer of modernism, combined Arts and Crafts ideals with the spirit of machine production (Houze 53–54; 54).

13. T. Craig, *Edith Wharton. A House full of Rooms: Architecture, Interiors and Gardens* (New York: The Monacelli Press, 1996), 163–65. Subsequent references to this work are included in the text.

14. See L. Orrinsmith, *The Drawing Room, Its Decoration and Furniture* (London: MacMillan, 1878) and Mrs. H. R. Haweis, *The Art of Beauty* (New York: Harper & Bros., 1878).

15. P. Sparke, "The New Homes of Elsie de Wolfe" in S. McKellar and P. Sparke, *Interior Design and Identity* (Manchester: Manchester University Press, 2004), 72–76; 76.

16. See S. Bennett, *Five Centuries of Women & Gardens* (London: National Portrait Gallery, 2000), 111. Subsequent references to this work are included in the text.

17. D. Ottewill, *The Edwardian Garden* (New Haven, CT and London: Yale University Press, 1989), 21–26. Subsequent references to this work are included in the text.

18. J. Waymark, *Modern Garden Design: Innovation since 1900* (London: Thames & Hudson, 2003), 9–10. Subsequent references to this work are included in the text.

19. See Peto's Italianate gardens at Iford Manor, Wiltshire, UK, and Buscot Park in Oxfordshire.

20. However, J. Dixon Hunt has shown that flowers were a more important feature of Italian Renaissance gardens than Wharton indicates. See Dixon Hunt's introduction to *Italian Villas and their Gardens* (A facsimile edition of the original 1905 printing of the first edition [1904]) (Rizzoli and the Mount Press, 2008).

21. See W. Miller, *What England Can Teach Us about Gardening* (New York: Doubleday, Page & Co., 1911). Contrary to the suggestion in the title, Miller called for a U.S. style of gardening, suited to the North American climate, topography, native plants and way of life, building on the achievements of great landscapists and horticulturalists such as Downing, Olmsted and Eliot.

22. A. Jennings, *Edwardian Gardens* (London: English Heritage and the Museum of Garden History, 2005), 32–39.

23. Landscapists and horticulturalists were challenged by the large number of new plants that were becoming available. See G. C. Taylor, *The Modern Garden* (London: Country Life, 1952), 13. Subsequent references to this work are included in the text.

24. T. Richardson, *English Gardens in the Twentieth Century: From the Archives of Country Life* (London: Aurum Press, 2005), 73–74.

25. D. Imbert, *The Modernist Garden in France* (New Haven, CT and London: Yale University Press, 1993), 35–40.

CHAPTER 19

Images of Wharton

Katherine Joslin

Edith Wharton had a considerable talent for sketching from life, literally sketching from life. One of her drawings survives in the Lilly Library at Indiana University.[1] In relatively few lines, Wharton brings into focus a wide-brimmed hat trimmed with a long scarf stylishly framing a confident face. The relaxed and knowing female comes to us through the soft black lines of a veil with tints of red in the hair and light in the eyes and lips; the eyebrows shade into an almost imperceptible nose, anchored in nostrils. One thinks, for a moment or more, that this must be a self-portrait. It is the sort of sketch Wharton draws of discerning female characters in her novels and stories. Lily Bart, the heroine of *The House of Mirth* (1905), comes to readers in similarly subtle lines: "Her vivid head, relieved against the dull tints of the crowd, made her more conspicuous than in a ball-room, and under her dark hat and veil she regained [a] girlish smoothness, [a] purity of tint" (*HM* 4). The face in the sketch actually belongs to Elisina Tyler, the executrix and residuary legatee of Wharton's wills, and provides a useful context for understanding the sort of stylishly modern woman that Wharton wanted to be, the image that she constructed and left to us in photographs as well as prose.

At the heart of the matter is Wharton's aesthetic preference for what she calls an artist's "tact of omission" (*DH* 198). *The Decoration of Houses* (1897), her first book, ends in a stark declaration about art and architecture: "Moderation, fitness, relevance – these are the qualities that give permanence ... *Tout ce qui n'est pas nécessaire est nuisible*" (*DH* 198). A work of art endures by what the artist knows how to leave out; tact of omission marks the master's hand. Later in *The Writing of Fiction* (1925), Wharton puts it more eloquently when she says of the short story that a true artist knows how "to suggest illimitable air within a narrow space" (*WF* 55). Although we think of Wharton's fiction as richly detailed and packed full of things, the truth is that she gave readers only the details she thought necessary to bring actual objects to mind. The later the work and

209

the earlier the setting, the more actual details of material culture readers will find in a Wharton novel or, especially, a short story.[2] "Tact of
omission" is retained throughout her oeuvre.

Images of her, at least those images that she had a hand in staging, can
be read with her aesthetic in mind. Every detail of dress and demeanor
carries meaning in her performances before a camera. In her images, both
photographic and literary, we see subtle shades of fabric and fabrication.
The reason that we believe we know Wharton, the writer and the person,
may well be because she left so many photographs and paintings in our
hands.[3] Images show her aging over time – a shy child, a wasp-waisted
young woman, a discerning middle-aged novelist, and finally a comfortably aging woman. We can see changes in her face from youthful puzzle-
ment through neurasthenic doubt into confident maturity and, finally,
into old age.

The series of images gives us reliable documents in the history of female
fashion, particularly couture designs, from the nineteenth into the twentieth century as women loosened corsets, lightened fabrics, and shed layers
of vestments to accommodate considerable changes in female mobility,
especially in the city. Women's fashion provides a useful context for reading not only Wharton's fiction but that of other modern writers as well.
The movement of a woman's body into more lissome garments signaled,
perhaps more than any other image, the progress and modernity of the
new century.

Wharton, as an image, makes an especially useful gauge of modern
dress because she belonged to a social class that made a fetish of clothes
in myriad rituals. Elisina Tyler in portraying Wharton wrote in 1930: "I
see why Edith makes such a fetish of dressing. She considers it an absolute
sign of civilisation to dress in the evening" (quoted in Lee 698). Wharton
had an eye for fashion, and money and time to collect a considerable
and representative wardrobe. The garments in her closet were tastefully
conventional, elegantly sewn in expensive fabrics, and finished in valuable antique laces, pearls, and furs. Women of Old New York during the
Gilded Age spent their days moving into and out of several costumes;
some winter ensembles reached a weight of twenty or thirty pounds.[4]
Even during summer months, the display of costumes demanded considerable time and energy. Consuelo Vanderbilt groused in her autobiography, *The Glitter and the Gold*, that women of her social class were obliged
to change clothes seven times in a typical summer day in Newport:

First, we put on a dress to dress in. Then we are ready for breakfast. After that
we dress for the beach, then for the bath, then for dinner, then for the drive,

then for the ball, and then for the bed. If that isn't being put through a regular course of dimity and diamonds, then I am no judge of such performances.[5]

In *A Backward Glance*, Wharton detailed the typical costume required for afternoon carriage rides in Newport, Rhode Island, up Bellevue Avenue and out onto Ocean Drive: "A brocaded or satin-striped dress, powerfully whale-boned, a small flower-trimmed bonnet tied with a large tulle low under the chin, a dotted tulle veil and a fringed silk or velvet sunshade, sometimes with a jointed handle of elaborately carved ivory, composed what was thought a suitable toilet for this daily circuit between wilderness and waves" (*BG* 82). The costume, worn for a single performance, left other garments lying in wait for events during the remainder of the day and evening.

Edith "Pussy" Jones was a wealthy child of fashionable parents and, like her mother Lucretia, loved dressing up. In *A Backward Glance*, she began her life story as a walk with her father in New York City and made the astonishing claim that this event awoke her to "the importance of dress, and of herself as a subject of adornment" and marked "the birth of her identity" (*BG* 1–2). She remembered surveying her image in the mirror and seeing a white satin bonnet detailed in pink and green velvet plaid with ruffles of "*blonde* lace" under the brim. As in her sketch of Elisina Tyler, she outlines the face in a "*bavolet*" or long scarf around the neck and a veil of gossamer wool across the face, allowing red cheeks to shine through as a "Valentine" (*BG* 1). An actual photograph of Pussy at five years of age shows her dressed more modernly in a flat hat, perched stylishly forward on the top of her head with a veil tied on the top and trailing down the back; she wears a cream-colored coat and dress with dark pointed-toe shoes. The camera caught a pensive face with large sad eyes.

The wealth of the Joneses accounted for a handful of family portraits by fashionable painters of the late nineteenth century. A first painting of her as a toddler reveals an undistinguished face ringed in a flare of red curls; a painting, unlike a photograph, offered color, and Pussy's hair was remarkable. In 1870, when she was eight, the family hired the English artist Edward Harrison May (1824–87) to paint their young daughter. May's work was noted for soft brush strokes and tints that depicted nineteenth-century females as delicate figures, perhaps just the image the parents wanted of their eight-year-old daughter whose brows tended to furrow and chin to jut out. He painted Pussy Jones in luxurious finery, a blue satin dress with a broad sash and fur trim at the neck and wrists. The painting captured the shine and curl in her red hair but smoothed the angles of her forehead and chin, erasing the complexities of her face.

Lucretia Jones engaged May again in 1881 to paint her daughter at nineteen as a stylish and marriageable young lady. Dressed in a red velvet ensemble of bustled skirt and puffed-sleeved jacket, trimmed in white lace ruffles, Edith Jones looks demurely at us from a face smoothed, once again, at the forehead and chin into an image of conventional beauty. Although the figure in the portrait looks ill at ease, Wharton liked the painting well enough to have it sent to the American Academy of Arts and Letters after her election to that august body in 1930. A miniature painting by the fashionable French artist Fernand Paillet (1840–1918) of her at twenty-eight after her marriage to Edward "Teddy" Wharton has also survived. The watercolor on ivory captures in detail a tightly corseted body dressed in a couture evening gown of yellow satin and lace with a cape stylishly draping her shoulders in black fur. Paillet transformed wealthy female clients into art nouveau beauties. As with May's paintings, the miniature mutes the distinctions of Wharton's face.

The clothing in these paintings and photographs can be read in the context of shopping in the late nineteenth century. Lucretia Jones taught her daughter how to follow the rituals of other wealthy families of Old New York by patronizing Parisian couture houses where exclusive ateliers employed hundreds of seamstresses in the production of rarified goods. The rise of couture fashion in Paris followed the coup d'état on December 2, 1851 that restored the French Empire, a Second Empire, with Louis Napoléon Bonaparte (1808–73) and his Spanish wife Eugénie (1826–1920) in power. Empress Eugénie set the fashion for women in France and indeed for women in Europe and the Americas by purchasing garments from the Houses of Charles Frederick Worth and Jacques Doucet in the rue de la Paix.[6] Rich women gained entry into the houses of fashion by virtue of their pocketbooks.

Wharton would always measure fashion by what she saw in the Paris of her youth. As she put it in *A Backward Glance*, living in Europe as a child "gave me, for the rest of my life, that background of beauty and old-established order!" (*BG* 44). During the early years of their marriage, the Whartons traveled to Paris as the Joneses had done, and continued to shop in the rue de la Paix. Rich clients of the House of Worth or Doucet viewed garments on live models and were pampered with individual fittings, under the eye of the designer himself. In Wharton's novels, wealthy patrons bought dozens of dresses at a time and left them in their wrappers for two or three years until the garments were safely stylish in New York and Boston. The writer remembered in *A Backward Glance* wearing a Doucet gown to lure Henry James, and later as a novelist, she would dress her daring heroines in Doucet dresses, the very ones Lily Bart unpacks at the end of *The House of Mirth* as she savors each "fall of lace and gleam of embroidery" (*HM* 512).

We know that Wharton resisted what she called Kodak realism in life and in fiction. She struggled with editors over every detail of her publications, including images of herself as a writer. "The last 'impression' I saw looked like a combination of a South Dakota divorcée & a magnetic healer," Wharton chided William Crary Brownell, her editor at Scribner's, in a letter of February 1901 (quoted in Lee 165). She hated to be photographed because, as she later confided to him, "the results are so trying to my vanity" (*Letters* 57–58). Beyond the chagrin of facing her prominent brow and chin, the intensely private woman felt the camera as an intrusion, and yet, such an intrusion was necessary if she wanted to sell her work to an inquisitive public. In contemplating ways to manipulate that exchange, Wharton quipped to Brownell, "I would do anything to obliterate the Creole lady who has been masquerading in the papers under my name for the last year" (*Letters* 57–58). By the "South Dakota divorcée" and the "Creole lady" she had in mind early photographs, all showing an hour-glass figure stiffly corseted into couture fashions. An 1884 photograph shows her in a chevron skirt, standing behind an ornately latticed stairway that has a Creole look to it. The nineteenth-century photograph of her that perhaps we know best shows her in a dark-colored, silk-beaded, and tightly bustled evening gown, probably the creation of the House of Worth (the heavy fabric and bustled skirt were signatures of Worth – although one cannot say for sure that any garment in a particular photograph comes from a specific designer). For safety's sake, skirts were bustled as a dress reform that moved heavy fabric away from the front of a gown where it might inadvertently catch fire from a hearth. Wharton's slim waist and well-gloved arms in this image (see Figure 4) have become iconic, so much so that Elaine Showalter used just the details of waist and gloves as a recognizable synecdoche on the paperback cover of *A Jury of Her Peers* (2010), a history of U.S. women writers.[7]

Photographs of Mrs. Edward Wharton as a young matron of Old New York can be read, too, in the context of her long bout with what we would call depression and, perhaps, anorexia. In the late nineteenth century, it was not uncommon for young ladies of wealth to suffer from what was then diagnosed as hysteria or neurasthenia, and Wharton confided to her friend Sally Norton that she lost a dozen years to the malady (*Letters* 139–40). In photograph after photograph she appears as a tense, gaunt figure. The oddest of these images depicts her pensive face, framed by

Figure 4: Edith Wharton, c. 1887, dressed in a bustled evening gown, perhaps designed by Charles Frederick Worth. Courtesy of The Lilly Library, Indiana University, Bloomington, Indiana.

equally pensive lapdogs, Miza and Mimi, on each shoulder. The strained young woman is dressed in a fashionable walking suit with leg-of-mutton sleeves that accentuate her tiny waist.

Our image of her as a modern writer comes from a handful of carefully posed photographs in the early years of the twentieth century as she worked with editors to stage her public life and create a modern image. Advertising exacts its own "tact of omission," and Wharton meant to be artful and canny.

A publicity pose for *Women Authors of Our Day in Their Homes* (1903) shows her arriving in an elegantly fashionable coat with layers of furs and a velvet hat trimmed with an entire bird (perhaps the creation of the famous Parisian milliner Madame Virot; and certainly anathema to Audubon supporters).[8] A second pose of her in the same location may have been shot on the same day. The coat is gone and the still-slender woman sits surrounded by furs in a well-corseted evening gown similar to a model that Jacques Doucet made for the French actress Réjane. In these twin publicity photos, Wharton emerged as a savvy Old New Yorker without a hint of South Dakota or the Creole South.

She wrote to Charles Scribner in 1905 blushing over her growing fame as a writer. *The House of Mirth* had delighted tens of thousands of readers, and she responded with pride and hope, "& if the number should ascend to 100,000 I fear my pleasure would exceed the bounds of decency" (*Letters* 95). That November, Wharton made an appointment with an author's agent, Elisabeth Marbury, about dramatizing the novel, and sent a new image of herself, as she teased, "with my eyes down, *trying to look modest*" (*Letters* 95).

The photograph Wharton sent to Scribner seems, at first glance, anything but tactful (see Figure 5). The truth is, however, that each and every item in her ornate ensemble is necessary to the image she hoped to construct. The photograph leaves no question about her knowledge of fashion in her monied class and no doubt about her authority to write as an astute novelist of Old New York. Her hair is coifed in a chignon, pushed foward like a crown and strung in pearls with a single pearl drop bringing light to the ear. The pose allows her body to act as a hanger for the layers of ceremonial goods that mark her authenticity. These vestments include valuable property she will leave in her will to friends and relatives.[9] Encircling her neck is an elaborate necklace that she called a "dog collar," a star-sapphire medallion encrusted with diamonds clasping several strands of pearls, a piece she bequeathed to her close epistolary friend Daisy Chanler. Across her bodice lies a long chain with diamonds and

Figure 5: Edith Wharton, Christmas 1905, dressed in holiday regalia, including a beaded dress, antique laces, furs, and pearls. Photo credit: Yale Collection of American Literature, Beinecke Rare Book and Manuscript Library.

pearls designed by Cartier, a piece that she wore in nearly every photograph taken of her and which she left to Bessy Lodge. The chain, when she was young, tethered her cigarette case (as such a chain does for Lily Bart) and, as she grew older, it more prosaically tethered her lorgnette.

The antique laces flowing from the arms of her cape later went to her niece Beatrix Ferrand and the sable wraps to Jane Clark. The beaded gown she is wearing, no doubt designed by Worth or Doucet, went as cast-off apparel to her maids. What may seem to our eyes an ostentatious, even absurd, display of goods was, to her mind, a symbolic performance. Dressing up for her readers, she used only those lines necessary to suggest her place in the literary and social pantheon.

Photographic efforts to cast her as a novelist at work come to us in a string of images of the writer at her desk (see Figure 6). In 1905, she sat for several poses in an elegant couture version of a tea gown, perhaps the creation of Jacques Doucet. The tea gown was a garment associated with intimate household scenes where a lightened corset or perhaps no corset at all allowed for comfort. Dress reformers moved tea gowns into public places and such loose-fitting garments were adopted by artistic and intellectual women as examples of "aesthetic dress." Wharton's costume mimics photographs of writers and artists in such fashion magazines as the *Delineator* and *Femina* and drawings made popular by Charles Dana Gibson. Her fashion and even her pose are conventional, albeit an haute couture version of female conventionality. The silken texture and sinuous lines of Wharton's gown with lace inserts at the shoulders and across the bodice and skirt suggest intimacy. Every prop is carefully selected. She sits on the edge of a caned chair at a desk with neatly tapered legs, a leather pad, and an inkstand. A be-ringed hand cradles a book atop a manuscript situated between brass and crystal candlesticks. A marble bust, a mantle, and a sculpture stand sentry, and a Persian carpet creates a dais for the folds of her gown. Not a single detail of the staging escapes Wharton's eye as she bends her reader's gaze toward the image.

In 1910, the photographer Peter Powell caught her in her most modern pose. Wharton's face, nearly in profile, looks out from a wrap of rich furs in the sort of pose Coco Chanel will later make famous. Her last formal photographic portrait in 1925 retains the stiffness of earlier poses, as she sits jeweled and majestically serious. In her seventies, she is photographed again at her desk, a plump figure in the relaxation of old age. She wears a favorite multicolored crocheted sweater (one that appears in several of the late snapshots), and she looks credibly at work. The truth is that she wrote in bed every morning, dressed in a pink silk sacque with a matching bed cap holding back her hair as the morning sun poured in across her shoulders. We have one last snapshot of her in such a dressing gown standing in a doorway of the Pavillon Colombe; she smiles contentedly into the informal camera in July 1937, just a month before her death.

Figure 6: Edith Wharton at her writing desk, c. 1905, dressed in a tea gown, perhaps designed by Jacques Doucet. Photo credit: Yale Collection of American Literature, Beinecke Rare Book and Manuscript Library.

Ironically, as much as Wharton shunned the camera, we find a relaxed and natural woman in the dozens of snapshots left to us by her friends. Katherine Haven took a candid shot, paparazzi style, of Wharton standing away from the crowd to take a deep drag on a cigarette. There is no question about her devotion to smoking. Another snapshot shows a

Figure 7: Edith Wharton, 1933, dressed in a modern suit and brimmed cloche hat. Photo credit: Yale Collection of American Literature, Beinecke Rare Book and Manuscript Library.

fashionable woman in a modern coat with a fur hat, stole, and muff, smiling fully into the camera in front of a trainload of supplies during World War I. Several casual shots show her riding in automobiles with Henry James, picnicking with Walter Berry in casual camaraderie, chatting with her many friends, and sweating through an unusually hot day as she receives an honorary degree from Yale in 1923. The handheld camera, in these less stylized shots, gives us a realism that the private woman may have thought she had reserved for her closest friends.

In the gallery of images we see Wharton becoming more and more decidedly the modern woman she sketches in the drawing of Elisina Tyler. In her sixties and seventies, she stands in the gardens of Château Sainte-Claire, her home in Hyères, wearing dresses and suits that are loosely corseted, if corseted at all. In one she wears a cubist-style dress that flows in angles across her body, and in others she wears knitted suits. These later snapshots reveal a woman content with herself, and comfortable in modern dress. One photograph of the older woman shows her sitting in a wicker chair beside a wooden bench on the floral-shaded patio of Sainte-Claire (see Figure 7). Clad in a jersey suit trimmed in lace cuffs, her body is free of corset and bustle. Her thinning hair is tucked under a brimmed cloche. She looks directly through the camera, smiles openly, and seems for that second to be one of us.

NOTES

1. The drawing is available via the online Lilly Library Collection of images at: http://www.indiana.edu/~liblilly/collections/overview/lit_american.shtml
2. See K. Joslin, *Edith Wharton and the Making of Fashion* (Hanover, NH and London: University Press of New England, 2009).
3. For the best collection of informal images of Wharton, see E. Dwight, *Edith Wharton, an Extraordinary Life* (New York: Harry N. Abrams, 1994).
4. For the story of dress reform, see P. Cunningham, *Reforming Women's Fashion, 1850–1920: Politics, Health, and Art* (Kent, OH: Kent State University Press, 2003).
5. C. Vanderbilt Balsan, *The Glitter and the Gold* (London: Heinemann, 1953), 20–21.
6. For the story of the couture industry, see V. Steele, *Paris Fashion: A Cultural History* (New York: Oxford University Press, 1985).
7. For the cover image, see E. Showalter, *A Jury of Her Peers: American Women Writers from Anne Bradstreet to Annie Proulx* (New York: Knopf, 2009; paperback 2010).
8. *Women Authors of Our Day in Their Homes: Personal Descriptions and Interviews*, ed. F. Whiting Halsey (New York: James Pott & Co., 1903), 245.
9. When she died on August 11, 1937, Wharton left two wills, one in France and the other in the United States. Elisina Tyler was named executrix and residuary legatee of both wills. See Benstock (456–59) and Lee (752–55) for a discussion of the controversies over the wills and a list of specific bequests.

PART V

Social Designs

CHAPTER 20

The Marriage Market

Pamela Knights

"'And you found it all out for yourselves – it was not in the least arranged for you?'" Ellen Olenska inquires of Newland Archer, in *The Age of Innocence*, as she expresses delight at his engagement. Incredulous, Archer repudiates any taint of a contract. "'Have you forgotten,'" he replies, "'that in our country we don't allow our marriages to be arranged for us?'" (*AI* 62). Here, as throughout her writings, Edith Wharton keeps readers aware of the maneuvers and settlements that underpinned even what might seem (as Archer claims), "'The most romantic of romances!'" (*AI* 62). Edith Jones herself was introduced into this arena at the age of seventeen, in 1879, as an awkward debutante. At twenty-three, with a broken engagement behind her, she became Mrs. Edward Wharton – an ultimately disastrous match, from which she would release herself in a Paris divorce court in 1913. This essay surveys the operations of the marriage "business," from debut to divorce, within the social worlds of Wharton's life and fiction. The evolving forms and perceptions of marriage outlined here influenced the climate of expectation more widely, stirring currents of change throughout U.S. society. As these were most conspicuous in the ranks of the monied elite, marriage in that social segment will be the primary focus – the conventions, rituals, and terms of negotiation, undertaken by prosperous or aspiring Americans, and the obligations associated with their roles at each stage.

When Kate Orme, in *Sanctuary*, contemplates the wreck of her engagement, or Susy, in *The Glimpses of the Moon*, worries over her ambiguous marital separation, Wharton was tapping into the most topical of public discussions. From the cautious decades of the mid-nineteenth century into the social turbulence of the Gilded Age and early twentieth century, the institution of marriage – and, increasingly, its breakdown – attracted keen attention. The prospects for women, the respective rights of each party, the possibility of alternatives, and the relationship of all these phenomena to the health of the nation, were matters of urgent debate.

Meanwhile, matters of etiquette appropriate to changing conditions were canvassed in a stream of publications addressed to the socially anxious. These guided their readers through the niceties of letter writing, introductions, courtship and ceremonies, and pronounced on the foundations for matrimonial harmony. The possibility of failure did not deter Americans from embarking on wedlock. While very youthful marriages were a rarity, the median age for first-time brides remained constant, at about twenty-two – an average taken slightly upward by the later marriages of working girls who might be family bread-winners; but by the age of twenty-nine (Lily Bart's position at the start of *The House of Mirth*), nearly three-quarters of all women could expect to be, or have been, married. For grooms, the average age of a first marriage was a little older: nevertheless, fifty-two percent of men had taken a wife before they were thirty, and only a quarter would remain bachelors beyond the age of thirty-four. Over a lifetime, more than ninety percent of men and women could expect to have been married.[1]

For many women of all classes, marriage seemed the route to economic security. Journalist Nixola Greeley-Smith, in "The Slump in the Marriage Market," quoted a "good-looking woman over thirty" who, despairing of finding a husband, as "the solution of the weekly bills," was contemplating the "grim spectre [of] ... the narrowing vista of oldmaidhood."[2] Ladies like Edith Jones or Lily Bart, untrained and restricted, had little scope to pursue activities and professions explored by New Women. As Lawrence Selden observes to Lily, "'Isn't marriage your vocation? Isn't it what you're all brought up for?'" Responding, "'I suppose so. What else is there?'" (*HM* 13), Lily speaks from a condition deplored by writers on the Woman Question. Charlotte Perkins Gilman's *Women and Economics* (1898) remains the preeminent critique, but others ventured similar analyses. *A History of Matrimonial Institutions*, published the year before Wharton's novel, summarized the degradation: many women, reliant on men for support, "look upon wedlock as an economic vocation. With them marriage tends to become a form of purchase-contract in which the woman barters her sex-capital to the man in exchange for life-support."[3]

Such forthright discourse was mingled, in newspapers and popular writing, with more sentimental perspectives. In the prevailing rhetoric, as echoed by Archer, "our marriages" in the United States arose from unmatched liberty of choice and opportunity. Matrimonial bartering was considered a foreign tradition; and nuptial trading practices, from Mexico to St. Petersburg, perennially served to fill "local color" slots in newspapers, framing exotic customs for U.S. consumption. Yet even these, at times, hinted at parallels nearer home. The New York *Sun*, for instance, placed "Berber Marriage Markets" next to illustrations of the winter fashions, as displayed at the great Horse Show: "Among the Kabyle tribes in northern Africa women are looked upon as chattels to be sold like other possessions, and they are accordingly disposed of to the person who makes the highest offer to the father or other male guardian." Alongside descriptions of the rows of Berber girls "decked in the most telling ... costumes," U.S. ladies' finery, at this key event in the New York calendar, took on a suggestive resemblance. Details of the latest array in loops and ribbons, or fur neck scarves (some with "animal heads at both ends and having diamonds for eyes"), hinted at an equivalence with the facial ornamentations and elaborate jewelry of the North African girls.[4] Sometimes, the links were explicit. The *New York Tribune* noted of the traditional Easter "Choros" dance at Megara, Greece: "Participated in by all the young girls of a marriageable age. It is considered as an announcement that they are in the market for husbands. A sort of debut into society."[5]

In the United States, this debut normally took place at eighteen. Parents of Wharton's generation and class still, in the late 1870s, preferred to present their daughter to society at home, or in another private house. As Wharton comments in *A Backward Glance*, her mother would never have countenanced an introduction in a public room (78). Fashionable New York hostesses (or those with social ambitions) might, instead, hire the ballroom of Delmonico's Restaurant for an evening reception and dance. From the 1880s, the "coming-out" might take place at "a tea," for "a large company," with "music and flowers ... to set off the entertainment";[6] or, for the growing numbers of super-rich, like Miss Blanche Stebbins (as reported in the *New York Times*, December 11, 1883) at a ball for up to 500 invitees at her parents' residence.[7] For those with restricted room (or income), introductions over a series of smaller teas could suffice. The settled place in the calendar for such events was during November or December, so making the most of the winter season before Lent imposed restrictions. (Mrs. Burton Kingsland's *Etiquette for All Occasions*, 1901, recommended a Saturday tea, as young men were more apt to be free to attend.[8])

Friends and selected acquaintances would receive an invitation card, with the daughter's name engraved beneath that of her mother – a notice that the debutante could now be added to their own guest lists. With her hair up, and suitably arrayed, the girl's duty was to "receive" with her mother, who formally introduced her to each guest on arrival; sometimes a few close girl friends, in harmonizing gowns, assisted with the general pleasantries. In a London presentation, white was obligatory, but a U.S. debutante might choose a color she found more becoming. All the same, to opt for black satin, as recalled of Wharton's Ellen Olenska (*AI* 37), would certainly have struck observers as inappropriate. An air of simple "girlishness" was essential – a light dainty frock, in contrast with the elegance and richness of the mother's attire, and flowers, with matching ribbons (Kingsland 126). Similar bouquets, all sent by friends, decorated the rooms – a popular girl, like Miss Annie G. Hall, as mentioned in *The Season* (1883), might receive up to fifty or sixty (Crandall 110). Whatever the scale, the debutante was the centerpiece. As Ward McAllister, the prominent social arbiter, declared, "A young girl should be treated like a bride when she makes her *début* into society. Her relatives should rally around her and give her entertainments to welcome her into the world which she is to adorn"; and he censured the excessive bad taste of any who proffered comment on expenditure.[9] For the self-conscious young woman, such attention must have been an ordeal – Wharton, in *A Backward Glance*, remembered her own debut evening as "a long cold agony of shyness" (*BG* 78). However, as Mrs. Kingsland counseled, "if our maiden can prevent her smile from becoming set and her manner mechanical, she will impress many in her favor" (Kingsland 118).

After this, the girl was "out" and could expect invitations to a round of amusements, all requiring attention to costume. Grand functions, such as the exclusive Assembly balls, or Delmonico's "Cotillion Balls," were social landmarks. The press would list the names of attendees, commenting on the relative "prettiness" of the fresh show of "buds" (or, less coyly, "army" of debutantes), and "handsomeness" of the "elder set" – the young married women and the girls who had been out for more than one season. Wealthy hostesses' dinners or private dances would also be documented, again, from the 1880s, with ever more personal remarks about dress and appearance. Accounts of winter delights (sleighing, skating, and tobogganing) filled the society columns; or, in the summer seasons at Newport or Bar Harbor, graceful sports (archery, croquet, boating, golf, drives in horse-drawn carriages). These were interspersed with features on the latest styles, or debutante "craze." (A *New York Times* item of 1885, satirized, in a mock interview with "Miss Satinskin," a brief fad for "cooking clubs," where girls took turns to host a series of fancy lunches; and an even more short-lived reading group, tackling Shakespeare's histories.[10]) New debutantes, or those still building up their circle, were advised that small entertainments might prove more rewarding, with less competition, than at fashionable gatherings: "Little dinners, followed by some merry games with prizes, dainty luncheons, small cotillions of not more than twenty or thirty couples, theatre parties properly chaperoned," were among Mrs. Kingsland's recommendations (Kingsland 121–22).

Although U.S. girls enjoyed greater freedom than their European counterparts, protocols governed every aspect of behavior. Any news spread quickly, as in Wharton's second season, when her name was first coupled with that of Harry Stevens in a paragraph of rumored engagements;[11] and as even a casual word might blemish a reputation, the chaperone's presence was key to averting misinterpretations. Besides, as Mrs. Kingsland hinted, restraint set "a higher value upon the object," particularly in the eyes of young men, "who are apt to sigh for the fruit that hangs highest" (Kingsland 194). Sweetness and tact were indispensable so, as the *New York Times* cautioned, a girl should avoid antagonizing rival debutantes by being "stiff" or by monopolizing the dressing-room mirror; she should be polite to older women, who, after all, could be powerful allies; and should charm men by listening sympathetically.[12] At balls, she should be lively and appreciative, although never first to arrive, nor last to leave; and she should distribute dances evenly. Gifts represented particular perils: only fruit, flowers, or confections were acceptable. As Maud C. Cooke explained, "notwithstanding that a small fortune may be lavished upon their purchase, [these] are supposed, in all probability from their perishable character, to leave no obligation resting upon the lady." Cooke also offered sample scripts for polite refusal: "Mamma never permits me to accept expensive presents."[13] Formulae were available, similarly, for turning down unexpected marriage proposals, but proper girls averted unwelcome attentions before the man declared himself; or, if they intended to accept, did not prevaricate unduly. While subtle encouragement was politic, being dubbed as a "trifler" could spell ruin.

Throughout, "Mamma," as mentor and social facilitator was all powerful. With neither mother nor effective guardian, Lily Bart justifiably deemed herself disadvantaged. The mother steered her daughter into her future duties as a "married maiden" (as the Social Register termed the group) – from hosting dinners to understanding the role of a chaperone. The rituals of "calling" were paramount – the daily routine of visits and card leaving, required of society matrons. The rule, with elaborate exceptions, ran, in brief: "You cannot invite people to your house until you have first called upon them in a formal manner and they have returned the visit."[14] Further sets of calls followed every social occasion. Although increasingly criticized as time consuming and taxing, it was through these exchanges that the wife supported her husband, established status,

consolidated introductions, and sustained valuable alliances. For the debutante, shepherded by her mother, calling broadened her chances to be
presented to potential husbands. For newcomers, or girls without extensive
networks, institutions such as the selective dancing classes (smaller-scale
public balls) enabled privileged subscribers to gain a footing. Outsiders
had a difficult passage, and the tactics of acquiring the crucial introduction (whether through association with outlying members of the upper
set, the hiring of an opera box, visits to fashionable resorts, staging of lavish entertainments, or through the "European route") gave rise to satirical
commentary. The career of Wharton's Undine Spragg might, for instance,
be compared with the imagined trajectory taken by Miss Detrimental
and her parents in C. W. de Lyon Nicholls' *The 469 Ultra-Fashionables of
America*, published the previous year. For the man, the passage could be
equally strenuous: for the would-be suitor, the practice was to gain the
requisite entrance through some mutual friend to the family. Parents, in
turn, scrutinized the character of anyone admitted over their threshold:
as Cooke urged, better go to the grave a "'forlorn spinster'" than for a girl
to marry a dissipated man (Cooke 121). Notes of eugenic caution and fear
of the foreign, or otherwise socially unacceptable, underpin many similar
warnings.

Once tacitly sanctioned, the man did not need parents' formal consent
before proposing, although good manners normally prompted approval
and, once engaged, he could expect cordial treatment. As Florence Howe
Hall reminded readers, it was not correct for parents to regard their
daughter's fiancé "as if he were a robber chief who intended to break up
their family and carry off the favourite of the flock."[15] Keepsakes sealed the
vows between the lovers – a ring for her and a ring or locket for him, aptly
inscribed, or containing a "likeness." Close friends and relatives received
the news first, at tea parties and "at homes." It was correct to "congrat-
ulate" the man, for his efforts and conquest, but to wish the woman "all
happiness." The official announcement, issued by the young woman's parents, launched further long rounds of "calling." Tributes celebrated the
event: Marian Lawrence [Peabody], of Boston, for instance, recorded in
her diary, in January 1906: "Flowers and presents arriving every minute
all day. Got over ninety boxes of flowers … One corner of the room was
all violets and another corner was solid gold and another white with
roses and jonquils and others."[16] To break a betrothal was serious and,
while neither party was obliged to make public any reason (and no blame
was imparted), it might be chronicled in the press (as was Wharton's
terminated engagement to Harry Stevens). All engagement or wedding

gifts were returned and the one-time lovers handed back all personal letters and tokens. The ideal length of an engagement remained a matter for
personal choice, but, throughout, care for propriety continued. The man
was supposed to forsake his former club cronies for his fiancée's company,
and the woman was to receive other gentlemen's attentions with courtesy,
now tinged with "reserve." The couple should also avoid demonstrative
shows of affection. Driving together in an open carriage was permissible,
but the long-suffering chaperone still accompanied any kind of journey,
visits to theaters, and other evening entertainments. The bride-to-be and
her mother would name the date (just after Lent, or in June, were favorite options), oversee preparations of the trousseau, and attend fittings for
the wedding gown (whatever the fabric, white, with high neck and long
sleeves, was mandatory). Managing the invitations for society weddings
required diplomacy. The New York Grace Church, for example, would
hold 2,000; and as the bride's guest list would also shape her future calling roster, good judgment was imperative.

Financial negotiations (handled by family lawyers) could be complex,
particularly so in marriages of U.S. women into European aristocracies.
As Maureen E. Montgomery explains, in *"Gilded Prostitution": Status,
Money and Transatlantic Marriages, 1870–1914* (1989), in the United States
a settlement normally provided for the daughter's income or trust fund.
American fathers could, then, be taken aback when encountering the
English tradition that, "pin money" aside, all fortune from his daughter's
side should pass irrevocably into her husband's hands. For those of lower
ranks, too, prenuptial agreement was recommended. The most excellent man might prove improvident, or "the beloved Charles, Henry, or
Reginald" fall into ruin: a young lady "should not, from a weak spirit of
romance, oppose her friends who advise it ... By making a settlement,
there is always a fund that cannot be touched."[17] (Such warnings would
be brought home to Wharton, with the revelations after twenty-five years
of marriage, that Teddy had embezzled her trust funds.) Mrs. Cooke
advocated business-like transactions even in the realm of the emotions.
Proposals, like any other contract, should be confirmed in writing and
ground rules fixed for the marriage: "[S]ay what each desires to do, and
have done; and draw out a definite outline plan." In sum: "Write down
and file all" (Cooke 129–30).

For established families, weddings, like debuts, were regarded as private, and traditionalists deprecated the intensifying culture of publicity.
The *New York Times* bewailed the intrusive power of the interviewer,
the public's appetite for detail, and the vulgarity of the class who sought

exposure: "[N]o convocation of politic bees in a glass hive could be more thoroughly open to observation than much of our so-called "society" is to-day." The *New York Times* society items contributed to this social buzz, at a low-level pitch; for less restrained treatment, readers of the period would have turned to *Town Topics*. The trend for "showing" presents was widely criticized, as was reporters' relish for cataloging displays, listing donors, and poring over price-tags – "like goods at an auction," as the *New York Times* complained as early as 1872. The Belmont/Howland wedding, for instance, was splashed as the high point of the 1877 Newport season, with $50,000 worth of presents.[18] The ceremonials of the new generations of millionaires – especially, as Montgomery's invaluable studies under-line, the high-profile transatlantic marriages of the 1890s – took ostenta-tion to hitherto unimaginable heights, inflaming interest to fever pitch. The famous accounts of the extravagant spectacle, and frenzied scenes of police holding back crowds of onlookers at beauty Consuelo Vanderbilt's wedding to the Duke of Marlborough in November 1895, might seem impossible to rival.[19] Yet others offered no mean show – among them, that year, the Burden/Sloane wedding at Lenox in June, with estimates of a $40,000 trousseau, two private trains, eighty broughams, transported in fifty freight cars, $700,000 of gifts, including jewels from Vanderbilt relatives, a diamond and emerald necklace from the bride's mother, and a honeymoon world tour.[20]

The press was also quick to sniff any subsequent marital trouble. One casualty was nineteen-year old finance heiress Anna Gould, whose showy alliance with the French Count Paul Ernest Bonniface de Castellane, in March 1895, would founder in a notorious divorce case ten years later. Across the United States, in the glare of such increasingly flamboyant nuptials, diverse groups lamented the rising scale of material ambitions in wedded life and pointed to soaring divorce figures as symptoms of social contagion. Public consternation about this "tide of divorce" was rein-forced by two major government reports, presenting statistics for more than forty years (1867–1906).[21] Noting 945,625 divorces in the 1909 census period (1886–1906), one analyst concluded: "Our rate [of increase] is twice that of Switzerland, thrice that of France, five times that of Germany, and many times that of England and Canada."[22] In William L. O'Neill's pré-cis: "In 1880 there was one divorce for every twenty-one marriages … by 1916 it stood at one in nine."[23] Although few (13 percent) sought alimony and fewer (9 percent) were granted it, the census revealed women as the main recipients[24] and, no matter who initiated proceedings, children, in most cases, were assigned to the mother.

Emotional dramas were aired in novels, plays, and songs, such as Frank Egerton's, "Don't Take the Children from Me: Or the Divorced Wife" (1885), and debate was kept fermenting by leading journals. The *North American Review*, for instance, published a series of themed essays (November 1889 to February 1890), gathering position pieces from clerics, politicians, and novelists. Among them were the Right Hon. W. E. Gladstone, and, representing the women's angle, Elizabeth Stuart Phelps. Its summing-up title, "Final Words on Divorce" (February 1890), proved overly optimistic, as the trend accelerated. "American Divorces by the Million," proclaimed the *New York Herald* in 1911. In an accompanying cartoon, a somber judge examined his papers while the jubilant ex-partners pranced in opposite directions flourishing beribboned decrees. Voicing fears about "the divorce germ that threatens to become a divorce epidemic," the article outlined the arguments, possible causes ("Is it the 'New Woman' ... [A]re marriages too lightly entered into?"), and tentative solutions.[25] Many regarded the weakening of the marriage tie as a symptom of the pressures (or greed) of modern times, or as the outcome of unrealistic expectations.[26] Moralists denounced divorce as inimical to the greater social good; others welcomed the changes, as offering hope for individuals for whom the bonds had become intolerable (Lichtenberger 172–89).[27] (Although in New York adultery was the only legal cause, nationally 60 percent of divorces were granted on grounds of cruelty and desertion [Lichtenberger 99; and Basch 105, 217].)

The press kept sensational elements in the spotlight, paying fascinated attention to the so-called "Divorce States," tracking their prowess in this lucrative new commodity: "A divorcee is to Fargo as the gold nugget is to the Klondike," remarked the *New York Times*; and, later, "competition is keen in the divorce business of South Dakota and Nevada."[28] Of keen interest were the activities of the socialites, waiting out the residence requirements in their "Divorce Colonies" – a dull imposition, much resented by the would-be divorced themselves. This cycle of the marriage trade gave fresh zest to society columns, which followed the careers and remarriages of "fair divorcées." Etiquette writers, too, adjudicated on dilemmas of modern manners: the correctness of reverting to one's maiden name (for a Boston judge, in 1903, a "fraud" where there were children[29]) and who should be received and how. Obituary tributes to social gatekeeper, Mrs. Astor, recalled her distressing difficulties, in later life, "in persuading New York society to assuage in the case of her daughter and some of her other relatives the severity of the very laws which she herself had instituted against divorcees."[30]

Wharton's efforts to end her own marriage discreetly in France failed to scotch rumors in U.S. newspapers. Speculation persisted, even after her decree; her photograph was published, and Teddy was pursued in Boston as he departed on a fishing trip: "'I won't talk to you,' exclaimed Wharton as he stalked away," while a companion (reported as "his son") expressed ignorance of Mrs. Wharton's plans.[31] However, as woman and writer, Wharton found her own passage out. She explored new territory in the dizzying reconfigurations of matrimony in the 1920s and 1930s, summed up in the movie title of *The Children*, "The Marriage Playground"; and, as Mrs. Edith Wharton, a respected divorcee, she enjoyed a form of freedom unavailable to most of her characters, and unthinkable in the strict sphere of her upbringing.

NOTES

1. From P. H. Jacobson, in collaboration with P. F. Jacobson, *American Marriage and Divorce* (New York: Rinehart, 1959); see particularly Table 23, 62.
2. N. Greeley-Smith, "The Slump in the Marriage Market," *The Evening World*, Final Results Edition, June 29, 1906, [n.p.] Image 15, at The Library of Congress, *Chronicling America: Historic American Newspapers*, chroniclingamerica.loc.gov. Subsequent references to this invaluable digital archive are referenced as *CA*.
3. G. Elliott Howard, *A History of Matrimonial Institutions* (Chicago: University of Chicago Press, 1904), vol. III, 249.
4. *The Sun*, New York, November 18, 1894 [5] Image 27; *CA*.
5. *New York Tribune*, April 12, 1908 [4] Image 20; *CA*.
6. C. H. Crandall (ed.), *The Season: An Annual Record of Society, 1882–1883* (New York: White, Stokes & Allen, 1883), 110. Subsequent references to this work are included in the text.
7. "Two Society Balls," *New York Times*, December 11, 1883, 5. All references to this newspaper were retrieved through the digital resource, ProQuest Historical Newspapers, *New York Times (1857–1922)*, www.search.proquest. com/hnpnewyorktimes, and subsequently referenced as *PQ*. Articles may also be accessed through the *New York Times Article Archive: 1851–1980*, www.query.nytimes.com/search/query?srchst=p
8. Mrs. B. Kingsland, *Etiquette for All Occasions* (New York: Doubleday, Page and Company, 1901), 126. Subsequent references to this work are included in the text.
9. W. McAllister, *Society As I Have Found It* (New York: Cassell, 1890), 243.
10. *New York Times*, October 18, 1885, 4; *PQ*.
11. *The Sun*, New York, October 17, 1880, 5, Image 5, *CA*.
12. *New York Times*, November 6, 1910, X 9; *PQ*.

13. M. C. Cooke, *Social Etiquette, or Manners and Customs of Polite Society* (Boston: George M. Smith, 1896), 123. Subsequent references to this work are included in the text.

14. Mrs. H. O. Ward (comp.), *Sensible Etiquette of the Best Society, Customs, Manners, Morals, and Home Culture,* 10th rev. edn. (Philadelphia: Porter & Coates, 1878), 43.

15. F. Howe Hall, *The Correct Thing in Good Society* (Boston: Dana Estes, 1902), 193.

16. M. Lawrence Peabody, *To Be Young Was Very Heaven* (Boston: Houghton, 1967), 362.

17. S. A. Frost, *Frost's Laws and By-Laws of American Society* (New York: Dick, 1869), 128.

18. *New York Times,* January 11, 1875, 4, *PQ*; June 23, 1872, 4, *PQ*; September 19, 1877, 1, *PQ*.

19. See P. Knights, *The Cambridge Introduction to Edith Wharton* (Cambridge: Cambridge University Press, 2009), 67–68.

20. *New York Times*, June 7, 1895, 8, *PQ*.

21. U. S. Bureau of Labor, *Marriage and Divorce 1867–1886* (1889); and U. S. Bureau of the Census, *Marriage and Divorce 1867–1887* (1909).

22. E. Alsworth Ross, *Changing America: Studies in Contemporary Society* (New York: The Century Company, 1912), 49.

23. W. L. O'Neill, "Divorce in the Progressive Era," *American Quarterly*, 17.2, Part 1 (Summer 1965), 203–17; 204.

24. Settlements were most ample in New York, although for New York women, legal separation often proved financially more rewarding: see N. Basch, *Framing American Divorce: From the Revolutionary Generation to the Victorians* (Berkeley and Los Angeles: University of California Press, 1999), 110, 114. Subsequent references to this work are included in the text.

25. *New York Herald* Magazine, August 13, 1911, 2, The Wilbur and Orville Wright Papers at the Library of Congress; Scrapbooks; December 1910– March 1914: 0146, //hdl.loc.gov/loc.mss/mwright.0500542

26. Canvassed in an early PhD study: J. P. Lichtenberger, "Divorce: A Study in Social Causation," diss., New York: Columbia University (1909), 142–71. Subsequent references to this work are included in the text.

27. See also G. Riley, *Divorce: An American Tradition* (Lincoln and London: University of Nebraska Press, 1997), 71–72.

28. *New York Times,* August 28, 1898, 16; *PQ*; October 11, 1908, 10; *PQ*.

29. *New York Times*, May 7, 1903, 1; *PQ*.

30. *New York Times*, Sunday Magazine, November 1, 1908, 3; *PQ*.

31. *New York Tribune*, June 2, 1913, 3, Image 3; *CA*.

CHAPTER 21

Leisured Lives

Maureen E. Montgomery

Edith Wharton's "most vivid" memory of her childhood summers in Newport were of the "picturesque archery club meetings: with the lovely archeresses in floating silks or muslins ... wide leghorn hats, and heavy veils flung back only at the moment of aiming." She attributes to these spectacles of "young gods and goddesses" her early ambition to "tell a story" (*BG* 46–47). She had a keen eye for spectacles of leisure and beauty in what she defined as the simple society of her youth. The archeresses appear in her historical novel, *The Age of Innocence* (1920) in their "pale muslins and flower-wreathed hats" (*AI* 214) at the August meeting of the Newport Archery Club, hosted by Mrs. Julius Beaufort, dressed "in a girlish cloud of mauve muslin and floating veils" (*AI* 211). Set in the 1870s, there is a hint that fashions are about to change. The social occasions for showing off "pretty dresses" in the graceful posture of drawing a bow and fiercely protecting unenhanced complexions "against sun and wind, and the arch-enemy sea air" with "veils as thick as curtains" were giving way to more energetic pastimes requiring a different approach altogether toward leisure apparel (*BG* 46).[1] Tennis was about to edge archery off Newport's lawns (*AI* 206).[2]

Wharton was acutely alert to the changes taking place around her in New York and Newport as she grew up and after she got married. She had a finely tuned register for changes in fashion, running a generous gamut from rules of decorum, clothing, furnishings, and architecture to pastimes, social entertainments, and dining habits. As an eyewitness to the momentous transformations in New York social life between the Civil War and World War I, she was, not unlike the fictional Mrs. Archer, able to "trace each new crack in its surface" (*AI* 258).[3] The social world of her parents' generation was, according to Wharton, "mild and leisurely" compared to the breathless pace of socializing at the turn of the century. It was populated by men of leisure of "middling prosperity" who supported their families with inherited income or the growing rentals from urban real estate. These were men who could sustain the demands of long, cere-monial dinners or formal social functions that began late in the evening. Nighttime entertainments mainly took place in private homes, dinner being the "most frequent distraction" (*BG* 57). The old New York of the Jones family constituted an intimate group of interrelated families who lived in lower Manhattan and whose chief nocturnal outing to a com-mercial venue was a visit to the theater.

What Wharton describes in her memoirs is a section of New York soci-ety that was deeply conservative and shunned any form of display and publicity. However, there were contemporaries of her parents who were more actively engaged in seeking to determine social distinction through more public forms of sociability and who were more amenable to includ-ing new men of wealth and their families. A landmark event was a cos-tume ball in 1854 hosted by Mrs. William Colford Schermerhorn at her home which cornered Lafayette Place and Great Jones Street. She issued 600 invitations and requested her guests to come dressed in the court costume of Louis XV. Reinforcing the French theme, she decorated her mansion in the style of Versailles – something that would be aped later in the nineteenth century – and introduced New York to the cotillion, also known as "the German," which became a standard dancing entertain-ment for the rest of the century.[4] There was nothing spontaneous or indi-vidualistic about the German. Set figures had to be rehearsed in advance; the assignment of leading roles reinforced status and cultivation; and the dance had to be performed as a group, thereby encouraging group iden-tity within a hierarchical framework. It was the highlight of the evening's entertainment and usually did not commence until after midnight.[5]

The tight provincial circle of wealthy New York families of Dutch and British descent had no need of a society page in a newspaper to alert them to what was happening in the social world. Everyone knew everyone else. As Mrs. Archer, the barometer of change but also prophet of doom and decline in *The Age of Innocence,* used to say: "When I was a girl ... we knew everybody between the Battery and Canal Street; and only the peo-ple one knew had carriages. It was perfectly easy to place any one then; now one can't tell, and I prefer not to try" (*AI* 100–01). Mrs. Archer's reference is to the days of the mercantile elite and the descendants of the great Dutch landowners in the early nineteenth century. By the time Wharton was a girl, there had already been several attempts to try and "place" people in society, but not by those who remained entrenched in lower Manhattan and who tried to ignore the encroachment of com-merce. Family networks and private forms of sociability alone were proving insufficient in maintaining the boundaries of elite identity that were constantly tested by the rise of new men of business. New York City underwent rapid expansion in response to its increasing importance as a port and railroad hub, which was accompanied by a multiplication in banking and insurance institutions and significant growth in the wholesale and retail trade.[6] While the extended family remained a vital institution in forging networks and creating a shared bourgeois culture, the public display of wealth and leisure became, in the 1850s, a feature in the assertion of social and economic power.

Mrs. George Jones nevertheless adhered to the tradition of conservative old New York when her daughter made her debut in society (see Pamela Knights' "Marriage Market," Chapter 20 in this volume). This was in 1879 just when there was a renewed effort to regulate the lives of New York's rapidly expanding bourgeoisie. It was associated with Mrs. Caroline Schermerhorn Astor who had become a force with which to be reckoned in facilitating the orderly integration of old and new money. With her husband's millions, her own impeccable family credentials, and the assistance of Ward McAllister, who was a cousin by marriage, she played a leading role in controlling access to the inner circles of New York's socio-economic elite. The scale of her operations far exceeded all previous attempts at social leadership, but then the challenge was that much greater with the phenomenal growth after the Civil War of multi-million dollar fortunes carved out of industrialization. The issue was: would money alone determine social status? Ward McAllister was determined that it should not.

In 1872, McAllister brought together twenty-five men to form the Patriarchs committee that would oversee the organization of three (later two) subscription balls at Delmonico's each winter. An invitation was supposed to signify that one was "in society." According to McAllister, the avowed purpose was "to make these balls thoroughly representative; to embrace the old Colonial New Yorkers, our adopted citizens, and men whose ability and integrity had won the esteem of the community, and who formed an important element in society. We wanted the money power, but not in any way to be controlled by it."[7] This was certainly not the first attempt to try and arbitrate membership of New York society nor to bring together wealth and lineage, but the fact that the Patriarchs lasted for twenty-five years is some indication of their success and of the effectiveness of using exclusiveness to define social boundaries. The balls became a prominent feature of New York's winter season and provided an opportunity to present debutante daughters. Huybertie

Pruyn of Albany, New York, for example, was taken by her mother to Delmonico's in December 1891 for the first Patriarchs Ball of the season. Her dress, of white chiffon over white satin with puff sleeves and a slight train, had been made at Kate Reilly's, a London-based couturiers on Fifth Avenue and 32nd Street. On the night of the ball, it was delivered directly to the Cambridge Hotel, just a block away, where Mrs. Pruyn and her daughter were staying. It was but a short distance down Fifth Avenue to Delmonico's where she was received by Mrs. Astor, whom she described as being "resplendent in brocade, with ropes and chains of diamonds, and her heavy tiara made her look even more imposing."[8]

An invitation to Mrs. Astor's annual ball at her home at 842 Fifth Avenue in January 1893 was a further confirmation of Huybertie Pruyn's place in society. She recalled: "Everything was extremely decorous and beautifully done. No doubt the present generation would call it very stiff. I can hear people say 'How typical of the gay nineties it must have been.' I suppose it was the essence of the best of that period. I am glad to have seen it, as even those then-new houses have vanished now" (Hamlin 247). Mrs. Astor's annual ball had become an institution in New York society. The guest list did not vary widely and thus it helped to consolidate group identity while allowing controlled access of newcomers to the inner circles. As with the Patriarchs, the guest list and what the women wore were recorded on the society pages of the New York press. The annual repetition for so many years of the ritual of Mrs. Astor receiving her guests in her grand drawing room had even caused the *New York Times* to engage in repetition of its annual report. In the waning years of Mrs. Astor's reign, perhaps with the consciousness that an era was ending, the *New York Times* devoted many more column inches to the details, providing a complete menu of the supper, and a listing of gowns and guests of note.[9]

Private balls denoted both an important public statement of wealth and position and the height of social formality, requiring weeks of preparation and planning. From the early 1880s on, they were highly publicized and the new society journalism pandered to the social ambitions of their hosts with their sycophantic accounts. The Vanderbilt costume ball of March 1883, held at the new Fifth Avenue mansion of William Kissam Vanderbilt, marked a high point in lavish outlay. The *New York World* ran with the headline: "How Mrs. Vanderbilt's Entertainment Distributed $250,000 Among The Working People." How differently fared the Bradley Martin costume ball of February 1897 at the Hotel Waldorf; it was excoriated for its extravagance at a time of severe economic recession. For three weeks, journalists were preoccupied with not only the details of the preparations but also with the criticism of clergymen about such wasteful expenditure. If it were Mrs. Martin's ambition to outdo the 1883 Vanderbilt ball, she achieved that in terms of publicity, but it was not of the kind she had anticipated and claims that her ball had provided employment fell on deaf ears.[10] A threshold appears to have been reached in terms of what was acceptable with regard to the public flaunting of wealth in the harsh economic times of the mid-1890s. Violent clashes between capital and labor gave rise to a greater self-consciousness among the wealthy, and dressing up in fancy costumes aping European royalty did not strike the right note in a democracy that sought to avoid class wars.

By the late 1890s the formality of leisure-class entertainments, as symbolized by the ball, had clearly begun to pall. The energy put into gatekeeping, with the endless hours of women calling and leaving cards along with the sometimes vicious competition over securing invitations to select gatherings no longer seemed worthwhile. The mood was captured by a new personality emerging on the social scene, Mrs. Stuyvesant Fish, who used private entertainments to parody her peers. Mrs. Astor was far from amused by Mamie Fish's burlesques that included, among others, a banquet for a hundred dogs, a formal dinner in honor of a monkey dressed in evening attire, who occupied Mrs. Astor's usual place at the table, and a plantation theatrical featuring a "young 'dud' darky" who regaled his friends back home about his experiences in New York high society (Morris 253).[11] More generally, the revolt against formality and exclusivity was marked by the flocking of fashionable society to the new restaurants and bars along the Great White Way and in the vicinity of Times Square amid the theaters. George C. Boldt at the Waldorf is credited with weaning New York from "the sanctity of their private homes to the public opulence of his hotel dining rooms," and this trend was pursued by the proprietors of Maxim's, Rector's, and Shanley's (Erenberg 34, 40).[12] The latter were spaces where theatrical celebrities and the wealthy could rub shoulders with members of the fast set in Mrs. Astor's Four Hundred. The commercialized world of entertainment centering on the theater and restaurants seemed to offer more interesting and spontaneous distractions than a cotillion – especially for men.

There were also signs of revolt in Newport, the premier summer resort of the social elite.[13] The new "cottages" of gilt and marble beseeched formal entertainments like many of their New York counterparts, recalling Wharton's description of the Wellington Brys' New York mansion – thought to be a copy of the Trianon – which lacked "a frame for domesticity" but "was almost as well designed for the display of a festal assemblage

as one of those airy pleasure-halls which the Italian architects impro-
vised to set off the hospitality of princes" (*HM* 212). Social gala occasions
reached a peak, or "ball point," in Newport in the summer of 1895 in
spite of the ongoing recession.[14] This was the year of Alva Vanderbilt's ball
for the Duke of Marlborough at Marble House (modeled on the Grand
Trianon at Versailles) for which $5,000 was spent on favors imported
from Paris for the cotillion.[15] It was also the summer when Cornelius and
Alice Vanderbilt staged a grandiose coming-out ball for their daughter,
Gertrude, at The Breakers, complete with white-wigged, liveried footmen
that evoked European court society.[16] Newport's male cottagers struck
back at this rigid formality and the rule of women and organized pastimes for their exclusive enjoyment. The Saunterer in *Town Topics* took
delight in declaring that men had at last rebelled against "the stupidity
of snobbishness and foolish worship of ridiculous customs at Newport"
and seceded from "a life of tedious and senseless conventionality." Center
Hitchcock was credited with organizing the Clam Bake Club, which
barred women on three days of the week, and Herman Oelrichs allegedly
compounded the situation with his Kat Bote Club, from which the men,
reportedly, came back the "worse for wear." Another segregated occasion
caused a stir when forty men completely deserted the women and went
"swimming, lunching and skylarking" at Mackerel Cove.[17] The Saunterer
laid the blame at women's door for making summer life too "artificial
and conventional" and noted the rudderless nature of Newport society
as it fragmented into cliques and lacked a "marked leader" now that Mrs.
Astor was "virtually retired."[18]

There were other, more substantial signs of change, particularly with
the move to life outdoors. The year 1895 also marked society's introduction to cycling and golf. Alva Vanderbilt became a devotee of both
and was reported to have been seen cycling along Ocean Drive wearing
a "thick dark veil." She subscribed to the Newport golf club, where her
future husband, O. H. P. Belmont, offered a silver prize for women golf-
ers.[19] Cycling was said to be all the rage at other summer resorts such
as Lenox, Stockbridge, Bar Harbor, and Long Island. The women golf-
ers at Shinnecock Hills, the first golf course in the United States, which
had a clubhouse designed by Stanford White, rode to the course on their
bicycles in their cycling suits that cleverly doubled up as golfing outfits.
Newport became a venue for national sporting contests: in 1895 it hosted
the first U.S. Golf Open at the country club; the casino was the home of
the U.S. Lawn Tennis Association; and, of course, that other rich man's
sport, yachting, was a seriously competitive affair with the venerable New

York Yacht Club holding annual races off Newport. For sixteen years, until his death on board his yacht at Cowes, Ogden Goelet offered a $1,000 and $500 prize for schooners and sloops during the key yachting week of the season in August.[20] Newport's cottagers sank considerable money into constructing sports arenas and into yachts and, in addition to participating in sports in exclusive venues, their spectatorship was yet another opportunity for self-display. The reporting of what women wore at the tennis championships at the casino was as detailed as that of the gowns worn at the horse show at the beginning of the New York winter season.

Nevertheless, nature was seen as a great restorative and living by the sea or camping and hiking in the mountains were among the physical recreations recommended as beneficial to one's health. Camping parties in the Adirondacks became popular among the fashionable and their thrills and virtues were extolled in the *Ladies' Home Journal*: "now that women have proved that they are not so frail and helpless ... and that they are quite as capable of enjoying the rough life and thriving on it as their masculine friends, camp life has taken on a new charm, and the men are glad to have the companionship of the fair sex."[21] The editor, Edward Bok, was an advocate of country life and attacked the formality and conspicuous display of fashion at summer resorts. "Some women," he wrote, "have an idea that God created the country especially as a sort of parade-ground for every vanity known to womankind." Neither the country nor the seashore were the place for vulgar display; they were supposed to be places of comfort, rest, and simplicity.[22]

By the 1890s, however, simplicity could no longer occupy the same sentence with society, neither at country resorts nor in the city. All notion of society being simple had long given way in the 1870s to a life lived in public and one that involved a fiercely competitive display of wealth and leisure. The era of Mrs. Astor's reign, from the 1870s to the late 1890s, witnessed an attempt to bring order to the perceived anarchy of arrivistes who descended on (or emerged from within) New York City. Formal rituals and insistence on compliance with strict codes of etiquette helped to construct and maintain class boundaries, and women were at the center of these efforts. Little, however, could be done to stem the fierce competitiveness of the wealthy. Albert Crockatt dubbed the years 1897 to 1908 as the "age of strut" (Crockatt 305). Although the influence of the established elite was waning at this time, still the nouveaux riches sought to emulate its social rituals and accrete themselves in order to claim social distinction. The concept of leisured lives, for all of its evocation of luxury, elegance, and privilege belied the anxiety, competition, and ruthlessness that exercised the wealthy. It also generated ample material for a consummate storyteller with an eye for detail.

NOTES

1. According to Henry Collins Brown, tennis required a distinctive form of dress to allow for greater movement of the body; until this time there were few sports, in which elite women engaged, which required specialized dress. See H. C. Brown, *Brownstone Fronts and Saratoga Trunks* (New York: E. P. Dutton, 1935), 152–54.
2. M. H. Elliot, a contemporary of Wharton, saw this as the beginning of the athletic era in Newport and records that it was Harry Stevens who helped to popularize tennis there. See M. H. Elliot, *This Was My Newport* (Cambridge, MA: The Mythology Company, 1944), 206–07.
3. Mrs. Penniston in *The House of Mirth* has a similar capacity as "a looker-on in life" whose "mind resembled one of those little mirrors which her Dutch ancestors were accustomed to affix to their upper windows, so that from the depths of an impenetrable domesticity they might see what was happening in the street" (*HM* 58). The Dutch ancestresses and their mirrors are reinvoked in *The Mother's Recompense*, in which Mrs. Clephane senior is accorded the role of noting new fashions (New York and London: D. Appleton Century, 1925), 44.
4. At the time it was a feature of entertainments at the court of Louis Napoleon and Eugénie at the Tuileries Palace. See L. Morris, *Incredible New York: High Life and Low Life of the Last Hundred Years* (New York: Random House, 1951), 17–19. Subsequent references to this work are included in the text.
5. L. A. Erenberg, *Steppin' Out: New York Nightlife and the Transformation of American Culture, 1890–1930* (Chicago: University of Chicago Press, 1981), 148. Subsequent references to this work are included in the text.
6. S. Beckert, *The Monied Metropolis: New York City and the Consolidation of the American Bourgeoisie, 1850–1896* (Cambridge: Cambridge University Press, 2001), 18–19.
7. W. McAllister, *Society As I Have Found It* (New York: Cassell, 1890), 214.
8. H. P. Hamlin, *An Albany Girlhood*, ed. A. P. Kenney (Albany, NY: Washington Park Press, 1990), 216. Subsequent references to this work are included in the text. While there is no record of Huybertie (of New York Dutch descent) meeting Wharton, she was well acquainted with Governor and Mrs. Levi P. Morton and spent a summer at Bar Harbor, Maine, living next door to Wharton's sister-in-law, Minnie.
9. See, for example, *New York Times*, January 8, 1901, 1; January 7, 1902, 7; January 12, 1904, 7. Even the menus of the food served were identical.
10. *New York Times*, February 7, 1897, 10. At both balls she went dressed as Mary Stuart, Queen of Scots.

11. See also M. E. Montgomery, *Displaying Women: Spectacles of Leisure in Edith Wharton's New York* (New York: Routledge, 1998), 78; the *New York Times*, January 21, 1900, 7. The latter was a double parody: it lampooned African Americans who were said to have ideas above their station using the well-known minstrel character, Zip Coon, who put on exaggerated airs and graces, and it ridiculed both social climbers and established high-society personalities.

12. See also, A. Stevens Crockatt, *Peacocks on Parade: A Narrative of a Unique Period in American Social History and Its Most Colorful Figures* (New York: Sears Publishing, 1931), 52–53. Sherry's restaurant and Delmonico's still offered exclusive dining for those less inclined toward more democratic and less formal establishments. Subsequent references to this work are included in the text.

13. As an alternative to U.S. summer resorts, fashionable society also flocked to European capitals to engage in yet more formal socializing or to recover from the hectic pace of the season by taking the waters at German spas such as Baden Baden or Wiesbaden. After Easter, London society was in full swing and then, of course, there was the requisite visit to the haute couturiers of the Rue de la Paix in Paris.

14. The phrase "ball point" was used by The Saunterer, the columnist of society news in the gossipy *Town Topics*, with reference to the social campaign of the Gould family (see *Town Topics*, December 6, 1894, 3).

15. The Duke married Consuelo Vanderbilt the following autumn in New York.

16. See C. Vanderbilt, Jr., *Queen of the Golden Age: The Fabulous Story of Grace Wilson Vanderbilt* (New York: McGraw-Hill, 1956), 4–9.

17. *Town Topics,* July 30, 1896, 5.

18. *Town Topics*, September 3, 1896, 6.

19. *New York Times*, July 21, 1895, 24 and July 22, 1894, 13. Her first husband was also a devotee and involved in the establishment of the Newport golf course.

20. *New York Times*, August 28, 1897, 7. He had inherited with his brother a massive fortune in New York real estate and had been a member of the Patriarchs committee.

21. J. Harte, "A Camp in the Adirondacks," *Ladies' Home Journal*, 9 (July 1892), 2–3.

22. E. Bok, "At Home with the Editor," *Ladies' Home Journal*, 7 (June 1893), 16.

CHAPTER 22

Wharton and Gender

Linda Wagner-Martin

Edith Newbold Jones Wharton, born January 24, 1862, was a fully developed professional writer long before her cultures – both United States and European – began thinking in terms of gender. Wharton, of course, had opinions about women's writing: she was less vehement than Hawthorne had been when he chastized what he called the tribe of scribbling women, those who wrote domestic fiction to earn a living. However, she believed similarly. She believed that if she were to become a truly significant literary figure, she must not write as if she were a woman. In her view, Sarah Orne Jewett was a sentimental local colorist (*BG* 293).[1] Like Willa Cather, Wharton was trying to avoid writing the somewhat predictable stories of women characters who managed to overcome social restrictions that coerced them into becoming less than they might be.

As recent important recovery efforts by scholar Laura Rattray have reminded us, Wharton's early writing was often about those unfulfilled female characters. The fiction that appears in Rattray's two-volume collection of Wharton's unpublished work differs in interesting ways from her early fiction – such as *The House of Mirth* in 1905 – that made her famous.[2] We have long been intrigued by *Bunner Sisters*, her novella about the despairing shopgirl sisters who open a store in their attempt to reach some modest economic level. The only promise available in their grim lives is the chance to marry, and the only candidate is an unscrupulous drug addict, a man who brutalizes the sister he does marry and steals the livelihood of both. A pastiche of gendered conventions, the novella was thought to be unpublishable when it was written (in 1892). It did not see print until 1916 when it appeared in Wharton's fourth collection of short fiction, *Xingu and Other Stories*.[3]

As Wharton presented Ann Eliza and Evelina Bunner, they break the pattern of "uplift" that most women writers in the 1890s were working to create. Without ability or money, these women knew their only hope was marriage. Unfortunately, the man who would marry a Bunner does so in search of money for his drug addiction. (The sisters seem to him inter-changeable; what he desires is the income from their shop.) One of the saddest turns in Wharton's remarkable novella is the fact that the cast-off wife comes back to the shop, a site now even poorer, and expresses her enmity toward her older sister, who had allowed her to make the mar-riage she herself desired. Hermione Lee rightly calls the story "a realist masterpiece of thwarted lives," comparing it to Balzac and emphasizing how "compressed" the women's lives are seen to be (Lee, "Introduction" ix–xi).[4]

Bunner Sisters was written during Wharton's early period of serious fic-tion, beginning five or six years after her marriage to Teddy Wharton in 1885. Shari Benstock groups the shorter stories, "Mrs. Manstey's View" and "The Fulness of Life" with *Bunner Sisters*, but admits that Wharton's writing practices during the 1880s remain a mystery (Benstock 70–72). Benstock also reflects on the fact that Wharton's isolation as a would-be writer made her overly dependent on the opinions of her editors, and when they disliked a work (as they did *Bunner Sisters*), she grew insecure about her own judgments. An example of Wharton's insecurity occurs in her July 1898 letter to Burlingame when she says she does not want to include these early writings in her first book of stories because, "They were all written 'at the top of my voice,' & The Fulness of Life is one long shriek." She wants instead to "write in a lower key" for her readers (*Letters* 36).

The themes of these early stories, however, draw on what Wharton knew about urban life, and particularly about the unhappiness of women's lives in whatever setting. Mysterious as well are the accounts of Wharton's erratic health during these years, and the fact that, with her beloved father dead in 1882 and her relationship with her quixotic mother always puzzling, Wharton was herself continuously unhappy. For Wharton to have worked so diligently to achieve her own marriage (first to Henry Stevens, whose family rejected her; then to Walter Berry, who never pro-posed; and finally to the least suitable of the three men, Teddy Wharton) only to be so bitterly isolated in that marriage was surely a turning point for her life – as well as for her fiction. Her lament in a poignant passage from "The Fulness of Life" – a selection she would not ever allow to be reprinted – spoke to more than the isolation of an unhappy wife:

I have sometimes thought that a woman's nature is like a great house full of rooms: there is the hall, through which everyone passes in going in and out; the drawing-room, where one receives formal visits; the sitting-room, where members of the family come and go as they list; but beyond that, far beyond, are other rooms, the handles of whose doors perhaps are never turned; no one knows the way to them, no one knows whither they lead; and in the innermost room, the holy of holies, the soul sits alone and waits for a footstep that never comes.[5] (*CSI* 14)

The same kind of resignation appears in a somewhat later story, "Autres Temps ..." as it had in "The Choice," "The Letters," "The Lady's Maid's Bell," and a few others. None of these stories, however, is a "classic" Wharton work, nor is it often anthologized.

Most of the writings of Edith Wharton, however varied, lent themselves to much more conventional (and sometimes non-gendered) interpretations. It is difficult to write an autobiographical study of Wharton only through her fiction, especially given the readings of it that were current in the early twentieth century. Precisely because Wharton was trying to avoid being read as a woman writer, it took half a century before critics paid necessary attention to the strong women characters she created. Wharton's fiction was more often valued for her portraits of male figures.

The Wharton of the earliest years of the new century had learned some very specifically gendered rules. She had learned that she would be allowed to lead her life, and publish her writings, so long as she obeyed the restrictions every woman – regardless of class – intuitively knew. She would be allowed to write (and publish, and receive good payment for her writing) so long as her editors and publishers saw her as a serious writer, one who did not fall into the category of "woman writer." In her view, she must avoid the ostensibly – or easily – sentimental. No reader cried at the end of a Wharton novel, and her conscious avoidance of the sentimental also explains in part the absence of children in much of her fiction.

There are at least three ironies in Wharton's position as author. The first is that – in the rationale of propriety and class – she was customarily known as "Mrs. Wharton," even twenty-five years after her divorce. Using this cognomen kept her in the province of the upper class and the elite, and marked her as the kind of advantaged writer whose life circumstances separated her almost completely from the retinue of the U.S. modernists – men who were not distinguished by either education or finances, and who made their literary fortunes by writing about such impoverished if daring, and usually male, characters.

The second irony is that Wharton handled all her own publication negotiations, and in her 220 letters to Frederick Macmillan (as well as many to Charles Scribner) she showed herself to be a real scrapper.[6] As Wharton's correspondence with friends as well as publishers shows, she did not want to settle for any polite position: she wanted what there was to be earned from writing. She was especially careful about rates for serialization (nearly all her novels appeared in serial form, and often in less prestigious magazines such as the *Pictorial Review* – the rights going to whomever would pay the highest fee). Shafquat Towheed concludes that Wharton was "consistently hard-headed" in all her negotiations (40).[7]

The third and perhaps most important irony was the criticism that followed Wharton's fiction: extant with each publication, critics repeated their mantra – that Edith Wharton was not a woman writer in any negative sense, that her best fiction was about male characters (many of whom resembled Wharton), and that her art relegated politics to a small corner of her work. By creating literature that replicated the universal, the abstract principles of human relationships, Wharton had earned a place in the pantheon of important writers. She herself encouraged this view by describing her writing as that of a male, explaining in a November 1907 letter to Robert Grant, "I conceive my subjects like a man – that is, rather more architectonically & dramatically than most women – & then execute them like a woman; or rather, I sacrifice, to my desire for construction & breadth, the small incidental effects that women have always excelled in, the episodical characterization …" (*Letters* 124). To succeed as a serious writer, Wharton seemed willing to extinguish many of her womanly traits – at least in her own self-conscious assessments.

It is easy to see Wharton's 1905 novel, *The House of Mirth*, as a test case for this latter irony. Lily Bart, the beautiful but penniless protagonist, must marry well to save her social position, and in some respects the honor of both herself and her family. In the opening scene, Lily seems to be manacled by her bracelets, caught in the trappings of the wealth that made a woman fashionable and desirable, the only qualities that mattered to her appropriate social class.

What Wharton did as well in this opening scene was to describe Lawrence Selden, the point-of-view figure, through whose eyes the tragic story of the naïve Lily is seen and told. A remarkable choice, Wharton's Selden begins as sympathetic, astute, worldly; the reader immediately follows the thread of impending romance, and for the course of the novel, Wharton surprisingly creates a narrative of disappointment.

Rather than instruct Lily, Selden misleads her. Rather than give her truly helpful information about the people of her (and his) class, Selden disappears at crucial moments. Rather than build a structure that might protect Lily, Selden uses his marginal stance in the social façade to show that he is keeping his distance from her. The overwhelming irony of his rush to her bedside – too late to either help her or love her – is that the character of Selden thinks he is saving her. Buffeted as she has been by the power brokers of her culture – the women as well as the men – Lily Bart has sacrificed both her reputation and her beauty in the service of Selden's reputation. It is the Bertha Dorset letters to him which she throws into the fire at their last meeting, the letters that would have permitted either Selden or Lily to have silenced the voices that were destroying Lily's life. Completely unaware that Lily has these letters, Selden shows himself to be in many respects even more naïve than Lily.

For decades of critique, the character of Selden was held up as a kind of astute – even noble – observer, saddened by Lily Bart's fall but seemingly separate from the events of her usually trusting life, events that led to her decline. It is this reading of Selden that critics used as a comparison to their sense of Edith Wharton, author, the sage purveyor of wisdom through her cultural commentary.

The House of Mirth, in the past thirty years, has been read very differently, and as a testament to what Wharton knew early on about the character of both men and women, detailed here in one of her most acidly gendered novels. Benstock places this novel at the heart of Wharton's immense, even spectacular, panoply of human character, and links it to her 1907 novel, originally titled *Justine Brent* (we know it as *The Fruit of the Tree*). In this later work, Wharton's women characters are not trapped by either social expectations or marriages. In her treatment of strong women (and the woman question, as well as euthanasia), Wharton challenges the very readers who objected to Lily Bart's death. These were financially able women, capable of making choices, even romantic ones. Sales for this novel were far below those of *The House of Mirth* (Benstock 153–55).

Interested as she was in marketing, Wharton tended to blame her publishers for differences in novels' sales. In many of her letters, and in her memoir, she does not attempt to explain why readers responded to one novel rather than another. Self-conscious as she was about protecting herself from the charges of being a woman writer, Wharton failed to comment on the qualitative differences in the women characters she drew. Had she been privy to the concept of gender, or to early notions of the feminism inherent in the struggle for women's vote, she might have broken away sooner from her need to give her readers socially acceptable female heroes.[8]

In an unpublished eulogy for Jean du Breuil de Saint-Germain during World War I, Wharton made one of her most political feminist comments; she said of him that "he made me see that the only thing that matters, in the feminist movement, is the fate of ... those poor hard-working women who accept their long misery with an animal fatalism because they do not know they have a right to a more humane existence."[9]

As a rule, the situation was not so much that Wharton's vocabulary lagged behind the times as it was that critics were somewhat stifled by their need to maintain the insistence that Wharton was a major writer. Yet years before Judith Butler's *Gender Trouble* made the use of that term an imperative, critics were adopting the concepts of gender to Wharton's successful works. Marilyn French's essay in the 1987 issue of *College Literature*, published after the first academic Wharton conference at The Mount in Lenox, Massachusetts, used the title "Muzzled Women" to reflect on the fact that many women writers never managed to draw women characters who were as adventurous, as bold, as acclaimed as those writers themselves had been or were.

Because of this artistic weakness, French argued, readers did not know how to read strong women – the reciprocal benefit of creating strong female characters and then having readers understand their creation was yet to come. French, herself an acclaimed feminist author, saw that women writers often blinded themselves to the "full range of possibility they knew was open to women. This disparity is so pervasive that one inclines to believe it is caused by censorship – external and internal, the more insidious sort."[10]

Wharton's career illustrates well French's analysis, with the added propensity to avoid what French calls "certain kinds of female figures" – women with power, and especially women with power over men. French notes, "Most readers cannot absorb, take in, such a character" (227). While French concludes her essay hopefully awaiting what she calls the second wave of feminism, a state in which "women authors [will be allowed] to use more of their experience in their work, allowing readers to accept such characters," a number of other critics were trying to place Wharton and her fictions in meaningful retrospective context (French 229).

Dale M. Bauer's 1994 *Edith Wharton's Brave New Politics* related Wharton's work to her culture, both war and postwar, and to the author's growing celebrity. Bauer discusses such a work as "Roman Fever" as a gender study, with the powerless widows kept from knowing even the simplest facts of their own narratives; and with her discussion of *Twilight Sleep*, Bauer ends equivocation about Wharton's sympathies: she states that Wharton had long since learned "that women under capitalist patriarchy form an oppressed class on their own, regardless of the class they enter upon marriage."[11] This too is the view of Martha Banta, a decade later, summarizing Wharton's women characters with a positive inflection that was years coming: Banta sees that Wharton often wrote about "trapped women ... History defined as the whiggish promise of progress toward social and personal perfection is mocked by Wharton's novels and tales about women suffocating in unsatisfactory marriages. She provides no promises that things will ever be better as succeeding generations move through the chain of time."[12]

Similarly confident, Susan Goodman draws the same set of conclusions: she writes about Wharton, "Always conscious of and concerned with questions of gender, Wharton played with its parameters and privileges" and did not hesitate to term herself, ironically, a "self-made man." Nevertheless, Goodman accurately points out (and wrote two different monographs about Wharton's inner circle of women friends, and the other of male colleagues) that she was subject to the aesthetic beliefs of her large male innermost circle, that art was the supreme goodness, and blessing, of life, and had in itself the "ability to bridge the limitations of time, history, and self."[13] As if avoiding the easier concept of gender, Goodman echoed in some ways the rubrics Wharton herself might have chosen – to place art, particularly her art, beyond considerations of gender politics.

NOTES

1. D. L. Chambers gives the best summary of Wharton's views in her *Feminist Readings of Edith Wharton* (New York: Palgrave Macmillan, 2009). See especially Chapter 1, "Wharton and Feminist Criticism," 15–24.
2. See particularly "Disintegration" in vol. II of L. Rattray (ed.), *The Unpublished Writings of Edith Wharton* (London: Pickering and Chatto, 2009), 65–118; both volumes are essential for any reader.
3. Hermione Lee recounts that Charles Scribner and Edward Burlingame were "nervous" about the novella's "unflinching grimness" and so would not publish it in *Scribner's Magazine* until 1916. H. Lee "Introduction" to *Edith Wharton: Ethan Frome, Summer, Bunner Sisters* (New York: Knopf, 2008), ix–xxviii; ix–x. Subsequent references to this work are included in the text.
4. Contrasted with *Bunner Sisters*, Gertrude Stein's *Three Lives* in 1909 might seem understated.
5. See J. Haytock, *Edith Wharton and the Conversations of Literary Modernism* (New York: Palgrave Macmillan, 2008), Chapter 5, "'The Readjustment of Personal Relations': Marriage, Modernism, and the Alienated Self," 131–58.
6. Shafquat Towheed points out that Macmillan was the preeminent world publisher, and that he paid Wharton rates that were much higher than those he paid most of his authors. Her standard royalty was twenty percent and she often used the threat of moving to a different publishing house to get her way. S. Towheed (ed.), *The Correspondence of Edith Wharton and Macmillan, 1901–1930* (New

York: Palgrave Macmillan, 2007), 15–33. Subsequent references to this work are included in the text.

7. See also C. J. Singley, Introduction, *A Historical Guide to Edith Wharton* (New York: Oxford University Press, 2003), 3–17; 7–10.

8. These are to come in the following decade, particularly Anna Leath in *The Reef* and the women of *The Age of Innocence*.

9. Quoted in D. L. Williams, *Not in Sisterhood: Edith Wharton, Willa Cather, Zona Gale and the Politics of Female Authorship* (New York: Palgrave, 2001), 122.

10. M. French, "Muzzled Women," *College Literature*, 14 (1987), 219–29; 225. Subsequent references to this work are included in the text.

11. D. M. Bauer, *Edith Wharton's Brave New Politics* (Madison State: University of Wisconsin Press, 1994), 100. While Bauer does not often use the word "gender," she relies on the phrase "Cultural dialogics."

12. M. Banta, "Wharton's Women: In Fashion, In History, Out of Time" in C. J. Singley (ed.), *A Historical Guide to Edith Wharton* (New York: Oxford University Press, 2003), 51–88; 70. For the argument that Wharton has always written about women characters somewhat subversively, see J. Dyman's *Lurking Feminism, The Ghost Stories of Edith Wharton* (New York: Peter Lang 1996).

13. S. Goodman, "Edith Wharton's Inner Circle" in K. Joslin and A. Price (eds.), *Wretched Exotic: Essays on Edith Wharton* (New York: Peter Lang, 1993), 43–60; 54.

CHAPTER 23

Race and Imperialism

Margaret Toth

Just five months after the close of the Philippine-American War (1899–1902), Edith Wharton published "The Mission of Jane" in *Harper's Monthly*. The story – narrating the trials a married couple, the Lethburys, faces raising Jane, an adopted orphan of unknown origins – engages several topics at play in contemporary debates about U.S. imperialism. Echoing alarmist views that Filipinos, if made wards of the United States, would contaminate and potentially annihilate the body politic, Wharton predicates "Jane's evolution," as the narrator describes it (*CSI* 423), on Mrs. Lethbury's regression. In a "monstrous fusion of identity" with the infant Jane, Mrs. Lethbury finds the "cave-mother" in her emerging, "centuries of animal maternity" hitherto repressed (*CSI* 421–22). As Jane grows older, her presence becomes even more troublesome; not unlike a resisting colonized subject, she gains power over the Lethburys through the ability to mimic and redeploy her guardians' discourse. The Lethbury household, which is unsettled and divided during Jane's upbringing, only reunifies once Jane – who remains an unassimilated "other" throughout the story – leaves to start her own family. While Wharton remained largely silent on her country's imperialist efforts at the turn of the century, "The Mission of Jane" indirectly draws on several topics circulating in pro- and anti-imperialist literature from the period, including benevolence, assimilation, the burden of duty to legal wards, and anxieties over racial heritage.

Representatives on both sides of the imperialism debate relied on popular race sentiment and oftentimes dubious race science to justify their arguments for and against expansion. Race, with respect to how it was both defined and experienced, was shifting dramatically during the period. This essay examines the mutually imbricated discourses of imperialism and race that governed Wharton's world and her work, considering her life and literature within an array of relevant contemporary contexts.

U.S. international politics experienced a seismic shift during Wharton's lifetime, first through overt expansionist efforts in territories like Hawaii, Cuba, and the Philippines – along with quieter imperialist operations in countries like Mexico and China – and later through World War I. While all these ventures were vital to the construction of a new transnational identity, it was perhaps the Spanish-American War and its aftermath that initially indicated, to European powers and U.S. citizens alike, the country's ascendant role in a shifting global hierarchy. In 1898, President McKinley, in retaliation for the sinking of the *USS Maine* and ostensibly in support of Cuba's quest for independence, led the country into war with Spain. The conflict, lasting four months, concluded with the Treaty of Paris, which granted the United States varying degrees of control over several territories formerly under Spanish rule, including Cuba, Puerto Rico, and the Philippines. Adopting different policies regarding the territories, the United States favored annexation of the Philippines; but McKinley's issuance of the Benevolent Assimilation Proclamation, laying out plans for rule in the Philippines, incensed Filipinos seeking independence and thereby instigated the Philippine-American War. These conflicts inspired fierce arguments, often referred to as the imperialism debates, among the U.S. populace. Although mainstream accounts have marginalized this chapter of U.S. history, it is difficult to overstate just how tumultuous and formative it was. The imperialism debates forced the United States, which had prided itself (however speciously) on exceptionalism with respect to imperial designs, to confront the task of constructing a new international identity.

Given the intensity of these national debates and Wharton's bold stance on World War I less than two decades later – not to mention her extensive intercontinental travel at the height of the debates – Wharton was surprisingly reserved about the changing international role of the United States. Many of her literary contemporaries, including Julia Ward Howe, Mark Twain, and William Dean Howells, staked firm claims on either side of the imperialism debate in their private and public writings. In contrast, Wharton's beliefs were less explicit, even though she humorously referred to herself as a "rabid Imperialist" in a letter to her friend Sara Norton in March 1901 (*Letters* 45). Although some digging is required to excavate Wharton's own perspectives on U.S. imperialism, many of her friends and acquaintances took unambiguous stances on the subject. Their writings offer a wide range of views, from enthusiastic pacifism to unapologetic imperialism, and exhibit several contexts with which Wharton herself was certainly familiar and that likely shaped what

Frederick Wegener describes as the "imperial sensibility" subtending her politics and fiction.[1]

When Wharton cagily described herself as a "rabid Imperialist" to Sara Norton, she surely was acquainted with Sara's father's anti-imperialist views. Charles Eliot Norton – a Harvard University professor of art history who guided her education in Italian culture and lent her valuable support as she worked on her historical novel *The Valley of Decision* (1902) – opposed the Spanish-American War and was a vocal critic of the U.S. involvement in the Philippines and so-called "benevolent assimilation." At the other end of the spectrum were figures like Wharton's lifelong friend Walter Berry, a strong supporter of annexation and imperialist economics in Puerto Rico, and acquaintance Theodore Roosevelt, perhaps *the* leading ideologue in the pro-annexationist movement (Lee 68). Roosevelt fought as a Rough Rider in the Spanish-American War, planting the seeds for his future political career. Later, as Vice President and then President of the United States, he supported a colonial state in the Philippines, which he viewed as a natural extension of Westward expansion.

For Roosevelt, the Philippines also emblematized the new anti-isolationist path his country should pursue. His view was quite popular, rearticulated by pro-imperialists in several leading newspapers and periodicals. For instance, Senator Henry Cabot Lodge – father of the aspiring poet Bay Lodge, of whom Wharton was fond – argued that the United States needed to fulfill its "noble task" by acquiring the Philippines and thereby "taking rank where we belong, as one of the greatest of the great world powers."[2] Wharton's friend and lover Morton Fullerton agreed with these views. In *Problems of Power* (1913), written in the aftermath of the turn-of-the-century imperialism debates, he took an expansive view, concentrating on the Panama Canal and Pan-Americanism but also gesturing toward more far-reaching global ambitions. The volume, which Wharton read in draft form and advised Fullerton on, expresses some skepticism about tools of imperialism like the Monroe Doctrine, but primarily champions the United States' new role and anticipates a world dominated, both fiscally and culturally, by the system of Western capitalism. In a section on China and the Far East, for instance, Fullerton envisions an Asian landscape "criss-crossed with railways built by Western capital, that will discipline in civilizing ways a population ready to take its part in the task of world organization."[3]

Although Wharton was no doubt conversant with her acquaintances' arguments for and against U.S. imperialism, she rarely wrote explicitly about the subject. However, both her life choices and several of her written works suggest pro-imperialist and colonialist leanings. In terms of biography, Wharton, at the height of the imperialism debates, moved into The Mount, her palatial estate in Lenox, Massachusetts. The Whartons, like many Old New York families building in the region, including the Stuyvesants and Vanderbilts, were weary of Newport and were attracted to the undeveloped land and quaint romanticism that the New England countryside offered. Like intrepid settlers, they tolerated the local "natives," the rural poor that the writer later would racialize in *Ethan Frome* (1911) and *Summer* (1917), in order to live out their dream of "colonizing" the territory. Wharton's contemporaries recognized the imperialist spirit underpinning these ventures. In *Problems of Power*, for example, Fullerton references Lenox in order to draw a comparison between the "rich families of New York [who] have created vast domains around their country houses" and "Roman and Gallo-Roman colonists" (24). Familiar with Lenox because of his visits at The Mount, Fullerton introduces Wharton and her milieu's colonizing tendencies in this passage in order to situate them as leaders of the United States' new "imperial movement" (25).

While Fullerton here stresses the "newness" of imperialism, Wharton's ambitions in Lenox in fact signal both a return to, and a revival of the colonialist–imperialist legacy bequeathed to her by her ancestors, particularly her great-grandfather Ebenezer Stevens. In *A Backward Glance* (1934), she proudly memorializes Stevens, who earned an illustrious name for himself as a general in the Revolutionary War. Wharton also paid homage to Stevens through her project in Lenox. Stevens, after the war, used "the fortune he had made as a [East India] merchant" – in other words, the profits of an entrenched agent of British imperialist machinery – to build Mount Buonaparte, later renamed simply The Mount, on Long Island (*BG* 13). A century later, Wharton trained an imperial gaze on her generation's version of "unsettled" territory, western Massachusetts, and, by christening her home The Mount, forged an explicit bond between herself and her colonialist–imperialist forefather. It is perhaps no coincidence, then, that in the letter wherein she labels herself a "rabid Imperialist," she also mentions her purchase of the land at Lenox and her plans to begin developing it (*Letters* 45).

Wharton's imperialist sympathies become even clearer when we situate her as a global citizen. After she abandoned her life at The Mount and settled permanently in France, she became a vocal supporter of her adopted country's imperialist and colonialist policies. Her intellectual circle in Paris included several key advocates of the French empire. As Wegener puts it, "Wharton's recollections of her milieu during this period [from 1907 to World War I] constitute a checklist of statesmen, aristocrats, scholars, and journalists whose work was instrumental in buttressing the implementation of French territorial designs overseas" (788). One of these acquaintances, Hubert Lyautey, Resident-General of Morocco, coordinated Wharton and Berry's trip to French-occupied Morocco in 1917. Wharton had traveled to Algeria and Tunisia in 1914, and in 1917, despite the war, she eagerly took advantage of the opportunity to travel to a part of the world that she repeatedly described throughout her life as "magical." The resulting travel narrative, *In Morocco*, dedicated to Lyautey and his wife, reads like a propaganda tract for French colonialism. While Wharton expresses some hesitation about making North Africa too accessible to European influence, fearing it might compromise the region's authenticity, she champions Lyautey's efforts, even devoting several pages to charts that numerically document the successes – commercial, educational, judicial – of the French Protectorate. Toward the end of the narrative, Wharton succinctly articulates her views about imperialism: if a country finds itself in a "demoralized condition," then "European powers" are "justified" in "assert[ing] their respective ascendencies."[4] No doubt these imperial sentiments also shaped her passionate perspectives on World War I (see Julie Olin-Ammentorp's essay in this volume).

These imperialist sympathies inflect Wharton's works, sometimes quite directly. For instance, the short story "The Seed of Faith," set in Morocco and published two years after the writer's trip there, holds the French administration in high regard even as it criticizes U.S. missionaries. While perhaps not as obvious, novels like *The Reef* (1912) and *The Children* (1928) reveal Wharton's understanding of the terms of U.S. imperialism and indicate her support for the Monroe Doctrine and anti-isolationism. As with *The Children*, other novels written after World War I – for instance *The Glimpses of the Moon* (1922), in which the characters' "denationalized" identities[5] and Orientalist proclivities appear to be codependent – invite reevaluation for their commentary on new imperial dynamics, ones restructured in the wake of the war.

While Wharton's imperialist propensities seem clear, they are complicated by her views on race. As Jennie Kassanoff has argued, her fiction expresses anxieties about the "racial hybridization" inherent in the processes of exploring and conquering new territories, including the "frontier," which is "a site of regrettable racial corruption."[6] While Kassanoff here refers to the "hybridization" that occurred in the settling of the Western frontier, racial mixing was still a live issue when Wharton embarked on her literary career. The question of amalgamation surfaced repeatedly in multiple discussions – from the imperialism debates to conversations about immigration reform and arguments for and against African American and American Indian enfranchisement – and it inspired counter-discourses of racial preservation, such as nativism and eugenics, among Anglo-Americans.

A familiar starting point for discussions of Wharton and race is the "crisis" of racial integration facing Old New York and New England toward the end of the nineteenth century. The influx of immigrant populations, which coincided with the emigration of young men of established families to the West, threatened to restructure the racial makeup of long-standing Anglo-American communities. Moreover, birthrate studies suggested that Old New York and New England "stock" was on the decline, raising the fearful specter of race suicide. Prominent figures in Wharton's U.S. circle, including Roosevelt, Norton, Henry Cabot Lodge, and Henry James, expressed concern over this possibility. Henry James suggested that "a prodigious amalgam ... a hotch-potch [sic] of racial ingredients" was accelerating biological decay in New England (quoted in Kassanoff 54), while Roosevelt, taking a proactive stance, argued that reproduction was a national duty and labeled those who refused parenthood "criminals." He issued dire warnings about the future of the United States: "If the tendency is not checked, ["the race"] will vanish completely – in other words, there will be race suicide."[7]

Such pleas for positive eugenics (encouraging reproduction among "desirable" populations) merged with more pernicious agendas of negative eugenics (limiting "undesirable" reproduction), with the latter becoming increasingly popular in the United States in the 1900s and 1910s. Texts like Robert Reid Rentoul's *Race Culture; Or, Race Suicide (A Plea for the Unborn)* (1906) and Madison Grant's *The Passing of the Great Race* (1916) advocated such measures as sterilization and segregation to prevent reproduction among those classified as "degenerates," including the mentally ill, the poor, and anyone not deemed racially "fit." For instance, Rentoul, writing in the United Kingdom, recommended that the U.S. government sterilize African Americans and railed against "inter-marriage of the white man and black, the white man with the redskin, the white man with the native Hindu, or the white man with the Chinese," which would only result in "terrible monstrosities."[8] Race science, such as Sir Francis Galton's studies in heredity, and particularly Herbert Spencer's treatise on Social Darwinism, figured prominently in these works and lent them a patina of authority. Spencer, whose work profoundly shaped Wharton's own understanding of race, contended that the "law of organic process is the law of all progress"; in other words, just as individual organisms evolve, so too does society.[9] To Wharton's contemporaries, who often perverted Spencer's vision, Social Darwinism seemingly offered clear justification against racial mixing: they needed to preserve not only their "species" but also their society and, more broadly, the nation. As a response, they mobilized nativist and sometimes explicitly eugenicist ideologies.

Wharton scholars have demonstrated that these concerns deeply inform novels like *The House of Mirth* (1905) and *The Age of Innocence* (1920), both of which refuse to integrate racialized others, Simon Rosedale and Ellen Olenska respectively, into the United States' body politic. However, Old New York nativism and eugenics provocatively connect with other race contexts that have received less attention in Wharton criticism, in particular the restructuring of the United States' racial geography through oppressive government legislation in the 1880s and 1890s. In this period, as nativist concerns among the writer's peers escalated, legislation like the Chinese Exclusion Act (1882) and the Dawes Act (1887), along with Supreme Court decisions like *Plessy v. Ferguson* (1896), sought in various ways to delimit how people of color entered into, occupied, and navigated the United States' landscape.

Several of these decisions reverberated long past Wharton's lifetime, coming up for appeal only to be amended and reified. Yellow Peril rhetoric, employed to pass legislation restricting Chinese immigration, drew from and redeployed the language of Roosevelt and others concerned with race suicide. As one 1882 *San Francisco Alta* article urged U.S. merchants, "self-preservation demands Chinese exclusion."[10] Meanwhile, as nativists bemoaned the future of the vanishing Anglo-American "native" race, the Dawes Act facilitated the deterioration of the United States' actual indigenous population. The Act, which reallocated collectively-owned tribal territory to individual owners in 160-acre increments, resulted not only in immense losses of American Indian land – the surplus was sold off to Anglo-American settlers – but also the weakening of indigenous cultural traditions. Along with other government practices like the Indian Boarding School system, the Dawes Act served as an insidious tool of assimilation, as it explicitly stated that the privileges of citizenship would be extended to those "to whom allotments shall have been made," provided they have "adopted the habits of civilized life."[11] While the Dawes Act established oppressive geographical borders, *Plessy v. Ferguson* restricted the mobility of African Americans by demarcating a strict color line. It also reinforced racist pseudo-scientific understandings of race, upholding such specious doctrines as the "one-drop" rule. This decision took its place alongside other racist legislation, such as the anti-miscegenation laws.

While we should be careful of collapsing these historical moments – as they were prompted by different (though sometimes overlapping) motives and had varied consequences among the affected populations – they are only a handful of many cases that illustrate a pattern in turn-of-the-century U.S. legislation: support for eugenicist and nativist doctrine through the construction and regulation of racial boundaries. Moreover, they exhibit important, and under-examined, frameworks for understanding Wharton's worldview, particularly when she still resided in the United States. When James and others urged Wharton to turn her literary attention to an "American subject" in 1902, for example, the country was experiencing a fierce debate over renewing the Chinese Exclusion Act. This rhetoric resonates in important ways with the anti-Semitic, nativist language that dominates Wharton's protectionist aesthetics in the resulting "American" novel, *The House of Mirth*. Similarly, Jennie Kassanoff's reading of *The Custom of the Country* (1913) – a novel that turns, she argues, on slippages between American Indians and vanishing Old New Yorkers, with the latter seeking to reject the title of "invader" and identify instead as "aborigine" (17) – demonstrates that the background of shifting American Indian policy is important to the work.

Moreover, these events certainly shaped Wharton's racial worldview and her racism. Kassanoff argues that we must acknowledge Wharton's racism (1) and how it evolved as she grew older (39). Similarly, Dale Bauer, charting several key changes across *Summer*, *The Age of Innocence*, and the unfinished last novel, *The Buccaneers*, suggests that the author's views on nativism, eugenics, and racial amalgamation shifted over time. Wharton's last novel, Bauer writes, implies that an "amalgamation of cultures – the English and Brazilian or the American and the British – leads to a more passionate, less reactionary society."[12] Other novels, such as *The Children*, in which the writer destabilizes racial identities in often playful ways, support Bauer's observation. Yet while it is true that Wharton's racial views may have opened up in some respects, they narrowed in others. For instance, her racism toward African Americans – evidenced in her disgust for the Harlem Renaissance – made its way into novels like *Twilight Sleep*, which in its first edition casually and repeatedly used the word "nigger," and the otherwise broadminded *The Buccaneers*, which trades in nostalgia for plantation mythology. In other words, it is not that Wharton's racist views disappeared as she grew older; rather, they simply changed.

For instance, as Wharton's attitudes on race shifted over time, one discourse emerged more and more frequently in her works: Orientalism. Wharton's Orientalism was shaped by a variety of experiences, including her reading of other Orientalist authors and her own excursions in North Africa. While traveling in Algeria, she wrote to Fullerton on April 9, 1914, enumerating the exotic experiences she was accumulating in "this magic land": "we saw a sort of epitome of it all – the caravans of camels, the nomads, the wonderful white figures in the silent sun-baked streets . . . the Ouled-Naïls [Algerian belly dancers] dancing ventriloquently on a white roof-terrace in the moonlight" (*Letters* 315–16). Dreading the day that she has to return to Europe and "look at ugly monkeys in comic clothes," Wharton exclaims, "*How* I understand Lady Hester Stanhope!" (*Letters* 316). Edward Said claims that "every writer on the Orient . . . assumes some Oriental precedent, some previous knowledge of the Orient, to which he refers and on which he relies," and Wharton was no exception.[13] That she feels a spiritual kinship with Lady Stanhope (1776–1839), a British citizen who traveled extensively in the Middle East and ultimately decided, somewhat scandalously, to settle in Lebanon, is revealing. Said lists Stanhope among several nineteenth-century proponents of Orientalism who played "the role of expert-adventurer-eccentric" (246) and, as scholarship on *Vanadis* and *In Morocco* has demonstrated, this is precisely the role Wharton crafts for herself in her travel narratives. In *In Morocco*, sweeping, authoritative claims about North Africa sit comfortably alongside – and, indeed, are licensed through – her racist representations of "natives," who are rendered variously as infantile, savage, and abject. In other words, it is impossible to separate out Wharton's imperialist and racialist ideologies.

Similarly, in Wharton's novels, especially her later works, imperialism and race intersect at the meeting point of Orientalism. Occasionally, she offers subversive commentary on the subject. In *The Glimpses of the Moon*, for example, Nick grooms himself for a career in academic Orientalism, dreaming of the book he will write about Asiatic history and Oriental art. Like many of the writers Said describes in *Orientalism*, from Chateaubriand to Flaubert, Nick plans to rely on his imagination, "which had been enchanted by the idea of picturing . . . the fabulous landscapes of Asia" (*Glimpses* 63), to invent his version of Orient: "he liked writing descriptions, and vaguely felt that under the guise of fiction he could develop his theory of Oriental influences in Western art at the expense of less learning than if he had tried to put his ideas into an essay" (*Glimpses* 63). Nick's musings lay bare the deep structure of Orientalist discourse: instead of resolutely devoting himself to a study of the East, Nick, as Western subject, would rather write a fantastical account that mixes fact and fiction. Yet should he find success in the literary market, his narrative, like those of Flaubert, would be consolidated as authoritative. In such passages, Wharton appears not to sanction but to critique, however subtly, the Orientalist apparatus. More often, however – and even throughout *The Glimpses of the Moon* – she exploits Orientalist practices. In *Twilight Sleep*, The School of Oriental Thought, run by the Mahatma (a "Hindu Sage") and championed by Mrs. Manford, herself a type of "expert-adventurer-eccentric," attracts the elite Anglo-American characters in part because of its sexually titillating atmosphere, wherein East/West boundaries are traversed. Quite tellingly, Arthur Wyant refers to the Mahatma as a "nigger chap" (*TS* 46), and cross-cultural boundaries are policed and, ultimately, fortified. In this subplot, Western views on Eastern subjects – shaped so profoundly by imperialism and colonialism – merge with and become inseparable from U.S. segregationist and protectionist policies.

As her Orientalist travel narratives and fiction pointedly reveal, imperialism and race intersect in complicated ways in Wharton's works. In fact, the two subjects are effectively interdependent and, at times, mutually constitutive. In order to tease out such complexities, we must contextualize Wharton's writing within relevant politico-social frameworks, attending to domestic concerns like Old New York nativism, the United States imperialism debates, and racist turn-of-the-century legislation as well as global ones, including European colonialism and Orientalism.

NOTES

1. F. Wegener, "'Rabid Imperialist': Edith Wharton and the Obligations of Empire in Modern American Fiction," *American Literature*, 72 (2000), 783–812; 784.
2. "Lodge Pleads for Peace," *New York Times*, January 25, 1899, 5.
3. M. Fullerton, *Problems of Power* (New York: Charles Scribner's Sons, 1915), 353. Subsequent references to this work are included in the text.
4. E. Wharton, *In Morocco* (New York: Charles Scribner's Sons, 1920), 257.
5. E. Wharton, *The Glimpses of the Moon* (New York; London: D. Appleton and Company, 1922), 46. Subsequent references to this work are included in the text.
6. J. Kassanoff, *Edith Wharton and the Politics of Race* (Cambridge: Cambridge University Press, 2004), 26, 25. Subsequent references to this work are included in the text.

7. Letter from Theodore Roosevelt to Albert Shaw, April 3, 1907, in L. Auchincloss (ed.), *Theodore Roosevelt: Letters and Speeches* (New York: Literary Classics of the United States, Inc., 2004), 520–22; 522.

8. R. R. Rentoul, *Race Culture; Or, Race Suicide?* (London: The Walter Scott Publishing Co., 1906), 31–32, 4–5.

9. H. Spencer, *Progress: Its Law and Cause*, rpt. in *Humboldt Library of Popular Science Literature*, 2 (June 1882): 233–85; 234.

10. "The Terrible Chinee," Rpt. *New York Times*, March 12, 1882, 3.

11. "An Act to Provide for the Allotment of Lands in Severalty to Indians on the Various Reservations (General Allotment Act or Dawes Act)," 1887. *OurDocuments.gov* (accessed January 15, 2011).

12. D. Bauer, *Edith Wharton's Brave New Politics* (Madison: University of Wisconsin Press, 1994), 181.

13. E. Said, *Orientalism* (New York: Vintage Books, 1979), 20. Subsequent references to this work are included in the text.

CHAPTER 24

Social Transitions

Adam Jabbur

From *The House of Mirth* (1905) to *The Age of Innocence* (1920), Edith Wharton's analytical gaze observes in fine detail the many social upheavals that coincided with the Gilded Age and the Progressive Era, the two momentous periods in U.S. history that shaped both the writer's life and her prolific career. Time and again, the worlds of industry, finance, and politics serve either as settings or as major themes in novels aimed at capturing the functions and dysfunctions of social mores both old and new. Schooled in the conventions of a social organization that, as Wharton describes it, prized above all else the conformity and propriety of its members, the author witnessed, often from the other side of the Atlantic, the decline of that system during the late nineteenth and early twentieth centuries, and with it the death of the traditions and customs that formed the moral and ethical foundation of her youth.

Although turned off by the excesses and eccentricities of her modernist successors, Wharton still claimed for herself a reasonably forward-looking stance on social matters, appearing genuinely frustrated at being defined as one of the "prigs and prudes who barred the way to complete expression" (*BG* 127). That is not to say that she wished to efface all of convention and tradition. Even as she denounced her parents' generation for their "blind dread of innovation" and "instinctive shrinking from responsibility," she also acknowledged the redeeming qualities of those "old obediences" from which she herself had sought to break free (*BG* 22). Yet Wharton knew that change must come, and that to face it with fortitude would be a virtue. As she declares in the preface to her autobiography, "one *can* remain alive long past the usual date of disintegration if one is unafraid of change" (*BG* xix).

With neither the polemics of a hardliner nor the disinterested observations of a spectator, Wharton's writings display an often conflicted yet courageous attitude toward the social transitions of her day. In a way, however, it is not so much the notable moments in history, or even the particular rituals of the past, that shape the writer's imaginative pursuits. Instead, it is her sense of passed and passing time, what she once called "the value of duration," that reshapes the tumultuous moments of her era into living portraits of a rapidly and dramatically evolving nation (*BG* 5). Satirical and biting though her novels often are, they retain at least the shadow of possibility – an image, however unclear, of a future that has not lost everything of the past. For Wharton, change is a natural process that, naturally enough, fosters both anxiety and relief, both hardship and hope. Yet despite her ambivalence, she manages to design a model of change tastefully accomplished: a kind of growth that takes the form of continuity; a spawning of new life in a world made stable by the observance of reliable old values.

Spanning from the end of the Civil War until the last decade of the nineteenth century, the Gilded Age is remembered largely for the burgeoning of the Second Industrial Revolution.[1] With the development of efficient new technologies, the postwar United States enjoyed accelerated economic growth in both farming and manufacturing. As Paul Kennedy reports, the decades following the Civil War saw wheat and corn production grow by more than 200 percent, steel rails by 523 percent, coal by 800 percent, and serviceable tracks of railway by more than 500 percent.[2] This last development not only led to greater mobility for people of all classes, it also joined the telegraph in marking a revolution in shipping and communication, opening new markets to large-scale corporate operations. Although the stock market remained centered in Wall Street, there was now great wealth to be made in rural America, and with this wealth came expanded influence peddling. As the national GDP soared, so too did corruption in local and federal government, only intensifying the political and class tensions of the day.

The Gilded Age produced especially dramatic consequences for Wharton's New York. By the early 1870s, "Boss" Tweed's Tammany Hall had become synonymous with underhanded dealings, and civic turmoil revealed growing political partisanship and social instability. The Orange Riots of 1870 and 1871, to name just one example, pitted Irish Catholics against Irish Protestants (the "Orangemen") in a street conflict that represented far more than an Old World grudge brought to U.S. shores. For Michael Gordon, these riots signified nothing less than a conflict over the United States' national identity. "Irish workers and many middle-class Irish allies," he explains, "believed that ... Orange principles would help to subvert republicanism and 'Anglo-Saxonize' America at the same time that industrialization was causing class lines to harden." Alternatively, the Orangemen and their backers saw Irish Catholics as the menace to republican principles, and wished "to reassert the values they believed should govern social relationships as immigrants like the Irish challenged their class authority."[3] Unrest was in the air as revolutionary politics, rampant racketeering, and mass unionization redefined the city's social and economic constitution.

New York's old aristocracy was not immune to these upheavals. Many of the city's wealthy residents were ruined when dozens of banks and investment houses collapsed during the Panic of 1873, and the remnants of the old order would soon find their social scene occupied by an invading force of *nouveau riche*.[4] Despite the financial hardships endured by some, New York offered great opportunities in finance and commerce. During the 1870s and 1880s, more than half of all United States imports landed in New York, and the city's banking system flourished in the last decade of the century, helping to complete a transition of economic power from New York's established patrician set to the newly monied class represented by figures such as Simon Rosedale in *The House of Mirth*. From local merchants, real-estate barons, and financiers to imported industrialists and entrepreneurs, the *nouveau riche* sought and paid for entry into the prestigious high society of Old New York.

Possessing enormous wealth but lacking validated social standing, the newly monied, as Wharton portrays them in many of her novels, used both marriage and elaborate (often gaudy) displays of affluence to demonstrate their worthiness. At the same time, those in possession of inherited wealth and repute, their fortunes in some cases depleted by failed investments or dwarfed by the holdings of the *nouveau riche*, feared alienating these unrefined, yet commanding and powerful, self-made men. For Wharton, however, the ascent of the *nouveau riche* fostered a consequent rise in the vulgarity of both taste and behavior. The once-closed society of her youth had opened itself to a looser moral system, and the old dispensation could not withstand the new assaults on its integrity.[5] Divorce rates drastically increased as judges began to extend greater custody rights to mothers, and the financial dealings of the city's elite, once grounded in principles of honesty and fairness, gave way to opportunism and exploitation. As Hermione Lee puts it, Wharton could not "abandon a concept of 'society' as some kind of recognisable stable entity" (Lee 441). Although suffocating and sometimes petty, the aristocracy of Old New York had, for Wharton, provided the order, manners, and civilizing influence that served as the foundation of a healthy society.

If the Gilded Age serves as background for Wharton's life and work, the Progressive Era serves as foreground. It was during this period she enjoyed some of her greatest popularity and success as a novelist, often representing in art the social transitions that began in her youth and persisted into her adult years. In fact, recent studies of the era have begun to stress the continuities, rather than the differences, between the Gilded Age and the Progressive Era.[6] In response to the corruption and opportunism of the postwar period, the 1890s brought about a series of reforms as activists sought to "purify" government, improve public education and working conditions, and overhaul the nation's financial system, often with broad middle-class support.[7] At the same time, the short-lived Populist Party, comprised mostly of lower-class farmers from the South and Midwest, fought to give voters a more direct role in governance. Many states, largely in response to these emerging populist sentiments, adopted new initiative, recall, and referendum laws that, it was hoped, would further democratize the nation, in part by creating a more informed citizenry capable of challenging widespread political abuses and corporate greed.[8]

As was the case during the Gilded Age, Wharton's New York again took a central role in shaping the national discourse of the Progressive Era, especially in the area of worker rights. By 1880, Samuel Gompers had already referred to the city as "the cradle of the American labor movement,"[9] and the twentieth century would bring to New York not only a drastic upsurge in worker strikes, but also a consequent expansion of collective bargaining rights for the men and women whose labor sustained the city's manufacturing industries. Especially prominent were the tensions between the wealthy capitalist class and the growing immigrant population, which included millions of Italian laborers and a relative handful of European intellectuals, some of whom had crossed the Atlantic with socialist sympathies that now infiltrated mainstream U.S. politics.[10]

Alongside these labor movements, and sometimes in partnership with them, was an intensifying women's rights campaign. Aided by a coalition of wealthy and working-class women called the National Women's Trade Union League of America, the New York Shirtwaist Strike of 1909 aimed at improving working conditions and wages for laborers in the garment industry. In addition, in 1916 Margaret Sanger opened the nation's first birth-control clinic in Brooklyn. Later, in 1920, local initiatives such as these gave way to two major nationwide victories for women's rights activists: the first coming with the establishment of the Women's Bureau in the United States Department of Labor; the second, and more profound, coming with the ratification of the Nineteenth Amendment, which granted women the right to vote and hold political office.

Despite the prevalence of shared goals, however, the progressive movement was far from monolithic. It was, in fact, a mixed bag of alliances that at times seemed at odds with one another. The campaigns for direct elections and recall rights, for example, tended toward an expansion of democratic principles whereas the frequent calls for replacing elected local officials with city managers seem antidemocratic. In a sense, Wharton seems to mirror the often conflicted nature of the Progressive Era. Far from devoting herself to political causes, the writer applied to Progressive Era reforms the same ambivalence that appears in her depictions of the Gilded Age. Dale M. Bauer, in an analysis of the later novels, argues that to see Wharton as merely a nostalgic, conservative atavist is to miss the nuances of her engagement with the social developments of her day. Wharton's ambivalence, Bauer suggestions, "emerges from her clear-sighted acknowledgement that the past was not utopian and her recognition that the present and the future are, for her, mired in incredible political and social follies."[11]

Indeed, much of Wharton's work takes a sympathetic approach to such issues as the oppression of women. Even so, she never devalues traditionally feminine domestic roles, and at times she appears to question the motives, if not the sense, behind some forms of women's liberation. In *Twilight Sleep* (1927), for instance, Pauline Manford sees no inconsistency in affiliating herself with both the Birth Control League and the National Mothers' Day Association. Together, her erratic political and therapeutic activities paint the portrait of an egoistic and aimless leisurist whose "artificial activity" amounts to nothing more than "spinning around faster and faster in the void, and having to be continually rested and doctored to make up for exertions that led to nothing" (*TS* 71). In *The Reef* (1912), however, Wharton assumes a more progressive stance, appearing to commiserate with Anna Leath's recognition of the sexual double standard in New York's high society.

Despite her often modern views, Wharton rarely, if ever, grants her characters absolute liberation from social norms. The sexual awakening of Charity Royall in *Summer* (1917), for instance, leads not to her longed-for escape from the town of North Dormer, but instead to pregnancy, marriage, and stability. This is not entirely new ground for Wharton, who decades earlier cautioned against reckless reform in *The Valley of Decision* (1902). Set in eighteenth-century Italy, this novel traces the intellectual development of the reform-minded Odo Valsecca, who, "like countless youths of his generation," is seduced by "the formation of a new spirit, the spirit that was to destroy one world without surviving to create another" (*VD* 91). The search for freedom, Wharton seems to imply, might lead only to greater hardship.

More than a century after Odo's epiphany, the progressive mill manager John Amherst would experience a comparable situation in *The Fruit of the Tree* (1907). Convinced that the dehumanizing industrial machine is to blame for the injury sustained by one of his workers, Amherst determines to improve the safety conditions at the Westmore mill. His goal seems within reach when he marries the mill's new owner, but his union with Bessy Westmore – a leisured heiress more motivated by high profits and the quest for greater luxury than by the wellbeing of those whose labor generates her lavish wealth – serves not to cultivate Bessy's sympathy, but instead to distance Amherst from his own cause.[12] After many twists and turns, including Bessy's death in a horse-riding accident, Amherst marries Justine, thus setting up the novel's greatest irony. Prior to her death, Bessy had developed plans for an elaborate, private gymnasium that Amherst later mistakes for a recreation center meant to serve the mill workers. Justine knows the truth, but keeps it to herself as Amherst builds the facility and dedicates it to the memory of his dead wife.

At the novel's close, the tension between middle- and upper-class interests might seem resolved. Amherst realizes his aim of materially improving the lives of the mill workers, and the wealthy receive the satisfaction of expanding their philanthropic ventures. Yet a façade of delusion and deceit covers the novel's closing episodes. As Amherst commemorates Bessy's legacy, "[a] wave of anger swept over Justine ... It was grotesque and pitiable that a man like Amherst should create out of his regrets a being who had never existed, and then ascribe to her feelings and actions of which the real woman had again and again proved herself incapable!"[13] Just as the novel's love story in effect marginalizes the plight of the mill workers, the false pretenses on which Amherst had built the gymnasium seem to reflect the spuriousness of cosmetic philanthropic gestures.

Yet understandably, Wharton's most poignant social critiques take aim at nineteenth-century New York high society, and not surprisingly, these novels also mourn the vanishing traditions and values of New York's antebellum aristocracy. In *The Custom of the Country* (1913), for example, the writer adapts the exploitative capitalist mindset to the commodified beauty of her antiheroine, Undine Spragg, the unrefined daughter of Midwestern *nouveau riche* whose travels in New York and Paris are aimed at finding for Undine a husband of high social standing. Although callous and shallow, Undine is not, however, Wharton's primary object of condemnation. As the narrator tells us, Ralph Marvell – Undine's second husband, and a member of an old, distinguished New York family – "sometimes called his mother and grandfather the Aborigines, and likened them to those vanishing denizens of the American continent doomed to rapid extinction with the advance of the invading race" (*CC* 73–74). It seems, as further developments in the novel suggest, that Ralph's elite sect had, in its primitivism, in fact created its own susceptibility to the "invading race" of ravenous, ill-mannered outsiders whose elevation to elite social circles results from the failures of the established aristocracy.

In another of Wharton's New York novels, *The House of Mirth*, the traditions that nearly suffocated the writer in her youth find a more susceptible victim in the figure of Lily Bart, an aging socialite whose aristocratic family has endured financial devastation. Lily's struggle is both her own and that of the society in which "she had been brought up to be ornamental" (*HM* 480). Although Wharton thematizes the democratic principle of choice, thus tempting her reader to place on Lily the full responsibility for her own condition, the novel repeatedly undercuts its own condemnations of Lily not only by exposing her intensely human compassion, but also by drawing clear distinctions between the worldly affairs of men and the limited affairs of women. Lawrence Selden offers Lily a future outside the comfortable yet corrupt world of the rich, but it seems like a choice that her training would never have allowed her to make. Once pushed into poverty, Lily appears fated by circumstance, if not by the cruel demands of irony, to meet with an unfavorable end.

Wharton's criticisms in the *The House of Mirth* extend beyond women's issues to include the corruption and greed that had taken hold of New York's wealthiest citizens. In fact, this development may represent a return to New York's historical beginnings. Unlike the colonial centers of Boston and Williamsburg – both of them founded by English immigrants in search of religious freedom – New York (originally New Amsterdam) has its roots in the commerce of the Dutch East India Company. The settlement at the mouth of the Hudson River, considered by some to be the birthplace of modern capitalism, grew out of nothing more than a quest for riches, and New York's last transition to British control in 1674 was followed by periods of remarkable prosperity that multiplied the fortunes of local manufacturers and merchants, many of them war profiteers and slave traders.[14] It seems unclear whether Wharton means to evoke this history in her analysis of New York's upper class. The references to Lily as "human merchandise," for example, and as "a slave preparing the ground and sowing the seed" (*HM* 412, 303), appear more than incidental.[15] Whatever the case, however, she consciously immerses us in a world of irresponsibility, moral hypocrisy, and self-delusion – one where marriage is a "vocation" and where a man can "take as much pride in his inheritance as though it had been his own work" (*HM* 13, 32).

Some fifteen years later, Wharton imagined an even more ambivalent world in *The Age of Innocence* where the disillusioned Newland Archer finds himself "imprisoned," much like Lily Bart, in the old New York aristocracy. Although betrothed to May – a woman perfectly suited to a man of high social status – Newland discovers an impossible love for May's cousin, the Countess Ellen Olenska, who has recently fled her husband in Europe and returned to her family in New York. Free-spirited and disdainful of the rigid social structures now imposed on her, she symbolizes for Newland an escape from the "unreality" of fashionable New York, where he merely drifts through "a parody of life" in which "nothing was ever to happen" (*AI* 327, 182, 228). Undertaking once again the relationship between private and public affairs – and Newland's dilemma represents both – the author infuses this love story with implications for the rights of women, the hypocrisy, irresponsibility, and pompous emptiness of the ruling class, and the fear of losing or abandoning familiar ways of life. Newland crystallizes the novel's social critique in his description of May's apparent vacuity: "There was no use in trying to emancipate a wife who had not the dimmest notion that she was not free" (*AI* 196).

Like Lily, Newland oscillates impetuously between his duty toward tradition and his desire to forsake social convention. Unlike *The House of Mirth*, however, which ends before Lily gets a chance to review her decisions with the benefit of hindsight, Newland's tale closes with a final chapter set twenty-six years after the main action of the story, affording him the luxury of reflecting on a personal history with which he is at peace. Although certainly formative, Newland's failed love affair with Ellen serves only as a preamble for what he now understands as his "real" life: the intervening twenty-six years of which we receive only a summary. For it is during these years when the real social, and thus personal, changes in Newland's world take place: the years of the Progressive Era when energized social debate enlivened the public consciousness and, thus, the world of ideas and actions for which the younger Newland had secretly longed. Wharton never implies that all of this change happened *in spite* of the old social conventions from which Newland had wished to escape. Instead, the changes grow out of Newland's traditions, or with them. Far from the sedentary and apathetic existence of his forbears, Newland's life expands, not contracts, into a commemoration of his inherited obligations. With May now dead, Newland comes to see that "Their long years together had shown him that it did not so much matter if marriage was a dull duty, as long as it kept the dignity of a duty: lapsing from that, it became a mere battle of ugly appetites. Looking about him, he honored his own past, and mourned for it. After all, there was good in the old ways" (*AI* 350). Yet, like Wharton, Newland sees the merit in acclimating to a new world. Reflecting on the more open and invigorating world now available to his offspring, Archer observes that there "was good in the new order too" (*AI* 350–51).

Highlighting the disparity between past and present, Wharton ends her novel with a subtle reflection on Newland's progress. When confronted by the "reality" of his domestic life with May, Newland slips into a kind of living death, "without sense of the lapse of time" (*AI* 317). Only when his attention remains fixed on Ellen does the clock seem to wind, if not, it sometimes seems, at an abnormally quick pace.[16] The lifeless standstill of "the old order," once Newland's greatest fear, becomes animated during the twenty-six-year interval of his "real life." Although Newland has many choices made for him in his early life, he discovers a way to make choices of his own, an option that Lily Bart had perhaps never really enjoyed. Newland undertakes the task of learning how to choose and live responsibly in a world like that of "Souls Belated," where social mores change even as they stay the same. As Selden puts it in his last conversation with Lily, "Things may change – but they don't pass" (*HM* 501). For Wharton, these transitions represent not the "terrifying 'trend'" (*AI* 351) that haunts Mrs. Archer in *The Age of Innocence*, but instead a difficult yet unavoidable course to the future.

NOTES

1. The Gilded Age takes its name from Mark Twain and Charles Dudley Warner's satirical novel *The Gilded Age: A Tale of Today*. See S. D. Cashman, *America in the Gilded Age: From the Death of Lincoln to the Rise of Theodore Roosevelt*, 3rd ed. (New York: New York University Press), 1–31, for an extended discussion of the burgeoning industrial milieu during the early years of the Gilded Age.
2. P. Kennedy, *The Rise and Fall of the Great Powers* (New York: Random, 1987), 242.
3. M. Gordon, *The Orange Riots: Irish Political Violence in New York City, 1870 and 1871* (Ithaca, NY: Cornell University Press, 1993), 5.
4. Wharton's father, George Frederic Jones, was not among those ruined during the panic. He had already begun to "economize" in 1866 when, according to Wharton, her father took the Jones family to Europe in order to escape postwar inflation. Shari Benstock adds that George's troubles "were caused in part by mismanagement of his inherited properties" (29).

5. Despite Wharton's misgivings, the Gilded Age produced some of New York's greatest cultural achievements, from the Metropolitan Museum of Art to the New York Public Library. See R. C. Crocker, "Cultural and Intellectual Life in the Gilded Age" in C. Calhoun (ed.), *The Gilded Age: Perspectives on the Origins of Modern America*, 2nd ed. (Lanham, MD: Rowman and Littlefield Publishers, 2007), 211–38; 213.

6. See R. Edwards, *New Spirits: Americans in the Gilded Age, 1865–1905* (New York: Oxford University Press, 2006) for a book-length study of the "long Progressive Era" (7). Nancy Cohen also breaks the mold of conventional historical thought by locating the origins of modern liberal ideology not in the Progressive Era, but instead in the Gilded Age, in her study *The Reconstruction of American Liberalism: 1865–1914* (Chapel Hill: The University of North Carolina Press, 2002).

7. New banking laws in the early twentieth century laid the groundwork for the creation of the Federal Reserve System in 1913. See J. L. Broz's *The International Origins of the Federal Reserve System* (Ithaca, NY: Cornell University Press, 1997) for a book-length study of the topic.

8. See K. Mattson's *Creating a Democratic Public: The Struggle for Urban Participatory Democracy During the Progressive Era* (University Park: Pennsylvania State University Press, 1998), 25, 40, 84.

9. M. Dubofsky, *When Workers Organize: New York City in the Progressive Era* (Amherst: University of Massachusetts Press, 1968), 1.

10. See Dubofsky's *When Workers Organize* for a brief introduction to labor developments in Progressive-Era New York (1–14, 34–45).

11. D. M. Bauer, *Edith Wharton's Brave New Politics* (Madison: University of Wisconsin Press, 1994), 3. Bauer cites "the eugenics movement, fascism, and Nazism." As Elizabeth Ammons points out, Wharton had once seen merit in "social Darwinist race theories." See E. Ammons, "Edith Wharton and the Issue of Race" in M. Bell (ed.), *The Cambridge Companion to Edith Wharton* (Cambridge University Press, 1995), 68–86; 73. See P. Ohler, *Edith Wharton's "Evolutionary Conception": Darwinian Allegory in Her Major Novels* (New York: Routledge, 2006) for a book-length study of Wharton's engagement with Darwinian thought.

12. Bessy had inherited the Westmore mill on the death of her husband.

13. E. Wharton, *The Fruit of the Tree* (New York: Charles Scribner's Sons, 1907), 628.

14. See J. Lepore, *New York Burning: Liberty, Slavery, and Conspiracy in Eighteenth-Century Manhattan* (New York: Vintage, 2005) for an introduction to New York's involvement in slavery (xi–xx).

15. Readers also find in this novel the same corruptive surrender to modern appetites that Wharton alludes to in *The Custom of the Country*. Here, Gus Trenor – a member of New York's elite society, and a married man – attempts in a roundabout way to purchase Lily's sexual attention.

16. See, for example, pages 166, 226, and 238.

PART VI

Time and Place

CHAPTER 25

Wharton and France

William Blazek

Charles Eliot Norton, one of Edith Wharton's early mentors in the literary life, spent five years traveling and studying in Europe from 1868 before taking up the position for which he is best remembered, as the first history of art professor at Harvard University. Writing from his rented villa outside of Siena in 1870, he declared: "[I]f the world were not so bad, and if America in especial were better, – I could be content to live here."[1] However, he was looking for an opportunity to return to the United States in order to confront his homeland's rampant materialism and commercialism, driven by a sense of duty to his young family and to his country, to draw the United States closer to the classical ideals of culture that he most admired. Seven years later he would write from Cambridge, Massachusetts: "[M]y life would doubtless be better in many ways in Europe; but I should be after all of less service there than here."[2]

Service to her native country merged in Wharton's life with the opportunity to create a life in Europe that Norton's career and family obligations prevented him from obtaining. She, too, felt the urge toward civic duty, and wondered in a March 1906 letter to Norton's daughter Sara whether "[i]f one lived in another country, [one would feel] the alien's inability to take part, help on, assert one's self for good ... The *social action* on the community would be impossible" (quoted in Benstock 159). The next dozen years would prove these doubts naïve, as she began her permanent residence in France and would feel compelled to take on an immense amount of work for her adopted *patrie* during World War I and for what she called the Land of Letters (*BG* 119). The contrast with her worthy but comparatively feeble efforts in New York in 1906 for the Society for the Prevention of Cruelty to Animals would become pronounced. "I have been giving this winter to the cause of the poor animals here," she explained to Sara from New York, "My last days here must be given to the sensiblerie of my S.P.C.A. fight." The insertion of the French *mot juste* (for sentimentality) conveys Wharton's divided loyalties, as does another sentence in the letter: "Oh, the curse of having been brought up there, & having it ineradically [sic] in one's blood!" (*Letters* 104).

Like Henry James' expatriation, Wharton's sense of herself as one of America's "wretched exotics" (*Letters* 84) was the product of her parents' European sojourns during her youth. Making financial economies, the Jones family lived mainly in Italy and France from 1866 to 1872, and again from 1880 to 1882. Learning modern languages, therefore, came to Edith Newbold Jones in a privileged fashion. She tells how as a child she learned Italian, tutored by "a charming young lady" in Florence: "My lessons amused me, and the new language came to me as naturally as breathing, as French and German had already" (*BG* 42). She follows this sentence with an aside that reveals something of the narrow social perspective of her wealthy upbringing: "Why do so few parents know what a fortune they could bestow on their children by teaching them the modern languages in babyhood, when a playmate is the only professor needed, and the speech acquired is never afterward lost, however deep below the surface it may be embedded?" (*BG* 42). When she took up residence in Paris at the age of forty-five, she arranged lessons to update what friends called her perfect seventeenth-century French, and a French composition exercise assigned by her tutor became the basis for *Ethan Frome*. Her charity work during World War I involved legal, commercial, and political correspondence in French, fields of expertise that required nuances of vocabulary and diction. The French critic Roger Asselineau asserts: "Edith Wharton's mastery of French was such that she could not only write [in 1916] to such a finicky stylist as [André] Gide without fear of being criticized, but she even published in the *Revue des Deux Mondes* a story which she had written directly in French: 'Atrophie' in July 1929."[3]

With French and German governesses and early reading in four languages, Wharton was from childhood drawn deeply into the beauty and romance of European cultures – not an inevitable consequence of her class privileges, as she was often to point out when describing other Americans abroad, but a result founded on her talented linguistic ability and natural curiosity. In addition, her youthful experience of Europe provided her with a strong sense of European cultural history and a deep admiration for the qualities of order and harmony that she found in the great European cities. The attraction in her mind was built on a contrasting repulsion toward the newness of the United States, and in her autobiography she recalls the immense contrast in the 1870s between the squalor around the New York docks and the architectural splendor of Rome and Paris (*BG* 44).

To foreground her early knowledge of France and the French language clarifies a particular emphasis that Wharton places in her autobiography, letters, and fiction on the concept of cosmopolitanism. Its importance lies beyond a casual description of her particular form of expatriation, for it is closely related to the kinds of practical and moral service that she devised in her literary career and was able to pursue through her decision to settle in France. The term has today become associated with political issues surrounding the mass movement of immigrants, displaced peoples, asylum seekers, political exiles and economic transients around the world – victims of lost duties and rights of hospitality, as Jacques Derrida argues.[4] Yet for Wharton in her time the condition among the *haut bourgeois* implied experience especially of Europe, aesthetic sensibilities across a range of literary and cultural traditions, a refined sense of cultivated taste and manners, and the means and most likely the family heritage to acquire these qualities. The term cosmopolitan could be applied in a less favorable way, also, to indicate wealthy individuals whose backgrounds would presume just such an inheritance, but whose behavior often expressed itself in self-indulgent excesses of pleasure seeking or in snobbishness, laziness, or arrogance. Wharton uses the phrase "fashionable cosmopolitan" to distinguish members of this crowd, who were "always ready to welcome new ideas, though they could seldom spare the time to understand them" (*BG* 219). Wharton's affiliations were with those cosmopolites who more purposefully and productively used the advantages of international travel and wide learning.

In 1907 Wharton began her long-term Paris residence in the Rue de Varenne, renting a large apartment (from the Vanderbilts) found by her brother Harry, who was living nearby. The French novelist and essayist Paul Bourget smoothed Wharton's entry into the salon society of the Faubourg Saint-Germain. He had first met her in the United States while he was researching his book *Outre-Mer: Impressions of America* (1895), with its admiration for the nation's achievements in fusing science and commerce. Among Wharton's closest new friends was the hostess of the most prestigious salon, Rosa de Fitz-James. Descended from a wealthy Viennese banking family, she expressed an "easy cosmopolitanism" (*BG* 265) and spoke nearly perfect English – a reliable feature of the multilingual circle of friends Wharton developed in France. Another devoted new acquaintance introduced to Wharton by Bourget was Charles Du Bos, who "was addicted to literature in English" (Lee 302) and translated *The House of Mirth* into French, a vital factor in the novelist's acceptance in the Paris literary and academic salons. Many in her coterie in Paris, and later in her postwar homes in Saint-Brice-sous-le-Forêt and Hyères, were English and American men of letters – some permanent expatriates, all cosmopolitan in the culturally productive sense. They included her dearest companion, Walter Berry, diplomat and author; the Anglo-American historian and academic Gaillard Lapsley; the English diplomat and painter Robert Norton; the Harvard-educated art historian and agent Bernard Berenson; the English banker John Hugh Smith; the museum director and cultural historian Kenneth Clark; and Wharton's lover William Morton Fullerton, a U.S. journalist and commentator on international relations. Hermione Lee writes in her biography of Wharton that "Paris was, in certain districts, just a high-class American town, Newport-by-the-Seine" and claims that "she does not seem to have become, ever, very intimate with the Faubourg set, and made only a few close French friends" but that at the heart of her social relations in France was, above all, literature (272, 279, 298).

That focus also points to the relationship between Wharton's cosmopolitan milieu in France and her need to engage in meaningful service. Writing gave her the means both to criticize the shortcomings of the United States and to express the merits of deeply rooted French culture. A further advantage of her cosmopolitan sympathies and the wealth that underpinned them was that she could assuage the pleasures and profits she made from writing satirically about New York and about Americans abroad. She could also pursue a full social and creative life in France, enjoy her liberty in the Land of Letters, and reconcile her ambiguous feelings about being an American exotic. Henry James addressed her as "dearest cunning cosmopolite," and he slyly recognized that "your only drawback is not having the homeliness and the inevitability and the happy limitation and the affluent poverty, of a Country of your Own (comme moi pour exemple!)."[5]

So Wharton was free to construct her own sense of national identity, especially after her divorce from Teddy Wharton in 1913. During their marriage the focus of their regular European trips had been Italy, although Teddy accompanied his wife on motor-flights in the French provinces and visits to Paris. Their decision in 1907 to divide their time between The Mount and Paris was to end with an acrimonious sale of the Massachusetts mansion estate and with their divorce in the French courts. One could speculate that Edith Wharton's obligations to France strengthened considerably owing to the privacy afforded by French divorce law, which prevented journalists from obtaining the court registers and allowed her to avoid a scandalous public outing of her married life in the newspapers back in the United States. In addition, staying in Europe provided the expatriate divorcee with the security of distance from relatives and old friends back in New York, where a divorced woman still faced strictures on her reputation and social mobility. As with the forcibly expatriated Ellen Olenska in *The Age of Innocence*, foreign residence for Wharton in the Faubourg, "a quiet quarter … in spite of its splendour and its history" (*AI* 363), protected and enabled her. It was to be a short-lived respite, however, with the coming of war in Europe and new reasons for Wharton to devote herself to France and the United States.

Just before the onset of World War I, Wharton was actually contemplating a permanent move to England, where she had already made arrangements for a long-term lease on a country house near London. This was motivated in part by the proximity to her Anglo-American friends and by an opportunity to draw away from reminders of the endings of her marriage to Teddy and her affair with Fullerton. With the outbreak of military hostilities in August 1914, however, she quickly turned to organizing war-relief charities and fundraising activities, working steadfastly throughout the next four years – organizing workrooms for women who had lost jobs because of the mobilization, setting up hostels for refugees, establishing sanatoriums for tuberculosis victims, and fundraising for these and other causes. She also edited *The Book of the Homeless* and wrote *Fighting France* and *French Ways and Their Meaning*, as well as the novels *The Marne* and *Summer* during the war years. Wharton's travel book *In Morocco* (1920), based on her 1917 journey to the French protectorate, and the novel *A Son at the Front* (1923) followed. Alan Price and Julie Olin-Ammentorp have thoroughly documented and analyzed her work during the war, and the latter critic's essay in this volume can be consulted for further context; however, a key point worth making here is that World War I consolidated Wharton's ties to France and provided a gateway through which her passionate defense of French civilization could meet her desire to lift the United States to the high moral and cultural standards that she consistently found lacking in her nation of birth. When, in April 1916, French President Poincaré made her a Chevalier de la Légion d'honneur, Wharton's adopted country claimed her.

Wharton saw France's war against German militarism as a fight to save Western Civilization, and she directed her energies to those displaced by what she felt was the atrocity of German invasion. Her polemical writing during the war was aimed primarily at convincing the United States to enter the conflict, by illustrating the threat of German barbarism and by explicating the virtues and values of France. *Fighting France* portrays the destruction of French towns and the shelling of Rheims Cathedral as signs that Germany's aggression was based not on military expediency but on a cultural vacuity so deep seated that "wherever the shadow of Germany falls, all things should wither at the root" (*FF* 157). The determination behind France's resistance against the Kaiser's army Wharton found in the nation's courage and intelligence, and she concludes *Fighting France* with a flourish to rouse her U.S. readership: "If France perishes as an intellectual light and as a moral force every Frenchman perishes with her; and the only death that Frenchmen fear is not death in the trenches but the extinction of their national ideal" (*FF* 238). When the vanguard of soldiers from the United States arrived in France and paraded along the Champs Élysées on July 4, 1917, Wharton thrilled at the sight of "our wonderful, incredible troops" (Lewis 410). *French Ways and Their Meaning* was intended as a primer for the best educated of the three million Americans who reached France during the next two years. The volume's chapter titles highlight French national characteristics – "Reverence," "Taste," "Intellectual Honesty," "Continuity" – that mirror the emphases of an earlier study in the genre, *French Traits* (1888), written by William C. Brownell, Wharton's editor at Scribners. The novelist's concern for explaining the long historical evolution of these traits can both excuse faults and encourage reform, particularly within France's younger fellow republic. In her Preface to the volume, she writes about the French:

They have used their longer experience and their keener senses for the joy and enlightenment of the races still agrope for self-expression. The faults of France are the faults inherent in an old and excessively self-contained civilisation; her qualities are its qualities; and the most profitable way of trying to interpret French ways and their meaning is to see how this long inheritance may benefit a people [America] which is still, intellectually and artistically, in search of itself. (*FWM* x–xi)

What Wharton fails to examine in *French Ways* and related non-fiction is how France continued to be a nation in search of its identity, too. In his historical analysis of the development of French civilization and nationalism, Theodore Zeldin notes that "*Civilisation* (like *nation*) was a new word, first used in 1766, and admitted into the dictionary of the French Academy only in 1798."[6] Moreover, the term "civilization," that key indicator of French exceptionalism, was used by both radicals and conservatives in France throughout the nineteenth century to pursue agendas of either change or stability; and nationalism was a source of division throughout the Third Republic (Zeldin, *French Passions* 5–28). Unstable governments (108 ministries between 1870 and 1940, each lasting on average only eight months)[7] and extremist factions of reactionary and leftist political groups regularly led to rioting in the streets before and after World War I. (Wharton herself feared the start of a civil war with the Paris riots of 1934 [Lee 739].) The number of foreign residents and naturalized immigrants from France's borders and colonies climbed to nearly 1.4 million by 1911 and grew rapidly in the 1920s (Zeldin, *French Passions* 16). The legacy of France's imperialist claims in North Africa remains one of the country's major sources of internal political conflict today.

Wharton's *In Morocco* is dedicated to the Resident General of the French Protectorate, Hubert Lyautey, and she expresses undivided praise for his colonial policy, "*un système colonial de bonne conscience*"[8] – bringing the fruits of French civilization to Morocco while supporting the local aristocracy, developing native arts and agriculture, and restoring historical buildings. However, in contributing through her writing to the imperial project herself, Wharton veils the reality of Lyautey's actions, which also involved "starving the tribesmen by driving them out of their pastures, machine-gunning any who tried to work in the fields, and finally burning their villages" (Zeldin, *French Passions* 925).[9] The progress of civilization is always brutal for some, and Wharton offers her readers only glimpses of an ambiguous and multidimensional France – although her fictional depictions of, for example, the Malrive family of aristocrats in *Madame de Treymes* and the de Chelles in *The Custom of the Country* reveal the disadvantages of continuity, rigid tradition, and settled civilization.

It is tempting to say that until the war arrived, Wharton was in search of France and what it could mean to her, in the way that Shirley Foster writes about the travel book *A Motor-Flight Through France* as the writer's effort to seize France as an acquisition and to penetrate the country's essential character.[10] And because of the war, Wharton was in search of a new self, too, as a resident cosmopolitan American and as a female writer now living independently. The obligations and duties she fulfilled in France after 1914, literary and otherwise, lifted the curse of her exotic upbringing with its geographical, psychological, and existential in-betweenness. The war confirmed her role as a mediator between France and the United States, assured her of her acceptance in France, and provided her with motivation to write intensely for the remainder of her life, despite or perhaps because of the war's losses. Henry James wrote to her in November 1914: "It's impossible to 'locate anything in our time' [presumably quoting from her preceding letter]. Our time has been this time for the last 50 years, & if it was ignorantly & fatuously so the only light in which to show it is now the light of tragic delusion. And that's too awful a subject"

(Powers 316). His compatriot mused on that subject carefully during and after the war, but with her own brand of optimism and with a sense that the United States could be improved by her endeavors, especially if she remained in France and designed a life for writing, within surroundings amenable to her work and leisure.

Despairing of the ways that the American Red Cross had high-handedly taken over and often mismanaged her war charities, annoyed at the crowds arriving in Paris for the peace negotiations in 1919, and seeking a quieter social life and more regulated pattern for her writing, Wharton found more secluded surroundings outside of the capital, in the Pavillon Colombe in Saint-Brice-sous-le-Forêt, a short drive north of Paris, where she lived for most of the year, and in Sainte-Claire-le-Château in Hyères, where she spent the winters, with twice-yearly stays in Paris at the Hôtel Crillon while her household staff (which grew to number twenty-two) conducted the transfers. She directed her exceptional energy to gardening as well as writing, and the ancient house that she transformed along with the extensive gardens that she created in Hyères are used today as the headquarters of the Parc National. The 1920s was her most productive decade as a writer, and her earnings soared with the vibrant market for short story and serial publications in U.S. magazines, as well as from her novels and film and theater adaptation rights. *The Glimpses of the Moon*, *The Mother's Recompense*, and *The Children*, along with *The Age of Innocence* and *A Son at the Front*, all include French settings and U.S. characters of the restless international set. Writing from her French fortresses, Wharton continued her argument with the United States by focusing on modernity's loss of historical foundations, the Jazz Age's easy gratifications, and the increasing standardization and commodification of Euro-American culture. She kept an eye on contemporary literary trends and met younger U.S. writers who were in closest sympathy with her own social fiction, who satirized U.S. types and institutions, and exposed the gap between American ideals and reality – including Sinclair Lewis, Anita Loos, and F. Scott Fitzgerald. While she enjoyed performances by Isadora Duncan and the Ballets Russes in the 1910s, and greatly admired the early work of Marcel Proust, Wharton did not meet the modernists who lived in Paris in the 1920s. In the work of James Joyce and Gertrude Stein she saw juvenile prurience and pointless stylistic excesses.

Defining her literary legacy in *A Backward Glance*, Wharton writes from self-awareness of her privileged cosmopolitanism and emphasizes her efforts to open up new subject matter for U.S. literature, freeing it to confront complex moral issues. Acknowledging the independence she enjoyed to work without daily financial worries, she offers her literary achievements as a debt and a model to U.S. colleagues obliged to earn their living from writing; and she declares: "the greatest service a writer can render to letters is to follow his conscience" (*BG* 140). Her spiritual and intellectual inspiration for that task was the regulated landscape and sophisticated society she found in France, a civilization as she understood it that was based on the clarity, logic, and eloquence of French language, literature, and conversation. In *French Ways* she argues that the French people, and in particular French women, are more "grown up" than their U.S. counterparts (*FWM* 100–01, 113), and she saw her work as a jeremiad guide to what U.S. maturity might bring.

A memorial article by Louis J. A. Mercier published after the death of William C. Brownell in 1928 analyzes the most prominent themes in the writings of Wharton's editor, elements to combat the "neo-bar-barism" of the age: standards, order, control. Mercier concludes with the observation: "[T]here had been ... much progress since the days when he had returned to New York with the purpose of helping to work out on this continent the vision he had caught, in France, of a people molded into a unity of aspiration toward the beautiful and the true by long developed standards, whose transcendental value they recognized." [11] The rhetoric contains the germ of what Wharton herself stayed in France for, to perform cultural service; and even as she profited financially from the transaction she repeatedly gave her U.S. readership French lessons in how to nurture the habits of thinking and to appreciate the art of living. Wharton's most recent biographer investigated the annotations that Wharton made in her private library collection. A passage in her copy of the Harvard philosopher George Santayana's *The Life of Reason* reads: "In some nations everybody is by nature so astute, versatile, and sympathetic that education hardly makes any difference in manners or mind"; and in the margin along-side Wharton wrote: "France!" (Lee 675). [12]

NOTES

1. C. E. Norton, *Letters of Charles Eliot Norton*, 2 vols., ed. S. Norton and M. A. De Wolfe Howe (Boston and New York: Houghton Mifflin, 1913), vol. I, 395.

2. C. E. Norton, *Letters of Charles Eliot Norton*, 2 vols., ed. S. Norton and M. A. De Wolfe Howe (Boston and New York: Houghton Mifflin, 1913), vol. II, 91.

3. R. Asselineau, "Edith Wharton – She Thought in French and Wrote in English" in K. Joslin and A. Price (eds.), *Wretched Exotic: Essays on Edith Wharton in Europe* (New York: Peter Lang, 1996), 355–63; 357.

4. J. Derrida, *Cosmopolitanism and Forgiveness*, trans. M. Dooley and M. Hughes (London and New York: Routledge, 2004), 5, 19–22.

5. L. H. Powers (ed.), *Henry James and Edith Wharton Letters: 1900–1915* (London: Weidenfeld and Nicolson, 1990), 201, 240. Subsequent references to this work are included in the text.

6. T. Zeldin, *A History of French Passions 1848–1945, vol. 2: Intellect, Taste and Anxiety* (Oxford: Clarendon Press, 1977), 6. Subsequent references to this work are included in the text.

7. T. Zeldin, *France 1848–1945: Politics and Anger* (Oxford: Oxford University Press, 1979), 223.

8. R. Bidwell, *Morocco under Colonial Rule: French Administration of Tribal Areas 1912–1956* (London: Frank Cass, 1973), 2.

9. General Lyautey was eventually forced to resign from his post amid allegations of graft and corruption. Wharton was following a path taken by her politically conservative French friends such as Bourget: "French writers were certain that the Moroccans loved them and their literature abounds in self-congratulation" (Bidwell, *Morocco* 3, 27–28).

10. S. Foster, "Making It Her Own: Edith Wharton's Europe" in K. Joslin and A. Price (eds.), *Wretched Exotic: Essays on Edith Wharton in Europe* (New York: Peter Lang, 1996), 129–45; 138–44.

11. L. J. A. Mercier, "W. C. Brownell and Our Neo-Barbarism," *Forum*, 81.6 (June 1929), 376–81; 381.

12. Wharton visited the United States only once between 1913 and her death in 1937, to accept an honorary doctorate from Yale University in 1923, stopping briefly in "Skyscraperville" (*Letters* 519) to meet with relatives and friends. All four members of her immediate family died in France, her father at Cannes in 1882, her mother and both brothers in Paris.

CHAPTER 26

Wharton and Italy

Robin Peel

Edith Wharton was born in the United States and died in France, and arguably these are the two countries that shaped and meant most to her. She was always the American abroad, and even when she became resident in Europe the majority of her closest friends remained American. From 1907 onward, she occupied a series of properties in France and lived there permanently from 1914 (returning to Paris deliberately when war was declared) until her death. Nothing was to match the traumatic effect on Wharton of the outbreak of World War I, the invasion of Belgium by Germany, the desperate plight of the civilian refugees and the arrival of the front line so close to Paris. Within that outer Franco-American frame, however, another country – Italy – defined her sensibility in ways possibly more profound and enduring. Wharton came to consciousness as a child in Italy; this is where she played as a five-year old among the ruins of the Roman Forum, and she was forever stimulated by Italian history and culture. Her family settled in Florence in 1870, when she was eight, but returned to New York when she was ten. She carried from Italy the strong impressions of the ruins, cardinals' carriages and grand buildings, and these were vividly recalled sixty years later in her 1934 autobiography, *A Backward Glance*.

From the beginning, Italy was an important part of her writing and reading. *Fast and Loose*, written between her fourteenth and fifteenth birthdays, has Italian scenes drawn from the memories of Rome. Thrust back into U.S. life, Wharton's reading of John Ruskin reconnected her with Italy and encouraged the precise observation of her surroundings so important to an author (*LI* 195). Wharton's father encouraged her early writing, and in 1878 her parents arranged for a privately printed collection of five translations (from German) and two dozen of her own poems to be published as *Verses* in a little booklet. One of these poems, a dramatic monologue called "The Last Token AD 107," is spoken by a Christian woman about to face the lions of the Coliseum, knowing her Roman lover is among the spectators (*Poems* 11–12). Wharton's father also read to her sections from Thomas Babington Macaulay's *Lays of Ancient Rome*. She learned the language early and as an adult spoke, wrote and read widely in Italian.[1]

Writing and travel were inextricably linked in Wharton's adult years. She visited Tuscany in 1894, returning in 1903. During this period, she wrote a number of stories with Italian backgrounds and draft versions of unpublished poems such as "Italy, March 1892" and a song for "Spring, Italy, March 1892," poems of romantic longing. She returned to Italy for asthma treatment in 1905 but the prospect of travel, art and architecture inspired further visits in each of the succeeding decades. The Italian influence continued until the end of her life, when it took a revealing turn. In her final years, Wharton was drawn to the Roman church and attended Catholic services such as High Mass and Vespers in St. Peters and San Anselmo, providing clues to the real significance of the country for her.

Italy satisfied an easily overlooked spiritual, even mystical need nurtured in her childhood. This was never fully satiated by either the more material United States, or the more intellectual France. Although in Wharton's short stories the presence of Italy is frequently a metonym for questions raised by history, art and architecture, at play in these texts is another, more powerful discourse signifying a profound fascination with the mystical, the sublime and the religious. The symbiosis of art and religion that she found in Italy was not replicated for her in other places such as Spain, North Africa and England. Italy, with its strong traditions, its history and its sense of hierarchy, offered an older, more romantic and more nationwide version of the Old New York Society whose disappearance she did not ostensibly regret. For most of Wharton's creative life, her writing exposed the flaws of a rigid society and the price paid by women who were forced to conform to its imprisoning marriage conventions. The rhetoric of much of her fiction espouses a progressive scientific rationalism that is suspicious of anything that trades in darkness and blind faith, an ideology that Lewis attributes to the "tutelage of Egerton Winthrop" (Lewis 510). She admired the naturalism of Balzac and Stendhal and their ability to view, in a scientific way, each character as "a product of particular material and social conditions" (*WF* 6–7), and it is a view reinforced by her own reading of Darwin. It is extremely likely, as earlier critics such as Nathalia Wright observed, that Italy represented an alternative to the materialism of the Gilded Age.[2] The love of Italy came from other, often more sensual inclinations, however, and these surfaced most strikingly during her brief passionate affair with Morton Fullerton, and they also demonstrated their deep influence in her final decade, during which (in 1934, the same year in which her autobiography *A Backward Glance* was published) she wrote the unpublished "Italy Again" and the story "Roman Fever."

Wharton's fondness for Italy provides evidence of the paradox that characterized her whole life. She was an acute observer of the material world but immersed herself in art. She loathed the U.S. preoccupation with products and hotels, but was a motorcar enthusiast. Italy entered her life for very material reasons, following her father's decision to move the family to Europe to save money during the economic banking crisis of the immediate post Civil War years. The Italy she recalls in *A Backward Glance*, however, is a place of enchantment, and in Wharton's account of her childhood impressions of the magic and beauty of Rome the delight in Italy is palpable.

Less attractive is the fact that Wharton's love of Italy did not include a love of Italians, from whom she had that disdain so striking in Anglo-Saxon rhetoric of the late Victorian and Edwardian period. In a 1903 letter to her childhood friend Daisy Chanler, she writes:

I think sometimes that it is almost a pity to enjoy Italy as much as I do, because the acuteness of my sensations makes them rather exhausting; but when I see the stupid Italians I have met here, completely insensitive to their surroundings, & ignorant of the treasures of art and history among which they have grown up, I begin to think it is better to be an American, & bring to it all a mind & eye unblunted by custom. (*Letters* 77–78)

It was not the people, but the art and architecture of Italy that she loved, as mediated by Anglo-Saxon art critics. She recalls her father's illness and the family's visit to Florence and Venice "and it must have been then that he gave me 'Stones of Venice' and 'Walks in Florence', and gently lent himself to my whim of following step by step Ruskin's arbitrary itineraries" (*BG* 87). Her enthusiasm embraced all parts of Italy. In the cruise diary that she kept in 1888 during the four-month Aegean voyage with Teddy, she writes lyrically of Sicily. She made visits to Italy in 1894, 1903, 1905 (partly to receive treatment for her asthma at Salsomaggiore), 1911, 1926, 1930 and 1931, and explored all parts of the country across this forty year period.

Italy was the inspiration for a travel book, a study of houses and gardens, and her first novel *The Valley of Decision* (1902). It is also a presence in a dozen of her short stories. Wharton's love of Italy was influenced strongly by the ideas and books of those she admired. She was familiar with Goethe's late-eighteenth-century *Italian Journey*, and had read Pater alongside Ruskin. She had read the travel sketches of William Dean

Howells and the *Italian Hours* of Henry James. *Italian Hours* was published in 1909, but contained essays written during the previous forty years – loving essayistic appreciations of the cities, landscape, art and people of Italy.[3] Florence, Rome, Venice and Tuscany form the subject of the majority of these travel essays and were the places favored by most visitors, then as now. Howells wrote two of his books on Italy as a consequence of being the United States consul in Venice during the Civil War. *Venetian Life* appeared in 1866 and *Italian Journey* in 1867. Wharton knew both writers, and was an intimate friend of James, whose own love of Italy permeates novels such as *Roderick Hudson* (1876), *The Portrait of a Lady* (1881), *The Aspern Papers* (1888) and *The Wings of the Dove* (1902). Her close friends also included other Italian enthusiasts such as Charles Eliot Norton and Walter Berry, while other acquaintances such as Vernon Lee and Bernard Berenson loved Italy enough to live there. Lee had written of an Italy that Wharton was keen to discover. Wharton drove out from Florence to visit her at her home, Il Palmerino, on the hillside of San Domenico in 1894, and wrote approvingly in *A Backward Glance* that "Vernon Lee was the first highly cultivated and brilliant woman I had ever known" (*BG* 132). Berenson, the art critic, lived in the Villa I Tatti, near Florence. An even closer friend was the French Catholic writer Paul Bourget, whose *Sensations d'Italie* had been published in 1890. Wharton's Italian novel, *The Valley of Decision,* is dedicated to Paul and Minnie Bourget and its central female character, Fulvia Vivaldi, may well have been based on Vernon Lee.

Wharton loved the Italy of the Roman period and the Renaissance, but the period that most interested her aesthetically and historically was that of the seventeenth, eighteenth and nineteenth centuries. During this time, Italy evolved from being the medieval group of contesting city states to the independent Italy of 1861. The move toward unity began in the late fifteenth century with the formation of the Italian league. In the period leading up to French Revolution, the Italian states saw ideas from the Enlightenment coming into collision with despotism, particularly in Tuscany. It is this reforming, revolutionary period that particularly interested Wharton historically. The nineteenth century, which saw the Napoleonic invasion and the formation of the French empire, was challenged by revolutionary movements, and led to unification only a year before Wharton's birth. As a single state, Italy was very young.

Wharton's works inspired by Italy first came in a cluster, in what might be called her Italian period at the turn of the twentieth century. Several of her short stories from this early period, such as "The Muse's Tragedy"

(*Scribner's Magazine*, January 1899), and "The Duchess at Prayer" (*Scribner's Magazine*, August 1900) along with stories that appeared first in *The Greater Inclination* (1899), such as "Souls Belated," have Italian settings, themes or references, as do "The Confessional" (1901), "The Letter" and "The House of the Dead Hand" (both from 1904), "The Hermit and the Wild Woman" (1906), "The Daunt Diana" (1909) and "Autres Temps" (1911). Her two expository works rode on the back of the success of *The Valley of Decision* (1902), which sold 25,000 copies in six months. The first of these was *Italian Villas and their Gardens* (1904), her lavish study of Renaissance and Baroque "palaces" and their traditional gardens, characterized by parterres, statuary, water features and ilex avenues, providing water and shade, and illustrated with photographs and pictures by Maxfield Parrish. *Italian Backgrounds* was published in 1905, the same year Wharton and Teddy, held up in Cannes by a combination of bad weather and ill health, abandoned a proposed motor cruise to Italy. Lewis concludes that "the decision to give up the Italian trip in favor of a French tour was a critical one" because it meant that the "Italian phase of Edith Wharton's life had in effect come to an end" (Lewis 129). However, if Gianfranca Balestra is correct in dating a manuscript exercise in the language, Wharton was still polishing and practicing her Italian in 1908. The exercise is an unpublished short tale with a contemporary setting and is told from the maid's point of view.[4]

Wharton was initially drawn to the sumptuous heritage of imperial Rome and the Italian Renaissance, but was later persuaded that there was a neglected Italy of the post-Renaissance period. Shari Benstock argues that her twenty-year mission was to discover and celebrate this Italy, particularly of the eighteenth century (Benstock 63). Not only did she write *The Valley of Decision*, a two-volume fictional account of this period and its politics, she also began work on its sequel. Wharton planned sections and identified characters, following Odo, the protagonist of *The Valley of Decision*, to his death and then continuing with an account of the life of his widow in the Napoleonic era – an idea abandoned in due course in favor of U.S. subjects for her next novel project. Nevertheless, *The Valley of Decision* was a commercial success. It received a qualified critical welcome, with reviewers praising the handling of background rather than the success of the characters, but it sold well and quickly went into a second printing.

The novel is set in Italy during the period before the French Revolution in the context of opposing historical forces, representing the old and the new worlds. There is a further complication, for alongside the forces of the traditional and the modern Odo experiences the lure of art and the theater, when his meeting with the former soprano singer Cantapresto teaches him of the Northern Italian cities' "tinsel world" of performers, Goldoni, and the expiring commedia dell'arte (*VD* 72). Wharton was well aware that however much the Italian Catholic Church might have disapproved of the perceived immorality of the theatrical life, the appeal of its own ceremonies was largely based on the fact that they were so theatrical themselves. Both *The Valley of Decision* and *Italian Villas and their Gardens*, which benefited from the success of the novel, celebrate the theatricality of Italy while her 1903 short story "A Venetian Night's Entertainment" revels in the dupes and deceptions practiced in the Venice of Carnival and masks, as a gullible young American is tricked into marrying a poor but beautiful young woman.

What conclusion can we draw from the presence of Italy in Wharton's early writing? Her depiction of convents provides one insight. Annette Benert contrasts George Sand's affectionate memories of French Catholic convent life, which was a reprieve from her dysfunctional family, with Wharton's depiction of Italian convents as places of entrapment for women, as they are in both "The Hermit and the Wild Woman" and *The Valley of Decision.*[5] As an American Protestant, Wharton might be expected to have reservations, but other strict aspects of Catholic life (the role of priests, for example) are treated in her fiction with more indulgent irony. Perhaps she felt she did not have Sand's fierce independence, and was suspicious of those institutions designed to control women, defining them as either wives or nuns. Benert reads "The Hermit and the Wild Woman" as confirmation of Wharton's investment in the outer journey rather than the inner (99). In one sense this is true. The Wild Woman, who traveled ceaselessly since escaping the convent (the parallel with Wharton is obvious), does good works, is admired by the people for ways she has helped them during a bout of plague, and it is she who becomes a saint. However, the story is a dialectic narrative, requiring both poles and, as Benert reminds us, the story is linked to the travel observations of "What the Hermits Saw" in *Italian Backgrounds*, published the year before (100). Here Wharton describes the huts, bridges and chapels occupied by anchorites, who seek to make connections with the old gods displaced by orthodox Christianity. The inner search is that of the artist, and Wharton wished to be an artist.

The outbreak of World War I determined that France was to remain Wharton's base until her death, and it became the European country that appears in her writing in this long period of maturity. Italy, however, significantly reappears in her fiction during the final decade of her life, most notably in "A Glimpse," a 1932 story of Americans in Venice, and in "Roman Fever" which remains one of her best-known short stories. "Roman Fever" was published originally in the magazine *Liberty* in November 1934 and in the collection *The World Over* in 1936, the year before her death.

At the end of James' *The Golden Bowl* (1904), one of the characters speaks of "the one irresistible voice of the ever-to-be-loved Italy."[6] Wharton was seduced by that siren voice, and we see it not only in the fiction and essays with an Italian setting, but also in her conception of the uncanny, illustrated by *Tales of Men and Ghosts*, which form a counterpoint to the narratives of social realism and manners for which she is best known (see, for example, "Afterward"). We also find it in some of the poems written at the time of the affair with Fullerton, such as in sonnet six in "The Mortal Lease" series:

> The Moment came, with sacramental cup
> Lifted – and all the vault of life grew bright
> With tides of incommensurable light –
> But tremblingly I turned and covered up
> My face before the wonder. (*Poems* 54–56)

Desire is represented as religious ecstasy, with the apparatus and architecture of the Church ("sacramental cup," "vault") preparing the ground for a moment of mystical epiphany, with the speaker covering up her "face before the wonder." The love of art, of tradition, and the controlled representation of desire, none of which Wharton found in the United States, was satisfied by Italy. Ultimately, she seems to have submitted to the dark and somewhat frightening mysticism of those figures who so fascinated her in *The Valley of Decision*, namely cardinals and priests. Lewis argues that Wharton's 1932 visit to Rome differed from all her others, because she began to "interest herself strongly in the rituals and ceremonies, in the liturgical experience of the Christian religion, and in the meanings they exemplified" (Lewis 509). Previously her interest had been in Christian art, architecture, spectacle and history. Hermione Lee is more circumspect, arguing that Wharton's attraction to Catholicism "was aesthetic as much as devotional" (Lee 719). Even though at the end of *The Gods Arrive* (1932) Vance immerses himself in reading St. Augustine, Lee argues that we should give more attention to the aesthetic than the spiritual because her final short stories are pagan rather than orthodox in their religion, and are concerned with the haunting of the present by the past

(719). As the last of these stories, "All Souls'," shows, however, these narratives are concerned with the possibility of a visitation by a spirit, whatever the location. Published posthumously in a collection called *Ghosts*, this and other stories of the supernatural world do indeed engage with the uncanny and with those spiritual presences found in Coliseum, church and New England gothic house alike.

The lure of Italy in Wharton's final years suggests the quiet triumph of sentiment and sensation over scientific materialism. It was partly anticipated by her fascination with the genre of the ghost story, where the invisible world seems to goad science into an explanation. It is perhaps unsurprising that as the death of those around her encouraged her to reflect on her own mortality, Italian mysticism triumphed over the ephemeral material world exemplified by the United States. Wharton's final years may have been spent in the congenially intellectual environment of France where she had chosen to live and own property, but for this restless wanderer, on the move throughout her life, Italy provided a spiritual home.

NOTES

1. See H. Killoran "Edith Wharton's Readings in European Languages" in K. Joslin and A. Price (eds.), *Wretched Exotic: Essays on Edith Wharton in Europe* (New York: Peter Lang, 1996), 365–87; 366–68.
2. N. Wright, *American Novelists in Italy: The Discoverers: Allston to James* (Philadelphia: University of Pennsylvania Press, 1965), 23.
3. See E. Dwight, *Edith Wharton: An Extraordinary Life* (New York: Harry N. Abrams, 1994), 69.
4. See G. Balestra "Edith Wharton's Italian Tale: Language Exercise and Social Discourse" in C. Colquitt, S. Goodman and C. Waid (eds.), *A Forward Glance: New Essays on Edith Wharton* (Newark: University of Delaware Press, 1999), 207–20; 216.
5. A. Benert, *The Architectural Imagination of Edith Wharton: Gender Class and Power in the Progressive Era* (Madison, NJ: Fairleigh Dickinson University Press, 2007), 98. Subsequent references to this work are included in the text.
6. H. James, *The Golden Bowl* (Harmondsworth: Penguin, 1973), 161.

CHAPTER 27

Wharton and World War I

Julie Olin-Ammentorp

In her memoir *A Backward Glance*, Edith Wharton recounts the summer of 1914, describing a "beautiful afternoon toward the end of June" when she stopped at the home of the painter Jacques-Emile Blanche in Auteuil, thirty miles west of Paris. Friends discussed the latest news: "'Haven't you heard? The Archduke Ferdinand assassinated ... at Sarajevo'" – and then talk drifted to other topics: "the newest exhibition, the Louvre's most recent acquisitions" (*BG* 336, 337). Even a month later, at a hotel in Poitiers, she recounted, "all night long I lay listening to the crowds singing the *Marseillaise* in the square in front of the hotel. 'What nonsense! It can't be war,' we said to each other the next morning ... Two days later war was declared" (*BG* 338).

For Wharton, as for millions of others, the outbreak of war was a shock. A century later, historians have argued that if the war was "tragic," it was also "unnecessary": "the train of events that led to its outbreak," as the historian John Keegan has stated, "might have been broken at any point during the five weeks of crisis that preceded the first clash of arms."[1] The war, which rapidly became "one of the most miserable chapters in human history,"[2] was so terrible for both soldiers and civilians that it is now difficult to imagine that on August 1, 1914, few people had any inkling of how catastrophic it would be. For most, "war came out of a cloudless sky, to populations which knew almost nothing of it and had been raised to doubt that it could ever again trouble their continent" (Keegan 9). Even harder to grasp is the fact that many greeted the war enthusiastically, expecting it to be a brief and exciting adventure, a way to confer manhood upon boys and a new resolve upon nations that many believed had been made "soft" by prosperity. The Germans expected a quick victory; the French and English expected an equally rapid repulsion of the German invasion of Belgium and northern France. The first Battle of the Marne (September 5–10, 1914) made it clear that Germany would not, after all, win swiftly; the high death counts in the battles fought that fall were harbingers of the fatalities to come. By December 1914, for instance, of two million French soldiers who had been mobilized, 306,000 had died; in the Battle of Ypres alone, 24,000 British soldiers and 50,000 German soldiers lost their lives, and 30,000 Belgians perished before the year's end, "a figure that was to recur with gruesome consistency" each year of the war (Keegan 135, 132, 136). By late 1914, the war had settled into a stalemate, with both sides firmly established in the trenches that would come to epitomize the war – until the stalemate itself was succeeded by the deadly battles of 1916 and 1917, which were notable "for two reasons," in the words of J. M. Winter: "The first is the scale of the casualties in these huge battles. The second is that these operations, in effect, led nowhere" (140).

Ultimately the war dragged on for more than four years, becoming truly a world war, one that involved not only most major European nations but their colonies as well. Senegalese and Algerian soldiers fought on the side of the French, for instance, and soldiers from Australia and New Zealand on the side of the British; battles were waged not only on two fronts in Europe, but in South Africa, German East Africa, and the Middle East. The war cost millions of lives on all sides; combat deaths alone came to about nine million (Winter 7), and millions more were left with injuries, amputated limbs, and other problems that would affect the rest of their lives, including psychological ailments like shell shock (post-traumatic stress disorder). World War I introduced modern warfare to the twentieth century: tanks, machine guns, poisonous gas, and airplanes came into military use.

More than previous wars, World War I also diminished the distinction between combatants and noncombatants, soldiers and civilians. One of the first civilian disasters of the war affected the Belgians, thousands of whom were forced to flee their homes when the German army invaded. By the war's end, uncounted numbers had been displaced or had died in the horrible conditions on the home front. As J. M. Winter has written, the "military front and the home front stood together and collapsed together ... The Allies won the war primarily because they were able to field their armies without starving their civilian populations" (18). Many historians consider it the first instance of what has come to be called "total war."

Living in Paris during World War I, as Wharton did, was living "virtually at the front line" (Winter 170). The war's immediate impact on civilians precipitated her involvement with what quickly became a wide array of charities. In early August 1914, Wharton, at the request of the French Red Cross, opened an *ouvroir*, a sewing workroom, that employed seamstresses and other women who had been put out of work by the war.[3]

In September, as refugees from Belgium and northern France flooded into Paris, Wharton co-founded the American Hostels for Refugees (Price 29–30; Benstock 306). Half a year later, in April 1915, when the German army renewed attacks on western Belgium, the Belgian government asked Wharton to help care for refugee children. She agreed; soon she had "one hundred nuns, a colony of old women, and six hundred children" on her hands, and the Children of Flanders Rescue Committee was created (Benstock 317). Problems proliferated as the war continued. For instance, tuberculosis became a serious issue among soldiers, who sometimes transmitted it to their families; to address this issue, Wharton created the Maisons Américaines de Convalescence (Benstock 330). "By June 1917," Shari Benstock notes, Wharton "managed twenty-one houses in Paris and outlying regions" (331). "Mrs. Wharton's Charities," as they came to be called, were the second-largest private charitable endeavor in wartime France (Benstock 303).

The cost of these charities was vast, and in addition to organizing and overseeing much of their work, Wharton was their principal fundraiser. In both areas she had significant help: her friend Elisina Tyler assisted her in administering the charities, and her beloved sister-in-law, Mary ("Minnie") Cadwalader Jones, was Wharton's right-hand woman in fundraising efforts in the United States (Benstock 317–24, 333). It is hard to know exactly how many people were assisted by these organizations, but the figure was clearly large. In November 1915, for instance, Wharton reported that between October 1914 and October 1915, the American Hostels and their affiliate, the Foyer Franco-Belge, assisted more than 9,000 refugees, served 235,000 meals, found employment for more than 3,000 refugees, and distributed more than 48,000 garments.[4] The overall success of her efforts was recognized when the French government made her a Chevalier of the Legion of Honor in March 1916; the award was made particularly distinctive for Wharton by the fact that it was the last such award to be "given to a civilian and a foreigner until after the war" (Benstock 324). The Belgian government awarded her the Queen Elisabeth Medal in 1918 and made her a Chevalier of the Order of Leopold (the equivalent of the French Légion d'Honneur) in 1919 (Benstock 343–44).

Given Wharton's involvement with this range of charities as well as her devotion to France, her adopted country, it is not surprising that she felt from the war's beginning that the United States ought to join the Allied efforts. When a German submarine sank the passenger ship *Lusitania* in May 1915, causing 1,201 deaths, including those of 128 Americans (Keegan 265), Wharton was among the many who were sure that now the United States would declare war on Germany. In fact, she would have to wait nearly two more years for United States involvement, and in letters to friends she voiced her incomprehension of U.S. neutrality. To Sara Norton, for instance, she wrote in June 1916, "France continues to be magnificent, & one envies the people who have a real 'patrie'" (*Letters* 380). Similarly, during the severe coal shortages of the winter of 1917, she parodied President Wilson's stance in a letter to Bernard Berenson: "I've adopted as my motto a variant of Wilson's 'Too proud to fight' which runs 'Too cold to sleep'" (*Letters* 389). It was with relief that she finally wrote again to Sara Norton in May 1917 that, after the U.S. declaration of war on Germany on April 6, 1917, "we can now hold up our heads with the civilized nations of the world" (quoted in Olin-Ammentorp 22).

From the early months of the war, Wharton had put her pen into the service of her charities and her beliefs. The effort she would normally have put into fiction was instead channeled into committee reports, descriptions of her charities, appeals for funds, and accounts of trips near the front. As early as November 1914, "Edith Wharton Asks Aid for Destitute Belgians in France" appeared in the *New York Herald*, and articles such as "My Work Among the Women Workers of Paris" and "Edith Wharton Tells of German Trail of Ruin" were soon appearing in the *New York Times Magazine* and other publications.[5] Despite the shift in her focus as a writer, she wrote steadily throughout the war and into the months immediately following it. From August 1914 through the end of 1919, she published fifty-seven magazine and newspaper articles (thirty-seven of them before the end of the war); an edited collection (*The Book of the Homeless*); two volumes of non-fiction (*Fighting France* and *French Ways and Their Meaning*); two novels *(Summer* and *The Marne)*; three short stories ("Coming Home," "The Refugees," and "Writing a War Story"); and ten poems. She began her longest and most complex treatment of the war years, her novel *A Son at the Front*, in 1918, but was unable to complete it until 1922.

These works vary widely in tone as well as in genre; to understand them, it is helpful to take into account their roots not simply in the war years, but in different particular moments during those years. For instance, *The Marne* (1918), which sold well initially but was eventually dismissed as too positive, reflects the Allied enthusiasm over their decisive victory in the Second Battle of the Marne in July 1918. On the contrary, *A Son at the Front*, completed after the war and with a full knowledge of the war's cost, provides a much more sober view of the war and of life on the home front in Paris. This critically neglected novel takes on many interwoven issues: Paris in wartime; the petty in-fighting that sometimes went on over the control of wartime charities; parents and step-parents struggling for "ownership" of their son; the crisis of a middle-aged artist in wartime, his occupation gone; the way in which a war that seemingly came out of nowhere altered not only the daily lives but the futures of all it affected. Perhaps the most difficult challenge Wharton gave herself in writing *A Son at the Front* was her choice to make her main character, the artist John Campton, a fundamentally unsympathetic character. It is an illuminating but also grim work – making it an appropriate representative of the war it depicts.

Her two main non-fiction works related to the war, *Fighting France* (1915) and *French Ways and Their Meaning* (1919), also differ significantly. The essays in *Fighting France* are essentially war reportage, composed in wartime Paris and following her five trips to the front in 1915, during which she saw sites from Alsace to Belgium, visiting field hospitals, speaking with doctors, curates, and military officers, witnessing the ruins of homes and towns, and on one occasion being taken through the trenches. Wharton's language in *Fighting France* is vivid, clear, and generally free of cant, frequently recreating the surreal quality of some of her experiences – as when, for instance, she describes a chapel with the Virgin Mary's halo constructed from bayonets (*FF* 114), or recounts the unreality of having a password whispered to her after curfew in the town of Châlons by "a young man who in Paris drops in to dine with me and talk over new books" (*FF* 88–89). In contrast, *French Ways and Their Meaning* was written late in the war; it had its genesis in a talk Wharton gave to U.S. soldiers in Paris that was intended to help them understand and appreciate the culture they had come to defend, and as such is transparently pro-French – and anti-German. It nevertheless remains interesting as an expression of Wharton's admiration of French culture.

Wharton's most purely literary production during the war years is her novel *Summer* (1917). Set in western Massachusetts and focusing on the coming-of-age of a provincial girl, Charity Royall, *Summer* "was written at a high pitch of creative joy," Wharton recounted, "but amid a thousand interruptions, and while the rest of my being was steeped in the tragic realities of the war" (*BG* 356). Despite its apparent remoteness from the war, *Summer* may echo wartime concerns in its description of the grotesque corpse of Charity's mother and in the author's portrayal of the utter poverty of the mountain community, which may have been suggested by her observation of destitute Belgian refugees.[6] Yet the writing of *Summer* provided Wharton with a psychological refuge from the concerns of the war years; moreover, it has proved an enduring and popular work.

Taken together, Wharton's war-related writings exhibit great consistency in many ways. Her love and admiration of France pervades them, as does her commitment to the war despite its huge human cost – of which she was increasingly aware. Read together with her letters and other documents, they also reveal a deepening and darkening view of the war. Personal losses brought the tragedy of the war home to her: in 1915, she grieved for three young French friends who died in the fighting. Between February and April 1916, her grief was intensified by the deaths of three long-time friends, including Henry James. The most heartbreaking losses came near the end of the war. In August 1918, her young friend Ronald Simmons, an American studying art in Paris who had assisted Wharton with her charities, became one of the first victims of the influenza pandemic that would soon kill more people than the war itself had. And in September 1918, her young cousin Newbold Rhinelander, an aviator, died when his airplane crashed behind German lines.

After the Armistice on November 11, 1918, Wharton composed a number of elegies, including one for Ronald Simmons (to whom she would also dedicate *The Marne* and *A Son at the Front*), and one for her friend Theodore Roosevelt, who died in January 1919. She composed two more general elegies for soldiers who had died in the war, "You and You," and one simply entitled "Elegy." The latter is a quiet but poignant expression of grief for "the young dead," concluding with the haunting image of buried soldiers "whose eyes / Strain through the sod to see these perfect skies...." (Olin-Ammentorp 241). The war over, she also allowed herself to tell some stories that might have seemed too mocking in wartime; in "The Refugees" and "Writing a War Story," she satirized some of her behind-the-lines experiences. The war remained an element in her work for the rest of her career, most notably in serving as the immediate background for her novel *The Mother's Recompense* (1925) and her story "Her Son" (1932).

The outbreak of war had surprised Wharton; its conclusion came almost as suddenly. In mid-November 1914, "Through the deep expectant hush we heard ... the bells of Paris calling to each other; ... till all their voices met and mingled in a crash of triumph"; at last "we knew the war was over" (*BG* 359–60). However, Wharton soon realized that the war's end did not mean a simple return to the pre-war world; in late November 1918, for instance, she wrote to Minnie Jones that "The real difficulty will be to make people realize that the situation of the refugees is worse than

ever" (quoted in Olin-Ammentorp 155). Much of her charity work continued long after the Armistice (Price 169–71). Moreover, she had devoted
so much energy to her charitable efforts during the war that her literary income "dropped to an all-time low" (Benstock 355). Furthermore,
the constant strain told on her health: she had three minor heart attacks
between May 1917 and July 1918 (Benstock 345).[7]

Perhaps as difficult for Wharton as the financial and health problems
was her sense of a changed world. Like many others, she came to perceive
World War I as a great rift in civilization: "It was growing more and more
evident that the world I had grown up in and been formed by had been
destroyed in 1914" (*BG* 369–70). She was not alone in this feeling; authors
as diverse as Robert Graves, Virginia Woolf, and Willa Cather sensed the
postwar world as profoundly and disturbingly altered. The historian John
Keegan has written that the war "damaged … the rational and liberal civilization of the European enlightenment permanently for the worse and,
through the damage done, world civilization also" (8). Wharton would
have agreed.

Almost before the conflict itself was concluded, authors and critics
were beginning to canonize certain texts from the Great War. Works
such as Wilfred Owen's beautifully written, deeply disillusioned portrait
of the war in his poem "Dulce et Decorum Est" (1920), the poems of
Siegfried Sassoon and others, and the French novelist Henri Barbusse's
realistic *Le Feu* (1916) were among the first to create the anti-idealistic
views and minimalist tone that would come to be seen as characteristic
of World War I writing. John Dos Passos' *Three Soldiers* (1921), Robert
Graves' memoir *Good-bye to All That* (1929), and Ernest Hemingway's *A
Farewell to Arms* (1929) continued the anti-idealistic, even ironic, view of
a war that many had romanticized at its outset. Paul Fussell's eloquent
The Great War and Modern Memory (1975) influentially argued that irony
was the dominant tone (indeed the only legitimate tone) in the literature of World War I. Samuel Hynes' *A War Imagined: The First World
War and English Culture* (1990) broadened Fussell's argument and articulated more fully the fundamental "myth of the war" underlying both the
canon and Fussell's views: "the early high-mindedness that turned …
to bitterness and cynicism; the growing feeling among soldiers of alienation from the people at home; … the bitter conviction that the men in
the trenches fought for no cause, in a war that could not be stopped."[8]
More recently, critics have pointed out that these works have their limitations. Fussell has been faulted for constructing an argument that "is too
exclusively Anglo-Saxon to do justice to the full range of war writing"

(Winter 228–29) and for describing as reality what is in fact a literary construct.[9] Nevertheless, *The Great War and Modern Memory* remains, as James Campbell remarks, "the single most significant interpretation of the war and an unavoidable point of reference for all subsequent work" (269). Fussell's and Hynes' studies provide important perspectives both for understanding why Wharton's works have been excluded from the canon, and (ironically) for grasping the ways in which her works do conform to "the Myth of the War" – for instance, in their decreasing idealism and even in their mistrust of civilian perspectives, especially in the perspectives of women, whom Wharton frequently portrays as failing to understand the war.

Perhaps more than in any other category of literature, gender has played a crucial role in what has been acknowledged and studied as the literature of war; "war" itself has been narrowly, if rarely explicitly, defined as "combat," or, in the case of World War I, the stalemate of the trenches. In the last twenty years, however, the canon of Great War literature has begun to expand. The collection *Behind the Lines: Gender and the Two Worlds Wars*, edited by Margaret Higonnet (1987), Sandra Gilbert and Susan Gubar's *No Man's Land*, Vol. 2: *Sexchanges* (1989), Claire Tylee's *The Great War and Women's Consciousness* (1990), and Dorothy Goldman, Jane Gledhill, and Judith Hattaway's *Women Writers and the Great War* (1995) have all contributed to a wider understanding of the intersection of gender and World War I. (Indeed, Hynes' *A War Imagined* treats a wider range of authors than Fussell's *Great War and Modern Memory*, including several women writers.) Higonnet's important anthology, *Lines of Fire: Women Writers of World War I* (1999), makes available a range of works from many nations and argues cogently that in an era of total war, the distinctions between soldier and civilian have become meaningless; preserving a distinction between the "authentic" voice of war, that of the combatant, and "other" voices, such as those from the home-front, makes little sense. Both perspectives have their validity.

Many works from the front emphasize that those who have not shared the frontline experience cannot understand what war truly is; paradoxically, one of these works also acknowledges that the reverse is true. In Barbusse's *Le Feu*, one character states, "They don't know what war is back there; and if you started talking about the rear, it'd be *you* that'd talk rot."[10] Early in the war, Wharton had traveled near the front and brought what Colm Tóibín has called her "novelist's eye for the perfect detail"[11] to her documentary writing in *Fighting France*. Later in the war and in its aftermath, Wharton trained her eye on the home front. Works like "The Refugees," "Writing a War Story," and *A Son at the Front* mirror Wharton's considerable and complex experiences in wartime France, creating stories that reflect the difficult realities of life behind the lines. Within the wider context now established for understanding the literature of World War I, Wharton's work not only remains important, but gains a new significance.

NOTES

1. J. Keegan, *The First World War* (New York: Alfred A. Knopf, 1999), 3. Subsequent references to this work are included in the text.
2. J. M. Winter, *The Experience of World War I* (New York: Oxford University Press, 1989), 18. Subsequent references to this work are included in the text.
3. A. Price, *The End of the Age of Innocence: Edith Wharton and the First World War* (New York: St. Martin's Press, 1996), 16. Subsequent references to this work are included in the text. See also Benstock 303.
4. E. Wharton, "My Work Among the Women Workers of Paris" in J. Olin-Ammentorp, *Edith Wharton's Writings from the Great War* (Gainesville: University Press of Florida, 2004), 250. Subsequent references to this work are included in the text.
5. For a complete listing of Wharton's wartime publications, see S. Garrison, *Edith Wharton: A Bibliography* (Pittsburgh: University of Pittsburgh Press, 1990), 453–57.
6. On Charity's mother, see B. Nevius, *Edith Wharton: A Study of Her Fiction* (Berkeley: University of California Press, 1953), 169–70. On Wharton's portrayal of the "mountain people," see J. Olin-Ammentorp, *Edith Wharton's Writings*, 62. See also C. Waid, "Introduction" to *Summer* (New York: Penguin Signet Classics, 1993), v–xvi.
7. In a slightly different tallying of Wharton's health problems, Hermione Lee counts three "minor heart attacks linked to anaemia" between May and July 1918 (505).
8. S. Hynes, *A War Imagined: The First World War and English Culture* (New York: Collier, 1990), 439.
9. J. Campbell, "Interpreting the War" in V. Sherry (ed.), *The Cambridge Companion to the Literature of the First World War* (Cambridge: Cambridge University Press, 2005), 261–79; 268–69. Campbell's essay provides an excellent overview of interpretations of World War I literature. Subsequent references to this work are included in the text.
10. H. Barbusse, *Under Fire (Le Feu)*, trans. F. Wray (New York: E. P. Dutton, 1917), 180.
11. C. Toíbín, "Foreword," *Edith Wharton: Fighting France* (London: Hesperus Press, 2010), xii.

CHAPTER 28

The 1920s

Gail D. Sinclair

Civilization attempted to right itself after the cataclysm it had just experienced in World War I, and this course alteration spawned polemic camps at odds with one another on many levels. Warren G. Harding in his 1920 bid for the United States Presidency would solicit "A return to normalcy," supporting the Wilsonian ideal that the world had been made "safe for democracy" and a belief that the pre-war Gilded Age's status quo still remained possible. Much of the mainstream of the United States hoped so as well. Rigid Victorian modes still lingered for the generation in power prior to World War I as they attempted to hold fast to a way of life challenged by the "flaming youth" cult for whom the old norms were no longer valid or palatable. The culture was rife with conflict as the flamboyant young men and women coming of age in the 1920s garnered attention from the media, which had become a mass-market enterprise. The result was a revolution imposed by those whom historian Roderick Nash would call "The Nervous Generation," ushering in the fast-paced cadence of a new era.[1]

Like many others of her age, Edith Wharton found herself on the brink of a dramatically different time. Positioned on the continental divide between old and new, she acknowledged a seismic shift from the pre-war world she had known to the postwar climate of rapid advancements in transportation, medicine, and modern conveniences. Wharton shared with icon of the age Henry Ford, a "nervous clinging to old values even while undermining them" (Nash 154). Ford reflected a tension "between old and new, between a belief in progress and a tendency to nostalgia," as he idolized a past way of life while seeming to be "fully at home in the alleged new era of the 1920s" (Nash 157, 159). Both Wharton and Ford navigated in a world shifting between radically different spheres. Running parallel to these more pragmatic challenges and also emblematic of the times was a movement toward sweeping philosophical re-evaluation. A balancing act existed for those struggling to hold fast to positive qualities of a bygone time even as they recognized the unstoppable and necessary forward momentum of the present.

German psychologist and Harvard professor Hugo Münsterberg (1863–1916) aptly described the era building toward modernity as, "The *adagio* of our forefathers [that] has become a *prestissimo* which must keep us breathless."[2] His use of a musical motif becomes even more appropriate for the postwar era given the moniker "The Jazz Age," and the music of the time may have been one of the most obvious indicators for where lines were drawn between past and present. Race was one element of those deeply embedded divisions, but it was the African-American musicians that established jazz. The genre's most celebrated stars – Louis Armstrong, Duke Ellington, and Bessie Smith – were equally popular, if not more so, among the white population who provided the majority of financial capital and audience base. The freedom from stricture that jazz represented, juxtaposed against rigid rules of adherence from earlier genres, serves as a synecdoche of the times as a whole. This decade of dramatic change, also known as "The Roaring Twenties," reflected the frenetic pace mirrored in the notes that punctuated its essence.

In relation to Wharton, the context of the age is two-fold. Trends and interests on U.S. shores were often quite different from those associated with European centers. The domestic scene was focused largely on politics, business and popular culture. In his 1931 publication *Only Yesterday*, noted social historian and *Harper's* editor Frederick Lewis Allen provided a retrospective of the period's major characteristics and highlighted social and political trends related to the U.S. scene.[3] Allen suggests emphasis on a return to normality, a distinct fear of factors that might threaten such a return, and efforts to override the sobriety of the age in two significant ways. In reaction to the sobering trauma of war and its aftermath, the nation embraced a counter response informally labeled the ballyhoo years. Allen describes this as an era where "the country had bread, but it wanted circuses" (158), and where with surprising unanimity, "the American people could become excited over a quite unimportant event if only it were dramatic enough" (161). Secondly, while Prohibition made the sale or consumption of alcohol illegal, the Eighteenth Amendment banning the substance only fanned the alcoholic fervor and subsequently sparked the rise of the speakeasy and its concomitant elements: the flapper, jazz, bathtub gin, and the seamier gangster activity of bootlegging tied to the illegal running of alcohol. F. Scott Fitzgerald, as the chronicler of the age, looked back in his 1930s *Crack Up* essays with nostalgia and regret describing the period as "the most expensive orgy in history" with a "whole race going hedonistic, deciding on pleasure."[4]

That pleasure-seeking impulse generated nearly a decade of unparalleled shifts in what was considered publicly appropriate. Earlier forms of entertainment – the Ziegfield Follies, vaudeville, and French-inspired cabarets – reached the peak of their popularity in the 1920s. Fads became the rage with dance marathons, crazes such as Mah-Jongg and crossword puzzles, flagpole sitting and all manner of publicity-seeking stunts. Hero worship emphasized sports figures such as Babe Ruth and Jack Dempsey, movie stars like Charlie Chaplin and Rudolph Valentino, music icons George Gershwin and Irving Berlin, folk legend Charles Lindbergh and others pushing the boundaries of what seemed possible, along with the contrasting fascination with notorious gangsters, most recognizably Al Capone. The allure of the famous and the infamous fueled a growing interest in the sensational and in tabloids glorifying these events. The public was hungry for *causes célèbres* that diverted their attention from the trauma of a new and uncertain world and the contrasting ordinariness of their day-to-day lives.

With the passage of the Nineteenth Amendment in 1920, women gained the right to vote, and they began participating in broadening spheres of opportunity. That same year, Congress created a bureau for women in the Department of Labor to champion and regulate the workplace, and females fought for better pay and conditions.[5] Socially, they took up formerly male activities such as smoking, drinking and sports, but on a more significant level, and in growing numbers, they entered politics, business and the academy. Activist Alice Paul proposed the Equal Rights Amendment (1923), Margaret Mead entered the male-dominated field of anthropology, Wyoming's Nellie Tayloe Ross became the nation's first female governor (1925–27), aviator Elinor Smith set multiple flight records, and Eunice Randall became a professional radio broadcaster. Wharton was the first female to win the Pulitzer Prize in 1921 for *The Age of Innocence*, the award, notes Lewis, given annually "for the American Novel which shall best present the wholesome atmosphere of American life and the highest standard of American manners and manhood" (Lewis in *Letters* 443). Wharton noted ironically to Bernard Berenson that at the same time *The Old Maid* had been rejected by "every self-respecting American magazine" claiming that the short story was immoral (*Letters* 441). Such success, frustrating as it was for Wharton on some levels, netted her wide acclaim and significant earnings, roughly calculated from 1920 through 1924 to be about $250,000, a sum "not much less than $3,000,000 before taxes today" (*Letters* 418).

On the political front, serious concerns rose as Americans fought to affirm their democratic ideals and reclaim a sense of perceived supremacy. Patriotic fervor gave the country an aura of unity and sense of comfort after the challenge to their way of life the war had posed. Intense patriotism functioned to build symbolic walls around their Americanism as the masses looked fearfully toward rising socialistic ideology at home and abroad. Concern over radical belief systems fostered xenophobic violence against foreign nationals, African Americans and Jews among other minority groups experiencing active hostility. As Nash reported, "Between 1920 and 1924 the KKK [Ku Klux Klan] grew from five thousand members to an estimated five million" and "became a major political force in at least a dozen states" (143). Throughout the decade, trials captured national headlines as alleged criminals of foreign descent or those whose racial or religious backgrounds lay outside the norm were prosecuted. The Sacco-Vanzetti murder case and the Scopes trial focusing on creationism versus evolution are prime examples. Intolerance was more often the rule than the exception as white, Anglo-Saxon Protestants fought to hold dominance.

In business, the bull market was king with capitalism and its resultant consumerism in full swing. Money flowed freely, and with an advantageous exchange rate the dollar fared even better in Europe. A number of Americans, famously including the young and yet-to-be-discovered Ernest Hemingway, used this advantage to travel extensively or take up foreign residence. Buying on speculation was rampant in stocks, bonds, real estate and other investments of sometimes questionable but alluring financial possibility. This was the age of mass production, important especially to the car industry and the manufacture of household goods. Advertising shifted from what was necessary to what was desired, and installment purchasing became a viable option. The United States was on a spending spree that would drive consumerism to remarkable heights.

Following in the footsteps of Wharton, Henry James, and earlier Americans, a notable group of intellectuals and artists in the early 1920s found the nation's path increasingly intolerable and rejected their country's provincialism for the promise of more liberal realms abroad. This exodus would encompass most of the already famous as well as those whose names would become synonymous with modernism. They settled primarily on the Left Bank in Paris and on the French Riviera – both locales already chosen by Wharton and her circle, although the established group and their newer counterparts seldom mingled. The American expatriates, or expats as they came to be known, found Paris exciting;

Wharton saw the city as "a kind of continuous earthquake" made less appealing "with hundreds of thousands of U.S. citizens rushing about" (*Letters* 432). T. S. Eliot, Ezra Pound, Gertrude Stein, Aaron Copland, and Cole Porter were among those arriving early in the 1920s and were followed closely by Sherwood Anderson, Man Ray, Ernest Hemingway, F. Scott Fitzgerald, Archibald MacLeish, John Dos Passos, Djuna Barnes, and Dorothy Parker among other names later associated with Americans shaping the most influential currents of a new age.

As the earlier generation of expatriated artists had chosen a largely American social circle, so too did this new group even while being drawn to the bohemian lifestyle of sidewalk cafes like Le Dôme and La Rotonde, frequent soirees at established salons, and proximity to the intellectual and artistic vanguard for which Paris was famous. They sought to escape the perceived provincialism of their native country for the promise foreign intellectual centers provided, but they also sought each other and, to a large degree, lived as Americans in exile rather than immersing themselves in the culture of their adopted country. Almost without exception, at least with the writers and the works they produced, they kept their thematic focus on Americans and were strongly influenced by homegrown intellectuals like H. L. Mencken. His particularly acerbic but persuasive voice found its way into works like Hemingway's *The Sun Also Rises* (1926) where the main character Jake Barnes muses, "So many young men get their likes and dislikes from Mencken."[6]

Beyond the familiarity of other Americans, Paris offered an enticing lifestyle fostering the free flow of money and an escape from war's lingering effects, mostly accomplished with alcohol and its attendant activities. The comparable French term for "The Roaring Twenties" was "Années Folles" or "Crazy Years," characterizing the surface frivolity that seemed an effort to recapture late nineteenth and early twentieth century's celebrated Belle Époque, a period where stability and prosperity appeared unending. The rouse was a shallow but hard-fought attempt to hold on to the allusion nonetheless. While this group's artistic production often focused on modernity's nihilistic aspects, their lifestyle reflected a spirited revelry.

Such affected optimism could not be sustained, however, and what became more relevant was the rise of "modernisms" characterized by serious philosophical scrutiny of civilization as they now perceived it. F. Scott Fitzgerald expressed this new sensibility at the end of *This Side of Paradise* (1920) when his central character proclaims:

Here was a new generation, shouting the old cries, learning the old creeds, through a reverie of long days and nights; destined finally to go out into that dirty grey turmoil to follow love and pride; a new generation dedicated more than the last to the fear of poverty and the worship of success; grown up to find all Gods dead, all wars fought, all faiths in man shaken ....[7]

Modernism expounded cynicism and its accompanying rejection of decadence while continuing to exhibit its own forms of excess. To a degree this was in keeping with *fin de siècle* intellectualism centered particularly in the French aesthetic movement. Artists such as Henri de Toulouse-Lautrec, Paul Cézanne, Vincent van Gogh, Paul Gauguin, and Georges Seurat adumbrated twentieth-century tensions. Their legacy spawned the next wave of innovators – Pablo Picasso, Fernand Léger, Henri Matisse, Marc Chagall, Marcel Duchamp, Juan Gris, and André Breton – whose canvases created visual paradigms of such philosophical concepts as Existentialism, Nihilism, Surrealism, Cubism, Dadaism, and other serious forms of critique. As art historian Herbert Read describes it, their work sought "to express a new dimension of consciousness," in efforts to find meaning or reflect a lack thereof in a world where belief systems had been obliterated or seriously damaged and were "alas, fragmentary and unconsoling."[8]

Although Wharton was geographically embedded in French intellectual and artistic centers from which the strongest modernist voices emanated, to a large degree she did not share the conceptual world inhabited by the younger Americans. A number of her contemporary critics viewed Wharton, nearly sixty by the dawn of the 1920s, as an anachronism living in close proximity to the cutting-edge world of fellow American writers with whom she appeared to have little in common but vocation and geography. Pamela Knights remarks that Wharton did share an interest in the period's focus on "the psychopathology of everyday life" (19), and we might add to this her concern for the plight of women, but on the whole she "did not mingle in flamboyantly avant-garde circles, and did not approve of the experimentation of much modernist art" (27). However, the easy categorization of artists working during this period of major cultural adjustment is difficult at best. Philippe Collas and Éric Villedary rightly note in *Edith Wharton's French Riviera* an underlying ambiguity in Wharton's beliefs that mirrors an inability to encompass the complexity that was true for the contemporary artists. They struggled between past ideals and present realities that saw ideological *terra firma* as an outdated and unsupportable concept. Collas and Villedary surmise that, "Wharton found herself caught between these two worlds; the past that she wished to flee but that gave her sustenance, and the present, which she was not sure she preferred but which gave her the liberty she craved."[9] Many of the younger artists experienced this same modernist angst.

The 1920s expatriated scene that rapidly supplanted its predecessors gravitated at least initially around Gertrude Stein, the daunting figure at its axis. Stein and Wharton had backgrounds of relative privilege in common, as well as childhood travels in European cultural centers, a passion for writing, and many mutual interests and friends, but the two most noted American female authors of the time had little contact and shared almost nothing of their life in Paris. Stein presided over her salon at 27 rue de Fleurus on the Left Bank and preached what Susan Goodman describes as "a private laboratory of self" aggrandizing the power of language as a chief vehicle of newness and expression.[10] Wharton articulated a general distaste for the avant-garde and what she interpreted as that artistic desire to "make new" simply for the sake of newness, and further complained that an "unsettling element in modern art is that common symptom of immaturity, the dread of doing what has been done before" (*WF* 17). As Lewis notes, these two women – who might have had more in common than either would acknowledge – never came to be associated with "the international assortment of poets and novelists, painters, playwrights, and socialites that flowed through" each other's milieu. Lewis goes on to observe: "While Gertrude Stein was offering counsel to James Joyce, Ernest Hemingway, Sherwood Anderson, and many others, Edith Wharton was playing hostess to Paul Valéry, André Gide, Sinclair Lewis, Aldous Huxley, and Kenneth Clark" (440).

Stein was especially in tune with the progressive movements so central to modernism and the 1920s, and her salon could boast regular participants from the most established practitioners as well as those on the cusp of fame. Matisse and Picasso were among the early figures whose work contributed to her growing collection of modern art. Stein remarked, "More and more frequently, people began visiting to see the Matisse paintings – and the Cézannes: Matisse brought people, everybody brought somebody, and they came at any time and it began to be a nuisance, and it was in this way that Saturday evenings began."[11] These gatherings also came to be populated by such U.S. writers as Hemingway, Fitzgerald, and Sherwood Anderson among others who joined the conversation about art as an ideological force in its broadest sense. The regular bringing together of the most influential in their various genres helped establish a remarkable cohesiveness among art forms and the thematic ideas they illustrated.

Further demonstrating this intermingling of arts, especially as related to the French atmosphere in which Wharton and other expatriates resided, were the entertainment genres of dance, music, and theater. In the previous decade, Serge Diaghilev's Ballets Russes had established itself as a preeminent company whose innovative performances offered a unique collaboration of dance, original music and stage sets, themselves viewed as an art form. Groundbreaking composer, Igor Stravinsky, had created for the Ballet such original scores as *The Rite of Spring*, which incited a riot at its 1913 premier performance. Isadora Duncan, also reaching her creative height in that decade, found inspiration in classical lines of Greek sculpture translated and reflected in what might be described as moving *tableaux vivants*. Josephine Baker would in the next decade transform such free-flowing motion to a unique and ribald dance style more appropriate to the hedonism of the Folies Bergère than the sophistication of the Ballet. Both women's oeuvres revealed the amalgam of influence and art forms represented by the era.

Paris with its intellectual salon life, highbrow art and entertainment arts epitomized the overall spirit of the 1920s and modernism at its core, but when the city's artistic community sought temporary escape, they found it on the French Riviera. Presiding at the social center of Lost Generation expats and their French counterparts were Gerald and Sara Murphy, a well-established American couple from a background of wealth and privilege. As Deborah Rothschild notes, "Together, they created a distinctly modern elegant style of living that ranged over art, literature, music, theater, fashion, design, gardening, child rearing, and entertaining."[12] As with Wharton who had arrived before them, the Murphys established themselves as mainstays in the expatriated artistic community of their generation, but unlike Wharton and her friends who wintered on the Côte d'Azur, the Murphys made it a summer haven. Living on inherited money, they purchased a home at Cap d'Antibe, named it Villa America, and from there hosted the brightest and most talented of their generation. As in Paris, little mingling occurred between Wharton's circle and the younger American implants. Only one of the Wharton biographies mentions the Murphys at all, and then only in a disclaimer that "The gregarious *joie de vivre* of rich bohemian Americans like the talented painter Gerald Murphy and his wife, Sarah [sic] ... was not at all Whartonian. A glossy French picture-book called *La Côte d'Azure au temps d'Edith*

Wharton, full of pictures of flappers, models, casinos and grand hotels in Cannes, gets it exactly wrong" (Lee 536).

Wharton did live well on the Riviera, but in a very different manner from the younger American artists. Where they preferred public revelry with friends, her style was one of mostly quiet seclusion and private time spent at home writing and in the company of a few well-chosen companions. Knights points out that Wharton resided "between two broad generations, represented above all, in the mid- and late nineteenth century, by Nathaniel Hawthorne and Henry James, whom she admired, and the 1920s generation of F. Scott Fitzgerald and Ernest Hemingway, with whom she was out of sympathy" (26). In a 1925 letter to Fitzgerald, Wharton confessed, "I feel that to your generation, which has taken such a flying leap into the future, I must represent the literary equivalent of tufted furniture and gas chandeliers" (*Letters* 481). Wharton pandered to this image in many ways. In 1922 she had written similarly: "I am so accustomed nowadays to being regarded as a deplorable example of what people used to read in the Dark Ages before the 'tranche de vie' had been rediscovered, that my very letter-paper blushes as I thank a novelist of your generation for his praise" (*Letters* 457). This self-deprecating, yet subtly defiant approach becomes her kind of calling card to the younger writers. She complains in some interviews in the 1930s about the "grande dame" image with which she has been characterized, albeit somewhat through her own application. Musing on critics' labels and "this violets and old lace affair" in a November 1936 interview in the *New York Herald Tribune*, Wharton provides what Laura Rattray has described as an "expert deconstruction of her mutating public image and reputation."[13]

The 1920s saw an explosion of talented artists employing new responses to their changing world, and Wharton resided at the movement's geographic epicenter. She was often mistrustful of its appeal, although not entirely immune to its impact. Recent criticism broadens our vision of her aesthetics, which actually fit into early definitions of modernism, although she continued to steer her own course (see Chapter 34 on Wharton and modernism by Jennifer Haytock). By decade's end, the Jazz Age party was over and its casualties counted. The 1929 Stock Market crash left in its wake unprecedented financial fallout spewing fresh challenges to all. Looking back over the previous decade and reminiscing about her life, she would write, "the present generation hears close underfoot the growling of the volcano on which ours danced so long" (*BG* 379). Wharton observed herself and those to follow her with a keen eye and continued to write.

NOTES

1. R. Nash, *The Nervous Generation: American Thought, 1917–1930* (Chicago: Rand McNally, 1970). Subsequent references to this work are included in the text.

2. H. Münsterberg, *American Problems: From the Point of View of a Psychologist* (New York: Mofat, 1910), 3–5. Cited in P. Knights, *The Cambridge Introduction to Edith Wharton* (Cambridge: Cambridge University Press, 2009), 19. Subsequent references to Knights' work are included in the text.

3. F. Lewis Allen, *Only Yesterday: An Informal History of the 1920s* (New York: Harper and Row, 1931).

4. F. Scott Fitzgerald, *The Crack-Up*, ed. E. Wilson (New York: Charles Scribner's Sons, 1931), 21, 15.

5. C. Gourley, *Flappers and the New American Woman: Perceptions of Women from 1918 Through the 1920s* (Minneapolis: Twenty-First Century Books, 2008), 14–35.

6. E. Hemingway, *The Sun Also Rises* (New York: Charles Scribner's Sons, 1926), 49.

7. F. Scott Fitzgerald, *This Side of Paradise* (New York: Charles Scribner's Sons, 1920), 260.

8. H. Read, *A Concise History of Modern Painting* (New York: Frederick A. Praeger, 1959), 81.

9. P. Collas and E. Villedary, *Edith Wharton's French Riviera*, trans. S. Pickford (Italy: Flammarion, 2002), 62.

10. S. Goodman, *Edith Wharton's Inner Circle* (Austin: University of Texas Press, 1994), 117.

11. J. R. Mellow, *Charmed Circle: Gertrude Stein & Company* (New York: Praeger, 1974), 84.

12. D. Rothschild (ed.), *Making It New: The Art and Style of Sara and Gerald Murphy* (Berkeley: University of California Press, 2007), 11.

13. L. Rattray (ed.), *The Unpublished Writings of Edith Wharton* (London: Pickering and Chatto, 2009), vol II, xlvi, l.

CHAPTER 29

Wharton and the Great Depression

Carol J. Singley

Born into a privileged New York society on January 24, 1862, Edith
Wharton was sixty-seven when the stock market crashed in late October
of 1929. The stunning statistics associated with the financial collapse
are well known: on October 24, the New York Stock Exchange fell an
unprecedented forty points in one day. Unemployment, at 3.2 percent in
the United States in 1929, jumped to 8.9 percent a year later. At least seven
million Americans were out of work. On December 30, 1930, the New
York Bank of America closed its sixty branches and erased the accounts
of 400,000 depositors in the largest bank foreclosures in the history of
the United States. By 1933, more than one quarter of the American population was unemployed.[1] The financial crisis spread quickly to Europe,
including France, where Wharton had made her home.

Conditions in Wharton's adopted country did not immediately dete-
riorate, as they did in the United States and Great Britain. The reason,
John Garraty explains, was that France was less committed to industry,
had not experienced a rise in unemployment in the 1920s because of a
low birth rate and shortage of manpower resulting from World War I,
and benefitted from a low valuation of the franc.[2] In addition, the French
people and government had an inflated sense of national well-being after
the stock market crash. Wharton, who returned only once to the United
States in the 1920s, was thoroughly immersed in French life and culture
and may have absorbed some of this optimism, even if short-lived: the
1929 French budget produced a surplus of five billion francs; the 1930
budget ran a deficit of five billion francs (Garraty 40).

Wharton's situation may have seemed comfortable initially. Before the
crash, she was earning impressive sums for her writing as a popular and
critically acclaimed novelist. By 1925 she was "rich by virtue of her pen,"
Shari Benstock writes, having recouped all of the losses of the war years
(390). In 1927, contracts for her work totaled almost $2 million (Benstock
395). However, the Depression forced widespread, permanent changes in

the publishing industry. Library circulation increased 40 percent from 1929 to 1933 because people could not afford books, and overall book sales in the United States dropped by nearly half.[3] Book and magazine publishers scaled back accordingly. The crisis affected new and aspiring authors more than acclaimed veterans like Wharton, but no one was immune. Moreover, Wharton's expansive lifestyle required funds, making "her primary concern ... money" (Benstock 394). She traveled extensively and had purchased impressive properties in France after residing in the fashionable Faubourg Saint Germain: Pavillon Colombe, a spacious estate in Saint-Brice-sous-Forêt, with acreage across the road; and Sainte-Claire le Château, with surrounding acreage, on the French Riviera in Hyères. These expertly designed homes boasted impeccably furnished interiors and gardens that required servants and significant cash flow. Wharton also continued to fund her World War I charities and its dependents. She was able to keep abreast of her expenses so long as she continued to write and her fiction continued to sell, which was the case up to the time of the crash. However, an altered financial landscape in the wake of the crash left her struggling in unfamiliar ways, with the result that money became a greater determining factor than before.

The Depression had a profound effect on U.S. writers and literature. Some expatriates, including Ernest Hemingway and F. Scott Fitzgerald, who had spent the 1920s in Europe, returned home. The Jazz Age came to an abrupt end, and the excesses and gaiety of the so-called Lost Generation were replaced by a more sober and critical realism. Many intellectuals and writers rejected the notion of progress and questioned economic and political institutions. Some, like Langston Hughes, John Dos Passos, Dorothy Parker, Sherwood Anderson, John Steinbeck, and Hemingway developed leftist politics and were attracted to the Communist Party. The U.S.S.R. provided an appealing model of growing prosperity with its emphasis on planning and social control although radical upheavals, even if they seemed warranted by high unemployment and low productivity, never materialized (Garraty 168, 165). Michael Gold's novel, *Jews without Money* (1930), exemplified the proletarian spirit, while Jack Conroy's *The Disinherited* (1933) described the disillusionment of industrial workers. Steinbeck chronicled the plight of farmers fleeing the Dust Bowl in futile attempts to realize the American dream in *The Grapes of Wrath* (1939), and Richard Wright dramatized racial and social injustice in *Native Son* (1940). Some writers joined the Popular Front, a leftist organization that opposed Fascism, as developed under Mussolini in Italy, under Hitler in Germany, and under Franco in Spain. Hemingway's protagonist in

For Whom the Bell Tolls (1940) fights in the Spanish Civil War against a Fascist regime.

At one extreme were writers associated with the Communist Party, who emphasized the solidarity of the working class and the need for the overthrow of an exploitative capitalism. At the other were writers who offered escape or answered a yearning to connect to roots and rediscover foundations, often conceived as rural and simple, that defined American life. Carl Sandburg's poems, *The People, Yes* (1936), epitomized this latter trend. William Faulkner developed a mythic Southern world in *Light in August* (1932) and *Absalom, Absalom!* (1936), although Ted Atkinson argues that his depictions are more informed by Depression-era social politics than is first evident.[4] Margaret Mitchell's immensely popular Civil War saga, *Gone with the Wind* (1936), captivated readers with its descriptions of turmoil, loss, and resilience. Despite a decline in ticket sales and a strict code of ethics, people flocked to the movies, making the 1930s a golden age for cinema. Musicals, gangster, and horror films, such as *Dracula* and *Little Caesar* of 1931, gave way to portraits of effective government as the New Deal took effect (*Bullets or Ballots* [1936], *Mr. Smith Goes to Washington* [1939]). Audiences also flocked to comedy and fantasy such as the Marx Brothers' *Duck Soup* (1933) and *The Wizard of Oz* (1939). If the 1920s had been, as Robert McElvaine notes, "a time of political conservatism and moral latitude, of great prosperity and grinding poverty," the 1930s proved a time of radicalism and experimentation.[5] The contradictions within these popular forms of art constitute the grotesque, and what Mark Fearnow calls "the hallmark of depression America."[6]

Wharton continued to write about money during the Depression, but her fiction makes oblique rather than direct reference to the crisis. Proponents of the proletariat were most successful in the fields of drama, as Sean McCann notes.[7] The stage plays of Wharton's 1924 and 1911 works, *The Old Maid* (1935) and *Ethan Frome* (1936), were produced alongside Erskine Caldwell's gritty *Tobacco Road* (1932), one of the longest-running plays in Broadway history (1933–41). Although these works describe struggle, Wharton's general preference for manners, international flair, and attention to taste and décor seems at odds with the challenges of the Depression. Nevertheless, fiction that Wharton composed during this decade reflects the times. Her representations are indirect, subtle, ironic, and sometimes comic, as they are in Faulkner's *The Hamlet* (1940), in which, according to Andrea Dimino, "economic decline generates ... dialogue of value" about "the basic tension of depression humor, the need to reconcile the Edenic abundance of America with the realities of waste and hardship."[8]

The Depression was especially challenging for three reasons. First, Wharton's work had begun to lose its appeal to large audiences, making it difficult to place with publishers. It suffered under the scrutiny of 1930s critics like Marxist Granville Hicks, who derided Wharton for her aristocrat focus, claiming her work "has ended in romantic trivialities."[9] Second, she was advancing in years, declining in health, and finding it increasingly difficult to maintain the pace of her earlier writing career. Third, she was overextended financially when the Depression began, having committed not only to an affluent lifestyle but also having assumed financial responsibility for several dependents, whom she generously supported even in tight fiscal circumstances. One of the highest-paid U.S. novelists of her time, she found it difficult to maintain her comfortable lifestyle and marketplace success. She scrambled to meet the demands of Depression-era readers and critics, who favored wholesome fare or escapism. There was less room than before for her ironic realism or for the sexual liberties of some of her characters, such as the unmarried Vance and Halo in *The Gods Arrive* (1932).

Difficulties over this novel and its prequel, *Hudson River Bracketed* (1929), encapsulate the issues that pressed on her. Toward the end of 1928, the publishers of the *Delineator* began running *Hudson River Bracketed* before it was finished, causing Wharton concern because she was recovering from a serious illness and was not well enough to meet deadlines. Her convalescence from this heart ailment was long and tedious. In July of 1929, just three months before the stock market crash, the publishers debated whether to shorten the serial run of *Hudson River Bracketed*, outraging Wharton (Lee 688). The novel appeared in book form with Appleton in November, before the serialization had finished its run, further annoying her. The Depression, Lee writes, "would profoundly affect Wharton's personal and professional life from now on" (688).

If the year leading up to the crash had not been kind, subsequent ones created greater obstacles. As Lee writes, Wharton was by no means impoverished, but the decline in the value of the dollar, lower rents on her New York properties, and diminished returns from a trust fund necessitated a new economizing. A new French tax law in 1934 doubled her taxes and created an obligation that she left unfulfilled at the time of her death in 1937. Her resources contracted, but her responsibilities did not. Wharton continued to fund her tuberculosis hospitals, her ex-secretary Dolly Herbert, and her mother, a "left-over protégé from her war work" named Gabrielle Landormy (Lee 689). The publishing industry was also facing retrenchment. Magazine publishers, an important outlet for Wharton's work, shortened the length of stories and issues as readers curtailed their purchases. Wharton's earnings declined accordingly, from "$95,000 in 1929 to $5,000 in 1930" (Lee 691). Cost-cutting measures continued as the decade progressed. In 1935, Penguin Books in England began publishing the 25-cent paperback in an attempt to make books inexpensive enough for the average reader (Carlisle 10–11). Despite a smaller market, Wharton published an impressive number of short stories and interviews in magazines in the 1930s, a testament to her professionalism and determination to counter devaluation of her work. These stories appear in two collections, *Human Nature* (1933), and *The World Over* (1936), the title of which conveys, befitting the Depression, both global reach and dire reality.

Much of this fiction revisits familiar upper-class settings and themes, with oblique references to the economic hardship across the United States and abroad. The stories feature comfortable, complacent upper-class Americans in Europe or New York, some of them smug dilettantes of the type made famous by Lawrence Selden in *The House of Mirth* (1905) and Newland Archer in *The Age of Innocence* (1920). Many plots involve restrictive marriages, illicit affairs, and the ambiguous security of membership in elite society. Characteristically, members of the upper class look down on or romanticize those of the lower class, but Wharton's irony is such that readers see these shortcomings even if the characters are oblivious to them. In "A Glimpse," which first appeared in the *Saturday Evening Post* in November 1932, John Kilvert accidentally boards "the wrong boat – the unfashionable boat" (*CSII* 609) en route to see his former lover when he observes a couple engaged in animated conversation. Fretting that he has missed the essence of life, he fantasizes a passionate romance between the man and the woman, fascinated by the way that "real people" lived (*CSII* 624), but insensitive to material difficulties they may be facing. His obsession with the "greatest emotional spectacle he had ever witnessed" (*CSII* 629) continues even after he learns that they are not lovers, but professional musicians working out the terms of their collaboration.

Suicide, which may be read as an allusion to the desperate measures of those who lost fortunes in the stock market crash, appears in two stories of the 1930s, both collected in *Human Nature*. "The Day of the Funeral" first appeared in January 1933 as "In a Day" in *Woman's Home Companion*. It opens with the shocking matter-of-fact description of a suicidal woman whose husband has been conducting an affair: "His wife had said: 'If you don't give her up I'll throw myself from the roof.' He had not given her up, and his wife had thrown herself from the roof" (*CSII* 587). Wharton's story mimics the violent emotions on Wall Street with its portrayal of illicit love and marital betrayal. The unfaithful husband, Ambrose Trenham, is so self-absorbed that he cares little about his wife, Milly's, suicide. He is relieved that he can now continue his affair with impunity. His lover, however, feels great sympathy for Milly and calls on Trenham to share in her remorse, which he cannot do. In another story, "Joy in the House" (*Nash's Pall Mall Magazine*, December 1932), Christine Ansley returns to her husband and son after a six-month affair with a struggling artist. The husband, a marvel of forgiveness and magnanimity, displays a banner with the words, "Joy in the House," to signal his delight at her return. However, he fails to disclose, because he "will not permit suffering my house" (*CSII* 643), that the abandoned artist has committed suicide. Hearing the news from the artist's destitute widow, Christine must confront her moral responsibility for the affair. She also must acknowledge that the "small sensual joys" of her wealthy home and neighborhood do not grant immunity from life's pain. They cannot "shut out something dark and looming on the threshold of her thoughts – the confused sense that life is not a matter of water-tight compartments, that no effort of the will can keep experiences from interpenetrating and coloring each other" (*CSII* 640).

Alluding to the years before the stock market crash, both stories raise questions of moral responsibility for reckless and selfish behavior. In "A Glimpse," a husband's callous attitude toward his wife's suffering prompts his lover to leave him. In "Joy in the House," the home that a wayward wife returns to for solace and comfort becomes an emotional prison. Both protagonists experience diminished expectations in keeping with Depression-era realities. Although the stories do not explicitly reference the Depression, we can read them in the context of the financial crisis to understand the social and moral issues Wharton associates with privilege, in a similar way that Shelley Newman reads Willa Cather's historical novel *Sapphira and the Slave Girl* (1940) against the Depression in order to analyze the meanings of remembered homes and the historical and cultural ideas of citizenship.[10] In Wharton's work, members of fashionable New York society are too myopic and self-centered to care about the needs of the rest of the world.

Wharton mentions the Depression in "Charm Incorporated," originally published as "Bread Upon the Waters" in *Hearst's* magazine in February 1934. James Targatt and his wife Nadeja go "to a different restaurant every night ... hunting out the most exotic that New York at the high tide of prosperity had to offer" (*CSII* 653). Targatt takes luxuries for granted in the 1920s. When he bothers to reflect on his good fortune, he is hardly sensitive to others' needs. Noting that "extortionate valeting establishments ... used to charge a dollar a minute for such services," he is gratified that "he found a stranded German widow who came to him on starvation wages" (*CSII* 654). He makes an impetuous marriage proposal to an Eastern European woman he refers to as part "of that struggling mass of indistinguishable human misery .... called 'Wardrift'" (*CSII* 654), but he is so lacking in global awareness that he does not know precisely her country of origin. To his credit, however, he supports his resourceful wife and the numerous relatives she imposes on him at considerable expense, especially as "Wall Street was beginning to be uneasy" (*CSII* 661). Despite market volatility, Targatt and Nadeja cleverly manage to align the newly arrived Kouradjines with rich Americans, many associated with Hollywood, by relying on Nadeja's "dogged optimism" (*CSII* 657) and the family's indescribable but indisputable charm. These efforts yield good returns and Targatt sees his investments grow in the process of helping his in-laws. The story is lighthearted, even madcap, in the spirit of escapist Depression-era fiction that lifts morale by celebrating resourcefulness and minimizing hardship. Even though, as Nadeja puts it, "it seems that people are no more as rich as they were" (*CSII* 664), the Targatt-Kouradjines venture succeeds beyond everyone's expectations.

Wharton also alludes to the economic crisis in "Diagnosis." First published in 1930 in the *Ladies' Home Journal* and reprinted in *Human Nature*, the story opens with a line applicable both to the Depression and disease: "Nothing to worry about –absolutely nothing. Of course not ... just what they all say!" The successful protagonist, Paul Dorrance, lives near "Wall Street[,] which was the visible center and symbol of his life's work."[11] After he learns, incorrectly, that he has a terminal illness, he proposes marriage to a woman with whom he has had an affair and whom he continues to see after her divorce. His motive is selfish: "He was marrying simply to put a sentinel between himself and the presence lurking on his threshold" (729). On a trip to Europe, Eleanor is solicitous, "watching over his comfort, sparing him all needless fatigue and agitation," as "perfect" a wife as she had been a mistress (730). Two years pass. When Eleanor falls ill with "bad bronchitis," Dorrance pays no attention until the diagnosis is dire: pneumonia. Just before she dies, Eleanor says cryptically to Dorrance, "it was worth it! I always knew –" (737). Dorrance later learns that his terminal diagnosis was meant for another patient and that the doctor had explained his mistake to Eleanor.

"Diagnosis" evokes the reversals of fortune common to the Depression: Dorrance thinks he is dying but is actually well; his nurturing wife is stricken with disease and dies. Both characters live in an economy of scarcity: Dorrance ostensibly has a limited number of days to live; Eleanor knows that Dorrance marries her out of need, not love. Yet Wharton's different descriptions of the characters represent gender inequities in the workplace during the Depression. The fiction of the 1920s trumpeted women's capabilities and right to work, with the result that few occupations seemed off limits to women.[12] The Depression focused attention not on women's employment but on men's. When men found themselves unemployed – which Wharton represents as Dorrance's presumed terminal illness – women's jobs came under greater scrutiny, with some demanding that women relinquish jobs to men and revert to traditional, caring roles, which Eleanor does as Dorrance's wife. Women's positions in the workforce were thus weakened – portrayed in Eleanor's case as bronchitis that becomes fatal pneumonia.

Yet Wharton gives Eleanor the last word. She marries Dorrance fully aware of his flaws, which allows her to capitalize on existing resources and invest in her future. When her husband divorced her after having learned of her affair, she was more dependent than she would have liked. Marriage to Dorrance brings affluence and allows her to recover the losses suffered in the divorce. More importantly, Eleanor possesses the truth about Dorrance's shallowness, which she controls by remaining silent. Eleanor speaks volubly on her deathbed with "an almost critical equality of expression" (735). Her elusive "I always knew" settles the score in her favor, making "Diagnosis" a feminist tale in which a demeaned woman asserts herself.

In "Duration," a similarly feminist tale first published in *The World Over*, a wealthy family habitually denigrates their dull relative, Martha Little. They dedicate resources to her – in the form of social invitations – only when they risk little by doing so. They are surprised when Martha, at the age of 100, achieves local fame. They are even more shocked when at the rehearsal for her birthday celebration she eliminates her competition for attention, another centenarian, Uncle Syngleton Perch. She deliberately trips the man with her cane, sending him reeling and procuring the position of honor for herself. It is tempting to see the aging Wharton in this story, expressing the triumph of old age. It is also possible to discern Wharton's advocacy of women. For the "duration" of the Depression, women found opportunities to demonstrate competence because men were unemployed or their economic positions weakened. (Philip Hanson discusses these Depression-era sexual politics in Hollywood films under the subheading, "Men Leaning on Women."[13]) In "Duration," a relative escorting Martha at the rehearsal expects her to "transfer her frail weight to Mr. Perch's," but she makes "an unexpected movement" that causes Perch to "fall over with a crash" (*CSII* 796–97). As Martha tells her guests, the scene in which Perch shares in her glory is merely a rehearsal; at the actual birthday celebration, Martha leans on no one but herself.

The causes of the Depression have been endlessly studied. Among many theories is one advanced by Peter Temin, who argues that the Depression was the result of unyielding commitment to the gold standard, which had become outmoded as a result of World War I. The deflationary effect of a gold-standard ideology was precisely wrong for the world economy at that time.[14] At the heart of Temin's argument is a point about the hazards of commitment to archaic policies and worldviews. This is a point Wharton knew well. Whether or not she was abreast of economic theories about the causes of the Depression, she knew that change is not only inevitable but also beneficial. Those least able to adjust to fluctuating and unpredictable circumstances suffer the most. The ability to adapt to new conditions can lead to prosperity and happiness; the failure to adapt, to illusion and suffering. This theme is reinforced in "Charm," "Diagnosis," and "Duration," in which female characters deftly surmise their situations and respond in ways that allow them not only to survive but to triumph.

Wharton responded to the challenges of the Depression with hardheaded realism, wit, and tongue-in-cheek feminism. Many of her male characters reflect what she found objectionable about elite New York complacency. Her female portrayals serve as foils and alter egos for the aging author, who wrestled daily with diminishing returns on her writing and declining reputation and health. Although Wharton seldom references the Depression explicitly, it forms a backdrop for her short fiction of the 1930s. She resists both tendencies that according to Fearnow typify literature of the Depression: a forward energy generated by reform politics and technological and cultural change, and a regressive nostalgia and retreat into the past (Fearnow 16–17). Although critical of social conventions, she eschews radical politics common to the era. Wharton's 1930s story, "Roman Fever," tacitly criticizes Fascism with its patriarchal repression; her enduring disdain for literature about "the man with the dinner pail" (*BG* 206) sums up her skepticism about New Deal reforms. Wharton's privileged existence was not free of financial concern during the Great Depression. Her fictional portrayals reveal the importance of wealth, and her depictions of material well being are suffused with moral value. Never polemical, she yet points toward a social economy wherein resources are matched by generosity and compassion.

NOTES

1. R. P. Carlisle, *The Great Depression and World War II: 1929–1949* (New York: Facts on File, 2009), vol. VII, 15.

2. J. A. Garraty, *The Great Depression: An Inquiry into the Causes, Course, and Consequences of the Worldwide Depression of the Nineteen-Thirties, as Seen by Contemporaries and in the Light of History* (San Diego, CA: Harcourt Brace Jovanovich, 1986), 39. Subsequent references to this work are included in the text.

3. E. Ausk, "Literature" in J. Ciment (ed.), *Encyclopedia of the Great Depression and the New Deal*, 2 vols. (Armonk, NY: Sharpe Reference, 2001), I, 175–78; 175.

4. T. Atkinson, *Faulkner and the Great Depression: Aesthetics, Ideology, and Cultural Politics* (Athens: University of Georgia Press, 2005), 5.

5. R. S. McElvaine, *The Great Depression: America, 1929–1941* (New York: Times Books, 1961), 13.

6. M. Fearnow, *The American Stage and the Great Depression: A Cultural History of the Grotesque* (New York: Cambridge University Press, 1997), 6. Subsequent references to this work are included in the text.

7. S. McCann, "Literature" in R. S. McElvaine (ed.), *Encyclopedia of the Great Depression*, 2 vols. (New York: Gale, 2004), II, 579–83; 580.

8. A. Dimino, "Why did the Snopeses Name their Son 'Wallstreet Panic'? Depression Humor in Faulkner's the Hamlet" in L. Wagner-Martin (ed.), *William Faulkner: Six Decades of Criticism* (East Lansing: Michigan State University Press, 2002), 333–53; 334–35.

9. G. Hicks, *The Great Tradition: An Interpretation of American Literature since the Civil War* (1933 rev. ed: New York: Biblo and Tannen, 1967), 219.

10. S. Newman, "No Place like Home: Reading *Sapphira and the Slave Girl* against the Great Depression" in A. Romines (ed.), *Willa Cather's Southern Connections: New Essays on Cather and the South* (Charlottesville: University Press of Virginia, 2000), 54–64; 54.

11. "Diagnosis" in R. W. B. Lewis (ed.), *The Collected Short Stories of Edith Wharton*, vol. II (New York: Scribner's, 1968), 723–40; 723. Subsequent references to this work are included in the text.

12. L. Hapke, *Daughters of the Great Depression: Women, Work, and Fiction in the American 1930s* (Athens: University of Georgia Press, 1995), 6.

13. P. Hanson, *This Side of Despair: How the Movies and American Life Intersected during the Great Depression* (Madison, NJ: Fairleigh Dickinson University Press, 2008).

14. P. Temin, *Lessons from the Great Depression: The Lionel Robbins Lectures for 1989* (Cambridge, MA: MIT Press, 1989), x.

PART VII

Literary Milieux

CHAPTER 30

Literary Influences

Judith P. Saunders

A passionate reader and lifelong bibliophile, Edith Wharton was widely familiar with English, American, and continental literary traditions, including their roots in the classics of Greece and Rome. She treasured this literary legacy. In her autobiography she pays homage to the "communion" she enjoyed from a very young age with "the great voices that spoke ... from books," emphasizing their essential contribution to her emotional, intellectual, and creative development (*BG* 69). The masterpieces of world literature unlocked doors to unexpected places, each in turn serving as "the gateway into some *paysage choisi* of the spirit."[1] She left direct evidence in her diaries and letters, as well as in her autobiographical and critical writings, of her encounters with *belles lettres* from the ancient and recent past. Indirect evidence of those encounters may be found in her own fiction and poetry, in the form of references, quotations, and allusions. Her titles, more often than not, are borrowed from her reading; mining the work of earlier writers for phrases apt for her purposes, she signals her intention to situate each story or novel in something larger, namely a linguistically and historically rich cultural tradition. Declaring that "the great originators draw as much from the past as from the present," she expresses her conviction that creative powers never thrive in a vacuum.[2] Rather, the achievements of previous generations provide vital inspiration and context for new accomplishment.

Wharton names Classical mythology as one of the earliest influences on her developing imagination. Even before she learned to read, as she explains in *A Backward Glance*, "the domestic dramas of the Olympians roused all my creative energy" (*BG* 33). Evidence of her ongoing enthusiasm for this subject matter is plentiful in her fiction, as well as in her letters and diaries. She invokes dryads, Furies, and sirens, for example, to describe both fictional and real-life predicaments. Diana, Artemis, Hermes, Cupid, Venus, and Perseus make significant appearances in her fiction, along with Psyche and Cupid, Daphne and Apollo, Sisyphus and

Tantalus. The Sphinx figures in her major novels, as does the Cretan labyrinth. Wharton's references to mythic persons, places, and events are never mechanical; they are woven subtly into the texture of her fiction and contribute compellingly to the presentation of character and theme. Drawing well-known myths into her own narratives, moreover, she typically modifies her originals intriguingly, challenging readers to recognize and interpret her imaginative reconfiguration of ancient stories.

Her fascination with "the Olympians" eventually led Wharton to the less well-known materials of Norse mythology; she refers frequently, for instance, to the early Icelandic collections gathered in the *Edda*. Exploration of fables and myths from other cultures supplemented a thorough-going familiarity with the Christian Bible: she names the Old Testament, Isaiah, the Song of Solomon, and the Book of Esther, among others, as early favorites. Although she does not exploit this reading with the intensity or frequency she manifests in her use of Classical sources, allusions to well-known Biblical stories and parables appear from time to time in her writing, for example, Adam and Eve, the lilies of the field, new wine in old bottles. Most memorably, she turns to Ecclesiastes for the title of *The House of Mirth*, the novel that was to establish her critical and popular success as a novelist.

Wharton's interest in ancient myth and scripture is firmly anchored in a wide acquaintance with Classical drama, poetry, and philosophy. Frequently mentioned works include the epics of Homer and Virgil, together with dramatic literature by Euripides, Aeschylus, Seneca, and Sophocles. Wharton voices vivid praise for the "supreme and poignant reality" of Greek tragedy. Even the poorly educated Sophy Viner from *The Reef*, woefully unaware of pertinent "literary or historic associations," responds with emotional intensity to the "ineluctable fatality" of the Oedipus story (as reworked by Corneille in *Oedipe*).[3] Wharton also admired St. Augustine's *Confessions*, and she was a dedicated reader of philosophical writings by Marcus Aurelius, Epictetus, and Plato. Her familiarity with great works of the Greek and Roman world laid a foundation for her remarkably thorough engagement with Anglo-European literatures of the modern era – that is, from the Renaissance through the early twentieth century. The names of sixteenth- and seventeenth-century poets and dramatists pepper her writings. She refers repeatedly to plays by Marlowe, Webster, and Shakespeare; she glories in the poetry of Donne, Herbert, Crashaw, Vaughan, Marvell, and Waller. She moves effortlessly from Bacon's essays to Bunyan's *Pilgrim's Progress*, to Milton's *Areopagitica*, *Comus*, and *Paradise Lost*. She also speaks admiringly of works by eighteenth-century writers such as Addison, Johnson, Lamb, Swift, and Pope; she offers knowing appraisals of novels by Defoe, Fielding, Richardson, Smollett, and Sterne.

Even in the face of her catholic tastes and unstinting responsiveness, it would be fair to say that Wharton expresses strongest admiration for immediate literary forebears – that is, for nineteenth-century writers who preceded her by only one or two generations. She cherished the Romantic poets throughout her life, with especial intensity. Recalling the "supreme day" in her girlhood when she was given editions of Keats and Shelley, she declares: "Then the gates of the realms of gold swung wide, and from that day to this I don't believe I was ever again, in my inmost self, wholly lonely or unhappy" (*BG* 71). Wordsworth and Coleridge, along with Keats and Shelley, were touchstones in her inner world, star-studded figures in the pantheon of her literary heroes. She classes them, along with Milton and Shakespeare, among "the supremely great English poets."[4] Reading and re-reading their work, she delighted in quoting from their poems, essays, and letters, in alluding to potent images and memorable characters. In this way, she integrated words and images from valued literary ancestors into her own imaginative constructions. Specific examples abound: among the most prominent, for instance, are thematically significant allusions to Keats' "Ode on a Grecian Urn" in *The Reef* and to Coleridge's "Kubla Khan" in *Hudson River Bracketed*.

Writers from the second half of the nineteenth century also earned Wharton's affection – among poets, most notably, Robert Browning and Elizabeth Barrett Browning. Frequent and favorable mentions of Tennyson punctuate her work, along with occasional references to Swinburne, Hazlitt, Morris, and the Rossettis. The "incredible verbal gymnastics" of Lewis Carroll and Edward Lear endeared themselves to her at an early age (*BG* 50). Edward Fitzgerald's translation of Omar Khayyam's *Rubaiyat* makes several appearances in her fiction, usually in an ironic context. Theoretical writings in the wider field of culture and aesthetics engaged her serious attention: she read Carlyle, Pater, and Ruskin with approbation, and she allied herself unreservedly with the critical principles of Mathew Arnold (whose poetry she also read with pleasure). Responding enthusiastically to many of her great nineteenth-century predecessors in fiction, she commended the novels of Austen, Scott, Butler, the Brontës, Trollope, Stevenson, Thackeray, Dickens, Eliot, Meredith, Conrad, and Hardy.

On the U.S. side of the English-language tradition, Wharton identifies little of interest in Colonial or seventeenth- and eighteenth-century writings. Except for Jonathan Edwards, U.S. literature seems for her

to begin with Washington Irving. She was familiar with the Fireside
Poets – Whittier, Longfellow, Bryant, Lowell, and Holmes – and with
Hawthorne, but she devotes more attention and praise to Emerson than
to any of the others. Because Poe, Melville, and Whitman were neither
valued nor read in her parents' social circle, she was left to discover them
on her own; that she did so is testimony to her adventurous inclinations
as a reader. Among late nineteenth-century American prose writers,
Wharton singles out Twain, Howells, Henry Adams, Santayana and, of
course, James for favorable mention. It was her overwhelmingly positive
response to Whitman's poetry, however, that came to rival her enthusiasm even for the British Romantics. For discussion of the role this critically important predecessor played in her life and career (together with
Emerson and other U.S. Renaissance writers), see Linda Costanzo Cahir's
essay (Chapter 31 in this volume), which examines Wharton in the context of American Romanticism.

Impressive in its depth and breadth as Wharton's familiarity with the
Anglo-American tradition may be, this material formed only part of
her vast store of literary resources. Having learned Italian, French, and
German in childhood, and having continued her study of languages well
into her adult life, she was able to read in the original major works of
European literature. During the early part of her career she dedicated herself to acquiring an intellectually well-grounded yet profoundly personal
relationship with Italian history, culture, and aesthetic achievements.
Idyllic childhood memories of playing in "the ruins of imperial Rome,"
buttressed by her introduction in early adolescence to the work of Dante,
stimulated a lifelong warmth for this country of "weather-worn sun-gilt
stone" (*BG* 30, 31). Her reading in Italian literature was wide ranging,
including Da Ponte, Casanova, Petrarch, and countless others, but against
this background her "abiding love" for Dante stands out with unmis-
takable prominence (Lewis 139). She read Dante with Walter Berry; she
quoted his poetry to her lover Morton Fullerton and in her private diaries;
allusions to his great trilogy spill into her fiction as naturally as breathing.
She compares the perpetually wandering, wealthy pleasure-seekers in *The
Glimpses of the Moon*, for example, to the tormented shades in Dante's
hell, who are condemned to endless repetition of their spiritually bank-
rupt behavior. In creating the Italian setting for her first novel, *The Valley
of Decision*, and in writing extensively about Italian landscaping and
architecture, she turned appreciatively to the work of eminent and knowl-
edgeable visitors who had preceded her, notably Goethe's *Italian Journey*
and Ruskin's *Stones of Venice* or *Walks in Florence*.

As with her love of Italy, Wharton's special relationship to France, the adopted home of her later years, is marked by reading begun in her first "ecstatic" explorations of "the kingdom" of her father's library (*BG* 69, 43). Her familiarity with French poetry and drama was extensive; it embraced the writings of Baudelaire, Verlaine, Rimbaud, Mallarmé, Corneille, Ronsard, Racine, Fontaine, Molière, Hugo, Chénier, Vigny, and more. The prose works of writers such as Rabelais, Montaigne, Pascal, Michelet, Diderot, and Sainte-Beuve were well known to her. She expressed strong admiration for the grand masters of French fiction, reserving her most laudatory comments for Flaubert, Stendhal, Balzac, Prévost, Constant, Proust, and Maupassant, but including in her reading such lesser figures as the Goncourts, Daudet, Lesage, and Dumas. She singled out Balzac and Stendhal, in particular, naming them the two principal figures in modern fiction: they are the "dividing geniuses" whose ability to integrate characters plausibly into an intricately realized social environment sets them apart from even their most gifted forerunners (*WF* 5). Hermione Lee identifies her "enormous and wide-ranging knowledge of French literature" as the chief source of Wharton's "mastery of style" in the French language (Lee 306). Her fluency was of a sufficiently high order to permit her to oversee and, indeed, sometimes to improve French translations of her own writings.

Wharton's knowledge of German literature and language also was extensive. She thanks her German governess, Anna Bahlman, for introducing her to "all the wealth of German literature, from the Minnesingers to Heine" (*BG* 48). Wharton refers as easily to the work of Walther von der Vogelweide, or Schiller, in consequence, as she does to more recent work by Naturalists like Hauptmann. She found much that pleased her in nineteenth-century fiction and drama by Keller, Hoffmannsthal, George, and Kleist. The extent of her acquaintance with German lyric poetry can be observed in her detailed lamentations over the deficiencies of an anthology of *Deutsche Poesie*. She reserved her most profound admiration for Goethe, whose work engaged her deeply throughout her life. Her ardent regard encompassed his whole career, from the early Sturm und Drang period through his contributions to Weimar Classicism and to German Romanticism. She read his plays, novels, poetry, and nonfiction, for example, *Prometheus*, *The Sorrows of Young Werther*, *Iphigenia in Tauris*, *The Elective Affinities*, and *Wilhelm Meister*. First and last, she was devoted to his *Faust*, naming it repeatedly on her lists of favorite literary works. She makes direct or indirect reference to it in nearly every one of her novels. The opening scene of *The Age of Innocence*, to name a memorable example, features an operatic performance of the Faust story, highlighting the seduction scene between Faust and Gretchen. May Welland's naïve obliviousness to the sexual treachery being enacted on stage leads seamlessly into the critique of innocence that is to follow. In two later novels, *Hudson River Bracketed* and *The Gods Arrive*, Wharton makes significant use of Faust's descent in part II to "the Mothers" – mysterious and primal sources of fertility – to explain the artist's need to plumb unconscious depths of self in the process of creative discovery.

Wharton augmented her substantial knowledge of the Italian, French, and German traditions with occasional forays into Spanish literature – chiefly Cervantes' *Don Quixote*. More significantly, she also undertook sustained reading in nineteenth-century Russian literature. She draws attention to the excellence of both writerly craft and human insight in the fiction of Gogol, Dostoevsky, Chekhov, and Turgenev, lavishing special praise on Tolstoy. She ranks him close to Balzac and Stendhal, near the top of her list of great novelists. The work of "the Russians" constitutes a critical piece in the late-won literary education of her protagonist Vance Weston in *Hudson River Bracketed*. Until he wins acquaintance with this part of his cultural inheritance, Wharton clearly implies, the young writer's apprenticeship in the art of fiction remains incomplete.

Any survey of Wharton's literary resources and preferences, however sketchy, risks degenerating into a catalogue. She encountered precisely this problem in writing her autobiography, observing that she could scarcely bear to leave "out of this record" a single one of her "best beloved companions": the spiritual soul mates she encountered in books (*BG* 91). Her dauntingly extensive reading encompassed nearly the whole body of Western literature, as it was defined in her lifetime. There is nothing particularly surprising about her literary choices: with few exceptions, she occupied herself with authors and works that other highly educated people of her day considered worth reading. Her friendship with the Harvard-educated Bernard Berenson is a case in point. Their lively correspondence was dominated by ongoing discussions of literary topics. Together "they cite Tennyson's *Ulysses*, Browning, Goethe and Dante to each other, exchange opinions on Petrarch, or Renan, or the *Oxford Book of German Verse*, or the relative merits of Dostoevsky and Tolstoy." Drawing "mainly ... on the same cultural fund," they derived great pleasure in trading "cherished quotations and allusions well known to them both" (Lee 415). Their mutually gratifying literary exchange was possible only because they had spent a lifetime cultivating familiarity with a common body of materials.

Even the abbreviated list of Wharton's favorite writers, although it sheds light on her temperament and helps to define her intimate concerns, does not distinguish her decisively from well-read contemporaries. A set of preferences that includes Dante and Goethe, Emerson, Pascal, and Arnold, Keats, Shelley, Wordsworth, and Coleridge, points to a many-layered sensibility, a responsiveness that encompasses philosophical speculation, social engagement, sensual delight, and emotional investment. In the arena of her own principal endeavors – fiction – Wharton invokes names that raise no eyebrows: her praise for the novels of Balzac, Tolstoy, Austen, Thackeray, and Meredith, for example, is unremarkable. Only her persistent high regard for Whitman is unexpected: her admiration for his poetry appears to defy the conservative impulse that typically marks her literary judgment. Her devotion to his formally innovative poetry, with its vigorous integration of metaphysical, political, aesthetic, and sexual concerns, compels readers in succeeding generations to give more serious consideration to her experimental tendencies as an artist, as well as to her frank acceptance of the sensuous-erotic side of human nature.

But what of *influence*? To examine the record of Wharton's reading and to ponder her lists of best-loved authors is not necessarily to identify shaping influences, theoretical or practical, on her own writing. The relationship between admiration and influence is a vexed one. One may admire a particular body of writing without wishing to imitate it and, conversely, one's capacity to imitate an admired structure or style may not be equal to the wish. Sources of genuine influence may be denied, for any number of reasons, or they may accomplish their work so stealthily as to go unrecognized. There is little evidence, in fact, that Wharton regarded even the writers she most praised as models in any individualized sense. Her most memorable statement on the topic of individual influence is one of repudiation, provoked by reviewers who persisted in comparing her to Henry James: "[T]he continued cry that I am an echo of Mr. James (whose books of the last ten years I can't read, much as I delight in the man) ... makes me feel rather hopeless," she laments in a June 1904 letter to William Crary Brownell (*Letters* 91). She had good cause to protest this particular attribution of discipleship: it was to persist beyond her death and relegate her for decades to the ranks of the "minor" and the derivative in textbooks and literary histories. The myth of the Jamesian influence on Wharton was not exposed as false until the 1960s, when Irving Howe and Millicent Bell examined the evidence in the case and found it wanting. In Bell's book-length study of the question, she offers detailed evidence of

Wharton's artistic independence from her supposed mentor.[5] Howe offers a definitive summing up: "the claim that Henry James exerted a major influence upon Mrs. Wharton's fiction, repeated with maddening regularity by literary historians, testifies to the laziness of the human mind."[6]

Wharton tends to speak of the writers and works she most values as "voices," "friends," and "companions," rather than as influences. Memorable characters, episodes, images, and phrases enter into her life, nourishing a rich interior world. Reading, she asserts, is an active process that fosters a continual "interchange of thought between writer and reader." Ever increasing numbers of literary works are drawn into a vast network of interconnection, transcending space and time, for inside the reader's mind "the books ... talk to each other." Wharton likens this activity to organic development: absorbed into a single human intelligence, literary works resemble "growing things that strike root and intertwine branches" ("Vice" 99, 102). The reader's mind becomes the locus of an ongoing conversation, one including writers who represent numerous historical moments and national origins. Contributing to this conversation, moreover, the reader engages in "a creative act."[7] Literary works themselves, as they enter into successive conversations in the minds of new readers, evince an essential "plasticity," since they are susceptible to "being diversely moulded by the impact of fresh forms of thought" ("Vice" 99). With such comments, Wharton salutes the collective influence of the past. She does not advise young writers to select specific models for imitation; she recommends, rather, "long training & wide reading, & a saturation in the best that the past has to give." In addition to "practice and discipline," which are vital to a literary apprenticeship, she emphasizes the need to "assimilate" the many-branched "influences" of great predecessors, "so that they become part of [one's] stock-in-trade" (*Letters* 411).

Wharton's views of the relationship between reader and writer, taken in large part from "The Vice of Reading" (1903), coincide unmistakably with those put forward some years later by T. S. Eliot in his well-known essay "Tradition and the Individual Talent" (1920). Like Wharton, Eliot argues that works of literature are interconnected, collectively forming a "living whole." Enjoying a "simultaneous existence," they exercise upon one another a two-way influence. The individual artist achieves full significance only in "his relation to ... dead poets. You cannot value him alone." By the same token, works from previous epochs are "altered by the present as much as the present is directed by the past." Eliot insists, in consequence, on the necessity of a thorough grounding in world literature for any serious writer: to remain satisfied with "one or two private admirations" or "one preferred period" is irresponsible. He assures both readers and writers that they cannot come into possession of a literary tradition by passive "inheritance" but must invest "great labour" in the project.[8] In sum, Eliot shares with Wharton a conception of literature as a hugely complex living body, within which individual works enjoy continually shifting interrelationships. He concentrates on the writer's potency (the ability to rearrange an existing "tradition" by the introduction of new work into it), while she highlights the reader's (the transformative impact on texts of individual intelligence). Such difference in emphasis notwithstanding, Wharton and Eliot describe historical influence and cultural transmission in essentially the same terms, identifying them as dynamic, nonlinear processes. This similarity in outlook tends to go unnoticed in assessments of Wharton's position in literary modernism.

Wharton's distinguishing qualities as a connoisseur of literature, as is increasingly apparent, are based less on *what* she read than on *how* she read. Throughout her life she was a zealously engaged reader. Works that spoke compellingly to her remained a part of her inner world forever. She was constantly renewing the immediacy of their presence, moreover, in sessions of reading that she initiated with gusto throughout her life (with Walter Berry, Henry James, and other friends). Identifying her ongoing private conversation with previous writers as "ecstatic communion," she underlines the reverence these inspired in her (*BG* 69). Throughout her career, she paid delighted homage to her spiritual homeland, the "country" of *belles lettres*: mentioning, naming, quoting, and alluding, she demonstrates its powerful and continuous effect on her imagination (*BG* 119). Each quoted passage, each borrowed title, and each allusion, brief or sustained, represents a strand in a vital network of intergenerational and cross-cultural relationships. Weaving words and images gleaned from literary predecessors into her writing, Wharton helped her "best beloved" and "most living companions" one more step of the way on their journey to posterity (*BG* 91, 69). Her allegiance to the "Land of Letters" was unwavering, and she forged connections, Whitman-like, with its diverse citizenry (*BG* 119).

NOTES

1. E. Wharton, "The Vice of Reading" in F. Wegener (ed.), *Edith Wharton: The Uncollected Critical Writings* (Princeton, NJ: Princeton University Press, 1996), 99–106; 102. Subsequent references to this work are included in the text.

2. E. Wharton, "A Reconsideration of Proust" in F. Wegener (ed.), *Edith Wharton: The Uncollected Critical Writings* (Princeton, NJ: Princeton University Press, 1996), 179–84; 182.

3. E. Wharton, *The Reef* (New York: D. Appleton, 1912), 58–59.

4. E. Wharton, "Preface to *Eternal Passion in Poetry*" in F. Wegener (ed.), *Edith Wharton: The Uncollected Critical Writings* (Princeton, NJ: Princeton University Press, 1996), 253–55; 254.

5. M. Bell, *Edith Wharton and Henry James: The Story of their Friendship* (New York: George Braziller, 1965).

6. I. Howe, "Introduction: The Achievement of Edith Wharton" in I. Howe (ed.), *Edith Wharton: A Collection of Critical Essays* (Englewood Cliffs, NJ: Prentice-Hall, 1962), 1–18; 6.

7. E. Wharton, "Preface to *Ghosts*" in F. Wegener (ed.), *Edith Wharton: The Uncollected Critical Writings* (Princeton, NJ: Princeton University Press, 1996), 270–74; 271.

8. T. S. Eliot, "Tradition and the Individual Talent" in *Selected Essays 1917–1932* (London: Faber and Faber, 1932), 13–22; 14–17.

CHAPTER 31

Wharton and the American Romantics

Linda Costanzo Cahir

Edith Wharton was born amid the dark and bright energies of American romanticism. While Cynthia Griffin Wolff rightly characterizes her as "a profoundly anti-Romantic realist" (Wolff 9), Wharton was deeply immersed in romantic literature and influenced by the modes and concepts of select romantic writers. She admits to having "plunged with rapture into the great ocean of Goethe," and by the age of fifteen she had read all of his plays and poems, describing *Faust* as one of her "'epoch-making' encounters" (quoted in Wolff 35). Her interest in Goethe was lifelong and self-defining, as she used a quotation from Goethe's *Wilhelm Meister* as an epigram for her autobiography: *Kein Genuss ist vorüubergehend* (No pleasure is transitory). Although Goethe died thirty years before she was born, his aesthetic values lived on in American romantic writers who were early, influential contemporaries of Wharton. Among these, most notably, is Ralph Waldo Emerson (1803–82).

Wharton was twenty years old when Emerson died. She read his work throughout her life, and we can clearly see that she returned to his writing during significant moments in her life. She referenced Emerson in her letters, her fiction, her non-fiction, and her verse. In 1899, she published *The Greater Inclination*; however, just prior to this, she considered changing the title of this first collection of her short stories to *Mortals Mixed of Middle Clay*, which is the first line of Emerson's poem "Guy" (*Letters* 36). In 1908, in a letter to Morton Fullerton, she adapted a line from Emerson's essay "Character" to describe the strong feelings that Fullerton stirred in her: "The moment my eyes fell on him I was content" (*Letters* 129). In 1910, when coming to terms with the painful realization that their affair was drawing to its end, Wharton wrote a poem in memory of a night spent with Fullerton in Charing Cross Hotel near Waterloo Station. The poem, rather straightforward and poignant, is written in a Whitmanesque style with its protracted lines and mounting rhythms, but it is called "Terminus," after the title of an Emerson poem. Wharton returned to his poetry in *The Gods Arrive* (1932), the title of which is a homage to the last line of his work, "Give All to Love." As late as April 1937, shortly before her death, she again invoked Emerson. In a letter written to Bernard Berenson, she asked him "to remember that, whether as to people or as to places & occasions, I've *always* known the gods the moment I met them" (*Letters* 604).

Throughout her letters Wharton writes of the respect that she had for Emerson. She makes repeated allusions to him throughout her writing, and she references his work in multiple ways relating to her relationship with Morton Fullerton. Emerson's philosophy influenced the departures from tradition that Wharton attempted in her own life. Emerson's insistence on the integrity of self-reliance, his absolute faith in the individual's prerogative to determine the lines of right conduct, and his resolve that one must listen to the truths spoken in one's private heart validated Wharton's decision to break rank with social customs and mores, particularly with regard to her affair with Fullerton.

However, in her fiction, where her assessment of Emerson's ideas are implied rather than openly stated, Wharton's opinion of his philosophy becomes far more ambivalent. As early as her first novel, *The Valley of Decision* (1902), we see the effects of Emersonian self-reliance in the protagonist, Odo Valsecca, who becomes the Duke of Pianura. Set in eighteenth-century Italy, the novel explores his personal history and how he envisions an Italy far better and greater than the feudal state of oppression and poverty that he witnesses. He becomes an activist for significant sociopolitical reform, in the process of which he chooses his commitment to national reformation above his personal desires and his love of Fulvia. However, his efforts at reformation fail wretchedly. The peasants are unable to envision any way of life beyond the harsh servitude they know; ironically, they – the very people Odo was attempting to liberate – lead the counter rebellion in which his beloved Fulvia is killed. Odo, a strict adherent to his moral and political convictions, ends alone and defeated, in a "deathlike isolation" (*VD* 651), the embittering price he pays for adhering to and acting on the deep moral and political truths spoken in his Emersonian private heart.

We see Wharton's ambivalence toward Emerson's philosophy particularly in *The House of Mirth*. Lawrence Selden's "republic of the spirit" is his reworking of Emerson's central creeds. Selden's philosophy disavows conformity, in general, and in particular the conventionality of formal religion, patriotism, and materialism for the transcendent realm. He argues the romantic tenet that to reach the transcendent, his republic of the spirit, one must trust intuition and recognize that society is in conspiracy against their individuality. He calls on Lily Bart to be a nonconformist, but his call, we see, is steeped in contradiction, dreamy impossibilities, double standards, and hypocrisy. His is a realm of words, but his articulated values strike an empathic, admirable chord in Lily, who, in some deep place of being, *is* Emersonian. However, her shaky attempts at self-reliance and her emerging unwillingness to adhere to deadening social customs arguably bring about her death.

In contrast to Lily Bart's demise, we see an ascendency to power and an actualization of individual will in Undine Spragg. As a bright romantic, Emerson believed that individual will is not driven by self-interest, but rather inspired by the divine. In *The Custom of the Country*, Wharton calls into question this intrinsic assumption central to Emerson's philosophy. In Undine, she creates the paradigmatic self-reliant character who trusts herself with absolute surety. Demonstrating the radical individualism of Emerson in her courage to follow her inclinations against all public disapproval, Undine operates with the fortitude of an iron-stringed heart and lives by her own law. Fully unconstrained by traditional standards of conduct and devoid of any homage to custom, she, arguably, carries Emerson's creed to its dangerously logical conclusion, and, consequently, dramatizes what Wharton understands to be the inherent flaw in Emerson's doctrine. At its extreme, Emersonian self-reliance can not only mortally harm others, but also carry its practitioner to a world fully void of humanity, decency, and, ironically, divinity.

In addition to Emerson's writing, Wharton was well read in the work of Walt Whitman (1819–92). In researching Wharton's complex collection of books of poetry, Hermione Lee found that "Above all, she treasured and marked the poetry of Whitman" (674). Lee reminds us that this interest was not merely intellectual, but also deeply emotional; she "developed a great passion" for his writing in spite of the fact, or perhaps even because, it was judged as "particularly shocking" in her time (32). In Wharton's conventional society, Whitman's verse was considered of questionable decency, and she explicitly acknowledged this, explaining that "*Leaves of Grass* was kept under lock and key, and brought out ... only in the absence of 'the ladies' to whom the name of Walt Whitman was unmentionable, if not utterly unknown" (quoted in Lee 32).

Whitman's verse was very well known to Wharton, however. There are anecdotes of Henry James reading aloud Whitman's poetry to Howard Sturgis and her, and of Wharton being encouraged to deliver a public address on Whitman at the Théâtre des Arts in Paris. In *The Spark*, the third novella of the *Old New York* quartet, Walt Whitman appears as a character who saves Hayley Delane's life, and, through his example of love, clearly effects his redemption.

At nineteen, Delane was critically injured in the Civil War. His battlefield experiences and the sights he witnessed in the military hospital revealed to him, with full force, the horrors that men do. These experiences had an enduring and conversionary effect as he came to believe that human beings lack humanity. The postwar older Delane endures the social rituals required of him, but he is, essentially, a man who has withdrawn from the world. He self-reliantly stands apart. The young narrator of *The Spark* grows increasingly intrigued by this "shut-up fellow" and wonders if he is "shut-up consciously, deliberately – or only instinctively, congenitally? There the mystery lay."[1] He goes about solving the riddle of the man, "exploring him like a geologist" (55).

As the narrator tells his story, Delane becomes a man of heroic strength and moral sagacity. The narrator comments: "Almost any man can take a stand on a principle his fellow-citizens are already occupying; but Hayley Delane held out for things his friends could not comprehend" (*Spark* 99). This brand of self-reliance, however, is not as radical as Emerson's. Rather than shun father and mother and wife and brother when his genius calls him, Delane shuns his own immediate needs when the needs of another seem greater. He is the Emersonian self-reliant man whose actions are mitigated by simple human kindness.

Under the narrator's direction we come to see the poignancy and the greatness of Delane, a fact that is lost on the trivial people who comprise his immediate society. He is reluctant to speak, but as the narrator questions him about the war, little by little, he learns of the "old heathen" who, when Delane was "all foggy with fever," used to come and talk to him "by the hour" (80–81). This man taught him, by example and through conversations, much about simple human kindness. As readers, we find out, along with the narrator and Delane, that this caring "old heathen" was Walt Whitman. The narrator insists on reading some of Whitman's verse to Delane, who responds: "'Old Walt ... He was a great chap: I'll never forget him. – I rather wish, though ... you hadn't told me that he wrote all that rubbish'" (109).

When Delane refers to Whitman's poetry as rubbish, he is reflecting old New York's preference for topically genteel verse of a traditional form and meter. Although depicted as a far finer man than those of his trivial society, he is, simultaneously, like that world in some ways. He is flawed and, in this case, foolish. This foolishness sparks an understanding – an alternate way of seeing – in the narrator. Naïve belief in the limitless, unflawed grandeur of Delane has been replaced by a more universal awareness: a tolerance, sympathy, and acceptance of people despite their flaws and a respect for those who stand self-reliantly apart from their society. Just as Whitman sparks understanding in Delane, the latter in turn brings about understanding in the narrator, who stands as a trope for Wharton herself, implying how Whitman coaxed her to alternate ways of seeing and being.

Whitman sparks the deeply worthy ethical and spiritual values that emerge in the fictional Delane, and, we assume, in the narrator. While Wharton clearly admired Whitman the man, she equally valued his poetry. In essence, she considered Whitman to be "the greatest of American poets," one whose verse fascinates its readers with "mysterious music" (*BG* 186). She shared this opinion with James who told her in conversation that the poet was "Oh, yes, a great genius; undoubtedly a great genius!" (*BG* 186). Wharton thought so highly of Whitman that she took the title of her memoir, *A Backward Glance*, from his autobiographical essay, "A Backward Glance O'er Travel'd Roads"; and her own copy of his *Leaves of Grass* is deeply marked through her repeated readings of it throughout the years. According to Lewis: "Walt Whitman was, of course, the lyric poet she esteemed above all others, ranking him even more highly than Keats and Shelly" (Lewis 237).

Wharton clearly conveys the respect she has for Whitman, Emerson, and Edgar Allan Poe in a letter written to William Crary Brownell, her literary editor at Scribner's. She knew that Brownell was working on an essay on Poe and, in referring to Brownell's essay, wrote: "I should like to get in that Nicaean bark with you – and in time gently steer it toward the 'far-sprinkled systems' that Walt sails among. Those two [Poe and Whitman], with Emerson, are the best we have – in fact, the all we have" (quoted in Lewis 236). Wharton read and returned to Poe at various points in her life and he appears as a sympathetic character in *False Dawn*, the first of the *Old New York* quartet, a work which has yet another Emersonian self-reliant character at the heart of the tale.

In *False Dawn*, Lewis Raycie, driven by the force of his beliefs, interferes – to a vastly destructive extent – with the destiny of his own family. The beginning of the story finds the young man embarking on old New York's maturation ritual: the Grand Tour. His father requests that, while in Europe, he begin the family's private art gallery by purchasing "a few original specimens of the Italian genius," works by established seventeenth-century masters like Domenichino, Albani, Carlo Dolci,

Guercino, Carlo Maratta, and Salvator Rosa.[2] However, once in Europe, young Raycie, influenced by none other than John Ruskin, is initiated into a new aesthetic that challenges the specters of past painting traditions. He emerges from the Grand Tour reborn into a more sagacious sense of beauty, but when he returns home with his purchases (paintings by Italian Primitives such as Mantegna, Giotto, and Piero della Francesca), his infuriated father disowns him. The remainder of the novella details Raycie's stouthearted attempts to educate his world in the new critical principles.

The largest portion of *False Dawn* is comprised of Raycie's failed efforts to teach his world what he has learned. His theories of art are derided and his collection of paintings is belittled. Throughout it all, his wife and his daughter must endure the humiliation. In response to the vitriol of the art critics who review his collection, Raycie retreats into "a little air-tight circle of aloofness" (*FD* 113). His "withdrawal from the world" (113) forces Treeshy (his wife) and Louisa (his daughter) to live in seclusion, too.

Raycie endures years of poverty and subjects his family to the same dreadful situation because "he would not admit that he was beaten" (*FD* 119). Whatever money he had, he spent to maintain his gallery; and, in consequence of their poverty, his daughter dies at eleven and he and Treeshy die in disillusionment and anonymity. The paintings are left to gather dust in a remote relative's home until, years later, long after Raycie's death, a distant cousin inherits the art collection and comes to understand its worth, when (quite by accident) she discovers that she is able to sell it off for "pearls and Rolls-Royces" and a "new house in Fifth Avenue" (*FD* 143). This irony is surpassed only by the fact that, years later, the greatness of the Italian Primitives is recognized, but this appreciation comes about in spite of Raycie's efforts, not because of them. The art world understands and acknowledges the aesthetic worth of Mantegna, Giotto, and della Francesca long before they know of Lewis Raycie or the Raycie collection.

In his all-consuming quest, Raycie (much like Melville's Ahab) generates an antithetical response in us. We feel that, at one extreme, an exorbitantly harmful and censurable pride compels him to persist in a private mission that has dire consequences for those people most directly subject to his decisions. However, at the other extreme, a noble perseverance and an admirable self-reliant perspicacity require him to aspire to the fulfillment of a vision that his far less visionary world seems anxious to doom.

In this quality, Raycie resembles the glimpses of Edgar Allan Poe that we see in the novella. Raycie's sister, Mary Adeline, brings food and money to the "poor young Mrs. Poe" who would "never see meat unless [she] can bring them a bit" (*FD* 30–31). Much like the Italian Primitives, Poe's writing is undervalued and underappreciated, and Mary Adeline worries that the poverty the family, particularly "Mr. Poe's" wife, endures because of his sacrifice for his art are taking their terrible toll. "I fear she's dying of a decline" (*FD* 31) she compassionately explains. Quieter in her ways than her brother, Mary Adeline nonetheless shares his strength of purpose. She visits the Poes despite her father's assumed displeasure in her doing so, explaining to her brother: "You see, Mr. Poe's an Atheist; and so father ..." (*FD* 32). Raycie does understand; he hands Mary Adeline money for the family and asks her to tell Poe that he is "a great poet – a Great Poet" (*FD* 32).

Wharton also considered Poe a great poet. However, she not only valued his poetry, she also valued his literary theory. Barbara A. White constructs a convincing case for Wharton having been influenced specifically by Poe in writing her essay, "Telling a Short Story." White contends that the essay is filled with "romantic metaphors" that are "all the more striking in a text seemingly devoted to order, form, tradition, and even the classical 'unities.'"[3] She further explains that in the essay Wharton emerges as a "believer" in Poe's theory of "'pre-established design,'" meaning that the story should "correspond to a skillfully constructed invention or an intricate story with a 'decorated surface'" (White 5).

Carole Shaffer-Koros' 2001 essay does a laudable job of supplying evidence for Poe's influence on Wharton's writing of ghost stories in general, and, in particular, "Kerfol."[4] Even more interestingly, Shaffer-Koros' work traces Poe's influence on the writing of *The Custom of the Country*. Lewis sees the effect of Poe in Wharton's short story, "The Bolted Door" (Lewis 237), a work White also labels particularly "Poe-esque" (White 73), while Lee argues that Poe "haunts" her story, "The Eyes" (Lee 219). While Wharton's ghost stories generally share Poe's gothic sensibilities and his chilling imagination, they do not share the complexity of structure and the density of prose that mark his stylistic conventions. Poe only lived to be forty (1809–49) and so, in the strictest sense, he was not a contemporary of Wharton. However, the dark romantic tradition in which he wrote was.

Yet another writer key to this romantic tradition was Nathaniel Hawthorne (1804–64). Wharton's home in the Berkshires was a generous walk from the cottage where Hawthorne wrote *The Tanglewood Tales*. She was widely read in Hawthorne, and surely had heard local stories about him. Overall, however, her opinion of Hawthorne is complex and contradictory. On one hand, she found his writing enervated; but on the other, she acknowledges his influence on her. In *A Backward Glance*, the author notes that *Summer* owes a debt to *The Scarlet Letter* (see Lee 512); and Wharton scholarship has traced the effect Hawthorne's "Ethan Brand" and *The Blithedale Romance* had on *Ethan Frome*. As Lee records, however, *Summer*'s Charity is "recognizably in the tradition of 'the woman who pays:' ... most of all Hester Prynne ... cast out by the Puritan community for adultery, more in tune with the wilderness than the town and listening, as Charity listens, to the patriarchal rhetoric of the preacher giving his great Election Day sermon on the values of America. Wharton plants the clues..." (Lee 512).

While the writer's opinion of Hawthorne was ambivalent, her opinion of Herman Melville (1819–91) was not. She read Melville's writing at different points in her life and *Moby Dick* emerged as a significant text to her during an emotionally crucial time in her life.[5] In October 1907, she invited Fullerton to The Mount, where she was left with the impression that the two shared a deep kindredness. That winter Wharton returned to Paris where, sometime during February or March of 1908, she began an impassioned affair that lasted, intermittently, until 1911. In her diary and letters, the writer describes the profundity of this union. From this we understand the freeing effect Fullerton had on the emotionally and sexually restrained Mrs. Wharton. However, by 1911, the novelty of their affair had worn thin for Fullerton; he grew more detached, and in her letters we see Wharton painfully pleading with him to end his bouts of silence, and strategizing ways of holding his interest. Clearly, Wharton understood that she could offer Fullerton what few women could: a provocative intelligence. Thus, in those letters, she speaks to him in the codes they share: writing, philosophy, and music. She quickly mentions Wagner, Flaubert, and Dostoievsky, among others, and in a very pointed way, mentions Melville's *Moby Dick*. Her question, "do you share my taste for Melville?" is an explicit invitation to Fullerton to share with her his view on this work and writer (*Letters* 238).

This May 12, 1911 letter, remarkable for the driving intellect and the apparent sorrow that infuse it, is equally remarkable if we consider the date within the context of Melville scholarship. Wharton expresses an enthusiasm for *Moby Dick* at a time when the novel was almost entirely forgotten. The resurgence in Melville interest did not come about until 1921. Wharton's recognition of Melville's greatness at a time when his writing was largely unnoticed and unknown is significant to the point of wonderfully curious. Several years later in *The Writing of Fiction* (1925) and in "The Great American Novel" (1927), she makes additional references to Melville. *Solitude and Society in the Works of Herman Melville and Edith Wharton* explains that, in addition to *Moby Dick*, Wharton had read Melville's South Sea novels (*Typee* and *Omoo*), as well as *Pierre: Or the Ambiguities*; her library contained copies of Melville's *Mardi*, *Redburn*, and *White-Jacket* (Cahir 13). Although there is no concrete proof that Wharton read these, there is the assumption. *Solitude and Society* traces the influence of Melville on the writer as well as the aesthetic and philosophical sensibilities that they shared. Worth noting is the fact that Wharton's final library at Hyères was a smaller, condensed version of her past libraries, and at that late point in her life, she valued Melville writing so fully as to retain five of his books in a library where no Emerson or Hawthorne, for example, survived her selection process.

At heart, Wharton was a traditionalist, or, in Wolff's phrase as cited at the outset of this essay, "a profoundly anti-Romantic realist" (9). However, while Wharton was a realist, she was also immersed in the writing of the American romantic tradition. Emerson, Whitman, Poe, Hawthorne, and Melville and their bright and dark romantic values impacted on her emotional and intellectual growth. Throughout her correspondence, fiction, poetry, and literary theory we see in the anti-Romantic realist, Edith Wharton, the deeply romantic values of the ascendency of personal authority, the duty and right to question doctrines, the prerogative of personal fulfillment, and the belief in the nonrational forces of creativity. One could never accuse Wharton of the foolish consistency that constitutes the hobgoblin of little minds.

NOTES

1. E. Wharton, *The Spark* (New York: D. Appleton and Company, 1924), 17. Subsequent references to this work are included in the text.
2. E. Wharton, *False Dawn* (New York: D. Appleton and Company, 1924), 53. Subsequent references to this work are included in the text (*FD*).
3. B. A. White, *Edith Wharton: A Study of the Short Fiction* (New York: Twayne, 1991), 5. Subsequent references to this work are included in the text.
4. C. Shaffer-Koros, "Edgar Allan Poe and Edith Wharton: A Case of Mrs. Mowatt," *Edith Wharton Review*, 17 (2001), 12–16.
5. See Linda Costanzo Cahir, *Solitude and Society in the Works of Herman Melville and Edith Wharton* (Westport, CT: Greenwood Press, 1999). Subsequent references to this work are included in the text.

CHAPTER 32

The Novel of Manners

Cecilia Macheski

Henry James observed in 1888, "We know a man imperfectly until we know his society, and we but half know a society until we know its manners."[1] By 1919, Edith Wharton would declare that the writer's perspective as well as the manners themselves had been radically altered:

The world since 1914 has been like a house on fire. All the lodgers are on the stairs, in dishabille. Their doors are swinging wide, and one gets glimpses of their furniture, revelations of their habits, and whiffs of their cooking, that a life-time of ordinary intercourse would not offer. Superficial differences vanish, and so (how much oftener) do superficial resemblances; while deep unsuspected similarities and disagreements, deep common attractions and repulsions, declare themselves. (FWM v–vi)

The crisis Wharton evokes in *French Ways and Their Meaning* offers insight into the context of the novel of manners. James' comment positions the writer as a sensitive investigator, a historian who documents the environment out of which character is construed. Wharton suggests that events can shatter assumptions, tossing the writer into the role of voyeur and journalist, but at the same time open new possibilities for understanding the society racing past.

To understand manners, the writer positions himself or herself as an outsider, an observer, an anthropologist taking notes on a culture, even as that culture is undergoing change. Understanding what is meant by "manners" as novelists approach the term prevents readers from expecting merely rules on table settings or wedding etiquette. For critic Lionel Trilling, manners are "a culture's hum and buzz of implication," revealing what a society truly values. Manners, he continues, are "hinted at by small actions, sometimes by the arts of dress or decoration, sometimes by tone, gesture, emphasis, or rhythm, sometimes by the words that are used with special frequency or a special meaning."[2] James W. Tuttleton favors limiting the definition to novels "concerned about how manners reflect the moral condition of humanity" and concludes that in the novel of manners, "the manners, social customs, folkways, conventions, traditions, and mores of a given social group at a given time and place" are set out for preservation and analysis.[3] As Wharton suggests with her image of the house on fire, such manners are more visible and accessible at a time when society is in transition, whether through war, economic upheaval, demographic shifts, or moral or cultural crisis.

Readers might conclude that all novels could be classed as novels of manners, but Wharton offered a more refined definition in 1925 when she published *The Writing of Fiction*. The novel, she wrote, is "the newest, most fluid and least formulated of the arts" (*WF* 3), which has its origins in the writer's desire "to draw his dramatic action as much from the relation of his characters to their houses, streets, towns, professions, inherited habits and opinions, as from their fortuitous contacts with each other" (*WF* 5). John P. Marquand's novel, *B. F.'s Daughter*, offers a succinct and witty example of a writer employing Wharton's strategy to help readers understand his protagonist, Polly Fulton, and her relationship to her society when the narrator notes that "Park Avenue did something to women, so that they all looked alike ... It was the strongest environment in the world." The women, their dogs, their jewelry, flowers and books share "some indefinable quality" that stamps their origin.[4]

Modern fans of Plum Sykes' *Bergdorf Blondes* or Candace Bushnell's popular *Sex and the City* might be surprised to learn that Marquand's work was published in 1946 and owes its style, as do many of the more recent "chick lit" titles, to the disruptions to U.S. society from World War II and from novels of manners written two centuries ago. This type of novel is distinct, Wharton argues, from novels of "character (or psychology) and adventure" (*WF* 66). She traces the roots of the form to the French writers Balzac and Stendhal, who viewed "each character first of all as a product of particular material and social conditions..." (*WF* 9). Without this social context, characters may remain "unvisualized and unconditioned (or almost) by the special outward circumstances of their lives" (*WF* 7–8). Moreover, the novel of manners sets characters in a predicament that leads to a clashing of forces; Wharton asserts that "the conflict engages not only individuals but social groups, and the individual plight is usually the product – one of the many products – of the social conflict" (*WF* 144). Thus Polly Fulton, like Newland Archer in *The Age of Innocence*, is studied not so much as an individual but as part of her "tribe" on a street that Archer would find remarkably familiar even after six decades, just as the women in *Sex and the City* are depictions of a city, its consumer culture, its dating rituals and its unique language. The

manners are a source of cultural power, creating barriers to prevent outsiders from invading the carefully limited inner circles.

The novel of manners is not anthropology or sociology, but novelists
certainly borrowed from these emerging disciplines in the early decades
of the twentieth century as they studied cultures through observation,
interviews and artifacts. As Wharton published her wartime books, Ruth
Benedict completed her PhD in 1919, studying under Franz Boas. She and
Margaret Mead later worked together as cultural anthropologists, establishing the validity of the new science. Wharton read carefully the work
of Darwin and Herbert Spencer on social Darwinism. Pamela Knights
marks the impact of this reading on her fiction: "The language of adaptation, adjustments, variants and dominant 'types,' with characters figured
in terms of insects or micro-organisms, often ... serves to prompt the
reader to keep an emotional distance, to move away from empathy with
individuals to an analysis of broader social schemes."[5] Wharton's *French
Ways and Their Meaning, Fighting France* (1915), *The Marne* (1918) and *In
Morocco* (1920) offer further evidence of her scientific lens. Unlike the scientist, however, the novelist "manipulates his data in terms of a narrative
rather than a scientific or 'logical' framework" (Tuttleton 11) and has the
freedom to offer subjective views of what he or she observes. Whereas
Wharton traces the origins of the form to the European novelists she
admired, such as Balzac, Stendhal, Tolstoy and Flaubert, most readers
and critics agree that Jane Austen set the standard in the English and
later the American novel of manners. Austen's representation of the conflict between the old social order and the rising middle class resounds in
the confrontations between Elizabeth Bennet and Fitzwilliam Darcy. The
young men in red coats and riding breeches may charm young Lydia into
a dangerous liaison with Wickham, but they also remind the reader that
England anticipated an invasion from Napoleon, and the soldiers parad-
ing in Merryvale were more than ornaments. If the invasion never came,
Austen nevertheless lived in the shadow of the French Revolution and
could visualize the lodgers on the stairs Wharton evoked. Recent tributes such as the BBC adaptation of *Pride and Prejudice* with Colin Firth
as Mr. Darcy and Jennifer Ehle as Elizabeth Bennet (1995) or *Pride and
Prejudice and Zombies* (2009) by Seth Grahame-Smith support Wharton's
assertion of the flexibility and endurance of the form.

A pervasive question for social critics in the late nineteenth and early
twentieth centuries became, do Americans *have* manners? If manners are
the product of long practice and social cohesion, the newness and diversity
of U.S. culture – geographical, ethnic, economic, religious – challenged

the conventional notions of society and manners. Visiting the United States from England in the early nineteenth century, Frances Trollope caused a great stir with her observations on the new republic, published in *Domestic Manners of the Americans* (1832). Speaking "of the population generally, as seen in town and county, among the rich and the poor, in the slave states and the free states," Trollope asserted, "I do not like them. I do not like their principles, I do not like their manners. I do not like their opinions."[6] In the 1820s and 1830s, Trollope found the new frontier dwellers prone to use "blue language" (that is, frequent swearing), and to read nothing but newspapers and magazines. She concluded that "a very general diffusion of literature [is] impossible in America" (Trollope I: 126). Her attack touched a nerve that was still raw when Henry James returned from Europe to visit the United States and write *The American Scene* (1907). Theodore Roosevelt attacked James as "the undersized man of letters who flees his country because he, with his delicate, effeminate sensitiveness, finds the conditions of life on this side of the water crude and raw..." asserting a view of manners in opposition to Trollope that James later labeled "puerile."[7]

James visited Ellis Island on his U.S. tour, predicting a future society in which the English language would be forever altered. A new generation of freed African Americans were migrating into northern cities, likewise altering society. Flapper dresses and bobbed hair were the outward signs of deeper unrest after World War I, as F. Scott Fitzgerald portrays in *The Great Gatsby* (1925). Rapid technological advances increased the speed and convenience of travel and communication as first bicycles and then automobiles made men and women more accessible to one another, since they could escape chaperones on their new wheels, as Wharton shows in *Summer* (1917) when Harney and Charity are free to cycle out of North Dormer.

Two early novels of manners illustrate the focus on the uncertainty of Americans about their manners. Henry James published *Daisy Miller: A Study* in 1878. This novella initiated many of the themes he would explore throughout his career and that would define the American novel of manners for decades: a transatlantic setting, a young American ingénue confronting European manners, and generational and cultural misperceptions. Meeting a young American man named Winterbourne in a Swiss resort, Daisy tells him that the only thing she dislikes about Europe "is the society. There isn't any society; or if there is, I don't know where it keeps itself. Do you? I suppose there is some society somewhere, but I haven't seen anything of it. I'm very fond of society, and I have always had a great deal of it ... I used to go to New York every winter. In New York I had lots of society."[8] Daisy's unrefined notion of society inspired responses in later years such as this from Mrs. May King Van Rensselaer's *The Social Ladder* in 1924: "Nothing in this republic has been more burlesqued and respected, more jeered at and aspired to, more violently attacked and more passionately envied than that intangible accolade termed 'social distinction.' People affect to scorn and make light of recognition by Society, and contrive and plan and spend to attain it."[9] However, the years between Daisy's debut and Mrs. Van Rensselaer's attempt to preserve a lost era were critical for the novel of manners. While a modern reader might find Daisy's excursions with "foreigners" little more than flirtations, to the members of the society she so longed to enter, Daisy's disregard for, or innocence about, local etiquette demands her exclusion. Speaking to his aunt about Daisy's "mystifying manners," Winterbourne takes some of the blame for her death on himself: "I was booked to make a mistake. I have lived too long in foreign parts" (152).

William Dean Howells edited *The Atlantic Monthly*, becoming friends with Henry James and earning the honorary title of "dean of American letters" by the time of his death in 1920. Earlier in his life, however, he wrote a campaign biography of Abraham Lincoln and was rewarded with a consular post in Venice, where he lived during the American Civil War. The opportunity to live in Italy and observe manners led to the publication of *Venetian Life* (1866) and *Italian Journeys* (1867), works that foreshadow Wharton's *French Ways and Their Meaning* and *In Morocco*, and anticipate the techniques of cultural anthropologists. Howells' detailed observations of daily life in Italy proved ideal preparation for writing the novels of manners. Rejecting the expatriate life James and Wharton would choose, he returned to the United States but continued to observe and record manners. Having missed living there for the duration of the Civil War, he returned alert to the changes in society that the war had wrought. As a character in his novel *The Rise of Silas Lapham* (1885) remarks, "'I suppose that in a new country one gets to looking at people a little out of our tradition; and I dare say that if I hadn't passed a winter in Texas I might have found Colonel Lapham rather too much.'"[10]

The main character, Silas Lapham, has made a fortune manufacturing paint, ruthlessly driving out his partner, Rogers, to become sole owner. The plot traces his rise as he moves from the country life of Vermont to the city life of Boston with his wife and daughter: "Suddenly the money began to come so abundantly that she need not save; and then they did not know what to do with it" (25). Pressed by his family, he begins to climb the social ladder. At a dinner party with an old-guard family, Lapham is determined to behave appropriately, but his awkwardness is apparent: "he had spent five minutes in getting into his gloves ... When he had them on, and let his large fists hang down on either side, they looked, in the saffron tint which the shopgirl said his gloves should be of, like canvassed hams. He perspired with doubt as he climbed the stairs" (174). He soon pulls them off as he sees his host is gloveless. He is "pallid with anxiety lest he should somehow disgrace himself, giving thanks to God that he should have been spared the shame of wearing gloves where no one else did, but at the same time despairing that Corey should have seen him in them" (175). Unused to wine but worried his manners will reveal his ignorance, he drinks too much and awakens the next morning to ask his wife, "'Was I drunk last night?'"(193). Money is one ingredient for social mobility, but as Lapham soon recognizes, an ability to grasp the innuendo of gesture, to decode the unspoken judgments and recognize the almost invisible webs of power and hierarchy, required lifelong training, much more than a shopgirl could provide.

As the "fiery house" exposed by World War I cooled, novelists found fertile ground, especially in the 1920s, exploring what the "dishabille" of the manners of the postwar Jazz Age revealed. Not only Wharton, but many younger U.S. writers saw the form as ideally suited for examining the "undressed" new society that was built as the postwar generation negotiated women's suffrage, racial integration, rapidly developing technologies, immigration, and the consequences of Prohibition. These U.S. novelists including Sinclair Lewis, Ellen Glasgow, and F. Scott Fitzgerald found in *Silas Lapham* and *Daisy Miller* prototypes for examining America's place in the new century, peopling their fictions with characters who become increasingly self-conscious of their roles as both anthropologist and artifact in the excavation to interpret the codes and rituals that surround them.

In Fitzgerald's *The Great Gatsby* (1925), Daisy Buchanan famously asks, "'What'll we do with ourselves this afternoon? ... and the day after that, and the next thirty years?'"[11] Her question reverberates in the novel of manners of the 1920s and 1930s. Carol Kendicott, protagonist of Lewis' *Main Street* (1920), dreams of traveling to Venice while living trapped in Gopher Prairie. Sinclair Lewis focused on the Midwest in his best-known novel of manners which exploded the persistent myth that small town life in the United States was idyllic and firmly rooted in neighborly kindness and morality. Lewis depicts the town of Gopher Prairie as such: "Ugly, materialistic, business-oriented, dead to art and complacent in its philistine middle-class values, Gopher Prairie is representative of all American small towns, from Ohio to the Carolinas." Lewis condemns the ugly architecture, the slow and nonstandard speech, the accumulation of "cheap motor cars, telephones, ready-made clothes, silos, alfalfa, kodaks, phonographs, leather-upholstered Morris chairs, bridge-prizes, oil-stocks, motion-pictures, land-deals, unread sets of Mark Twain..." (quoted in Tuttleton 146–47). The society he describes abjures social climbing in favor of consumerism.

Ellen Glasgow wrote twenty-one novels between 1897 and 1941, working primarily at her family home in Richmond, Virginia and focusing on the manners of the South, a choice derived from her belief that "We write better ... when we write of places we know, and of a background with which we are familiar."[12] She creates the fictional city of Queensborough, Virginia, as a setting for her trilogy of novels of manners, *The Romantic Comedians* (1926), *They Stooped to Folly* (1929) and *The Sheltered Life* (1932), delineating the "houses, streets, towns, professions, inherited habits and opinions" (*WF* 5) of the rapidly disappearing Old South. Unlike Carol Kendicott and Newland Archer, many of her characters have accepted the society they inhabit. An exception is young Jenny Blair in *The Sheltered Life*, who regrets abandoning a dream of going to New York to become an actress: "I want to go away. I'm tired of Queensborough. I'm tired of everything."[13] John Welch replies with the voice of an anthropologist: "The trouble is we imagine we can change ourselves by changing the scenery ... I'd like to go away and be free, and I know perfectly well the kind of freedom I am looking for has not yet been invented ... People who have traditions are oppressed by tradition, and people who are without it are oppressed by the lack of it – or by whatever else they have put in its place" (219). Asking, like the Countess Olenska, "Where is that country?" when Archer envisions escaping to a place where they can be happy, Welch continues:

Where? There isn't any place far enough away for a man who asks for more civilization, not less ... Our civilization [that of The South] is as good as the rest, perhaps better than most, because it's less noisy; but the whole thing is a hollow crust everywhere. A medical man is expected to take it easier when he calls it anthropology, but I can't see how that helps. They forget that living in anthropology may be quite as disagreeable to a sensitive mind as living in civilization. (219)

Like Glasgow, Wharton reserved some nostalgia for the world before the war, when life seemed more defined by widely agreed upon codes of behavior, but likewise she saw that society through the astringent lens of the satirist. In *Old New York* (1924) she excavated her society in four novellas, each of which portrays a decade, starting with the 1840s in *False Dawn* and concluding with the 1870s in *New Year's Day*. Taken in sequence, the novellas are comparable to the results of an archaeological dig: four strata neatly preserved, each recording a distinct cultural moment. Wharton's tales are rich in details of clothing, interior design, dialogue and social behavior; each small volume catalogues the evolution of manners from one decade to the next. The first novella evokes an era when young men like Lewis Raycie were sent to Europe on a Grand Tour, and commanded to purchase an Old Master painting or two as evidence of the family's power, wealth and status. Young Raycie comes into conflict with his father over the paintings he selects in Italy, where he meets John Ruskin and learns to admire the early Italian painters like Giotto, and Mantegna and Piero della Francesca, not yet valued by Old New York collectors, but to grow beyond price to the next generation, becoming recognized as "one of the most beautiful collections of Italian Primitives in the world"[14] whereas the Raycie name has vanished from the social register. *The Old Maid*, capturing the manners of the 1850s in which "a few families ruled, in simplicity and affluence" (3), uncovers an illegitimate birth, undercutting the appearance of "simplicity." *The Spark* contrasts a young man's appreciation for Walt Whitman's poetry with an old soldier's dismissal of *Leaves of Grass* as "rubbish." Finally, *New Year's Day* takes readers to the 1870s and studies the sexual mores as "Life has become too telegraphic for curiosity to linger on any given point in a sentimental relation; ... 'Fifth Avenue Hotel? They might meet in the middle of Fifth Avenue nowadays, for all anybody cares'" (4). Once again, Wharton perches outside the fiery lodging to catalogue the material culture artifacts and the moral baggage the residents cling to as they escape the flames.

Violation of social codes can be fatal. Lewis Raycie's choice to abjure his father's taste for Ruskin's leads to his poverty and early death. Daisy's risky visit to see the Colosseum results in her fatal contagion with Roman fever. Silas Lapham, morally reclaimed, is nevertheless condemned to leave Boston and return to rural life. While many novelists of manners could resolve social conflict by marriage or moral reform, for Wharton too much had changed. Near the end of her life, she would write: "Everything that used to form the fabric of our daily life has been torn in shreds, trampled on, destroyed"("A Little Girl's New York," quoted in Knights, 119).

NOTES

1. H. James, "Life of Emerson" in D. Massin et al. (eds.), *Macmillan's Magazine,* 57 (London: Macmillan, 1888), 86–98; 88.

2. L. Trilling, *The Liberal Imagination* (Garden City, NY: Doubleday, 1950), 145.

3. J. W. Tuttleton, *The Novel of Manners in America* (New York: Norton, 1972), xii; 10. Subsequent references to this work are included in the text.

4. J. P. Marquand, *B. F.'s Daughter* (Boston: Little, Brown, 1946), 19.

5. P. Knights, *The Cambridge Introduction to Edith Wharton* (Cambridge: Cambridge University Press, 2009), 35. Subsequent references to this work are included in the text.

6. F. Trollope, *Domestic Manners of the Americans,* vol. II (London: Whittaker, Treacher & Co., 1832), 295. Subsequent references to this work are included in the text.

7. F. Kaplan, *Henry James: The Imagination of Genius* (New York: William Morrow, 1992), 488.

8. H. James, *Daisy Miller* in *The Turn of the Screw and Other Short Novels* (New York: Signet, 1962), 101. Subsequent references to this work are included in the text.

9. M. K. Van Rensselaer, *The Social Ladder* (New York: Henry Holt, 1924), 3.

10. W. D. Howells, *The Rise of Silas Lapham* (New York: Signet, 1963), 60. Subsequent references to this work are included in the text.

11. F. Scott Fitzgerald, *The Great Gatsby* (London: Heinemann, 1987), 102.

12. E. Glasgow, *The Woman Within: The Autobiography of Ellen Glasgow* (New York: Harcourt, Brace, 1954), 129–30.

13. E. Glasgow, *The Sheltered Life* (New York: Hill and Wang, 1979), 216. Subsequent references to this work are included in the text.

14. E. Wharton, *Old New York* (New York: Appleton, 1924), 137. Subsequent references to this work are included in the text.

CHAPTER 33

Naturalism

Donna Campbell

Although Edith Wharton has often been characterized primarily as a novelist of manners, throughout her career she made a series of original and substantial contributions to the school of naturalism. Well versed in evolutionary theory and the emerging sciences of human behavior, including anthropology, Wharton wrote about her upper-class culture from the scientific perspective of the naturalists, and her fiction includes naturalistic themes of imprisonment, confinement, and struggle. Examining Wharton's novels in the context of naturalist writers such as Stephen Crane, Frank Norris, Theodore Dreiser, and Jack London leads to a more complete understanding of the naturalistic tradition during Wharton's time and of the complex response that her novels offered to it.

Naturalism is a late nineteenth-century literary movement that promoted a scientific approach to the writing of fiction, one based in objective observation and informed by the evolutionary theories of Charles Darwin and Herbert Spencer. Sometimes considered simply as a more brutal offshoot of realism, naturalism has always been difficult to define in terms both of its subject matter and of its established canon. One commonly cited brief definition is that of George Becker, who called it "pessimistic materialistic determinism," although critics have consistently argued that such a definition is too narrow.[1] As Eric Carl Link suggests, "the defining characteristic of 'naturalistic' narrative ... [is] the artistic integration of naturalist theory as theme,"[2] including plots that highlight its engagement with the concept of determinism, characters and settings that illustrate the determining forces of heredity and environment, and symbolism that announces naturalism's consistent themes of economic instability, the "brute within," and imprisonment. Naturalistic characters are governed by hereditary drives and passions that they cannot understand, yet they resist these forces that control them. They struggle in settings that reduce human beings to the level of animals or automata, such as those of urban poverty, a hostile wilderness, or a stiflingly bourgeois milieu. Rarely do naturalistic characters number among the elite, educated, or powerful members of their culture; instead, they are often working-class figures or those otherwise marginalized by society, poised on the cusp of some disaster such as poverty or addiction. Subjecting these characters, whom they regarded as more primitive and elemental than those of the middle class, to the pressure of social ills such as alcoholism, drug addiction, and violence, naturalist writers pressed them to their limits in order to demonstrate true human nature beneath the veneer of civilization. Nor were the naturalists afraid to displease audiences by presenting a frank portrayal of sexuality or by denying them a happy ending. As David Baguley notes, naturalist plots "are always dysphoric" and "[submit] man (or, more frequently, woman) to an ironic, humiliating destiny."[3] The characteristic trajectory of the naturalistic novel is that of decline or, in Baguley's terms, entropy, as the individual crumbles under the weight of forces and moves from a more or less coherent state of subjectivity to disorder, chaos, and death. Yet as Donald Pizer has pointed out, naturalistic characters strive to assert their human dignity even within a deterministic universe, and the American naturalistic hero's tragedy is that an innate "potential for fineness" is blocked by circumstance.[4]

Naturalism originated in France in the 1860s and 1870s with the writings of Edmond and Jules de Goncourt (1822–96; 1830–70), Guy de Maupassant (1850–93), and especially Émile Zola (1840–1902), the most noted practitioner and theorist of the movement. In "The Experimental Novel" (1880), Zola proposed that the novelist should take the same clinical approach toward his subject matter as the experimental scientist, using the novel as a medium within which to strip away the false veneer of social conventions. The novelist, like the scientist, could thereby study the effects of heredity and environment in the elemental human beast. By studying "the two-fold question of temperaments and environments," Zola explained in his preface to the Rougon-Macquart series, "I shall try to find and trace out the thread which leads mathematically from one man to another." Assembling "documents" or materials gathered from charts and notebooks full of his observations, Zola published twenty Rougon-Macquart novels, tracing several generations of two families whose "prime characteristic" was "the overflow of appetite."[5] As this description suggests, its narrative style may have promised detachment and restraint, but naturalism's subject matter was excess, and it attracted criticism for its violation of literary and social norms. Yet as naturalism spread through Europe and to the Americas, it found defenders: in Spain, Benito Pérez Galdós (1843–1920), Leopoldo Alas (1852–1901), and Emilia

Pardo Bazán (1851–1921); in Italy, Giovanni Verga (1840–1922); and in South and Central America, Argentina's Eugenio Cambaceres (1843–88), Mexico's Federico Gamboa (1864–1939), and Brazil's Raul Pompéia (1863–95), Julio Ribéiro (1845–90), and Aluísio Azevado (1857–1913). Closer to Wharton's practice were British and Irish novelists often considered naturalists, including George Gissing (1857–1903), George Moore (1852–1933), Thomas Hardy (1840–1928), and Arnold Bennett (1867–1931).

When Wharton began writing fiction in the 1890s, naturalism was enjoying as much critical esteem and popularity as it would ever know in the United States. In the short span of a few years at the end of the century, a host of naturalistic novels appeared, including Stephen Crane's *The Red Badge of Courage* (1895) and *Maggie: A Girl of the Streets* (1893, 1896), Harold Frederic's *The Damnation of Theron Ware* (1896), Ellen Glasgow's *The Descendant* (1897), Kate Chopin's *The Awakening* (1899), and Frank Norris' *McTeague* (1899), followed by Theodore Dreiser's *Sister Carrie* (1900), Paul Laurence Dunbar's *The Sport of the Gods* (1902), and Jack London's *The Call of the Wild* (1903). These novels reflected a shift away from the realism of W. D. Howells and Henry James, in which ethical choice was a key theme. Instead, they used naturalistic themes of imprisonment, entrapment, and struggle to portray both the classic determinants of heredity and environment and to critique a society that imprisoned its members through a misapplication of the era's social Darwinism. Naturalism shined a spotlight on hypocritical morality, as in *Maggie: A Girl of the Streets*; racism, as in *The Sport of the Gods;* the confining position of women, as in *The Awakening*; and the maltreatment of the poor and working class, as in London's *The People of the Abyss* and, more subtly, *The Call of the Wild*. A clearer picture of Wharton's contribution to naturalism emerges when considered in the context of that of her contemporaries Stephen Crane, Frank Norris, Theodore Dreiser, and Jack London as well as her own critical statements about the movement.

Journalist, novelist, and war correspondent Stephen Crane (1871–1900) wrote in an impressionistic, experimental style that emphasized the ironic distance characteristic of naturalism. In Crane's fiction, authorial irony emphasizes the distance between the subject's consciousness and that of the author, and it mocks the institutional pieties of bourgeois culture. In *Maggie*, for example, Crane uses irony to dismantle the 1890s genre of the sentimental slum story and to represent a truth that he believed would shock his readers. His protagonist, Maggie Johnson, at first "blossom[s] in a mud puddle"[6] amid the squalor of her surroundings, yet after being seduced and abandoned by the bartender Pete, she sinks into prostitution and death. Maggie's romantic idealism about Pete suggests that in such a setting, a failure to recognize the constraints of the slum environment is as destructive as the slum environment itself. Crane emphasizes this point by having Maggie's mother, whose drunken fits of violence are legendary in their tenement block, piously order Maggie from the family flat when Maggie stays out all night with Pete. A similar failure of romantic idealism occurs in *The Red Badge of Courage* (1895), in which a country youth, Henry Fleming, dreams of glory during the Civil War. Henry must confront his own initial cowardice in the battle of Chancellorsville, recalling "the red sickness of battle" when he felt that "He had been an animal blistered and sweating in the heat and pain of war," before ridding himself of it and learning that death was "after all … but the great death."[7] As shown in this passage, symbolism in naturalistic novels often blurs the boundaries between human beings and objects, with human beings portrayed as animals or machines and vice versa: Henry must recognize that he has behaved like an animal before he can become a man. Another example occurs in "The Open Boat," in which four shipwrecked men, including "the correspondent," try to stay afloat in a dinghy until they can be rescued. Seeing a "tall wind-tower," as they drift close to land, the correspondent reflects that it "was a giant, standing with its back to the plight of the ants. It represented … the serenity of nature amid the struggles of the individual." The correspondent recognizes that to nature, men are insignificant insects and that nature is "flatly indifferent" to the plight of human beings, the characteristic stance of nature in naturalism.[8]

Another of Wharton's naturalist contemporaries was Frank Norris (1870–1902), whose contributions to naturalism included his theoretical essays on naturalism and his treatment of economic determinism. Writing about Zola for *The Wave* in 1896, Norris explained that realism's "small passions, restricted emotions, [and] dramas of the reception-room," were insufficient to represent the truth about life; to be truthful, fiction must instead portray lives "twisted from the ordinary … and flung into the throes of a vast and terrible drama that works itself out in unleashed passions, in blood, and in sudden death."[9] Three years later, Norris put these concepts into practice in *McTeague* (1899), his tale of a working-class dentist described as a brute who is stupid, ignorant, and preternaturally strong. The "brute" in McTeague awakens when he can no longer fight the stirrings of sexual desire, the "foul stream of hereditary evil … the evil of an entire race" that causes him to violate the anaesthetized Trina by kissing her "grossly, full on the mouth."[10] Norris' perspective on sexuality as an overwhelming force that causes the brute to erupt is characteristic of naturalism, as is the novel's thesis that a combination of heredity and environment destroys McTeague: only when he is pressed by the loss of his occupation and Trina's hereditary miserliness does he turn to alcohol and violence. Moreover, the fortunes of the McTeagues fluctuate based on their possession of, and response to, gold, which functions symbolically as a deterministic variable not merely for the McTeagues but for those around them. Like Wharton, Norris insists that economic determinism governs lives not only on the individual level, but on the national and international level too, as shown in *The Octopus* (1901) and *The Pit* (1903), which chronicle the production and distribution of wheat. *The Pit,* of which Wharton owned a copy, even anticipates the parallel between commodities trading and the marriage market in *The House of Mirth*.

Dreiser, whom Wharton praised, and London, whom she did not discuss in print, shared her interest in Spencer and Darwin as well as in the determining power of social class. Dreiser's first novel, *Sister Carrie* (1900), follows the naturalistic plot of a woman alone in the city. Unlike Lily Bart of *The House of Mirth*, who cannot bring herself to marry for money, Carrie Meeber succeeds by adapting to her circumstances, molding herself to the desires of successively more powerful men and, as an actress, more discerning audiences.[11] She compartmentalizes her feelings, transforming the sense of inchoate longing that she projects into an asset to stimulate male desire. The emptiness at her core, satisfied materially but not psychologically with publicity and consumer goods, makes Carrie the perfect embodiment of the culture whose values she reflects back to her audiences. Dreiser continues this critique of sexual and consumer desire in *An American Tragedy* (1925), which demonstrates the ways in which U.S. culture encourages a conflation of the two. The novel chronicles the life of Clyde Griffiths, whose work in his wealthy uncle's collar factory is less compelling to him than the glimpses he has of the city's social elite. Like Carrie, he gazes at what he desires through the literal and figurative medium of a glass window that initially bars his entry to the social world above him. Trapped by biology, by environment, and by class aspirations, Clyde drifts into an affair with Roberta Alden, a factory girl, just as the wealthy Sondra Finchley takes an interest in him; after Roberta becomes pregnant, he decides to murder her by staging an accidental drowning on a remote lake. Although the question of Clyde's guilt is never resolved, since he merely fails to save her when she drowns, the trial, conviction, and execution of Clyde for Roberta's death is presented as the novel's real American tragedy. The novel indicts class stratification and consumer culture as the forces that killed Roberta, with Clyde as a mere passive agent psychologically conditioned to do whatever is necessary to achieve the American dream.

Instead of desire and psychological determinism, London focuses on Darwinian and Spencerian themes of atavism, heredity, and survival of the fittest in fiction such as "To Build a Fire" and *The Call of the Wild*. In the latter, Buck, a pampered California dog kidnapped and taken to the Yukon, endures abuse as a sled dog, learns that the law of nature dictates the survival of the fittest, and atavistically reverts to his ancestral type as he hears the howl of a wolf pack. London's wilderness subject matter and his socialism mark his difference from Wharton, yet his depiction of Darwinian competition over scarce resources and the choice of the most desirable mate recalls Wharton's *The House of Mirth* or "Roman Fever." In this late story, Mrs. Slade and Mrs. Ansley shed their polite pretenses of friendship and gradually revert to primitive emotions as they revive their past competition over the ideal mate, Delphin Slade. Their present-day competition over the marriage prospects for their daughters, a competition geared toward genetic survival, is as savage in its way as the struggle for survival in London's fiction.

Two variants of naturalism, the Progressive-era social problem novel and the "revolt from the village" exposé of small-town life, are exemplified by other writers whom Wharton singled out for praise: David Graham Phillips (1867–1911) and Sinclair Lewis (1885–1951). Known as a muckraking journalist (like Upton Sinclair, whose *The Jungle* sparked a public outcry that led to the Pure Food and Drug Act), Phillips wrote novels of social critique that mirrored Wharton's own topics: divorce, the "New Woman," and the incursions of the upstart manufacturing class and stock market millionaires into old society. Shortly before his death, he completed *Susan Lenox: Her Fall and Rise* (1917), which Wharton considered a neglected masterpiece. Like *Maggie* and *Sister Carrie*, it is the story of a woman who sells herself as a matter of economic survival, but unlike Carrie, Maggie, and Lily Bart, Susan Lenox frankly negotiates the terms of the exchange and thereby preserves her autonomy. With its vivid depictions of the rape and beatings that Susan experiences, *Susan Lenox* brought a new level of sexual frankness and practical economic realism to the naturalistic fallen woman tale. In *Main Street* (1920) and *Babbitt* (1922), Sinclair Lewis uses the techniques of naturalism, including detailed descriptions of unsavory sights, to prick bourgeois pretensions and complacency. As Wharton does with Ralph Marvell in *The Custom of the Country*, Lewis pits a character of sensitivity and culture – in *Main Street*, Carol Kennicott – against the shallow absence of tradition and culture, as embodied by Undine Spragg and small-town America. Through Carol Kennicott and George F. Babbitt of *Babbitt*, a realtor who mildly rebels against the dull conformity of his life, Lewis satirizes U.S. society – its cult of efficiency, its boosterism, and its lack of appreciation for a truly cosmopolitan culture.

As might be expected, Wharton's response to naturalism was complicated. While incorporating its evolutionary principles into her work, she disdained its formulaic applications in the fiction she read. She had, of course, read Zola; her references to his work suggest this, and among the surviving volumes from her library are copies of his *Le Naturalisme au Théâtre* (1881) and two novels of the Rougon-Macquart series, *La Conquête de Plassans* (1874) and *Germinal* (1885). More central to her practice of naturalism was her avid reading in evolutionary theory. Wharton devoured not only volumes of Darwin and Spencer but T. H. Huxley's *Discourses Biological and Geological* (1897), Ernst Haeckel's *The History of Creation* (1876; the copy in Wharton's library an edition from 1893), Kellogg's *Darwinism Today* (1907) and Robert Lock's *Recent Progress in the Study of Variation, Heredity, and Evolution*, published in 1906 (Lee 70–71, 330). Equally important in her self-education were evolutionary accounts of social and literary forms, such as William Lecky's *History of European Morals from Augustus to Charlemagne* (1869) and Hippolyte Taine's scientific account of literary history as an expression of the author's race, milieu, and moment rather than the exclusive product of individual genius. In writing to her friend Sara Norton in March 1908 about a "very interesting but rather painful book" that "demolishes Taine's methods as a scientific historian," Wharton explains, "As Taine was one of the formative influences of my youth – the greatest after Darwin, Spencer & Lecky – I feel as if things were falling in ruins . . ." (*Letters* 136). Yet despite such challenges to theories that had served as scientific touchstones for her, Wharton continued to integrate their insights into her writing. As Tricia M. Farwell, Linda Kornasky, and Bert Bender have shown, she incorporated Darwin's theories of sexual selection into her novels, and studies by Jennie Kassanoff, Judith Saunders, Paul Ohler, and Laura Saltz demonstrate that Wharton applied Darwinian concepts of survival, competition, inheritance, and evolutionary development. Characters such as Ralph Marvell and Lily Bart are presented as failures of adaptation and rare specimens ripe for extinction, just as Undine Spragg is a living example of Spencer's dictum of survival of the fittest, a predator whose weapons are beauty, dissimulation, and the naïveté of the men she ruthlessly collects. In a Darwinian world, the selfishness of an Undine, a Zeena Frome of *Ethan Frome* or a Bessy Westmore of *The Fruit of the Tree* is a primitive force that consistently triumphs over the hesitations and self-sacrificing natures of those around them.

Yet Wharton did not hesitate to criticize what she saw as the limitations of naturalistic subject matter. She wrote to her editor William Crary Brownell in 1902 to express irritation about reviewers' "assumption that the people I write about are not 'real' because they are not navvies & char-women" (*Letters* 91). A quarter of a century later, years of being pigeonholed as a writer of upper-class subjects caused her to renew her complaint: "The idea that genuineness is to be found only in the rudimentary, and that whatever is complex is unauthentic, is a favorite axiom of the modern American critics ... [T]he modern American novelist is told ... that only the man with the dinner-pail is human, and hence available for his purpose."[12] Like the other naturalists, Wharton did not question the idea that lower-class subjects – "the man with the dinner-pail" – were "rudimentary" or further from civilized behavior in managing their emotions, suggesting in the 1922 preface to *Ethan Frome* that the air of artificiality that mars some fiction can be avoided "if the looker-on is sophisticated, and the people he interprets are simple." Yet Wharton disagreed that this quality of simplicity made lower-class characters the only subjects for fiction. In addition to naturalism's limited subject matter, Wharton also objected to the limitations of its method. In a late essay, "Tendencies in Modern Fiction," she notes that the "feebler [realists] beat their brains out against the blank wall of 'Naturalism,'" drawing "helpless puppets on a sluggish stream of fatality," a cutting indictment of naturalistic determinism. Her solution to such formulae is the application of what she sees as the true foundation of literary art, the selection and transformation of the raw materials: "Transmutation is the first principle of art, and copying can never be a substitute for creative vision."[13]

Recent critical perspectives on Wharton and naturalism have analyzed the ways in which Wharton exercised this "creative vision" by transforming the genre. Critics such as Barbara Hochman, Jennifer Fleissner, and Donna Campbell have found evidence of Wharton's naturalism in allusions to highbrow reading materials and a focus on women's bodies as well as in more conventional measures such as deterministic themes and scientific imagery. *The House of Mirth*, long considered one of Wharton's most naturalistic novels, illustrates these ideas: the classical allusions and references to Selden's and Percy Gryce's book collections reveal the inadequacy of such civilized tools to aid the men's understanding of Lily, and Lily's performance in the famous *tableaux vivants* scene recalls similar forms of visual display of women's bodies in other naturalistic novels. Wharton's other novels demonstrate a range of naturalistic practices as well. With its plethora of controversial subjects, including divorce, the New Woman, the plight of the factory worker, euthanasia, and drug addiction, *The Fruit of the Tree* fits into the genre of the muckraking naturalistic social problem novel, and the paired narratives *Ethan Frome* and *Summer* address some of naturalism's most significant themes, including sexuality, poverty, racial inheritance, and the effects of the physical environment on character. *The Age of Innocence* analogizes naturalism's scientific perspective through its sophisticated handling of narrative voice and point of view as well as its use of the language of anthropology. An objective upper-class or middle-class observer was a common figure in early naturalism, for, as June Howard has observed, such a perspective reassured readers threatened by the proletarianization that naturalism's plots of decline and lower-class characters seemed to promise. In creating not a "simple" but a "sophisticated" character such as Newland Archer and an even more sophisticated narrative perspective from which to reveal Archer's blindness, Wharton adds an additional level of complexity to naturalistic representation, one that Donald Pizer has called "naturalism in its 'perfected' state."[14]

What Wharton brought to naturalism was significant. Firstly, by expanding its subject matter beyond that demonstrably recognizable as naturalistic, she refutes the idea that naturalism must focus on "the man with the dinner-pail." In addition, she challenges strict notions of determinism through her sophisticated use of the themes of imprisonment, entrapment, and struggle. Wharton's depiction of the internalizing of external forces such as manners, social customs, or gender expectations replaces the more overt forces of imprisonment with psychological ones, for despite their intelligent assessment of their plight, characters such as Lily Bart, Ethan Frome, and Newland Archer are as hamstrung by the environments in which they live as their more brutish counterparts in London or Norris. Although she is given choice after choice in *The House of Mirth*, Lily Bart can escape being trapped in a gilded cage only by death, an indictment of the society in which she lives. This naturalistic approach to the "society novel" genre thus forces the reader to look past the gilding and see the cage forged by a culture that treats women as commodities. Ethan Frome is likewise trapped, but his situation occurs through a heritage of duty and self-abnegation that he feels compelled to uphold until death can set him free. Charity Royall is trapped by biology – her pregnancy – as well as by custom. Her "swarthy" complexion and origins in the disreputable Mountain community suggest that, as in *McTeague* and other naturalistic novels, one cannot escape the evidence of one's ethnic heritage.[15] Finally, Wharton's sophisticated use of narrative voice renders key features of naturalism, such as its detached and ironic perspective, capable of handling not merely the "simple" characters of traditional naturalism but the "sophisticated" ones of her fiction. Despite her subject matter, which was unconventional for naturalism, among her contemporaries no author more deftly shows the imprisoning power of the forces of heredity and environment in a deterministic universe, and the struggles of characters as resisting agents within it, than Edith Wharton.

NOTES

1. G. J. Becker, "Modern Realism as a Literary Movement" in G. J. Becker (ed.), *Documents of Modern Literary Realism* (Princeton, NJ: Princeton University Press, 1963), 3–41; 35.

2. E. C. Link, *The Vast and Terrible Drama: American Literary Naturalism in the Late Nineteenth Century* (Tuscaloosa: University of Alabama Press, 2004), 20.

3. D. Baguley, "The Nature of Naturalism" in B. Nelson (ed.), *Naturalism in the European Novel: New Critical Perspectives* (New York: Berg, 1992), 13–26; 19.

4. D. Pizer, "The Three Phases of American Literary Naturalism" in D. Pizer (ed.), *The Theory and Practice of American Literary Naturalism: Selected Essays and Reviews* (Carbondale: Southern Illinois University Press, 1993), 13–35; 22.

5. E. Zola, "On the Rougon-Macquart Series" in G. Becker (ed.), *Documents of Modern Literary Realism* (Princeton, NJ: Princeton University Press, 1963), 159–61; 160, 161.

6. S. Crane, *Maggie: A Girl of the Streets* in J. C. Levenson (ed.), *Stephen Crane: Prose and Poetry* (New York: Library of America, 1984), 7–78; 24.

7. S. Crane, *The Red Badge of Courage* in J. C. Levenson (ed.), *Stephen Crane: Prose and Poetry* (New York: Library of America, 1984), 81–212; 212.

8. S. Crane, "The Open Boat" in J. C. Levenson (ed.), *Stephen Crane: Prose and Poetry* (New York: Library of America, 1984), 885–909; 905.

9. F. Norris, "Zola as a Romantic Writer" in D. Pizer (ed.), *Frank Norris: Novels and Essays* (New York: Library of America, 1986), 1106–08; 1106, 1107.

10. F. Norris, *McTeague* in D. Pizer (ed.), *Frank Norris: Novels and Essays* (New York: Library of America, 1986), 263–572; 285, 284.

11. For comparisons of Carrie Meeber and Lily Bart, see B. H. Gelfant, "What More Can Carrie Want? Naturalistic Ways of Consuming Women" in D. Pizer (ed.), *The Cambridge Companion to American Realism and Naturalism* (Cambridge: Cambridge University Press, 1995), 178–210; A. Kaplan, *The Social Construction of American Realism* (Chicago: University of Chicago Press, 1988); and A. Price, "Lily Bart and Carrie Meeber: Cultural Sisters," *American Literary Realism, 1870–1910*, 13.2 (1980), 238–45.

12. E. Wharton, "The Great American Novel" in F. Wegener (ed.), *Edith Wharton: The Uncollected Critical Writings* (Princeton, NJ: Princeton University Press, 1996), 151–59; 155.

13. E. Wharton, "Introduction to Ethan Frome" and "Tendencies in Modern Fiction" in F. Wegener (ed.), *Edith Wharton: The Uncollected Critical Writings* (Princeton, NJ: Princeton University Press, 1996), 259–61; 260; and 170–74; 172, 171.

14. D. Pizer, "American Naturalism in Its 'Perfected' State: *The Age of Innocence* and *An American Tragedy*" in A. Bendixen and Z. Zilversmit (eds.), *Edith Wharton: New Critical Essays*, (New York: Garland, 1992), 127–41; 127.

15. E. Wharton, *Summer* (New York: D. Appleton and Company, 1917), 8.

CHAPTER 34

Modernism

Jennifer Haytock

Edith Wharton did not like modernism. She was quite clear on this point, both in her private letters to friends and in her published critical pieces on writing. In "Tendencies in Modern Fiction," published in the *Saturday Review of Literature* in 1934, Wharton laments the apparent indifference to the past and lack of principles in the work of the new generation of writers. Still, to study Wharton requires an awareness of modernism, for she lived and wrote during the era in which it flourished. In regard simply to chronology, one might look at the recent *Cambridge Companion to American Modernism* (2005), which covers the years 1890–1939, a span that comprises entirely Wharton's professional life. However, modernism is not defined merely as an era; rather, it encompasses, addresses, and provokes a number of issues, including subject choice, writing style, relationship to the marketplace, ideas about gender, sexuality, race, technology, and many more. Modernism further demands an acknowledgment of the literary criticism that first defined it as well as an engagement with later and current generations of critics who have challenged and expanded the modernist canon.

Writers and critics in the early part of the twentieth century defined modernism largely through aesthetics and a need to represent the realities of modern life. A small group of modern writers formed a school of criticism that established the value of particular kinds of literature. In "Tradition and the Individual Talent," T. S. Eliot called for the erosion of personality in literature, arguing that "the poet has not a 'personality' to express, but a particular medium ... in which impressions and experiences combine in peculiar and unexpected ways."[1] Hence, he laid a foundation for the school of New Critics who, in subsequent decades, insisted on regarding a poem or story as an artifact to be examined by itself alone, apart from its author and the historical moment of its production. In *Axel's Castle* (1942), Edmund Wilson follows Eliot's lead by regarding modern literature as founded largely on symbolism, and of all the authors he considers, only one is a woman (William Butler Yeats, Paul Valéry, Eliot, Marcel Proust, James Joyce, and Gertrude Stein), although he also published an essay in 1938 titled "Justice to Edith Wharton." Other early critics of modern writing, however, took a different approach. Alfred Kazin, for example, in *On Native Grounds* (1942), insisted that all of American experiences shaped American writing, and, unlike Wilson and others who regarded modern writing as originating with World War I, he dates "modern literature" as beginning around the time of the Civil War and identifies such writers as William Dean Howells as its originators.[2] Unlike many other literary studies from the early and mid-twentieth century, *On Native Grounds* includes women writers such as Wharton, Willa Cather, and Ellen Glasgow, although Kazin considers that Wharton stuck to writing about New York society because she "could do no other" (77). Wharton herself regarded modernism as "anarchy" caused by the author's "distrust of technique and the fear of being unoriginal" (*WF* 14). Essentially she objected to Ezra Pound's cry to "Make it new!" for she found no value in newness for its own sake.

More recently, however, critics have seen how Wharton's aesthetics actually fit into early definitions of modernism. Her subtle deployment of irony combined with a carefully controlled use of point of view contribute to the success of *The Age of Innocence* (1920) in that they align the reader with Newland Archer in his shocking discovery that his entire family has conspired against him and Ellen Olenska. Wharton's use of the same techniques was less successful, or at least less immediately recognized, in *A Son at the Front* (1923), published just three years later. She also experimented with point of view in *The Reef* (1912), shifting between the perspectives of two main characters. In *Ethan Frome* (1911), the tale of a decades-old tragedy told by an outsider, Wharton composed what is frequently regarded as her masterpiece in construction. And like Joyce, Wharton structured many of her characters' growth around epiphanies.[3]

Questions of style and technique are closely connected to modern writers' interest in new ideas about human psychology. William James' *Principles of Psychology* (1890) was well known in educated circles, and much of Sigmund Freud's work was translated into English in the early decades of the twentieth century. Whether the growth of psychology developed or merely fed an interest in the workings of the mind, many modernists used literary forms to explore the inner life of their characters. In *The Writing of Fiction* (1925), Wharton herself acknowledges that "[m]odern fiction really began when the 'action' of the novel was transferred from the street to the soul" (*WF* 3) and articulates an interest in "the exultations and agonies succeeding each other below the surface" (*WF* 4). Modernists approached the representation of a character's inner life using a wide range of techniques: Virginia Woolf's lyrical portrayal of Clarissa Dalloway and Septimus Smith in *Mrs. Dalloway* (1925); Cather's architectural rendering of Godfrey St. Peter in *The Professor's House* (1925); Joyce's and William Faulkner's stream-of-consciousness representations of Leopold Bloom in *Ulysses* (1922) and of Benjy, Quentin, and Jason Compson in *The Sound and the Fury* (1929), respectively. Wharton's representations of her characters' psychology is often more traditional, although in *The Reef* she experimented with point of view to convey the emotional and moral quandaries of characters caught in a love triangle.

In part because many modernists believed that the artist needed to separate himself from his homeland to develop creative distance and, for Americans, the sense that the United States was too conventional for intellectual pursuits, many modernist authors were expatriates. Henry James, Eliot, and H. D. moved to England; Stein, Joyce, Sherwood Anderson, Ernest Hemingway, F. Scott Fitzgerald, and Pound clustered in Paris, some more permanently than others. Wharton's home in Paris was within walking distance of the homes of Sylvia Beach, Natalie Barney, Colette, Stein and Alice B. Toklas, and others. Yet proximity did not make friends, and Wharton's social and intellectual circles did not overlap with her geographic one. Still, Wharton had in common with these women and other expatriate writers the fact of expatriatism itself. Stein left the United States to escape a stuffy American sensibility that blocked her career ambitions in medicine and shunned lesbians; Wharton left to escape a traditional New York society that regarded artists as an embarrassment. In 1911, just before she made her permanent home in Paris, she wrote to a friend that "at the present stage of [America's] strange unfolding it isn't exactly a propitious 'ambiance' for the arts" (*Letters* 253). It was also not a "propitious" home for a divorced woman; like her character Ellen Olenska, Wharton found Paris to be free of a stifling morality that intruded on her vision for her life. Many of her works focus on expatriates as main characters, including Anna Leath and George Darrow of *The Reef*; Kate Clephane of *The Mother's Recompense* (1925), whose experience in Europe is exile from her family, especially her daughter; Susy and Nick Lansing of *The Glimpses of the Moon* (1922), who seek refuge from poverty in the drifting life of expatriates; the lost characters of *The Children* (1928), whose rootlessness serves as a metaphor for the lack of permanence in their personal relationships; and the artists Vance Weston and Halo Spear of *Hudson River Bracketed* (1929) and *The Gods Arrive* (1932), who seek inspiration abroad but only truly find it back in the United States. A number of Wharton's short stories also focus on expatriates, such as the adulterous couple in "Souls Belated" (1899) and the bereaved mother in "Her Son" (1932). Although Wharton herself seems not to have felt the effects of displacement that appear in many modernist texts as alienation and displacement, she uses expatriatism in her works as a cause and sign of inner disturbances.

The sense of dislocation and alienation in so much of modern literature may also be considered to be a response to technological changes of the late nineteenth and early twentieth centuries, changes that profoundly altered the way humans in the Western world live. Many of these technological advances – the radio, telegraph, telephone, automobile – contributed to what Wharton called "this day of general 'speeding up'" (*WF* 20) in human relationships with space and each other. In Fitzgerald's *The Great Gatsby* (1925), for example, characters oscillate pointlessly from New York to Long Island via the glorious convenience of automobiles. In John Dos Passos' *Manhattan Transfer* (1925) and *U.S.A.* trilogy, the mechanics of modern life result in characters' increasingly impersonal and isolated existence. Wharton loved many of these changes; she owned cars and enjoyed motor trips through New England, France, England, and Italy. Her travel writing, such as *Italian Villas and Their Gardens* (1904), *Italian Backgrounds* (1905), *A Motor-Flight through France* (1908), and *In Morocco* (1920), reveal not only her eye for physical and cultural detail, but also her awareness of the lure of travel as well as its difficulties. *In Morocco* in particular conveys her feelings of alienation – of being a visitor in an impenetrable culture.

Some of the most profound technological developments during Wharton's lifetime were related to warfare, and these were put on display during World War I, a cataclysm to which Wharton almost literally had a front seat from her home in Paris. For some writers and critics, participation in the war was a key hallmark of modernist experience, but only if the experience was soldiering, an exclusively male prerogative at the time. The literal and metaphorical "war wound" served as both cause and marker of alienation in the poetry of Wilfred Owen and Siegfried Sassoon and in novels such as Hemingway's *The Sun Also Rises* (1926) and *A Farewell to Arms* (1929), Fitzgerald's *The Great Gatsby*, and Faulkner's *Soldiers' Pay* (1926). Wharton, Cather, Glasgow, Mary Borden, and other women who wrote about the war from a non-combatant perspective were often ignored or disparaged, and thus both the validity of their representations of war and the connection to modernism that such representations might bring were denied. Wharton wrote about the war in short stories, novels, travel literature, and *The Book of the Homeless* (1916), a collaborative project to raise money for war charities. Although generally not regarded as a modernist work, her novel *A Son at the Front* experiments with point of view and registers a war wound in the main character's loss of his son; the son dies in the war near the end of the novel, but his father registers his loss much earlier in the disconnection he feels from his son's inner life. Only in the last decades of the twentieth century have the previously mentioned women writers received recognition for their representations of war and acknowledgment of a different kind of war trauma, a psychological response to the carnage and to the perceived damage to civilization that these writers experienced.

As part of their insistence on truth and true experience, modernist writers often repudiated consumerism and commercialism, which were associated with artificiality, superficiality, and femininity.[4] The 1920s saw the rise of a full-blown consumer culture, and this decade was the first golden age of advertising, notably satirized in *The Great Gatsby*. Many modernists believed that mass culture was for the everyday reader, particularly for the increasing number of women with leisure and funds to purchase books.[5] Wharton, who had been a best-selling author since the publication of *The House of Mirth* in 1905 and whose novels frequently appeared first as serial installments in popular women's magazines such as *Scribner's*, *Century*, and *McClure's* and many of which were made into films, was thus situated inside the very literary marketplace that came to signify the stodgy, conventional, and middlebrow – a literature seen as feminized and lacking in rigor compared to the vigorous and difficult works produced by Eliot, Joyce, Woolf, Pound, and others. Ironically, Wharton had worked hard to be considered not only a successful but also a professional writer, and she benefited from shrewd bargains with her publishers that she often negotiated herself. Still, she was not above satirizing the culture that supported her. As early as 1904, with the publication of the short-story collection *The Descent of Man*, she mocked the ignorance of the reading public: in the title story a science professor publishes a pseudo-scientific book and is horrified when readers love it; in "Expiation," a woman writes what she believes to be a shocking novel, only to find her audience not at all shocked, and she asks her uncle, a bishop, to denounce the book to raise its sales. Wharton later offered incisive portrayals of the damage of consumerism in *The Custom of the Country*'s Undine Spragg (1913), a voracious purchaser of clothes and jewelry who learns about the society she wishes to join through magazine articles, and *Twilight Sleep*'s Pauline Manford

(1927), a mother who seeks emotional satisfaction from massages, mani-
cures, and spiritual "cures."

The growth of feminist literary criticism in the 1980s brought about a
reassessment of both modernism and women writers, including Wharton.
In particular, Sandra Gilbert and Susan Gubar's *No Man's Land* trilogy
investigates not only neglected women writers, but also how those writers came to be overlooked and what the implications of their inclusion
in modernism and the literary canon might be.[6] Critics recognized that
much of modernist thinking figured woman as the "Other" which defined
modernism itself.[7] Reexamining the role of women in modern literature
not only demanded a reconsideration of women's lives and stories but also
expanded the canon of modern literature. Kate Chopin's *The Awakening*
(1899), for example, became regarded not only as a realist tale of a woman's constricted life in New Orleans but also as a modernist story of a
woman's rejection of a patriarchal system that denies her desire. This shift
in critical thinking also sparked a reassessment of women in modern literature written by men, such as Joyce's Molly Bloom, and Hemingway's
Brett Ashley and Catherine Barkley. By telling women's stories with blunt
honesty – by revealing their passions in *The Reef* and *Summer* (1917), the
hypocrisies that limit their imagination in *The House of Mirth* and *The Age
of Innocence*, and the forces that hold them hostage to patriarchal power
structures in *Bunner Sisters* (1916), *The Old Maid* (1924), and *The Mother's
Recompense* – Wharton exposed the challenges of modern life for women.

Further, modern writers believed that the expression of the human
experience required the representation of human sexuality and desire.
Joyce's *Ulysses* (1922), which Wharton found to be a "turgid welter of por-
nography (the rudest schoolboy kind)" (*Letters* 461), and D. H. Lawrence's
Lady Chatterley's Lover (1928) may be the most well-known examples, but
representations of sexual desire abound in modernist literature. This literature also allowed for representations of previously unspoken desires,
such as Nora Flood's lesbian desire for Robin Vote in Djuna Barnes'
Nightwood (1936), which also portrays an aging transvestite. Wharton's
published representations of sexual desire are less explicit but no less compelling and groundbreaking. Biographers conclude that Wharton's marriage to Teddy Wharton was largely devoid of sexual desire and may never
have been consummated, but Wharton's affair with Morton Fullerton,
beginning in 1907, apparently awakened her sexual passions, an awareness
that permeates her subsequent works. *The Reef* opens with a sexual affair
between George Darrow and Sophy Viner and then follows Anna Leath's
bewildered attempt to comprehend such an affair even as she struggles

with her own desire for Darrow. In *Summer*, Wharton created one of American literature's earliest portrayals of a young woman's awakening to sexual desire; Charity Royall not only acts on that desire, but also accepts responsibility for its resulting pregnancy.

The rise of modernism corresponded to the formalization of anthropology, which was established in academic institutions in the late nineteenth and early twentieth centuries. The methods of anthropology became useful for modern writers, including Zora Neale Hurston, who traveled in the southern United States to collect African-American folktales, which she later published and also used in her novels *Jonah's Gourd Vine* (1934) and *Their Eyes Were Watching God* (1937). Modernism's interest in the "exotic" or the primitive, seen in the visual art of Paul Gaugin and in Eugene O'Neill's play *The Emperor Jones* (1920), posed disturbing questions about the uses of the racial "other" for Western civilization. In the United States, the cohesion of anthropology was connected to the study of Native Americans; this line of thinking considered Native Americans as primitives in the modern world, representatives of an unevolved or partially evolved humanity. Wharton, who read widely in the field of anthropology, seems to have followed this line of thinking in her New England narratives, *Ethan Frome* and *Summer*,[8] and in Ralph Marvell's perception of his family as "Aborigines" to be "exhibited at ethnological shows" (*CC* 73–74). Franz Boas, in contrast, viewed humanity as divided into cultures that were simply different rather than at different stages on a scale of progress and argued against evolutionary and eugenic attitudes toward racial categories. Dale M. Bauer articulates the contradictions in Wharton's thinking about race, pointing out that Wharton follows Boas in her representation of Old New York as "tribal" in *The Age of Innocence*, yet persisted in believing stereotypes about African Americans as uncivilized.[9]

Questions about race cannot be separated from modernism. During the early decades of the twentieth century, African-American writers engaged in debates about literature, culture, and nationality. How to represent African-American life, what aspects to represent, what audiences to address: these questions engaged such authors as Hurston, Claude McKay, Langston Hughes, Nella Larsen, Jessie Redmon Fauset, and Jean Toomer. Collectively they offered a wide array of representations of African-American life and culture, some of which were brought together by Alain Locke in his anthology *The New Negro* (1925). These artists were not a unified voice: Hughes and Hurston, for example, broke on the question of whether to portray both the negative as well as positive sides of African-American characters, Hurston choosing to create rounded characters that might give white readers ammunition for their preconceived ideas about African Americans. In *Cane* (1923), Toomer offered a range of representations of African-American experiences, from a brutal lynching in rural Georgia to issues of courtship in Washington, DC. Larsen and Fauset chose to explore the lives of middle-class African-American women. Wharton seems to have been unaware of this body of literature, taking her impressions of African Americans mainly from Carl Van Vechten's *Nigger Heaven* (1926). One wonders what she might have thought of Larsen's *Quicksand* (1928) and *Passing* (1929), stories of oppressed women that speak to many of the issues that also concerned Wharton. She also had a disturbing tendency to ignore the possibilities of African-American characters in her own works; they appear rarely and usually as servants. In *Twilight Sleep*, she portrays them by evoking disturbing stereotypes. In *Edith Wharton and the Politics of Race*, Jennie Kassanoff argues that Wharton's conservatism is a problem that her more liberal critics must confront, for Wharton feared the consequences of immigration and mass culture. Further, Kassanoff suggests that these anxieties are at the root of her objection to modernism.[10]

Although Wharton disliked the work of quite a few modernist writers, singling out Joyce, Lawrence, Stein, Woolf, and Faulkner for criticism, she responded positively to that of others. She delighted in Anita Loos' *Gentlemen Prefer Blondes* (1925), recommending it to several friends, and she wrote to Fitzgerald that she (mostly) liked *The Great Gatsby*. She admired Joseph Conrad, Yeats, and Colette, and later in life she became neighbors and friends with Aldous Huxley. Although she preferred traditional European visual art, she enjoyed the work of Cézanne and Gauguin, and she admired other forms of modernism, such as Stravinsky's *Rite of Spring* and the performances of Isadora Duncan (see Lee 615–16; 620). Wharton's response to different modern forms, artists, and writers may be considered a case study for defining the sprawling category that is today's idea of modernism. After all, must one like all modern art to like, or to be, a modernist?

At the end of his essay on "Modern American Literary Criticism," Douglas Mao wonders why critics persist in clinging to a belief in a modernism that can be defined even while those critics redefine and expand the modernist canon; he posits an answer to his own question in the "capacity for criticism" that modernism itself creates.[11] Wharton, perhaps, might have conceded the point. In *The Writing of Fiction*, she admits that her own attempts to theorize writing are necessarily limited:

> Is all seeking vain, then? Is it useless to try for a clear view of the meaning and method of one's art? Surely not. If no art can be quite pent-up in the rules deduced from it, neither can it fully realize itself unless those who practise it attempt to take its measure and reason out its processes. It is true that the gist of the matter always escapes, since it nests, the elusive bright-winged thing, in that mysterious fourth-dimensional world which is the artist's inmost sanctuary and on the threshold of which enquiry perforce must halt; but though that world is inaccessible, the creations emanating from it reveal something of its laws and processes. (*WF* 118–19)

Wharton may not have considered herself a modernist, nor may her fellow writers of the early twentieth century have done so. However, their attempts to exclude her, and her desire to exclude herself, reveal much about what modernism is, its politics and its prejudices, and critics' more recent insistence on including her does the same. And her "creations" reveal her to be more invested in modernist aesthetics and concerns than perhaps she saw.

NOTES

1. T. S. Eliot, "Tradition and the Individual Talent," reprinted in *Selected Essays 1917–1932* (London: Faber and Faber, 1932), 13–22; 19–20.
2. A. Kazin, *On Native Grounds: An Interpretation of Modern American Prose Literature* (New York: Renal & Hitchcock, 1942), viii. Subsequent references to this work are included in the text.
3. See S. Kim, "Edith Wharton and Epiphany," *Journal of Modern Literature*, 29, (2006), 150–75.
4. See T. Strychacz, *Modernism, Mass Culture, and Professionalism* (New York: Cambridge University Press, 1993).
5. Recently some scholars have demonstrated that many modernists and their publishers were in fact quite engaged in marketing their books to a broad audience. See K. J. H. Dettmar and S. Watt (eds.), *Marketing Modernisms: Self-Promotion, Canonization, and Reading* (Ann Arbor: University of Michigan Press, 1996) and C. Turner, *Marketing Modernism Between the Two World Wars* (Amherst: University of Massachusetts Press, 2003).
6. See also L. Wagner-Martin, "Women Authors and the Roots of American Modernism" in R. P. Lamb and G. R. Thompson (eds.), *A Companion to American Fiction, 1865–1914* (Oxford: Blackwell Publishing, 2005), 140–48, and C. Waid and C. Colquitt, "Toward a Modernist Aesthetic: The Literary Legacy of Edith Wharton" in the same volume, 536–56.
7. See, for example, A. Huyssen, "Mass Culture as Woman: Modernism's Other" in *After the Great Divide: Modernism, Mass Culture, Postmodernism* (Bloomington: Indiana University Press, 1986), 44–62.

8. See P. A. Stevenson, "Ethan Frome and Charity Royall: Edith Wharton's Noble Savages," *Women's Studies*, 32 (2003), 411–29.

9. D. M. Bauer, *Edith Wharton's Brave New Politics* (Madison: University of Wisconsin Press, 1994), 178.

10. J. Kassanoff, *Edith Wharton and the Politics of Race* (Cambridge: Cambridge University Press, 2004), 33.

11. D. Mao, "Modern American Literary Criticism" in W. Kalaidjian (ed.), *The Cambridge Companion to American Modernism* (Cambridge: Cambridge University Press, 2005), 305.

Further Reading

EDITH WHARTON: CONTEXTUAL REVISIONS

Goodman, S., *Republic of Words: The Atlantic Monthly and Its Writers, 1857–1925* (Hanover and London: University Press of New England, 2011).

Haytock, J., *Edith Wharton and the Conversations of Literary Modernism* (New York: Palgrave Macmillan, 2008).

Kassanoff, J., *Edith Wharton and the Politics of Race* (Cambridge: Cambridge University Press, 2004).

Orlando, E. J., *Edith Wharton and the Visual Arts* (Tuscaloosa: University of Alabama Press, 2007).

Rattray, L. (ed.), *The Unpublished Writings of Edith Wharton*, 2 vols. (London: Pickering and Chatto, 2009).

Totten, G. (ed.), *Memorial Boxes and Guarded Interiors: Edith Wharton and Material Culture* (Tuscaloosa: University of Alabama Press, 2007).

Wagner-Martin, L., "Women Authors and the Roots of American Modernism" in R. P. Lamb and G. R. Thompson (eds.), *A Companion to American Fiction,1865–1914* (Oxford: Blackwell Publishing, 2005), 140–48.

BIOGRAPHY

Broughton, T. L. and L. R. Anderson (eds.), *Women's Lives/Women's Times: New Essays on Auto/Biography* (Albany: SUNY Press, 1997).

Goodman, S., *Edith Wharton's Women: Friends and Rivals* (Hanover, NH: University Press of New England, 1990).

Edith Wharton's Inner Circle (Austin, TX: University of Texas Press, 1994).

Heilbrun, C. G., *Writing a Woman's Life* (New York: Ballantine Books, 1989).

Marcus, L., *Auto/biographical Discourses: Criticism, Theory, Practice* (Manchester: Manchester University Press, 1994).

Preston, C., *Edith Wharton's Social Register* (New York: St. Martin's, 2000).

Wagner-Martin, L., *Telling Women's Lives: The New Biography* (New Brunswick, NJ: Rutgers University Press, 1994).

Williams, D. L., *Not in Sisterhood: Edith Wharton, Willa Cather, Zona Gale, and the Politics of Female Authorship* (New York: Palgrave, 2001).

COMPOSITION AND PUBLICATION

Barbour, J. and T. Quirk (eds.), *Biographies of Books: The Compositional Histories of Notable American Writings* (Columbia: University of Missouri Press, 1996).

Charvat, W., *The Profession of Authorship in America* (New York: Columbia University Press, 1992).

Davidson, C. N., *Reading in America: Literature and Social History* (Baltimore, MA: The John Hopkins University Press, 1989).

Garrison, S. (ed.), *Edith Wharton: A Descriptive Bibliography* (Pittsburgh, PA: University of Pittsburgh Press, 1990).

Vita-Finzi, P., *Edith Wharton and the Art of Fiction* (New York: St. Martin's, 1990).

Wegener, F., *Edith Wharton: The Uncollected Critical Writings* (Princeton, NJ: Princeton University Press, 1996).

Williams, D. L., *Not in Sisterhood: Edith Wharton, Willa Cather, Zona Gale, and the Politics of Female Authorship* (New York: Palgrave, 2001).

PORTRAITS OF WHARTON

Auchincloss, L., *Edith Wharton: A Woman in Her Time* (New York: Viking Press, 1971).

Bell, S. G. and M. Yalom (eds.), *Revealing Lives: Autobiography, Biography, and Gender* (Albany: SUNY Press, 1990).

Benstock, S., *No Gifts from Chance: A Biography of Edith Wharton* (New York: Charles Scribner's Sons, 1994).

Dwight, E., *Edith Wharton: An Extraordinary Life* (New York: Harry N. Abrams, 1994).

Lee, H., *Edith Wharton* (New York: Alfred Knopf, 2007).

Lewis, R. W. B., *Edith Wharton: A Biography* (New York: Harper & Row, 1975).

Proby, E. *Sexing the Self: Gendered Positions in Cultural Studies* (London and New York: Routledge, 1993).

Wolff, C. G., *A Feast of Words: The Triumph of Edith Wharton* (New York: Oxford University Press, 1977).

CONTEMPORARY REVIEWS 1877–1938

Golden, C. J., *Images of the Woman Reader in Victorian British and American Fiction* (Gainesville, FL: University Press of Florida, 2003).

Kaestle, C. et al, *Literacy in the United States: Readers and Reading since 1880* (New Haven: Yale University Press, 1991).

Killoran, H., *The Critical Reception of Edith Wharton* (Rochester, NY: Camden House, 2001).

Lewis, R. W. B. and N. Lewis (eds.), *The Letters of Edith Wharton* (New York: Charles Scribner's Sons, 1988).

Ramsden, G., *Edith Wharton's Library* (Settrington: Stone Trough Books, 1999).

Totten, G. (ed.), *Memorial Boxes and Guarded Interiors: Edith Wharton and Material Culture* (Tuscaloosa: University of Alabama Press, 2007).

Tuttleton, J. W., K. O. Lauer, and M. P. Murray (eds.), *Edith Wharton: The Contemporary Reviews* (Cambridge: Cambridge University Press, 1992).

Wharton, E., *The Writing of Fiction* (New York: Charles Scribner's Sons, 1925).

OBITUARIES

Colquitt, C., "Bibliographic Essay: Visions and Revisions of Edith Wharton" in C. J. Singley (ed.), *A Historical Guide to Edith Wharton* (Oxford: Oxford University Press, 2003), 248–80.

Fowler, B., *The Obituary as Collective Memory* (New York: Routledge, 2007).

Lauer, K. O. and M. P. Murray (eds.), *Edith Wharton: An Annotated Secondary Bibliography* (New York: Garland, 1990).

Starck, N., *Life after Death: The Art of the Obituary* (Victoria: Melbourne University Press, 2006).

Stone, D., "Edith Wharton Seen in Full," *Sewanee Review*, 116.1 (2008), 149–55.

Tuttleton, J. W., K. O. Lauer, and M. P. Murray (eds.), *Edith Wharton: The Contemporary Reviews* (Cambridge: Cambridge University Press, 1992).

Vidal, G., "Of Writers and Class: In Praise of Edith Wharton," *The Atlantic Monthly*, 241 (February 1978), 64–67.

EARLY CRITICAL RESPONSES

Bell, M., "Edith Wharton and Henry James: The Literary Relation," *PMLA*, 74 (1959), 619–37.

"Lady into Author," *American Quarterly*, 9 (1957), 295–315.

Brown, E. K., *Edith Wharton: Étude Critique* (Paris: E. Droz, 1935).

Lubbock, P., *Portrait of Edith Wharton* (New York: Appleton-Century-Crofts, 1947).

Lyde, M. J., *Edith Wharton: Convention and Morality in the Work of a Novelist* (Norman: University of Oklahoma Press, 1959).

Nevius, B., *Edith Wharton: A Study of Her Fiction* (Berkeley: University of California Press, 1953).

Ozick, C., "Justice (Again) to Edith Wharton," *Commentary* (October 1976), 48–57.

Wilson, E., "Justice to Edith Wharton," *New Republic*, 95 (29 June 1938), 209–13.

MODERN CRITICAL RECEPTIONS

Ammons, E., *Edith Wharton's Argument with America* (Athens: University of Georgia Press, 1980).

Bell, M. (ed.), *The Cambridge Companion to Edith Wharton* (Cambridge: Cambridge University Press, 1995).

Colquitt, C., S. Goodman, and C. Waid (eds.), *A Forward Glance: New Essays on Edith Wharton* (Newark: University of Delaware Press, 1999).

Haytock, J., *Edith Wharton and the Conversations of Literary Modernism* (New York: Palgrave Macmillan, 2008).

Kassanoff, J., *Edith Wharton and the Politics of Race* (Cambridge: Cambridge University Press, 2004).

Knights, P., *The Cambridge Introduction to Edith Wharton* (Cambridge: Cambridge University Press, 2009).

Rattray, L. (ed.), *Edith Wharton's* The Custom of the Country: *A Reassessment* (London: Pickering & Chatto, 2010).

WHARTON AND HER EDITORS

Charvat, W., *The Profession of Authorship in America* (New York: Columbia University Press, 1992).

Coultrap-McQuin, S., *Doing Literary Business: American Women Writers in the 19th Century* (Chapel Hill: University of North Carolina Press, 1990).

Tebbel, J., *Between Covers: The Rise and Transformation of Book Publishing in America* (New York: Oxford University Press, 1987).

Towheed, S. (ed.), *The Correspondence of Edith Wharton and Macmillan, 1901– 1930* (New York: Palgrave Macmillan, 2007).

West III, J. L. W., *American Authors and the Literary Marketplace since 1900* (Philadelphia: University of Pennsylvania Press, 1988).

Williams, S. S., "Authors and Literary Authorship" in S. Casper, J. Groves, S. W. Nissenbaum, and M. Winship (eds.), *History of the Book in America, Vol III: The Industrial Book, 1840–1880* (Chapel Hill: University of North Carolina Press, 2007), 90–116.

Wolfe, G. R., *The House of Appleton* (Metuchen, NJ: Scarecrow Press, 1981).

SELLING WHARTON

Bell, M., "Lady into Author: Edith Wharton and the House of Scribner," *American Quarterly*, 9 (1957), 295–315.

Glass, L., *Authors Inc.: Literary Celebrity in the Modern United States, 1880–1980* (New York: New York University Press, 2004).

Holt, H., "The Commercialization of Literature," *The Atlantic Monthly*, 96 (1905), 577–600.

Howells, W. D., "The Man of Letters as a Man of Business," *Scribner's Magazine*, 14 (1893), 429–45.

Madison, C., *Irving to Irving: Author-Publisher Relations 1800–1974* (New York: R. R. Bowker Company, 1974).

Totten, G. (ed.), *Memorial Boxes and Guarded Interiors: Edith Wharton and Material Culture* (Tuscaloosa: University of Alabama Press, 2007).

West III, J. L. W., *American Authors and the Literary Marketplace since 1900* (Philadelphia: University of Pennsylvania Press, 1988).

SERIALIZATION

Altick, R. D., *The English Common Reader: A Social History of the Mass Reading Public 1800–1900*, 2nd ed. (Columbus: Ohio State University Press, 1998).

Lund, M., *America's Continuing Story: An Introduction to Serial Fiction, 1850–1900* (Detroit, MI: Wayne State University Press, 1993).

McDonald, P. D., *British Literary Culture and Publishing Practice, 1880–1914* (Cambridge: Cambridge University Press, 1997).

Okker, P., *Social Stories: The Magazine Novel in Nineteenth-Century America* (Charlottesville: University of Virginia Press, 2003).

Thornton, E., "Selling Edith Wharton: Illustration, Advertising, and Pictorial Review, 1924–1925," *Arizona Quarterly*, 57.3 (2001), 29–59.

Turner, M. W., "'Telling of my weekly doings': The Material Culture of the Victorian Novel" in F. O'Gorman (ed.), *A Concise Companion to the Victorian Novel* (Oxford: Blackwell, 2005), 113–33.

SHORT STORY MARKETS

Levy, A., *The Culture and Commerce of the American Short Story* (Cambridge: Cambridge University Press, 1993).

Matthews, B., *The Philosophy of the Short Story* (New York: Longmans, Green & Co., 1901).

McMullen, B. S., "'Don't Cry – It Ain't that Kind of a Story': Wharton's Business of Fiction, 1908–1912" in L. Rattray (ed.), *Edith Wharton's* The Custom of the Country: *A Reassessment* (London: Pickering and Chatto, 2010), 43–58.

Mott, F. L., *A History of American Magazines, Vol. III, 1865–1885; Vol. IV, 1885–1905* (Cambridge, MA: Harvard University Press, 1938, 1957).

Peterson, T., *Magazines in the Twentieth Century* (Urbana: University of Illinois Press, 1964).

Showalter, E. (ed.), *Scribbling Women: Short Stories by 19th Century American Women* (New Brunswick, NJ: Rutgers University Press, 1997).

STAGE ADAPTATIONS OF WHARTON'S FICTION

Akins, Z., *The Old Maid: Dramatized from the Novel by Edith Wharton* (New York: Appleton-Century, 1935).

Davis, O. and D. Davis, *Ethan Frome: A Dramatization of Edith Wharton's Novel* (New York: Scribner's, 1936).

McDowell, M. B., "Edith Wharton's 'The Old Maid': Novella/Play/Film," *College Literature*, 14:3 (Fall 1987), 246–62.

Rattray, L. (ed.), *The Unpublished Writings of Edith Wharton, Vol. 1: Plays* (London: Pickering & Chatto, 2009).

Wharton, E. and C. Fitch, *The House of Mirth: The Play of the Novel*, ed. G. Loney. (Toronto: Associated University Presses, 1981).

Wiggins, C. M., "Edith Wharton and the Theatre," Diss. Case Western Reserve University, 1996.

WHARTON'S WRITINGS ON SCREEN

Boswell, P. A., *Edith Wharton on Film* (Carbondale, IL: Southern Illinois University Press, 2007).

Cahir, L. C. "Wharton and the Age of Film" in C. J. Singley (ed.), *A Historical Guide to Edith Wharton* (Oxford: Oxford University Press, 2003), 211–28.

Marshall, S., "Edith Wharton on Film and Television: A History and Filmography," *Edith Wharton Review*, 13.2 (April 1996), 15–26.

Mintz, S. and R. Roberts, *Hollywood's America: Twentieth-Century America Through Film* (New York: Brandywine Press, 2001).

Musser, C., *The Emergence of Cinema: The American Screen to 1907* (New York: Charles Scribner's Sons, 1990).

Scorsese, M. and J. Cocks, *The Age of Innocence, A Portrait of the Film*, ed. R. Standefer. (New York: Newmarket Press, 1993).

VISUAL ARTS

Dwight, E., "Wharton and Art" in C. J. Singley (ed.), *A Historical Guide to Edith Wharton* (Oxford: Oxford University Press, 2003), 181–210.

Holloway, D. and J. Beck (eds.), *American Visual Cultures* (London: Continuum, 2005).

Johnston, P. (ed.), *Seeing High and Low: Representing Social Conflict in American Visual Culture* (Berkeley: University of California Press, 2006).

Killoran, H., *Edith Wharton: Art and Allusion* (Tuscaloosa: University of Alabama Press, 1996).

Lynes, R., *The Lively Audience: A Social History of the Visual and Performing Arts in America, 1890–1950* (New York: Harper & Row, 1985).

Orlando, E. J., *Edith Wharton and the Visual Arts* (Tuscaloosa: University of Alabama Press, 2007).

Zorzi, R. M., "Tiepolo, Henry James, and Edith Wharton," *Metropolitan Museum Journal*, 33 (1998), 211–29.

ARCHITECTURE

Benert, A., *The Architectural Imagination of Edith Wharton: Gender Class and Power in the Progressive Era* (Madison, NJ: Fairleigh Dickinson University Press, 2007).

Denenberg, T. A., *Wallace Nutting and the Invention of Old America* (New Haven, CT: Yale University Press, 2003).

Edwards, S. and J. Charley (eds.), *Writing the Modern City: Literature, Architecture, Modernity* (London: Routledge, 2011).

Lowe, D. G., *Stanford White's New York* (New York: Watson-Guptill Publications, 1999).

Sullivan, L. H., *The Autobiography of an Idea* (New York: American Institute of Architects, 1924).

Wilson, W. H., *The City Beautiful Movement* (Baltimore, MA: The Johns Hopkins University Press, 1989).

Wiseman, C., *Twentieth Century American Architecture: The Buildings and their Makers* (New York: W. W. Norton & Company, 2000).

INTERIOR AND GARDEN DESIGN

Calloway, S. and L. F. Orr (eds.), *The Cult of Beauty: The Aesthetic Movement 1860–1900* (London: V & A Publishing, 2011).

Craig, T., *Edith Wharton: A House Full of Rooms: Architecture, Interiors and Gardens* (New York: The Monacelli Press, 1996).

Friedman, A. T., *Woman and the Making of the Modern House: A Social and Architectural History* (New York: Abrams, 1998).

Hellman, C., *Domesticity and Design in American Women's Lives and Literature: Stowe, Alcott, Cather, and Wharton Writing Home* (New York: Routledge, 2011).

Imbert, D., *The Modernist Garden in France* (New Haven, CT: Yale University Press, 1993).

Livingstone, K. and L. Parry (eds.), *International Arts and Crafts* (London: V & A Publishing, 2005).

Massey, A., *Interior Design Since 1900*, 3rd ed. (London: Thames & Hudson, 2008).

Waymark, J., *Modern Garden Design: Innovation since 1900* (London: Thames & Hudson, 2003).

IMAGES OF WHARTON

Balsan, C. V., *The Glitter and the Gold* (London: Heinemann, 1953).

Cunningham, P., *Reforming Women's Fashion, 1850–1920: Politics, Health, and Art* (Kent, OH: Kent State University Press, 2003).

Dwight, E., *Edith Wharton: An Extraordinary Life* (New York: Harry N. Abrams, 1994).

Groseclose, B. and J. Wierich (eds.), *Internationalizing the History of American Art: Views* (University Park, PA: Pennsylvania State University Press, 2009).

Halsey, F. W. (ed.), *Women Authors of Our Day in Their Homes: Personal Descriptions and Interviews* (New York: James Pott & Co., 1903).

Joslin, K., *Edith Wharton and the Making of Fashion* (Hanover and London: University Press of New England, 2009).

Showalter, E., *A Jury of Her Peers: American Women Writers from Anne Bradstreet to Annie Proulx* (New York: Knopf, 2009).

Steele, V., *Paris Fashion: A Cultural History* (New York: Oxford University Press, 1985).

THE MARRIAGE MARKET

Basch, N., *Framing American Divorce: From the Revolutionary Generation to the Victorians* (Berkeley and Los Angeles: University of California Press, 1999).

Dimock, W. C., "Debasing Exchange: Edith Wharton's *The House of Mirth*," *PMLA: Publications of the Modern Language Association of America*, 100.5 (1985): 783–92.

Hartog, H., *Man and Wife in America: A History* (Cambridge, MA and London: Harvard University Press, 2000).

Kingsland, F., *Etiquette for All Occasions* (New York: Doubleday, Page, and Company, 1901).

Knights, P., *The Cambridge Introduction to Edith Wharton* (Cambridge: Cambridge University Press, 2009)

Montgomery, M. E., *"Gilded Prostitution": Status, Money, and Transatlantic Marriages, 1870–1914* (New York and London: Routledge, 1989).

Rattray, L. (ed.), *Edith Wharton's* The Custom of the Country: *A Reassessment* (London: Pickering and Chatto, 2010).

Riley, G., *Divorce: An American Tradition* (Oxford: Oxford University Press, 1991).

Rogers, A. A., *Why American Marriages Fail and Other Papers* (Boston and New York: Houghton, 1909).

Wershoven, C. J., *The Female Intruder in the Novels of Edith Wharton* (East Brunswick, NJ: Associated University Presses, 1982).

LEISURED LIVES

Beckert, S. and J. B. Rosenbaum, *The American Bourgeoisie: Distinction and Identity in the Nineteenth Century* (New York: Palgrave Macmillan, 2010).

Elliott, M. H., *This Was My Newport* (Cambridge, MA: The Mythology Company, 1944).

Erenberg, L. A., *Steppin' Out: New York Nightlife and the Transformation of American Culture, 1890–1930* (University of Chicago Press, 1981).

Homberger, E. J., *Mrs. Astor's New York: Money and Social Power in a Gilded Age* (New Haven, CT: Yale University Press, 2004).

Kasson, J. F., *Rudeness and Civility: Manners in Nineteenth-Century America* (New York: Hill and Wang, 1990).

Montgomery, M. E., *Displaying Women: Spectacles of Leisure in Edith Wharton's New York* (New York: Routledge, 1998).

Van Rensselaer, M. K., *The Social Ladder* (London: Nash and Grayson, 1925).

WHARTON AND GENDER

Ammons, E., *Edith Wharton's Argument with America* (Athens: University of Georgia Press, 1980).

Chambers, D. L., *Feminist Readings of Edith Wharton, From Silence to Speech* (New York: Palgrave Macmillan, 2009).

Dyman, J., *Lurking Feminism: The Ghost Stories of Edith Wharton* (New York: Peter Lang, 1996).

Goodman, S., *Edith Wharton's Women: Friends and Rivals* (Hanover, NH: University Press of New England, 1990).

Haytock, J., *Edith Wharton and the Conversations of Literary Modernism* (New York: Palgrave Macmillan, 2008).

Holbrook, D., *Edith Wharton and the Unsatisfactory Man* (London: Vision Press, 1991).

Nettels, E., *Language and Gender in American Fiction: Howells, James, Wharton and Cather* (Charlottesville, VA: University Press of Virginia, 1997).

Rattray, L. (ed.), *The Unpublished Writings of Edith Wharton*, 2 vols. (London: Pickering and Chatto, 2009).

Wagner-Martin, L. and C. N. Davidson, *The Oxford Book of Women's Writing in the United States* (New York: Oxford University Press, 1995).

Waid, C., *Edith Wharton's Letters from the Underworld: Fictions of Women and Writing* (Chapel Hill: University of North Carolina Press, 1991).

RACE AND IMPERIALISM

Ammons, E., "Edith Wharton and the Issue of Race" in M. Bell (ed.), *The Cambridge Companion to Edith Wharton* (Cambridge: Cambridge University Press, 1995), 68–86.

Foner, E. (ed.), *The Anti-Imperialist Reader: A Documentary History of Anti-Imperialism in the United States, Vol. 2: The Literary Anti-Imperialists* (New York: Holmes and Meier Publishers, 1986).

Kaplan, A. and D. Pease (eds.), *Cultures of United States Imperialism* (Durham: Duke University Press, 1993).

Kassanoff, J., *Edith Wharton and the Politics of Race* (Cambridge: Cambridge University Press, 2004).

Said, E., *Orientalism* (New York: Vintage Books, 1979).

Sundquist, E. J., *To Wake the Nations: Race in the Making of American Literature* (Cambridge, MA: Harvard University Press, 1993).

Wonham, H. B., "Edith Wharton's Flamboyant Copy," *Playing the Races: Ethnic Caricature and American Literary Realism* (Oxford: Oxford University Press, 2004), 127–91.

SOCIAL TRANSITIONS

Cashman, S. D., *America in the Gilded Age: From the Death of Lincoln to the Rise of Theodore Roosevelt*, 3rd ed. (New York: New York University Press, 1993).

Chambers, J. W., *The Tyranny of Change: America in the Progressive Era, 1900–1917*, ed. V. P. Carosso (New York: St. Martin's Press, 1980).

Cohen, N., *The Reconstruction of American Liberalism, 1865–1914* (Chapel Hill: University of North Carolina Press, 2002).

Edwards, R., *New Spirits: Americans in the Gilded Age, 1865–1905* (New York: Oxford University Press, 2006).

Frankel, N. and N. S. Dye, *Gender, Class, Race, and Reform in the Progressive Era* (Lexington: University Press of Kentucky, 1991).

Goodman, S., "*The Custom of the Country:* Edith Wharton's Conversation with the *Atlantic Monthly*" in L. Rattray (ed.), *Edith Wharton's* The Custom of the Country: *A Reassessment* (London: Pickering and Chatto, 2010), 15–29.

Gould, L. L., *The Progressive Era* (Syracuse: Syracuse University Press, 1974).

Marcus, R. D., *Grand Old Party: Political Structure in the Gilded Age, 1880–1896* (New York: Oxford University Press, 1971).

WHARTON AND FRANCE

Bellringer, A. W., "Edith Wharton's Use of France," *The Yearbook of English Studies*, 15, (1985), 109–24.

Berman, J., *Modernist Fiction, Cosmopolitanism, and the Politics of Community* (Cambridge: Cambridge University Press, 2001).

Blazek, W., "French Lessons: Edith Wharton's War Propaganda," *Revue Française d'Études Américaines*, 115 (March 2008), 10–22.

Green, N. L., "The Comparative Gaze: Travelers in France before the Era of Mass Tourism," *French Historical Studies*, 25.3 (Summer 2002), 423–40.

Joslin, K. and A. Price (eds.), *Wretched Exotic: Essays on Edith Wharton in Europe* (New York: Peter Lang, 1993).

Lesage, C., *Edith Wharton en France* (Paris: Editions des Equateurs, 2011).

Nowlin, M., "Edith Wharton's Higher Provincialism: *French Ways* for Americans and the Ends of *The Age of Innocence*," *Journal of American Studies*, 38.1 (2004), 89–108.

Singley, C. J., "Race, Culture, Nation: Edith Wharton and Ernest Renan," *Twentieth Century Literature*, 49.1 (Spring 2003), 32–45.

Wegener, F., "'Rabid Imperialist': Edith Wharton and the Obligations of Empire in Modern American Fiction," *American Literature*, 72.4 (December 2000), 783–812.

Wright, S. B., *Edith Wharton's Travel Writing: The Making of a Connoisseur* (New York: St. Martin's Press, 1997).

WHARTON AND ITALY

Balestra, G., "'Edith Wharton's Italian Tale': Language Exercise and Social Discourse" in C. Colquitt, S. Goodman, C. Waid (eds.), *A Forward Glance: New Essays on Edith Wharton* (Newark, DE: University of Delaware Press, 1999), 207–20.

Buzard, J., *The Beaten Track: European Tourism, Literature, and the Ways to 'Culture'* (New York: Oxford University Press, 1993).

Joslin, K. and A. Price (eds.), *Wretched Exotic: Essays on Edith Wharton in Europe* (New York: Peter Lang, 1993).

Mulvey, C., *Anglo-American Landscapes: A Study of Nineteenth-Century Anglo-American Travel Literature* (New York: Cambridge University Press, 1983).

Peel, R., *Apart from Modernism: Edith Wharton, Politics and Fiction before World War I* (London: Associated University Presses, 2005).

Salenius, S. (ed.), *American Authors Reinventing Italy: The Writings of Exceptional Nineteenth Century Women* (Padovo: Il Prato, 2009).

Wright, N., *American Novelists in Italy: The Discoverers: Allston to James* (Philadelphia: University of Pennsylvania Press, 1965).

WHARTON AND WORLD WAR I

Fussell, P., *The Great War and Modern Memory* (London: Oxford University Press, 1975).

Higonnet, M., J. Jenson, S. Michel and M. C. Weitz (eds.), *Behind the Lines: Gender and the Two World Wars* (New Haven: Yale University Press, 1987).

Higonnet, M. (ed.), *Lines of Fire: Women Writers of World War I* (USA: Penguin Plume, 1999).

Keegan, J., *The First World War* (New York: Alfred Knopf, 1999).

Olin-Ammentorp, J., *Edith Wharton's Writings from the Great War* (Gainesville, FL: University Press of Florida, 2004).

Price, A., *The End of the Age of Innocence: Edith Wharton and the First World War* (New York: St. Martin's, 1996).

Sherry, V. (ed.), *The Cambridge Companion to the Literature of the First World War* (New York: Cambridge University Press, 2005).

Winter, J. M., *The Experience of World War I* (New York: Oxford University Press, 1989).

THE 1920s

Allen, F. L., *Only Yesterday: An Informal History of the 1920s* (New York: Harper & Row, 1931).

Benstock, S., *Women of the Left Bank: Paris, 1900–1940* (Austin: University of Texas Press, 1986).

Collas, P. and E. Villedary, *Edith Wharton's French Riviera*, trans. Susan Pickford (Italy: Flammarion, 2002).

Mellow, J. R., *Charmed Circle: Gertrude Stein & Company* (New York: Praeger, 1974).

Nash, R., *The Nervous Generation: American Thought, 1917–1930* (Chicago: Rand McNally, 1970).

Pound, E., *Make It New: Essays* (London: Faber and Faber, 1934).

Rothschild, D. (ed.), *Making It New: The Art and Style of Sara and Gerald Murphy* (Berkeley: University of California Press, 2007).

WHARTON AND THE GREAT DEPRESSION

Badger, A. J., *The New Deal: Depression Years, 1933–40* (Basingstoke: Palgrave Macmillan, 1989).

Garraty, J. A., *The Great Depression: An Inquiry into the Causes, Course, and Consequences of the Worldwide Depression of the Nineteen-Thirties, as Seen by Contemporaries and in the Light of History* (San Diego: Harcourt Brace Jovanovich, 1986).

Hapke, L., *Daughters of the Great Depression: Women, Work, and Fiction in the American 1930s* (Athens: University of Georgia Press, 1995).

McElvaine, R. S., *The Great Depression: America, 1929–1941* (New York: Times Books, 1961).

Pells, R., *Radical Visions and American Dreams: Culture and Social Thought in the Depression Years* (New York: Harper and Row, 1973).

Staub, M. E., *Voices of Persuasion: Politics of Representation in 1930s America* (Cambridge: Cambridge University Press, 1994).

Wilson, E., *The Thirties: From Notebooks and Diaries of the Period*, ed. L. Edel (New York: Farrar, Straus and Giroux, 1980).

LITERARY INFLUENCES

Bell, M., *Edith Wharton and Henry James: The Story of Their Friendship* (New York: G. Braziller, 1965).

Cassuto, L., C. V. Eby, and B. Reiss (eds.), *The Cambridge History of the American Novel* (Cambridge and New York: Cambridge University Press, 2011).

Goodman, S., *Edith Wharton's Inner Circle* (Austin: University of Texas Press, 1994).

Howe, I., "Introduction: The Achievement of Edith Wharton" in I. Howe (ed.), *Edith Wharton: A Collection of Critical Essays* (Englewood Cliffs, NJ: Prentice-Hall, 1962), 1–18.

Killoran, H., *Edith Wharton: Art and Allusion* (Tuscaloosa: University of Alabama Press, 1996).

Wegener, F., "'Enthusiasm Guided by Acumen': Edith Wharton as a Critical Writer," *Edith Wharton: The Uncollected Critical Writings* (Princeton, NJ: Princeton University Press, 1996), 3–52.

Wharton, E., *The Writing of Fiction* (New York: Charles Scribner's Sons, 1925).

WHARTON AND THE AMERICAN ROMANTICS

Bank, S., *American Romanticism: A Shape for Fiction* (New York: Putnam, 1969).

Cahir, L. C., *Solitude and Society in the Works of Herman Melville and Edith Wharton* (Westport, CT: Greenwood Press, 1999).

Gilmore, M. T., *American Romanticism and the Marketplace* (Chicago: University of Chicago Press, 1985).

Goodman, R. B., *American Philosophy and the Romantic Tradition* (New York: Cambridge University Press, 1990).

Hoffman, M. J., *The Subversive Vision: American Romanticism in Literature* (Port Washington, NY: Kennicat Press, 1972).

Hurley, J. A., *American Romanticism* (San Diego, CA: Greenhaven Press, 2000).

Shaffer-Koros, C., "Edgar Allan Poe and Edith Wharton: A Case of Mrs. Mowatt," *Edith Wharton Review*, 17 (2001), 12–16.

THE NOVEL OF MANNERS

Bentley, N., *The Ethnography of Manners: Hawthorne, James and Wharton* (New York: Cambridge University Press, 1995).

Claridge, L., *Emily Post: Daughter of the Gilded Age, Mistress of American Manners* (New York: Random House, 2008).

Goodman, S., *Civil Wars: American Novelists and Manners, 1880–1940* (Baltimore: The John Hopkins University Press, 2003).

Kasson, J. F., *Rudeness and Civility: Manners in Nineteenth-Century America* (New York: Hill and Wang, 1990).

Lindberg, G., *Edith Wharton and the Novel of Manners* (Charlottesville: University Press of Virginia, 1975).

Lyde, M. J., *Edith Wharton: Convention and Morality in the Work of a Novelist* (Norman: University of Oklahoma Press, 1959).

Milne, G., *The Sense of Society: A History of the American Novel of Manners* (Rutherford, NJ: Fairleigh Dickinson University Press, 1977).

NATURALISM

Bender, B., *The Descent of Love: Darwin and the Theory of Sexual Selection in American Fiction, 1871–1926* (Philadelphia: University of Pennsylvania Press, 1996).

Campbell, D. M., "The 'Bitter Taste' of Naturalism: Edith Wharton's *The House of Mirth* and David Graham Phillips's *Susan Lenox*" in M. E. Papke (ed.), *Twisted from the Ordinary: Essays on American Literary Naturalism* (Knoxville: University of Tennessee Press, 2003), 237–59.

Fleissner, J. L., "The Biological Clock: Edith Wharton, Naturalism, and the Temporality of Womanhood," *American Literature* 78.3 (2006), 519–48.

Newlin, K. (ed.), *The Oxford Handbook of American Literary Naturalism* (Oxford and New York: Oxford University Press, 2011).

Pizer, D., "American Naturalism in Its 'Perfected' State: *The Age of Innocence* and *An American Tragedy*" in A. Bendixen and A. Zilversmit (eds.), *Edith Wharton: New Critical Essays* (New York: Garland, 1992), 127–41.

"The Naturalism of Edith Wharton's *The House of Mirth*," *Twentieth Century Literature: A Scholarly and Critical Journal*, 41.2 (1995), 241–48.

Saltz, L., "'The Vision-Building Faculty': Naturalistic Vision in The House of Mirth," *MFS: Modern Fiction Studies*, 57.1 (2011), 17–46.

MODERNISM

Benstock, S., *Women of the Left Bank: Paris, 1900–1940* (Austin: University of Texas Press, 1986).

Campbell, D., "Edith Wharton's 'Book of the Grotesque': Sherwood Anderson, Modernism, and the Late Stories," *Edith Wharton Review*, 26.2 (2010), 1–5.

DeKoven, M., *Rich and Strange: Gender, History, Modernism* (Princeton, NJ: Princeton University Press, 1991).

Hadley, K. M., *In the Interstices of the Tale: Edith Wharton's Narrative Strategies* (New York: Peter Lang, 1993).

Haytock, J., *Edith Wharton and the Conversations of Literary Modernism* (New York: Palgrave, 2008).

Kalaidjian, W., *The Cambridge Companion to American Modernism* (Cambridge: Cambridge University Press, 2005).

Strychacz, T., *Modernism, Mass Culture, and Professionalism* (New York: Cambridge University Press, 1993).

Turner, C., *Marketing Modernism Between the Two World Wars* (Amherst: University of Massachusetts Press, 2003).

Wagner-Martin, L., "Women Authors and the Roots of American Modernism" in R. P. Lamb and G. R. Thompson (eds.), *A Companion to American Fiction, 1865–1914* (Oxford: Blackwell Publishing, 2005), 140–48.

Index

Academy, 148
Adams, Henry, 42, 46, 49, 328
Aeschylus, 75
Aesthetic movement, 183
Aestheticism, 202
Akins, Zoë, 161
   The Old Maid (adaptation), 158, 163, 171
Allen, Frederick Lewis
   Only Yesterday, 303
Allen, Joan, 172
American Critical Archives series, 105
American Hostel for Refugees, 295
American Red Cross, 282
American Renaissance, 328
Ammons, Elizabeth, 6, 100, 103–04
Anderson, Gillian, 173, 174
Anderson, Sherwood, 133, 308, 313, 366
Anna Karénina, 75
Anti-Semitism, 47, 258
Appleton, 58, 59, 117, 123, 124, 125, 126, 130, 131, 133, 138, 144, 152, 153, 168, 315
Appleton, William Sumner, 195
Appleton's Booklovers Magazine, 56, 123
Arnold, Matthew, 67, 327
Arquette, Patricia, 172
Art Nouveau, 202
Arts and Crafts Movement, 201, 202, 203, 204, 205, 206
Asselineau, Roger, 276
Association of American Authors (Authors League of America), 128
Astor, Caroline, 231, 236, 237, 238, 239, 240
   Four Hundred, 238
Athenaeum, 148, 151
Atherton, Gertrude, 49
Atherton, William, 174
Atkinson, Brooks, 163
Atkinson, Ted, 314
The Atlantic Monthly, 4, 9, 11, 12, 44, 52, 54, 55, 56, 118, 120, 127, 138, 143, 147, 153, 348

Auchincloss, Louis, 3, 8, 12, 19, 67
Austen, Jane, 346

Baguley, David, 354
Bahlmann, Anna, 3, 7, 9, 10, 11, 12–13, 14, 15, 16, 17, 18, 69, 329
Balestra, Gianfranca, 289
Balzac, Honoré de, 94, 244, 286, 345
Banta, Martha, 248
Barbusse, Henri
   Le Feu, 299, 300
Barnes, Djuna
   Nightwood, 369
Barnes, Margaret Ayer, 158, 161–62
Barney, Natalie, 366
Barrymore, Katherine Harris, 168
Bauer, Dale M., 67, 106, 248, 258, 266, 370
Bayne, Beverly, 169
Beach, Sylvia, 85, 366
Becker, George, 353
Beckert, Sven, 241
Belknap, Jeremy
   The Foresters, 137
Bell, Millicent, 67, 96, 105, 331
Bender, Bert, 359
Benedict, Ruth, 346
Benert, Annette, 107, 204, 290
Benevolent Assimilation Proclamation, 252
Benstock, Shari, 14, 43, 44, 48, 49, 50, 52, 53, 55, 57, 59, 60, 66–67, 105, 120, 123, 128, 129, 130, 139, 190, 244, 247, 275, 289, 295, 299, 312, 313
Bentley, Nancy, 41
Berenson, Bernard, 42, 49, 62, 65, 67, 89, 177, 180, 187, 278, 288, 296, 304, 330, 336
Berenson, Mary, 6, 49, 177
Bernini, Gian Lorenzo, 178–79
Berry, Walter, 7, 11, 12, 41, 49, 53, 57, 68, 95, 99, 167, 186, 219, 244, 253, 255, 278, 288, 328, 333
"Big Five" film companies, 168